W9-BTI-794

Attributions, Accounts, and Close Relationships

John H. Harvey Terri L. Orbuch
Ann L. Weber
Editors

Attributions, Accounts, and Close Relationships

Springer-Verlag
New York Berlin Heidelberg London Paris
Tokyo Hong Kong Barcelona Budapest

John H. Harvey
Department of Psychology
University of Iowa
Iowa City, IA 52242, USA

Terri L. Orbuch
Department of Psychology
University of Iowa
Iowa City, IA 52242, USA

Ann L. Weber
Department of Psychology
University of North Carolina
Asheville, NC 28804, USA

With 8 figures.

Library of Congress Cataloging-in-Publication Data
Attributions, accounts, and close relationships/John H. Harvey,
Terri L. Orbuch, Ann L. Weber, editors.
p. cm.
Includes bibliographical references and index.
ISBN 0-387-97461-X (alk. paper)
1. Interpersonal relations. 2. Attribution (Social psychology)
I. Harvey, John H., 1943- . II. Orbuch, Terri L. III. Weber, Ann L.
HM132.A874 1991
158'.2—dc20 90-24345

Printed on acid-free paper.

Typeset by Best-set Typesetter Ltd., Chai Wan, Hong Kong.
Printed and bound by Edwards Brothers, Inc., Ann Arbor, MI.
Printed in the United States of America.

9 8 7 6 5 4 3 2 1

ISBN 0-387-97461-X Springer-Verlag New York Berlin Heidelberg
ISBN 3-540-97461-X Springer-Verlag Berlin Heidelberg New York

This book is dedicated to our parents and loved ones, whose interactions with us have made the study of attributions and accounts in close relationships both illuminating and passionate.

Preface

In Chapter 1, our introduction to this book, we describe the main objective of the book as an attempt to bring together works by scholars who use the concepts of attribution and account in studying close relationships. We have assembled many of the leading scholars in these areas of work. The book also represents parts of the proceedings from two symposia held in 1990 on this topic. One of these symposia was held at Oxford, England, in conjunction with the meeting of the International Society for the Study of Personal Relationships in July 1990, and the other was a symposium on this topic at the meeting of the American Psychological Association in Boston, Massachusetts, in August 1990. We are most grateful both to our writers for this book and the speakers at those symposia for agreeing to participate in this dialogue. We also thank Robin Gilmour, Coordinator of the Personal Relationships Meeting, and Mahzarin Banaji and Peter Salovey, planners of the Division 8, APA Program, for facilitating the production of these symposia.

The reader of this book will find an international cast of writers and such disciplines on display as clinical and social psychology, sociology, communication studies, family studies, and psychology-law interface studies. Why do the qualities of international focus and interdisciplinary origin presently characterize the study of attributions, accounts, and close relationships? In part, this question may be answered by considering the breadth and heuristic value of the accounts and attributions concepts and the current popularity of trying to unravel some of the complexity of close relationships. We would suggest that this book may be used as a main text or supplement in graduate or advanced undergraduate courses concerned with close relationships or with applied aspects of attribution and accounts conceptions.

As the book's final set of commentaries argue, there remains much theoretical and empirical work to be done in order for maturity to be attained by this interface of work on accounts and attributions and their applications to the study of close relationships. Diversity in definition, theoretical direction, and empirical operations now is the theme. There also are on display different levels of analysis, with some workers focusing more on intrapsychic events and others more on interpersonal events. But an overarching position of most, if not all, of the chapters is the importance of the social context and people's mutual causal influence on one another in developing their understandings of the world. Further, fundamental questions common to all of the contributions concern how and with what consequences people interpret events within and relevant to their close relationships. The editors hope that this diversity is more appealing than confusing to the reader. We trust that it will challenge the reader and scholar to work toward greater theoretical cohesion, as such cohesion seems to do justice to relationship phenomena.

Finally, we owe a debt for their strong support to the people at Springer-Verlag.

John H. Harvey
Terri L. Orbuch
Ann L. Weber

Contents

Contributors

BERNICE ANDREWS, Department of Social Policy and Social Science, Royal Holloway and Bedford New College, University of London, London WC1B 3RA, UK

ROY F. BAUMEISTER, Department of Psychology, Case Western Reserve University, Cleveland, OH 44106, USA

DAVID O. BRAATEN, Business Communication, University of Southern California, Los Angeles, CA 90089-1421, USA

CHRIS R. BREWIN, MRC Social and Community Psychiatry Unit, Institute of Psychiatry, DeCrespigny Park, London SE5 8AF, UK

MICHAEL J. CODY, Communication Arts and Sciences, University of Southern California, Los Angeles, CA 90089-1694, USA

NANCY L. COLLINS, Department of Psychology University of California Los Angeles, Los Angeles, CA 90024-1563, USA

ROSALEEN CROGHAN, Psychology Disicipline, The Open University, Milton Keynes MK7 6AA, United Kingdom

RISA DICKSON, Communication Arts and Sciences, University of Southern California, Los Angeles, CA 90089-1694, USA

FRANK D. FINCHAM, Department of Psychology, University of Illinois, Champaign, IL 61820, USA

KENNETH J. GERGEN, Department of Psychology Swarthmore College, Swarthmore, PA 19081, USA

MARY M. GERGEN, Department of Psychology, Penn State University at Delaware, Media, PA 19063, USA

JOHN H. HARVEY, Department of Psychology, University of Iowa, Iowa City, IA 52242, USA

MILES HEWSTONE, Department of Psychology, University of Bristol, Bristol BS8 1HH, UK

AMY HOLTZWORTH-MUNROE, Department of Psychology, Indiana University, Bloomington, IN 47401, USA

LARRY KERSTEN, Communication Arts and Sciences, University of Southern California, Los Angeles, CA 90089-1694, USA

Sally Lloyd-Bostock, Centre for Socio-Legal Studies, Wolfson College, University of Oxford, Oxford OX2 6UD, United Kingdom

Dorothy Miell, Psychology Department, The Open University, Milton Keynes MK7 6AA, UK

Terri L. Orbuch, Department of Sociology, University of Michigan, Ann Arbor, MI 48109, USA

Sally Planalp, Department of Communication, University of Colorado, Boulder, CO 80309-0270, USA

Stephen J. Read, Department of Psychology, University of Southern California, Los Angeles, CA 90089, USA

Peter Schönbach, Fakultät für Psychologie, Ruhr-Universität Bochum, D-4630 Bochum, Germany

John Shotter, Rijksuniversiteit te Utrecht Faculteit der Sociale Wetenschappen, 3508 TC Utrecht, The Netherlands.

Arlene M. Stillwell, Department of Psychology, Case Western Reserve University, Cleveland, OH 44106, USA

Catherine A. Surra, Department of Human Ecology, University of Texas, Austin, TX 78712, USA

Anita L. Vangelisti, Department of Communications Studies, University of Texas, Austin, TX 78712, USA

Ann L. Weber, Department of Psychology, University of North Carolina at Asheville, Asheville, NC 28804, USA

Attributions, Accounts, and Close Relationships

1 Introduction: Convergence of the Attribution and Accounts Concepts in the Study of Close Relationships

John H. Harvey, Terri L. Orbuch, and Ann L. Weber

"The attributional approach is nonetheless complemented by, and sometimes merges into, the work on accounts, especially where issues of accountability are at stake." (Hewstone, 1989, p. 160).

Why an Interface Between Attribution and Accounts Work?

In this chapter, we will review the logic behind our assembling of scholars who use the concepts of attribution and accounts in their inquiry into the dynamics of close relationships. In the first section, we will try to provide a bridge partially for linking and contrasting some of the key ideas in this book. We will define and compare the attribution, accounts, and narratives approaches to understanding relationship phenomena. Next, we will discuss some of the strengths and limitations of the attribution and accounts/narratives perspectives on close relationships. In the course of this discussion, we will note some points of research rapprochement between these perspectives. Finally, we will briefly describe a further application of our account-making approach for the study of close relationships.

A central question of this chapter pertains to why this book and related symposia at the International Society for Personal Relationships-Oxford and APA-Boston meetings seemed necessary to us. The answer may not be as obvious as it would seem to the uninvolved scholar. The insightful quote from Hewstone (1989) above speaks to a natural boundary between these areas. But as strange as it may seem, the fields of attribution theory in social and clinical psychology and accounts/account-making, or related concepts such as narratives and stories, in several disciplines have emerged along parallel but seldom intersecting avenues of logic. These concepts often are defined in ways that preclude much attention to each other, and certainly theory and research on these concepts have proceeded in quite different ways.

Defining and Comparing Attribution, Account, and Narrative

Attribution

A mainstream definition of attribution is the perception of the causes of behavior (Jones, Kanouse, Kelley, Nisbett, Valins, & Weiner, 1972). The primary focus in attribution theory is on processes by which the "person on the street" forms an understanding either of observed or of personal events. This is the "naive psychology" that Heider (1958) so perceptively presented and that has had such an enduring impact over the last three decades. This definition has been broadened over time to include a concern with attributions of responsibility and blame (see Shaver, 1975; Weary, Stanley, & Harvey, 1989). In recent years, too, numerous other perspectives have been usefully brought to bear on the nature of attribution and the conditions in which it occurs. These works have extended attributional analysis beyond commonsense notions of causality to encompass consideration of the social conditions of attribution (e.g., Hewstone, 1983, 1989; Jaspars, Fincham, & Hewstone, 1983). Another interesting direction, especially for close relationship research, has embraced viewing attribution as a persuasive or communicative act that is as often concerned with convincing others about some state of affairs (Orvis, Kelley, & Butler, 1976; Newman, 1981). Vangelisti's chapter (Chap. 8, this volume) reports valuable research that amplifies on this "attribution as persuasion" theme.

In a powerful exposition on the dynamics of marital separation, Weiss (1975) used the concept of account to refer to a crucial activity of the person trying to cope with the loss of a close other. This work was influential in introducing the account concept to relationship research and in setting a foundation for bridging from attributional to accounts work on close relationships in the next decade. Weiss did not provide a detailed theoretical statement but did argue that the person's account for why a marital separation occurred helped the person to organize often confusing events and to achieve a degree of catharsis and closure. He also suggested that the account was motivating to the grieving individual and that it facilitated a greater sense of control in the person and the will to move on with his or her life.

Harvey, Wells, and Alvarez (1978) reported two studies that first examined attributional conflict in young romantic partners and then, following up on Weiss's treatment of the accounts concept, asked a small sample of newly separated persons to provide diary and interview evidence about their loss, how they explained it, and their plans for the future. For our purposes here, this article is noteworthy because it was one of the first works to note the value of the accounts concept within the context of work on attributional processes in close relationships. Harvey et al. defined the account essentially as "packaged attributions." Their results not only pointed to key attributional divergences among couples who were experiencing conflict (e.g., males' greater emphasis on sexual compatibility as a source of conflict than females' emphasis on this factor), but also provided evidence about accounts-explanations themes reported by the separated persons (e.g., perceived affairs by the partner, perceived insensitivity or lack of affection). This line of work on attributional divergence in close relationships has been extended and refined most effectively by Fincham and colleagues (e.g., Fincham & Bradbury, in press) and by Jacobson and colleagues (Berley & Jacobson, 1984).

In this same genre of research is the work by Huston, Surra, and colleagues on account-like perceptions for turning points in relationships (e.g., Huston, Surra, Fitzgerald, & Cate, 1981; Surra, 1985) and Vaughan's (1986) work on couples' accounts for relationship turning points leading to termination of the relationship. The studies by Huston, Surra and associates build on the 1970's era of research in the attribution field on close relationships, and at the same time provide useful account-type data with methodology that has focused on the development of reliable coding techniques. Although Vaughan's work does not emphasize an attributional or an accounts perspective, it does present interesting account-type evidence about the processes leading to termination of relationships.

Account

The present authors have defined accounts as story-like constructions that contain a plot or story line, characters, a time sequence, attributions, and other forms of expression such as affect (Harvey, Weber, & Orbuch, 1990). As the reader will quickly see, this definition of accounts is fairly broad and not necessarily the same as the one that appears to be espoused by other writers in this volume, such as Cody and McLaughlin (see also Cody & McLaughlin, 1990). The latter scholars have pursued accounts in the traditional "Goffmanian way" (Goffman, 1959; Scott & Lyman, 1968; Snyder, Higgins, & Stucky, 1983; Semin & Manstead, 1983; Schönbach, 1990), which emphasizes people's tendency to protect self and try to justify, make excuses, or exonerate themselves in situations in which their behavior is potentially blameworthy. In effect, this approach is concerned principally with social situations that embody predicaments and how we try to use attributions and other types of communications to alter others' perceptions of our role in creating these predicaments and their negative aftereffects. In addition, McLaughlin, Cody, and French (1990) have provided data that reveal how one party's account regarding alleged traffic violations led to other's attributions of responsibility for the outcome involved in the violation. Thus, in the latter line of work the account served as a basis for attribution.

Let us provide examples of the types of material/situation that illustrate these two different approaches to the study of accounts. In their well-known article, Scott and Lyman (1968) provide the following example of an account by a "mental patient" that presumably was communicated so as to highlight "an extremely dismal past" (Scott and Lyman's interpretation) and thus ameliorate others' negative evaluation of the individual in light of the present situation: "I was going to night school to get an M.A. degree, and holding down a job in addition, and the load got too much for me" (p. 54).

As another example, McLaughlin, Cody, and French (1990) obtained the following challenge-type account presented in court by a person charged with speeding in a 35 mph zone: "I might have been going 60, but I was not going anything like 70. I think the officer added those extra miles on just to make me more upset" (p. 254). McLaughlin et al. found that such a challenge led to relatively great attribution to personal traits by observer-respondents who read about the court case. As expected, they also found considerable attribution to personal influence when an accused person offered a justification (e.g., "was rushing home to turn off . . . [curling iron]").

Schönbach (1990, Chap. 3, this volume) has broadened the latter approach to accounts in his argument that an account episode contains minimally two agents—an actor and an opponent—and four phases: a failure event in which the actor is held at least partly responsible for the violation of a normative expectation; a reproach phase in which the opponent reacts to the failure event with a mild or severe reproach; an account phase in which the actor offers an excuse or justification; and an evaluation phase in which the opponent evaluates the account, the failure in light of the account, or the actor's personality in light of the failure and the account (cf. to Jones & Davis, 1965, correspondent inference theory of attribution in which inferences about another person's personality are based on the person's acts and inferred intentions, choices, and so on).

Contrast the foregoing type of material with the following example, which represents the fuller type of construction the present authors investigate under the rubric of account-making. This excerpt of an account appeared in the June, 1990, issue of *Esquire*. It is a story by Larkin Warren entitled "P.S., I Love You: A Letter From an Ex-Wife" and poignantly tells about a couple's early romance and eventual parting, and of an ex-wife's desire that peace and gentle memories will now prevail for her ex-husband and herself:

> The summer night you strolled up to our house, dressed in a white linen suit and carrying lilacs you'd lifted from your mother's yard—that was when I knew that all was lost for love. It was like hearing the metal tumbler fall and drop in a dead-bolt lock, so absolute was my conviction. . . .
>
> My father got over being dazed halfway through the summer, when the hot, blue light that shot through any room we were in together suddenly became

visible to his naked eye. He realized, as any boy-turned-father must, the edgy presence of secrets and sex. . . .

It was the sixties, the era of gestures, empty and full ones. This was a full one, a pregnancy, making the decision for us that we swore we would've made anyway. . . . We had money enough for plane tickets, and passion enough for a small opera. We eloped.

. . . The baby was perfect, my novice cooking less so, your hunt for a good job that would feed all of us less perfect than that. . . . We fled to a ski town, where the residency requirements were youth and beauty and money. We were reasonably confident of the first two, a little shaky on the last, but goofily hopeful.

After a winter or two, you began coming home a little later each night. Sometimes when I'd pick up a ringing phone, nobody would be there, and then nobody would hang up. . . . Minor indignities grew into major battles. . . . You lied about how much money you'd really taken out of the checking account, and I started a savings account in another bank, secretly feeding my lunch money into it. . . .

When the first separation came, then the second, and finally the last, we both cried, because this wasn't the way it was supposed to be, not for us. If I didn't love you, then what was this shooting ache, kind of like a constant side stitch, doing under my heart every time I looked at you?

"You were lucky that it all happened when you were so young," a friend once said, as though youth and stupidity lessened the pain or prevented loss when dreams, even childish ones, didn't come true. But there was nothing and nobody to blunt what we felt for each other, or what we did to each other. Now, a lifetime later, we are both grown up at last, with grown-up marriages and a recovered capacity for joy. . . .

I am letting you off the hook, and ask you to let me off any hooks hanging around in your memory too. I only regret the losses now, where once I raged at them, but I don't want them to be all there was. Remember the touch on the cheek, the child, the Notre Dame game we didn't see. (pp. 211–212. Reprinted by permission of Sterling Lord Literistic, Inc. Copyright © 1990 by Larkin Warren.)

Why have Harvey et al. defined accounts in terms of such detailed, story-like, explanatory constructions for all types of events occurring in a variety of social situations? The answer is embodied in the richness of psychological processes in this example. We wish to embrace a fuller gamut of processes as revealed in account-making than would be possible if we focused mainly on situations involving people's concern with protection and maintenance of self-esteem. While we are concerned with people's tendencies to develop accounts as justifications for their behavior (it might be contended that the entire story of the ex-wife constitutes a justification of her behavior), we also are concerned with these additional motivations: how people develop accounts to understand and feel a greater sense of control in dealing with their environment; how they develop accounts to engage in emotional purging or catharsis; how they use accounts as ends in themselves (a form of reaction to unfinished business, viz., the Zeigarnik Effect); and how they develop accounts so as to stimulate an enlightened feeling and greater hope and will for the future. All of these motivations may be imputed to the ex-wife's story presented above. For example, the overall thrust and certainly the final lines point to the writer's desire that an enlightened state, containing hope, now represent her and her husband's understanding of their years of marriage.

There are other reasons why we prefer to concentrate on accounts as stories. First, with this emphasis, we learn something about emotion and affect-laden memory (Harvey, Flanary, & Morgan, 1986). We have found that accounts for past relationships often contain reports of vivid memories of critical benchmark events such as a couple's first encounter, first sexual experience, and terminal episodes. We believe that such affect-laden memory may be more readily understood in the context of fuller account-like expressions than as it appears in more singular attributions and emotional responses. This point seems particularly tenable in situations involving severe stress (see Harvey, Orbuch, & Weber, 1990, for an elaboration of the affective, cognitive, and memorial concomitants of account-making in traumatic circumstances). Second, as will be elaborated below, this broader focus permits a stronger link to be formed with the literature on narratives and storytelling.

Narrative

Our book title could have included the term *narrative* in it. As the reader will see, narrative, which refers to the telling of stories, is a central concept in Baumeister and Stillwell's and Shotter's chapters and overlaps considerably with the accounts concept, as the editors use this concept. Baumeister and colleagues provide interesting data regarding the psychology of victim and perpetrator that derive from "micronarratives" (using Gergen & Gergen's, 1988, term).

Gergen and Gergen's writing has been influential in defining narrative as a useful psychological concept (e.g., Gergen & Gergen, 1987, 1988). They suggest that the well-formed narrative contains the following components: (a) the establishment of a goal state (e.g., an end point of the story, such as "how I escaped death in a recent car accident"); (b) selection of events relevant to the goal state (e.g., the acts involved in my escape); (c) arrangement of events in chronological order; (d) establishment of causal linkages (e.g., "My escape, therefore, was due to . . ."); and (e) demarcation signs (e.g., "Have you heard how I escaped death . . . ?"). Gergen and Gergen's arguments are especially informative about the social character of narratives and how they often are presented in order to persuade others. In their 1987 paper, Gergen and Gergen write about the role of narrative language in contributing to defense of the status quo in interpersonal (male-female) relations and in unifying individuals and groups toward certain lines of action (e.g., a couple's behavior of "becoming close" has such a rhetoric). Similar to the motives the present writers ascribe to account-making, Gergen and Gergen suggest that narratives may serve a wide variety of pragmatic functions, including creating expectations, challenging positions, gaining sympathy, and creating a sense of union.

Within the purview of his work on accountability, Shotter also has made important contributions to our understanding of narratives (e.g., Shotter 1984, 1987). One general idea that derives from his analysis is that narratives are always constructed and contextualized within larger explanatory systems (all-embracing accounts for particular events; e.g., a lover's overall account for his or her love-life, which subsumes and helps explain any particular love relationship—this idea corresponds to what Weber, Harvey, & Stanley, 1987, have referred to as a "master account"). Shotter's writing is informative with regard to naive attributors' narration, but also important with regard to scientists' attempts to understand and their consequent narrations. His chapter (Chap. 2, this volume), on the nature of a personal relationship, is illustrative of this dual concern. Shotter's concern with how scientists go about studying relationships is eloquently reflected in the following quote from his analysis of accountability, narratives, and close relationships:

> What we need is a better story, a better way of formulating the nature of personal relationships than the current "causal story," a story that makes "rationally visible," so to speak, the processual, formative nature of such relationships. . . . and a story that fits in with the *practice* of personal relationships, rather than in with the established practices of science—for in personal relationships, too, we can check, evaluate, and elaborate the truths we make, as we make them. Practically, even love is not blind. (1987, p. 245)

An apparent major difference that we have noted in comparing our approach to accounts with these scholars' treatment of narratives is that we wish to emphasize the private as well as the public nature of account-making. We believe that private grappling, including record and diary keeping, worrying, musing, and story-like problem solving are prominent aspects of account-making (see Tait & Silver, 1989, for an inviting discussion of rumination). But we also endorse Mead's (1934) view of the mind as a social entity that imports into its counsel the imagined reactions of others to privately held attitudes and beliefs or planned actions. Thus, even private reflection represents a social act from this perspective. It follows, then, that the emphasis upon public communicative acts that seems to permeate the writing of narrative scholars is quite congenial to our approach. At the same time, however, we believe that our approach may more explicitly serve as a bridge than does the narrative approach to work in social-cognitive psychology which is well-represented by Read and Collins (Chap. 7, this volume). This mainstream social-cognitive school of thought appears to be much less committed to an explicit view of the omniscience of social influence in attributional and cognitive activity than are the account-making and narrative positions.

Other scholars have treated the ideas of stories and storytelling, without prominent reference to the concepts of attributions, accounts, and narratives. Coles (1989) has written eloquently about the value of stories and storytelling in various life callings. For example, he urges teachers to use storytelling (personal as well as literary masterpieces) to make education more inviting to students, and to teach ethics and morality in a way that is compelling. Birren (1987) has presented ideas about the merits of autobiographical writing. He suggests that when both young and old make their autobiographical statements, this step gives new meaning to their present lives by helping them understand their past more fully: "Writing an autobiography puts the contradictions, paradoxes and ambivalences into perspective. It restores our sense of self-sufficiency and personal identity that has been shaped by the crosscurrents and tides of life" (p. 91). Bruner (1987) also has suggested that storytelling is stimulated by events that are out of the ordinary. He argues, "While the act of writing autobiography is new under the sun—like writing itself—the self-told life narrative is, by all accounts, ancient and universal. People everywhere can tell you some intelligible account of their lives" (p. 16). And in advocating the study of stories, Bruner says,

> I cannot imagine a more important psychological research project than one that addresses itself to the "development of autobiography"—how our way of telling about ourselves changes, and how these accounts come to take control of our ways of life. Yet I know of not a single comprehensive study of this topic. (p. 15)

Some Strengths and Limitations of These Approaches

We turn now to a selective discussion of strengths and limitations of the attributional, accounts, and narratives approaches to the study of close relationships.

The attributional theoretic approach to close relationships, and especially to the differentiation of distressed and nondistressed relationships, has yielded highly informative, replicable data (Fincham & O'Leary, 1983; Fincham & Bradbury, 1987; Berley & Jacobson, 1984; Holtzworth-Munroe & Jacobson, 1985; Holtzworth-Munroe, Chap. 9 this volume; Fletcher & Fincham, in press). This work is theory-driven, hypothesis-oriented, and solidly linked to traditional work in attribution theory and to other developments in the area of cognitive-social psychology. As Hewstone (1989) argues, the greatest strength of the attributional approach is its theoretical breadth and sophistication. It also is systematic in its pursuit of causal relations. For example, in their impressive research program, Fincham and Bradbury (1987) report longitudinal data that indicate distressed spouses' use of negative attributions (e.g., mimimizing the impact of positive events—"He's being nice because he wants to have sex with me tonight.") are predictive of marital quality over a 12-month period. A limitation that the attribution approach shares with the other approaches to be discussed is that too little research has been done with different populations in terms of age, socioeconomic, and cultural factors. Also, self-selection of respondents appears to be the rule rather than the exception in all of these domains of work. This limitation suggests that, at the minimum, there needs to be greater recognition of the qualifications of evidence collected with populations that select themselves for participation in relationship research.

The attributional approach to close relationships might benefit from a complementary focus on couples' thinking and behavior in broader texts. It also might benefit from studies done outside of the laboratory/clinic, across different types of social settings, not unlike some of the ethnographic inquiries of Csikszentmihalyi and colleagues, (e.g., Csikszentmihalyi & LeFeure, 1989). This supplemental tactic might also include consideration of larger chunks of explanatory material, or accounts/narratives. Basically, the argument is that there is an inherent limitation in terms of ecological validity in focusing on restricted populations, settings, behavior, and/or thought units. As the example of the ex-wife's statement suggests, attributions of causality, responsibility, and blame often occur in subtle and not easily condensed or summarized structures of thought and feeling. Antaki's (1985, 1990) recent work is influential in this regard. He has very usefully analyzed explanation within naturalistic discourses and, in so doing, has emphasized the need to treat such explanation within naturally occurring contexts.

The above emphasis on context represents a strength of the accounts and narratives approaches. But their major limitation overall is that they have not been pursued in the same systematic manner as the attributional approach. Both theory and method are in the quite early stages of development for accounts and narratives. Coding and classification of "free response" material still is open to the problem of generalizability of technique, despite some attempts to provide concepts of standardization (see Planalp & Surra, Chap. 5, this volume; Brewin, Chap. 11, this volume; Holtzworth-Munroe & Jacobson, 1985; Harvey, Turnquist, & Agostinelli, 1988; and Antaki, 1988).

In treating the two types of accounts work described above, we offer the following sets of separate remarks. As is evident from Cody and McLaughlin's (1990) and Shönbach's (1990) recent works, much strong integrative work on accounts as justifications is now occurring. Theory-driven research clearly is progressing in studying accounts in this more narrow sense than the work on accounts as stories. This work is being closely linked to attribution and self-presentation theory (e.g., Arkin & Shepperd, 1990). In addition, the methodology is sometimes experimental, thus more conducive to cause-effect analysis, and well-controlled and generally superior to the accounts-as-stories methodology because it involves less room for confounding of variables or misinterpretation of respondents' responses.

The accounts-as-stories and narratives approaches probably provide the broadest treatments of cognition and emotion found in the social and behavioral sciences to date. This breadth surely is the basis for such reach of these perspectives in their ability to connect with other positions such as that of storytelling and rhetoric in communication studies (e.g., Burke, 1945; Simons & Melia, 1989). This point would be truer to the extent that such approaches are also concerned with cross-cultural perspectives on account-making and narratives—at present, a neglected topic. Also, it is important that bridges be drawn between this area and such relevant but so far neglected areas as self-disclosure work (e.g., Jourard, 1971). Nonetheless, the breadth of these approaches is a major advantage. In this breadth, the scholar will find great richness and naturalism of phenomena and social psychological processes.

The accounts-as-stories approach will become stronger to the extent that it makes a clear, useful contact with other fields that contain more advanced theory and methodology. Read and Collins (Chap. 7, this volume) provide leads about how such a connection might occur with social-cognitive theory in general. Also, the possible linkage between account-making and scripts and stories as studied by cognitive psychologists (e.g., Mandler, 1984) deserves attention. One other point of integration is discussed by Orbuch (1990) and Harvey et al. (1990). It involves the use of accounts material as stimuli in affecting person perception and behavioral reactions to the presenter of the account. Modeled in part after Hovland, Janis, and Kelley's (1953) approach to communication, this program of research so far has identified a set of independent variables associated with accounts (e.g., themes, emotion displayed) and presentation episodes (e.g., gender of audience and presenter, credibility of presenter, empathy of audience) that have been found to influence trait ratings of, liking for, and behavioral reactions toward the presenter.

Further Application of the Account-Making Approach to the Study of Close Relationships

In recent years, our own work on account-making has been concerned with the role of account-making in people's coping with severe stress. In this section, we will briefly trace some of this work and indicate what implications it may have for advancing theory and research on close relationships.

We have developed a model (Harvey et al., 1990) that extends Horowitz's (1986) proposed stress response sequence. When severe stressors occur (e.g., sudden death of a loved one), Horowitz suggests that people go through several stages from shock, outcry, and denial to working through and completion. As can be seen in Figure 1.1, we have added the final stage of identity change and have hypothesized at what points account-making is most likely to occur. We suggest that account-making may occur in a limited way early in a stress response sequence but that it becomes more prominent and beneficial at the working-through stage (and at that point is accompanied by a greater sense of control over one's reaction to the event). The culmination of the sequence is change in one's identity. Following Bem's (1972) logic, the survivor of a major trauma near the end of the stress response sequence may be able to say, "Look at all that I have gone through. Now, I'm a much stronger person." A perceptive corollary to this logic, which Shotter (1987) attributes to Kurt Vonnegut, is that we must be careful about the stories we tell ourselves because we may become what they say about us.

Another crucial addition to the stress response model is the act of confiding in close others. We propose that confiding (which involves disclosing some part of one's account to a caring other or others) also occurs during the working through stage. A key aspect of this idea is that the confiding attempt must be met with a caring, empathic response from others.

Our ideas about the role of account-making and confiding in coping are similar to those advanced by Pennebaker (1985, 1989) in his influential program of research. Pennebaker has postulated and provided evidence showing that survivors of traumatic events often have improved psychological and physical health if they have confided about their trauma. Our focus differs somewhat from Pennebaker's in that we are concerned with the contents and nature of the confiding, the account-making, and the accompanying social dynamics. In our conception, accounts begin in private reflection and often progress quite far before they begin to be reported substantially in confiding activity. Pennebaker does not appear to emphasize the importance of the reception of the confiding attempt—that is, that it must be met with empathy by others—in order for confiding to work its beneficial effect on the survivor. We also believe that for many major traumas, the confiding or account-making often requires much cognitive-emotional work, and years thereof, in order for a sense of completion and tranquility to develop. On the other hand, Pennebaker and colleagues have found that brief confiding experiences (e.g., told by college students in laboratory circumstances regarding personal events such as date rape or loss of grandparents) may have positive effects on individuals and that writing, in particular, appears to be an effective agent in these types of confiding activities.

A recent study by Harvey, Orbuch, Chwalisz, and Garwood (in press) addresses the roles of account-making and confiding in coping with major traumas. In this study, 12 incest survivors and 13 nonincestuous sexual assault survivors responded to a questionnaire concerning a sexual assault

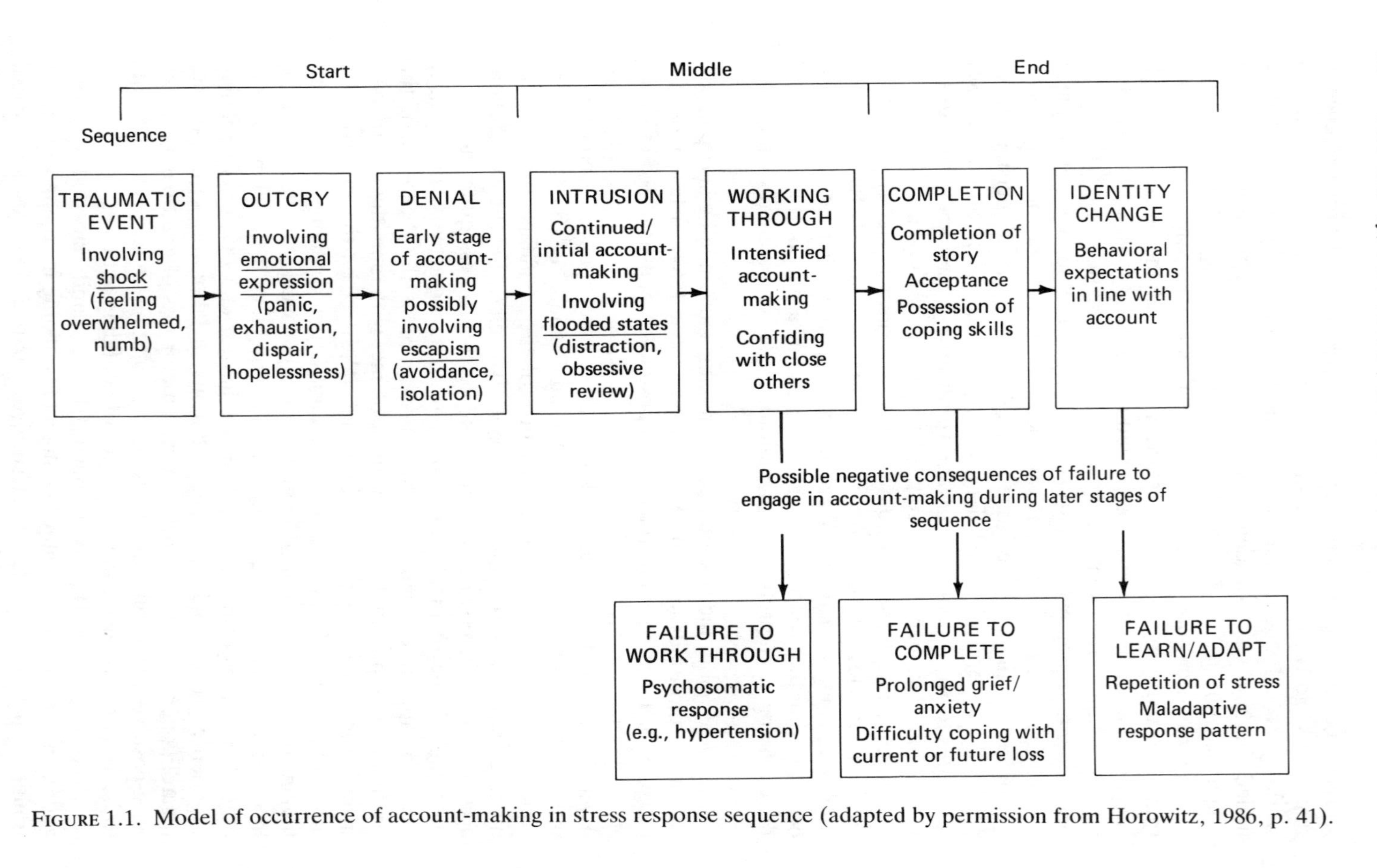

FIGURE 1.1. Model of occurrence of account-making in stress response sequence (adapted by permission from Horowitz, 1986, p. 41).

they had suffered at some time in the past. They were asked to provide accounts of the assault experience; whether or not they had confided in others about this experience and, if so, with what effect; how they had coped in general; and their beliefs about how the experience had affected their close relationships. The respondents ranged from 20 to 44 years old and were generally well-educated, middle-class, middle-income women living in the midwestern United States. Their answers were coded along dimensions relevant to the following: extent of account-making activities in coping (e.g., formal therapy, informal discussions with friends, diary or record keeping, private reflection about the event and its whys and wherefores); the nature and success of confiding attempts; success in coping; impact on close relationships; and present negative affect about the assault.

The findings of this study were strong in showing that the group of incest survivors exhibited a much greater sense that the assault had negatively influenced their close relationships, success in coping, and present affect than did the group of survivors assaulted by nonrelatives. Further, consistent with our theory, it was found that account-making activity was significantly positively correlated with successful coping ($r = .53$) and significantly negatively correlated with present negative affect ($r = -.35$). Regarding confiding evidence, it was found that confiding that led to an empathic response from others was significantly, positively associated with successful coping and was significantly, negatively correlated with negative affect. On the other hand, confiding that was met with relatively indifferent responses resulted in comparatively low success in coping and comparatively high present negative affect.

There are many limitations of this study, not the least of which is the small, self-selected nature of the sample. One derivative possibility is that because of self-selection, the respondents may have been much more likely to have engaged in account-making and confiding than were persons who did not elect to participate. Nonetheless, we believe that the data are representative of what one would find in general in studying how people deal with major personal trauma such as incest. The data are consistent with evidence for a group of incest survivors provided by Silver, Boon, and Stones (1983). The findings for confiding also resonate with data reported by Andrews and Brown (1988) and summarized by Andrews in her chapter for this volume.

Perhaps an example of an excerpt of an account presented in the study by Harvey et al. (in press) will reveal more powerfully the importance of caring/effective others in the coping sequence. The following account was provided by a woman who between the ages of 8 and 18 was assaulted repeatedly by her brother:

> The first time I revealed the abuse to DHS [Department of Human Services] and my parents was when I was 12. DHS concluded it was normal sibling curiosity.

My parents reacted with anger towards me, yelling about my brother's reputation if it should get around own. Their reactions left me feeling totally isolated and alone . . . forcing me to be victimized for another four years. (p. 14)

Overall, we believe not only that accounts about people's pain and anguish and their confiding about them may enhance their own recovery over time, but also that such accounts have great potential to affect all of us in salutary ways and help us connect better with a world of suffering that is always right at our doorstep. The reader is also referred to the account-like evidence reported by Croghan and Miell (Chap. 13, this volume) and by Holtzworth-Munroe (Chap. 9, this volume) for further perspective on account-making under trying conditions in or relevant to close relationships.

Finally, as reported both in Weber et al. (1987) and Harvey, Agostinelli, and Weber (1989), we have provided other data that pertain to the account-making/stress-reduction argument. These data, for example, point toward the value of account-making in helping people formulate new directions for intimacy after the loss of close others, either by separation or death.

Conclusion

This chapter has introduced this book and has discussed similarities and dissimilarities among the attributional, accounts, and narratives approaches to close relationships. Early on, we indicated that there are solid grounds for rapprochement among these approaches both in terms of theory and research. We hope that our treatment has convinced the reader of the merit of this integration theme. As a specific bridging example for the future, it makes sense to us to think of research being designed that combines an interest in specific types of attributions about relationship events with a focus on participants' fuller stories or narratives about those events. We presently know of no work that explicitly combines these types of probes.

At this point, the critic may suggest that in our advocacy of synthesis across these different positions, we are trying to assimilate too much diversity. The chapters in this book readily illustrate such diversity. For example, is the traditional attribution position, with its emphasis on experimental methodology and cause–effect relations, basically disparate from the narrative position that emphasizes nonexperimental methods, social constructivism as process, and the view that human relations cannot be readily interpreted within traditional scientific frames? It is possible. But even at this potential impasse, it makes sense to think that a dialogue between the two camps is possible and potentially useful. Beyond this point of exchange, we believe that there is considerable bridging possible between these schools of thought via the work on accounts as stories. The latter approach builds on attributional analysis and methods but quickly branches into more contextually relevant ideas and techniques. Further, the accounts-as-stories approach is less committed to the rhetoric of science than is traditional attributional theory. Although we as accounts theorists believe that our work is relevant to understanding people's understanding of social events, we do not believe that our understanding has to be developed via any particular research or intellectual strategy. We also believe that this work must be flexible in consideration of the reflexive character of social life, as is eloquently implied in the earlier quote from Shotter (1987). At the same time, traditional attributional conceptions have provided such a wealth of stimulation and evidence that it would be folly to disregard this literature as we try to develop better understandings of accounting and narrating activities.

In the end, we believe that these approaches bring together ideas that not only span many areas of the social and behavioral sciences, but that also move these disciplines into close contact with the humanities. As such, we believe that the current book goes quite a long way toward achieving the status of an interdisciplinary work that duly respects the diversity and specialness of close relationships. We truly hope that, at the minimum, this volume will provide further foundation for greater appreciation of the value of attributional and accounts-type approaches to the study of close relationships.

References

Andrews, B., & Brown, G.W. (1988). Social support, onset of depression and personality: An exploratory analysis. *Social Psychiatry and Psychiatric Epidemiology, 23*, 99–108.

Antaki, C. (1985). Ordinary explanaion in conversation: Causal structures and their defence. *European Journal of Social Psychology, 15*, 213–230.

Antaki, C. (Ed.) (1988). *Analysing everyday explanation: A casebook of methods*. London: Sage.

Antaki, C. (1990). Explaining events or explaining oneself? In M.J. Cody & M.L. McLaughlin (Eds.), *The psychology of tactical communication* (pp. 268–282). Clevedon, England: Multilingual Matters.

Arkin, R.M., & Shepperd, J.A. (1990). Strategic self-presentation: An overview. In M.J. Cody & M.L. McLaughlin (Eds.), *The psychology of tactical communication* (pp. 175–193). Clevedon, England: Multilingual Matters.

Bem, D.J. (1972). Self-perception theory. In L. Berkowitz (Ed.), *Advances in Experimental Social Psychology* (Vol. 6, pp. 1–62). New York: Academic Press.

Berley, R.A., & Jacobson, N.S. (1984). Causal attributions in intimate relationships: Toward a model of cognitive-behavioral marital therapy. In P.C. Kendall (Ed.), *Advances in Cognitive-Behavioral Research and Therapy* (Vol. 3, pp. 1–60). Orlando, FL: Academic Press.

Birren, J.E. (1987, May). The best of all stories. *Psychology Today*, pp. 91–92.
Bruner, J. (1987). Life as narrative. *Socia Research, 54*, 11–32.
Burke, K. (1945). *A grammar of motives*. New York: Prentice-Hall.
Cody, M.J., & McLaughlin, M.L. (Eds.). (1990). *The psychology of tactical communication*. Clevedon, England: Multilingual Matters.
Coles, R. (1989). *The call of stories*. Boston, MA: Houghton Mifflin.
Csikszentmihalyi, M., & LeFeure, J. (1989). Optimal experience in work and leisure. *Journal of Personality and Social Psychology, 56*, 815–822.
Fincham, F.D., & Bradbury, T.N. (1987). The impact of attributions in marriage: A longitudinal analysis. *Journal of Personality and Social Psychology, 53*, 510–517.
Fincham, F.D., & Bradbury, T.N. (in press). Cognition in marriage: A program of research on attributions. In D. Perlman & W. Jones (Eds.), *Advances in Personal Relationships* (Vol. 2). Greenwich, CT: JAI Press.
Fincham, F.D., & O'Leary, K.D. (1983). Causal inferences for spouse behavior in maritally distressed and nondistressed couples. *Journal of Social and Clinical Psychology, 1*, 32–57.
Fletcher, G.J.O., & Fincham, F.D. (Eds.). (1991). *Cognition in close relationships*. Hillsdale, NJ: Lawrence Erlbaum.
Gergen, K.J., & Gergen, M. (1987). Narratives as relationships. In R. Burnett, P. McGhee, & D.C. Clarke (Eds.), *Accounting for relationships* (pp. 269–315). London: Methuen.
Gergen, K.J., & Gergen, M. (1988). Narrative and the self as relationship. In L. Berkowitz (Ed.), *Advances in Experimental Social Psychology* (Vol. 21, pp. 17–56). Orlando: Academic Press.
Goffman, E. (1959). *The presentation of self in everyday life*. Garden City, NY: Doubleday-Anchor Books.
Harvey, J.H., Agostinelli, G., & Weber, A.L. (1989). Account-making and the formation of expectations about close relationships. *Review of Personality and Social Psychology, 10*, 39–62.
Harvey, J.H., Flanary, R., & Morgan, M. (1986). Vivid memories of vivid loves gone by. *Journal of Social and Personal Relationships, 3*, 359–373.
Harvey, J.H., Orbuch, T.L., Chwalisz, K.D., & Garwood, G. (in press). Coping with sexual assault: The roles of account-making and confiding. *Journal of Traumatic Stress*.
Harvey, J.H., Orbuch, T.L., & Weber, A.L. (1990). A social psychological model of account-making in response to severe stress. *Journal of Language and Social Psychology, 9*, 191–207.
Harvey, J.H., Turnquist, D.C., & Agostinelli, G. (1988). Identifying attributions in oral and written explanations. In C. Antaki (Ed.), *Analysing everyday explanation: A casebook of methods* (pp. 32–42). London: Sage.
Harvey, J.H., Weber, A.L., & Orbuch, T.L. (1990). *Interpersonal accounts*. Oxford: Blackwell.
Harvey, J.H., Wells, G.L., & Alvarez, M.D. (1978). Attribution in the context of conflict and separation in close relationships. In J.H. Harvey, W. Ickes, & R.F. Kidd (Eds.), *New directions in attribution research* (Vol. 2, pp. 235–259). Hillsdale, NJ: Erlbaum.
Heider, F. (1958). *The psychology of interpersonal relations*. New York: Wiley.

Hewstone, M. (Ed.). (1983). *Attribution theory: Social and functional extensions*. Oxford: Blackwell.

Hewstone, M. (1989). *Causal attribution: From cognitive processes to collective beliefs*. Oxford: Basil Blackwell.

Holtzworth-Munroe, A., & Jacobson, J.J. (1985). Causal attributions in marital couples. *Journal of Personality and Social Psychology, 48*, 1398–1412.

Horowitz, M.J. (1986). *Stress response syndromes* (2nd ed.). Northvale, NJ: Jason Aronson.

Hovland, C., Janis, I., & Kelley, H.H. (1953). *Communication and persuasion*. New Haven, CT: Yale University Press.

Huston, T.L., Surra, C.A., Fitzgerald, N.M., & Cate, R.M. (1981). From courtship to marriage: Mate selection as an interpersonal process. In S. Duck & R. Gilmour (Eds.), *Personal relationships 2: Developing personal relationships* (pp. 53–88). London: Academic Press.

Jaspars, J., Fincham, F.D., & Hewstone, M. (Eds.). (1983). *Attribution theory and research: Conceptual, developmental and social dimensions*. London: Academic Press.

Jones, E.E., & Davis, K.E. (1965). From acts to dispositions: The Attribution process in person perception. In L. Berkowitz (Ed.), *Advances in Experimental Social Psychology* (Vol. 2, pp. 219–266). New York: Academic Press.

Jones, E.E., Kanouse, D.E., Kelley, H.H., Nisbett, R.E., Valins, S., & Weiner, B. (Eds.). (1972). *Attribution: Perceiving the cause of behavior*. New York: General Learning Press.

Jourard, S.M. (1971). *Self disclosure*. New York: Wiley.

Mandler, J.M. (1984). *Stories, scripts, and scenes: Aspects of schema theory*. Hillsdale, NJ: Erlbaum.

McLaughlin, M.L., Cody, M.J., & French, K. (1990). Account-giving and the attribution of responsibility: Impressions of traffic offenders. In M.J. Cody & M.L. McLaughlin (Eds.), *The psychology of tactical communication* (pp. 244–267). Clevedon, England: Multilingual Matters.

Mead, G.H. (1934). *Mind, self, and society*. Chicago: University of Chicago Press.

Newman, H. (1981). Communication within ongoing intimate relationships: An attribution perspective. *Personality and Social Psychology Bulletin, 7*, 59–70.

Orbuch, T.L. (1990, July). *Person perception through accounts*. Paper presented at International Conference on Personal Relationships, Oxford, England.

Orvis, B.R., Kelley, H.H., & Butler, D. (1976). Attributional conflict in young couples. In J.H. Harvey, W.J. Ickes, & R.F. Kidd (Eds.), *New directions in attribution research* (Vol. 1, pp. 353–386). Hillsdale, NJ: Erlbaum.

Pennebaker, J.W. (1985). Traumatic experience and psychosomatic disease: Exploring the roles of behavioral inhibition, obsession, and confiding. *Canadian Psychology, 26*, 82–95.

Pennebaker, J.W. (1989). Confession, inhibition, and disease. In L. Berkowitz (Ed.), *Advances in Experimental Social Psychology* (Vol. 22, pp. 211–244). Orlando: Academic Press.

Scott, M.B., & Lyman, S.M. (1968). Accounts. *American Sociological Review, 33*, 46–62.

Schönbach, P. (1990). *Account episodes: The management or escalation of*

conflict. Cambridge: Cambridge University Press.
Semin, G.R., & Manstead, A.S.R. (1983). *The accountability of conduct*. London: Academic Press.
Shaver, K.G. (1975). *An introduction to attribution processes*. Cambridge, MA: Winthrop.
Shotter, J. (1984). *Social accountability and selfhood*. Oxford: Blackwell.
Shotter, J. (1987). The social construction of an 'us': Problems of accountability and narratology. In R. Burnett, P. McGhee, & D.D. Clarke (Eds.), *Accounting for relationships* (pp. 225–247). London: Methuen.
Silver, R., Boon, C., & Stones, M. (1983). Searching for meaning in misforfune: Making sense of incest. *Journal of Social Issues, 39*, 81–102.
Simons, H.W., & Melia, T. (Eds.). (1989). *The legacy of Kenneth Burke*. Madison, WI: University of Wisconsin Press.
Snyder, C.R., Higgins, R.L., & Stucky, R.J. (1983). *Excuses: Masquerade in search of grace*. New York: Wiley.
Surra, C.A. (1985). Courtship types: Variations in independence between partners and social networks. *Journal of Personality and Social Psychology, 49*, 357–375.
Tait, R., & Silver, R.C. (1989). Coming to terms with major negative life events. In J.S. Uleman & J.A. Bargh (Eds.), *Unintended thought* (pp. 351–382). New York: Guilford.
Vaughan, D. (1986). *Uncoupling: Turning points in intimate relationships*. New York: Oxford University Press.
Weary, G., Stanley, M.A., & Harvey, J.H. (1989). *Attribution*. New York: Springer-Verlag.
Weber, A.L., Harvey, J.H., & Stanley, M.A. (1987). The nature and motivations of accounts for failed relationships. In R. Burnett, P. McGhee, & D.C. Clarke (Eds.), *Accounting for relationships* (pp. 114–133). London: Methuen.
Weiss, R.S. (1975). *Marital separation*. New York: Basic Books.

2
What Is a "Personal" Relationship? A Rhetorical-Responsive Account of "Unfinished Business"

JOHN SHOTTER

The love story is the tribute the lover must pay to the world in order to be reconciled with it. (Barthes, 1983, p. 8)

In their discussion of narratives of relationship, Gergen and Gergen (1987) discuss relationship difficulties, in which talk of a "we" or an "us" changes into talk of "I" and "you"—instead of "*We* must think about this," the couple begin to say, "*You* and *I* must talk about it." Such phrasings are often constituents of a "regressive narrative" in a failing relationship, they say (p. 283). What I want to do in this chapter is partially to agree—such a change often does indicate difficulties in an intimate relationship—but also to explore other than "narrative" reasons why this is so. However, as I feel that the problem of distress in personal relations cannot be properly understood until the problem of what, conceptually, a personal relationship is, has been clarified, that is the main task that I shall set myself in the analysis below, only to return to the problem above right at the very end.

My general concern in this chapter, then, is to explore some of the problems raised (especially those of a moral kind)—not just for us as professional social scientists, but for modern, Western societies at large—by the question, "What is a close or intimate personal relationship?" and to explore the nature of the symbolic resources we might draw upon in formulating an answer to it. I want to do this within the context of my own concern with social accountability and selfhood (Shotter, 1984, 1987, 1989), i.e., the twofold claim that: (a) our experience and understanding of our *reality*, the form of our social *relationships*, and our *selves*, are all constituted for us very largely in the ways of talking that we *must* use, if we are to be accounted by the others around us as competent adults, in accounting for it (and for ourselves) in our society, but (b) that competency is developed within essentially dialogical, but intrinsically unaccountable, *joint* transactions with those others. Hence my interest also in Billig's (1987) recent rhetorical approach to social behavior, in which he emphasizes the two-sided, argumentative or dilemmatic nature of much everyday (and scientific) thought and talk, as it draws upon the communicative resources provided in the form of "topics" (*topoi*), loci, themes, or "commonplaces" in the common sense of our society. These are the common "stopping places" in the otherwise continuously changing stream of thought that enable members of a social group to attribute a shared significance to shared circumstances (Shotter, 1986) but that also import a degree of intrinsic argumentation and contest into the negotiation of accounts of events, things, and circumstances.

Theories and Traditions

When I was invited to contribute to this book, I decided to tackle the question as to what actually is a close relationship for two reasons: One was because, in my earlier excursion into this particular sphere of relationship research to do with an intimate "us" (Shotter, 1987), it had seemed to me that here, just as in many other areas of socio-developmental research in psychology, there was little or no concern with conceptual questions such as these and that this neglect was bound sooner or later to cause trouble. The other reason, however, was a substantive one, to do with a long-term interest of mine in the special properties of what I have called *joint action*—those ambiguous, uncertain social activities in our highly individualistic culture, in which people do *not* seem to act in a wholly individualistic and autonomous manner and which are intrinsically *unaccountable* because they are in some sense extraordinary, outside of normal, everyday life. These are activities that are exemplified in general in social "movements" or "transitions" rather than in stable social "states" or "institutions" (Alberoni, 1984), but in particular, in that extraordinary phenomenon of falling in (and out of) love, in which, in a special private zone of our lives, someone who was external to us, a complete stranger, is internalized and becomes such a needed part of ourselves that his or her loss is a loss we mourn. It is the nature of these both extraordinary and private, normally unaccountable regions of human conduct that I wish to investigate.

I go into this little bit of history because I now find that Duck (1990), in his "1990 state of the union" message, has to an extent "scooped" me by raising some of the same issues, in precisely the same terms, that I myself wanted to raise here—the problem of the degree to which something like a personal relationship can be said to exist independently of what the people involved in it (and the people studying it) *say* about it. Especially when all this talk has the character, as Duck claims also under Billig's (1987) influence, of unfinished business. In accepting Billig's claim that the dialectical, rhetorical, argumentative side of human life has been neglected in our theorizing, Duck is, I feel, absolutely right to suggest that we must now conceive of personal relationships as both constituted or mediated by talk and phenomenally as always in process or in transition, as still open to dialectical or argumentative change. Indeed, to go a step further, we might even suggest that, to the extent that "relational events are perceived not in a direct way but in mediated ways, through memory, recall, dialogue and conversation" (Duck, 1990, p. 24), all such events always occur on the boundary between two dialogically interlinked persons, and because of this there is no simple or single account of what a relationship is—it only has its being within a zone of intrinsic uncertainty. At least, I would suggest this, and would agree with Duck if—and this is where I shall probably depart from almost every other professional psychologist—I thought that our problem is that of formulating the right kind of general theory.

But my claim here is that this is *not* our problem. My claim in this chapter is that the unsatisfactory state of theory outlined by Duck (1990) as to what a personal relationship is, does *not* arise out of a continual failure yet to formulate the correct kind of theory, as if one day we might finally hit upon the right formulation. The problem, I think, arises out of another kind of difficulty altogether: a failure to grasp—if we actually take Billig's (1987) views about the neglect of rhetoric in our theorizing seriously—what theorizing or theory in a research area such as this should be like. It is still thought that proper theory in this area should copy natural scientific theory, as this is the only sort of theorizing that is respectable. Thus at present, because scientific theories in general are "free creations of the mind" (to quote Einstein), we feel free to formulate general theories in terms of any abstract principles which come to mind. But, as Duck points out, this results in "descriptive impositions" becoming treated (often without warrant) as "real properties of relationships" (pp. 12–13). However, if we accept that *normally* (and the normative nature of the issues in this sphere is something that has been crucially ignored) a relationship is constituted in the talk and other experiences of those who are involved in it and cannot exist as something imposed upon them by outsiders, then our theorizing must be of a very different kind. My purpose is to clarify its special nature and the degree to which it can only have its life, so to speak, within a tradition.

Accountability and Traditions

My aim in taking the two themes of (a) accountability, and (b) the two-sided, rhetorically organized, topically rooted nature of social behavior together is to use them as resources in raising a number of interconnected issues to do with the nature of thought and talk within a *tradition*: First, following Gauld and Shotter (1977), Shotter (1984), and MacIntyre (1981), we can note that human beings can only be held to account for that of which they are the authors (Shotter, 1984); an action is something for which it is *always* appropriate to ask the agent for an intelligible account. And people account for their actions by hermeneutically placing them within a larger whole; the action is rendered intelligible in terms of the part it plays within a possible sequence of other actions. However, because it is clearly possible to characterize a particular action under a large number of different possible descriptions (Menzel, 1978), we need to know in what way the persons themselves made sense of their actions. We need to know the basic "pre-understandings"—the internalized or embodied form of life with its associated *topoi* into which the person has been socialized (Shotter, 1984; Wittgenstein, 1969)—in terms of which the person him- or herself made sense of his or her own actions such that, had these pre-understandings been different, the person would not have acted as he or she did. In other words, we need to know the tradition within which people make sense of what they take to be their primary intention(s) (i.e., those for which they are prepared to be accountable).

This leads me to my second point: Following Bakhtin (1981, 1986), Bellah et al. (1985), Billig (1987), Billig et al. (1988), and MacIntyre (1981, 1988), we can note that the meaning of many important distinctions within Western life—such as those between public and private, personal and impersonal, individual and collective, uniquely individual and socially representative intimate and merely personal relations; between public institutions and everyday life activities; between the stable and the changing; between the moral and the technical, and so on—are not in any sense fully predetermined, already decided distinctions but that they are expressed or formulated in different ways in different, concrete circumstances by the use of a certain set of historically developed (and to an extent, morally maintained—see below) topological *resources* within the Western tradition. Thus, what might be called a living tradition does not give rise to a completely determined form of life but to dilemmas, to different possibilities for living, among which one must choose.

Thus, third, a living tradition, in consisting of a set of shared two-sided topics, loci, themes, or commonplaces, gives rise to the possibility of formulating a whole ecology of different and indeed unique positions, each offering different possibilities for the best way to continue and/or develop the tradition, hence its characterization as a "living" tradition. As MacIntyre (1981) puts it: "A living tradition . . . is an historically extended, socially embodied argument, and an argument precisely in part about the goods which constitute that tradition" (p. 207), and "Traditions, when vital, embody continuities of conflict" (p. 206). This is a very different idea, of course, as to what a tradition is, from that we are used to. For, under the influence of modern individualism, which was meant to free us from restrictive traditions, we have tended to equate all traditions with hierarchically structured, closed systems of knowledge, which are supposed to provide members with ready-made solutions to problems. But, as Bellah et al. (1985) have said, those who think of tradition in this way deeply misunderstand tradition even when they seek to embrace it. They defend not tradition but traditionalism, . . . whereas tradition is the living faith of the dead, traditionalism is the dead faith of the living. A living tradition is never a programme for automatic moral judgments. It is always in a continuous process of reinterpretation and reappropriation. Such a process assumes, however, that tradition has enough authority for the search for its present meaning to be publicly pursued as a common project. (pp. 140–141)

If it does have that authority (and this is an issue to which we must return), then although those with whom one argues may still find reasons to disagree, they will have to agree that one's arguments are grounded in more than just one's personal feelings, preferences, or opinions. They will have to agree that they do in fact relate agreed common goods. So, although the grounding of one's views or claims may not be sufficient to settle an argument—because one's opponents may also, as one must also agree, have grounded their arguments in agreed goods—it does mean that people can get to the position of mutually respecting each other's views. The argument must then be resolved, for instance, by moving to a larger realm of considerations, in which more impersonal goods may play a part.

Thus, fourth, it is worth noting, as Billig and his colleagues have made clear, that whether it is in public, professional, and scientific or private spheres of life, rooting one's speech or thought in the topics or themes of a living tradition is a *necessity* if one is to be a proper participant in it and to make genuine contributions to debates about its problems: "The very existence of these opposing images, words, evaluations, maxims and so on is crucial, in that they permit the possibility not just of social dilemmas but of social thinking itself" (Billig et al., 1988, p. 17). In fact, such traditions do not just constrain thought; they both enable and motivate it—they are "the *seeds*, not *flowers* of arguments," they say, quoting Bacon (1858, p. 492). For instance, as we all now realize, we cannot avoid arguments about the nature of freedom, but what one person calls "cultural hegemony" (the lack of public debate) another calls "the right of individuals to decide their own lives"; what others call "the road to serfdom" is what yet others feel makes people "free and equal"; what some call "poverty and exploitation" government ministers call "being less equal"; and so on. "It is amazing," say Perelman and Olbrechts-Tyteca (1969), "that even when very general *loci* are concerned, each *locus* can be confronted by one that is contrary to it. . . . It is accordingly possible to characterize societies not only by the particular values they prize most but by the intensity with which they adhere to one or the other of a pair of antithetical *loci*" (p. 85).

In fact, this means that when it comes to the scientific tradition itself, we can also find such two-sided *loci* or *topoi* at work (Mulkay, 1985; Potter, 1984; Potter & Mulkay, 1982; Prelli, 1989). While in the main, the scientific tradition can be characterized in terms of universalism (public testability), communality (public not personal knowledge), skepticism (the avoidance of quick conclusions), and disinterestedness (not the pursuit of self-interest) being positively valued, one can always find cases in which the actions of accredited scientists may be characterized in just the opposite terms—as displaying individuality, particularity, dogmatism, and interestedness (Prelli, 1989). Indeed, even the criterion of testability, which might be thought to be what separates factual from fictitious claims, can be interpreted in different ways, in different contexts (sometimes by the same speaker): as something that works independently of the scientist's own desires, or as something open to strategic use (Potter, 1984). In other words, all the main themes making up the scientific tradition can be used in a two-sided, rhetorical fashion, as resources in justifying one's own theories and in criticizing one's rivals. The answer to this is not somehow to try harder to be more clear about the criteria for good science but, as Billig (1989) puts it, to examine more deeply the nature of "those scientific arguments which deny their own rhetoric" (p. 142), thus to discover why they would rather hide than reveal the sources of their influence. (This point will be expanded further below.)

We must turn now to a fifth point to do with the nature of traditions, which MacIntyre (1981) raises in *After Virtue*: Central to his account of the concept of a tradition is his claim that we identify a particular action by placing the agent's intentions in doing it, both within the individual's own history, and within the history of the setting or settings to which they belong.

> In doing this, in determining what causal efficacy the agent's intentions had in one or more directions, and how his short-term intentions succeeded or failed to be constitutive of long-term intentions, [*we ourselves*] write a further part of these histories. Narrative history of a certain kind turns out to be the basic and essential genre for the characterization of human actions. (p. 194)

It is this, in MacIntyre's view, that allows us (as investigators) to establish a true identification of an action. For, as in a court of law, a witness's story can, if told appropriately, work to specify quite precisely the evidence required to corroborate or refute it; this is also the case with narratives generally: Even in an area where no proofs are available as such, narratives can themselves function to establish the requirements in terms of which the reality they specify can be checked out.

But do ordinary people in the living of their everyday lives need to identify their own actions in this way, if they are to act accountably (i.e., in a way that is routinely accountable)? No, surely not. Although we must act in a routinely accountable way in our everyday, practical living, we must also fit our own unique actions to our own unique circumstances. And we can do this as long as our actions are informed by the thematic or topical resources available to us in the tradition within which our actions play their part. Thus, although our actions may appear to outsiders as the "disjoined parts of some possible narrative," this does not mean, as MacIntyre (1981, p. 200) seems to suggest, that they do not have any meaning at all for us. They do; they have a practical meaning, in their own immediate context. What they lack is a meaning that can be grasped reflectively and theoretically; thus it is not meaning they lack but *intelligibility*. And this, of course, makes it impossible to pose and to investigate questions concerning their nature systematically and intellectually. Thus, pace MacIntyre, I think that to present human life in the form of a narrative—in order to render it reflectively intelligible—*is* to falsify it. The fact is, our life *is* lived as a sequence of disjoined parts, with each disjoined part gaining its local and immediate meaning from the context of its performance at the time of its performance—hence the importance of the primary intentions condition mentioned above. Thus, the retrospective coherency of a narrative (and the resulting intelligibility of people's actions) is achieved at the expense of rendering the local and changing context of actual, individual actions rationally invisible; the narrative's value, however (e.g., Freud), is in rendering the character of people's otherwise unaccountable actions visibly rational for intellectual purposes—an oscillation between the local and particular, the overall and general, between the voice of the individual and the voice of an intellectual group.

The sixth point I want to raise in this section concerns personal (and social) identity: One thing that is crucial in genuinely personal relationships with others, is being answerable to them for all that one has been with them in the past. MacIntyre (1981) takes a rather more strict (and more general) view of one's moral duties here: "I am forever whatever I have been at any time for others—and I may at any time be called upon to answer for it—no matter how changed I may be now" (p. 202). He takes this view because, as he points out (quite rightly), there is no way of *founding* or *rooting* my identity solely in my feelings of psychological continuity; publicly criticizable criteria of continuity, he would say, are required. Again, MacIntyre suggests that they are to be found within a twofold narrative concept of selfhood: that on the one hand, "I am what I am taken by others to be in the course of living out a story that runs from my birth to my death; I am the *subject* of a history that is my own and no one else's . . ." (p. 202), but on the other hand, "the narrative of any one life is part of an interlocking set of narratives . . . . Asking what you did and why, saying what I did and why, pondering the differences between your account of what I did, and *vice versa*, these are essential constituents of all but the very simplest and barest of narratives" (p. 203). But again we must ask, is all this necessary for an understanding of how ordinary persons can act in an accountable manner, as the unique persons they are? And perhaps of even more importance to us, interested as we are in private, intimate or love relationships: Is all this emphasis upon *public* accountability of relevance in a relationship that, by its special nature, is extraordinary, outside the larger schemes of mundane accountability? What MacIntyre sets out, I think, is a public ideal, and what we need to understand are the activities involved, not only in individual people doing the best they can practically, but also that very special form of morality operating only *within a private relationship*, between an intimate couple—where the morality of the larger, public tradition to which they belong makes its appearance only upon the breakdown of their intimacy.

This leads me to the seventh and final issue I want to raise, to do with conversations: Having made the point about narratives above, it is only fair to add that MacIntyre (1981) himself considers the claim, "that the supplying of a narrative is not necessary to make [an] act intelligible" (p. 196), that the placing of it in the context of a conversation may be sufficient. And about conversations he makes the following most important points:

> We allocate conversations to genres, just as we do literary narratives. Indeed, as conversation is a dramatic work, even if a very short one, in which the participants are not only the actors, but also the joint authors, working out in agreement or disagreement the mode of their production. . . . Conversation, understood widely enough, is the form of human transactions in general. (pp. 196–197)

About this, I could not agree more, and in a moment I shall be turning in more detail to Bakhtin's (1986) work on speech genres, in an attempt to clarify the special nature of the speech genre, which makes a private and intimate social life, as distinct from public life, possible. But when MacIntyre goes on to say that he is "presenting both conversations in particular . . . and human actions in general as enacted narratives" (p. 197), then I must disagree and reiterate the point I made above about the intrinsically, publicly unaccountable nature of joint action, of jointly authored activity (Shotter, 1984, 1987): In many of our ordinary, everyday activities, as we must interlace our actions with those of others, their actions will determine our conduct just as much as anything within ourselves. The final outcomes of such exchanges cannot strictly be traced back to the intentions of any of the individuals concerned; they must be accounted *as if* external to the participants concerned, *as if* a part of the natural world. Such activity, in giving rise to unintended and thus to publicly unaccountable outcomes, is not easy to control. Hence the creativity (and danger) of conversational or dialogical relationships, and of free speech in general.

Thus MacIntyre (1981) ignores, I think, a number of issues: One is the special nature of private life as a distinct conversational enclave within the public life of the world of Western individualism—and it is precisely its nature that we must investigate further below. Another is, I think, that it is a special feature of our tradition of individualism, that it allows many different forms of life to go on within different regions and/or moments of everyday, social life at large, without them all having to form "an interlocking set of narratives"—the tradition of individualism gives rise, one might say, to an order of possible orders, or versions, of individualism, not just one. And, establishing a private life, is one way in which we can act legitimately, precisely to avoid the necessity to interlock our actions with those of others, which MacIntyre feels necessary—hence, to appropriate to ourselves a degree of freedom at the expense of time spent contributing to one or another public order. The significance of this time out from public life, of this haven in a heartless world, is what, I think, we must make sense of. Yet another important fact he fails to acknowledge is the first-person right we assign to people to act freely, as long as their actions are routinely accountable, as long as they make sense (Shotter, 1984). But what he does not ignore, and what I think is of great importance to mention here, is the relation he introduces between our personal (or self-identity) and our social identity, for, as he sees it,

> we all approach our own circumstances as bearers of a social identity. I am someone's son or daughter, . . .; I am a citizen of this or that city, . . . hence what is good for me has to be good for one who inhabits these roles. As such, I inherit from the past of my family, my city, . . . a variety of debts, inheritances, rightful expectations and obligations. These constitute the given of my life, my moral starting point. This is in part what gives my life its moral particularity. (pp. 204–205)

This suggest that, as a version of individualism, we might propose the concept of the social individual (Sampson, 1990; Shotter, 1990), where social individuals are known in terms of their relations to others. This would be in stark contrast to the liberal concept of the possessive individual, where possessive individuals are known for those properties they possess solely within themselves, owing nothing to society for them (Macpherson, 1962)—a kind of individual MacIntyre clearly does not like.

What has begun to emerge in this section, then, are a number of oscillations as to where the authority in accounting for one's actions should be located: in one's immediate local situation or in the larger tradition of one's community, in something essentially unsystematic or in something systematic, within something private or public, in the topological resources of a tradition or in an intellectually produced narrative ordering of them, or in the people or an intellectual elite. But, as I have already hinted, all these oscillations are themselves located within a living tradition, that of Western individualism and modernism, which contains the seeds of all our arguments here. It contains the dilemmatic resources for the fashioning of a whole range of different possible accounts as to both what the social and self-identities of individuals might be and as to what a personal relationship between such individuals might be.

To look toward my conclusion for a moment: Contrary to Gergen and Gergen's (1987) claim that various narratives are involved in sustaining a love relationship, I want to claim that to be in love, is to be involved in pure *joint action*, action that, because it is intrinsically unaccountable, is extraordinary; it takes place in regions outside those in normal, everyday life—hence the point of the quote from Barthes: The love story is required to bring the extraordinary and creative phenomenon of love within the bounds of the ordinary and the routine, to make sense of it in mundane terms. It is the nature of these private and extraordinary, normally unaccountable regions of human conduct that I wish to investigate below. To understand the fashioning of these regions, it is to the communicative practices and commonplaces, the traditions and the speech genres that embody them, that we must now turn.

Speech Genres and Styles: Individuals and Their Identities

Following Chomsky (1965), a certain dogma—that anyone who has mastered a natural language is able to produce freely and understand an infinity of essentially novel sentences in that language—has enjoyed a considerable consensus in much empirical and theoretical work in psychological linguistics. It rests upon a paradigm of speech communication derived from Ferdinand de Saussure (1867–1913), which assumes that the only problem faced in communication is that of what might be called passive understanding, that is, of how an idea in the head of a speaker might come to be duplicated in the head of a listener. But as Bakhtin (1986) points out, what is involved in understanding a speaker in almost all day-to-day situations is something quite different—indeed, as we shall see, the duplication of ideas is a possible, final step but not at all a crucial step in the process of communication. As Bakhtin sees it:

> All real and integral understanding is actively responsive, and constitutes nothing other than the initial preparatory stage of a response . . . . And the speaker himself is oriented precisely toward such an actively responsive understanding. . . . [He or she] expects response, agreement, sympathy, objection, execution, and so forth (various speech genres presuppose various integral orientations and speech plans on the part of speakers or writers). (From *Speech Genres & Other Late Essays* by M.M. Bakhtin, translated by Vern McGee, p. 69, © 1986. By permission of the University of Texas Press.)

Thus, for Bakhtin (1986), the production of an utterance in an actual, everyday setting, must be distinguished from the production of an isolated, grammatical sentence: With all its individuality and creativity, an utterance can in no way be regarded as a completely free combination of linguistic forms. It is always a link in an unbroken chain of speech communication, linked both to what precedes it and to what might follow it. Futhermore, it takes into account both the identity of the speaker and the addressee, and from the very beginning it is constructed, in part, in anticipation of certain possible responses. Thus *addressivity*—the quality of it being directed toward someone—is a constitutive feature of an utterance; without it the utterance as such does not exist. A part, then, of what it is that defines a speech genre is that each sphere of speech communication has its own typical conception of its addressee, and of its addressee's speech, as Bakhtin says:

> This addressee can be an immediate participant-interlocutor in an everyday dialogue, a differentiated collective of specialists in some particular area of cultural communication, a more or less differentiated public, ethnic group, contemporaries, like-minded people, opponents and enemies, a subordinate, a superior, someone who is lower, higher, familiar, foreign, and so forth. And it can also be an indefinite, unconcretized *other*. . . . All these varieties and conceptions of the addressee are determined by that area of human activity and everyday life to which the given utterance is related. (From *Speech Genres & Other Late Essays* by M.M. Bakhtin, translated by Vern McGee, p. 95, © 1986. By permission of the University of Texas Press.)

But also within a speech genre, we must note the speaker's style, that is, how the voice in which he or she speaks takes into account both the interlocutor's position and expresses a way of dealing with what he or she might give as a response: trust, doubt, surprise, concern, earnest search for deep meaning, the acceptance of shared conventions, and so forth. Indeed, the voice of the other whom one is addressing is always present in one's own utterance, sometimes to such an extent that within many speech genres—in the giving of a paper at a psychology conference, for instance—it is not difficult at all for one's own personal voice to be almost absent.

But in everything I say, I also make a claim to sincerity, justice, truthfulness, beauty, and so forth, a claim that will occasion a response. Thus, if I am to speak in my own voice, to express myself (at least to some degree) as the author of my own actions, then I must express my own relation to what I say. To answer in my own voice—and not just in the voice of science, claiming that what I say must be true because I have observed certain conventional procedures in warranting it—I must *myself* be able to account it. Thus my *answerability* for my claims is the other side of addressivity: Besides speaking with an actively responsive understanding of what I am saying, with an anticipation of my interlocutors' response, I must not only know how they are placed, but also how I myself am placed in relation to what I am saying.

The different forms of addressivity and answerability contribute, then, to the responsivity constitutive of a speech genre. Typical genres might be in business, science, bureaucracies, education, philosophy, everyday life, families, and so forth. In these speech genres, the addressee's social position, rank, and importance are reflected in speakers' utterances. Finer nuances of style are determined by the nature and degree of personal proximity of the addressee to the speaker. We have here, then, a way of characterizing the style or the form of people's consciousness, both of themselves, and of the time-space in which they live. And what Bakhtin (1986) has done in his studies is to trace the different chronotopes (the different time-spaces)—and hence the different forms of consciousness and self-consciousness made available by the invention of different genres in Western literature—in particular, that genre that makes the expression of intimate relationships possible. Now, in studying Bakhtin's proposals in this sphere, it is necessary to say that he does not pretend to completeness or precision in his formulations and definitions, nor, of course, can I; the serious study of the representation of time-space relations in literature has hardly begun. His intention (and mine here) is just to explore in a solely hypothetical manner, the possible relations between speech genres and both the forms of identity and modes of interpersonal relations to which they give rise, in order to give an impetus to further work in this area.

Turning first to the broad distinctions between public and private speech genres, Bakhtin (1986) begins by making a fundamental distinction: "With all the immense differences among familiar and intimate speech genres (and consequently styles)," he says, "they perceive their addressees in exactly the same way: more or less outside the framework of the social hierarchy and social conventions, 'without rank,' as it were" (p. 97). Thus in speaking in an intimate speech genre (as opposed to a public one), in trying to anticipate the responses of their addressees, people do not take into account either their own or their addressee's title, class, rank, wealth, social importance, or age, but address those to whom they speak almost as if, says Bakhtin, they had merged completely. Returning now to the problems of personal (and social) identity raised by MacIntyre (1981), we can see that one aspect of the task—of accounting for oneself now in terms of a sequence of relations between what had happened to one in the past—involves the development and use of an appropriate speech genre. In the notes he offers toward the development of what he calls a historical poetics for the expression of genres, Bakhtin begins with the so-called Greek romance and ends with the Rabelaisian novel. To give the flavor of his analysis, I shall draw from the third period he discusses, what he calls the biographical novel.

Whereas in earlier Greek writing, events took place in an alien world of adventure-time, such that they lay outside the biographical time of the heroes involved and changed nothing in their lives, it is a time that left no traces. In later novels, they took place in a mixture of adventure-time with everyday time, where the transformational events occurring in the novel (e.g., Lucius's metamorphosis into an ass) provided a method for portraying the whole of an individual's life in its more important moments of crisis: for showing how an individual becomes other than he was—these are times that do leave a trace. In discussing the different kinds of identity generated by these two genres, Bakhtin (1981) has this to say: that first, we must take into account that, as distinct from all classical genres of ancient literature, the image of human beings in these novels is of people as individuals, as private persons. They are not parts of a social whole. This gives rise to problems, for this private and isolated person in the Greek romance

> often behaves, on the surface, like a public man, and precisely the public man of the rhetorical and historical genres. He delivers long speeches that are rhetorically structured and in which he seeks to enlighten us with the private and intimate details of his love life, his exploits and adventure—but all in the form of a *public accounting*. (*The Dialogic Imagination* by M.M. Bakhtin, translated by Caryl Emerson and Michael Holquist, pp. 108–109, © 1981. By permission of the University of Texas Press.)

Thus, in this chronotope (time-space representation), the unity of the human being is characterized precisely by what is rhetorical and juridical in it. Turning now to the second genre—in which Lucius as an ass has the chance to spy upon the inner, intimate details of much of Greek life—Bakhtin has this to say:

> The everyday life that Lucius observes and studies is an *exclusively personal and private life*. By its very nature there can be nothing *public* about it. All its events are the personal affairs of isolated people. . . . By its very nature this private life does not create a place for the contemplative man, for that "third person" who might be in a position to mediate upon this life, to judge and evaluate it. . . . Public life adopts the most varied means for making itself public and accounting for itself (as does its literature). Therefore, the particular positioning of a person (a "third person") presents no special problem. . . . But when the private individual and private life enter literature (in the Hellenistic era) these problems inevitably were bound to arise. *A contradiction developed between the public nature of the literary form and the private nature of its content*. . . . The quintessentially private life that entered the novel at this time was, by its very nature as opposed to public life, *closed*. In essence one could only *spy* and *eavesdrop* on it. (*The Dialogic Imagination* by M.M. Bakhtin, translated by Caryl Emerson and Michael Holquist, pp. 122–123, © 1981. By permission of the University of Texas Press.)

The *biographical novel* is the genre that, to an extent, solved this problem.

The essence of biographical time is the fashioning of a form of individual who passes through the course of a whole life. Because the development of this genre is much more multiform than the other two, I will limit my comments to just one of its forms, what Bakhtin (1986) calls the rhetorical autobiography—typified in the "encomium," the civic funeral or memorial speech. It is in such forms as these, suggests Bakhtin, in which people gave a public account either of others or themselves, that the self-consciousness of the Greek individual originated. Here, there was at first

> no internal man, no "man for himself" (I for myself), nor any individualized approach to one's own self. An individual's unity and his self-consciousness were exclusively public. Man was completely *on the surface*, in the most literal sense of the word. (p. 133)

The concept of silent thought only first appeared with the mystics and its roots in the Orient; even in Plato, the process of thought—conceived of as a conversation with oneself—did not entail any special relationship with oneself, says Bakhtin: "Conversation with one's own self turns directly into conversation with someone else, without a hint of boundaries between the two" (p. 134). So, what was the origin of what one might call an internal self-consciousness?

This begins, suggests Bakhtin (1986), with two further developments: One is the directing of the encomium toward an account of an idealized image of a particular life type, a specific profession—that of military commander, ruler, political figure—thus to import into it a *normative* character. Another was (with a degree of breakdown of the Greek public wholeness of the human image) the rise of the Roman patrician family. Here, self-consciousness begins to organize itself around the particularized memory of a clan and ancestors. The traditions of the family had to be passed down from father to son, and an account of a person's works is thus written, not for a general "someone" but rather for a specific circle of readers, the readers of one's works. Public and rhetorical forms evaluating the unity of a person's life became stereotyped and stilted.

> Moreover, the available public and rhetorical forms could not by their very nature provide for the expression of life that was private, a life of activity that was increasingly expanding in width and depth and retreating more and more into itself. Under such conditions the forms of *drawing-room rhetoric* acquired increasing importance, and the most significant form was the *familiar letter*. In this intimate and familiar atmosphere . . . a new private sense of self, suited to the drawing room, began to emerge. A whole series of categories involving self-consciousness and the shaping of a life into a biography—success, happiness, merit—began to lose their public and state significance and passed over into the private and personal plane. . . . Other categories as well undergo analogous transformations in this new little private drawing-room world. Numerous petty details of private life begin to take on an importance; in them, the individual feels "at home," his private sense of self begins to take its bearings from these petty details. The human begins to shift to a space that is closed and private, the space of private rooms where something approaching intimacy is possible, where it loses its monumental formedness and exclusively public exteriority. (*The Dialogic Imagination* by M.M. Bakhtin, translated by Caryl Emerson and Michael Holquist, pp. 143–144, © 1981. By permission of the University of Texas Press.)

Here, then, suggests Bakhtin, we can begin to find the origins of intimacy, of intimate speech genres, which have their currency within these private enclaves, away from public life at large. They are genres in which people account for their lives, not just to anyone in general, publicly, but to a limited group of others located in a familiar (family) setting. This, of course raises problems for us, as scientists facing the task of accounting for close relationships in general, publicly agreed terms.

Two Kinds of Theory

If we take Bakhtin's comments about the origins and nature of speech genres seriously, the possibility of our being able to use language in the sphere of research into personal relationships in the same way that it is used in the natural sciences—with each term having a discreet, unambiguous meaning—is remote. For, as Bakhtin (1981) says, with regard to language in general:

> As a living, socio-ideological concrete thing, as heteroglot opinion, language, for the individual consciousness, lies on the borderline between oneself and the other. The word in language is half someone else's. It becomes "one's own" only when the speaker populates it with his own intentions, his own accent, when he appropriates the word, adapting it to his own semantic and expressive intention. Prior to this moment of appropriation, the word does not exist in a neutral and impersonal language (it is not, after all, out of a dictionary that the speaker gets his words!), but rather it exists in other people's mouths, in other people's contexts, serving other people's intentions: it is from there that one must take the word, and make it one's own. (*The Dialogic Imagination* by M.M. Bakhtin, translated by Caryl Emerson and Michael Holquist, pp. 293–294, © 1981. By permission of the University of Texas Press.)

Thus someone who wants to speak to someone intimately but tries to do it in the scientific language of personal relationships, finds him- or herself, as Bakhtin points out, literally unable to speak in his or her own words, unable properly to express an authentic inner self—besides, the person's own intentions, his or her talk has hidden in it other intentions, and this is bound to raise the kind of conflicts in his or her relations that Billig et al. (1988) have formulated as "ideological dilemmas." For us as researchers too, there are consequences: If in our talk about our research into people's intimate, personal relations we use the kind of specially invented, abstract terms we usually feel free to use in our theorizing in psychology, we put *their* words into *our* terms, yet again inviting ideological dilemmas. How are we to react to *this* dilemma: of our words colonizing, so to speak, the modes of being of those we study?

If we are to analyze and illuminate the nature of the transactions in intimate personal relations (and perhaps to explain them), then we must, I think, as in our everyday communicative practices, oscillate not only between both sides of a number of different topics but also between the general and the particular (Billig, 1985). We must realize that although relationship dilemmas—those to do with, for instance, autonomy-connection, openness-closedness, and predictability-novelty (Baxter, 1988, 1990)—can be argued over in general theoretical, political, and ethical debates in society at large, they must also be faced and resolved in their own different particular and practical ways, in different particular sites or situations. In such circumstances, whatever theory we have to offer does not function as a set of laws or principles giving us as professionals perspicuous access to a reality that is otherwise hidden from us, thus easily to manipulate it—we all now accept, surely, that theory has never worked for us in the human sciences like this. Nor, surely, even if the invitation is there to act as if it does should be apply it in this way: that is, silence the "voices" (to use another term of Bakhtin's, 1986) to be heard at all the different particular sites where problems are being faced and resolved, in different ways in different circumstances. As Said (1985) says about the West's colonization of the Orient (hence my reference to colonization above):

> Yet what gave the Oriental's world its intelligibility and identity was not the result of his own efforts but rather the whole complex series of knowledgeable manipulations by which the Orient was identified by the West. . . . [Thus] it does not occur to Balfour [lecturing the House of Commons in 1910 about Egypt], to let the Egyptian speak for himself, since presumably any Egyptian who would speak is more likely to be "the agitator [who] wishes to raise difficulties" than the good native who overlooks the "difficulties" of foreign domination. . . . [Hence] truth becomes a matter of learned judgment, not of the material itself, which in time seems to owe even its existence to the Orientalist. . . [who receives] these cultures not as they are but as, for the benefit of the receiver, they ought to be. (pp. 40, 33, 67)

And this could be said of any field in which a group of academic experts speak on behalf of those they study: The characterization of what is being studied is influenced just as much, if not more, by matters of professional selection and judgment as by its own actual character.

At present, it is still thought that proper theory in psychology, and thus also in the psychological investigation of personal relationships, should copy natural scientific theory, as this is the only sort of theorizing thought respectable in our scientistic culture. And this, as I have already mentioned, allows us to formulate general theories in terms of any abstract principles or laws (or rational models) we please—as long as we subsequently attempt to prove them true, to prove that they correspond with reality in some way. We can do this by selecting a number of "sites" for their test (at best one or two, say, marital or nonmarital relations, same or different sex relations, ect.), and if our theory holds up, then we can publish it with the suggestion that such laws or principles can generalized and used to control and predict what is the case elsewhere in social life. This, however, is a recipe that not only leads to what Duck (1990) politely calls the field's "subtly changing *Zeitgeist*"—the fact that theories come and go like comets with a slowly fading tail research that disappears almost completely when another comet appears on the scene. It also blinds us to the very real complexities in the nature of personal relationships themselves (and in particular to the nature of genuinely private relationships). But perhaps even more important, it blinds us to the nature of our relations with/to those we study. In particular, it obscures from us the fact that we share with them a traditional set of ideological dilemmas and a common set of topical, symbolic resources in terms of which we must necessarily make sense, if we are to be seen by them as contributing to *their* dilemmas in our investigations. Otherwise, we run two interconnected risks: We run the very risk that science was supposed to avoid, of accepting as literally true what is merely a cultural convention (that the only real knowledge is scientific knowledge), and in refusing to open our position to argumentation and debate, of closing off new avenues of thought—just what was said to be wrong in the older moral traditions. We also, to the extent to which scientific traditions of thought are to do with manipulation and control, run the risk of being accused of doing this in the name of mastery and domination.

This can be avoided, I think, if we apply Billig's (1987; Billig et al., 1988) proposals to do with the argumentative, dilemmatic nature of our actual everyday thought, variously rooted as it is in a particular collection of two-sided "topics"—so that it recursively oscillates between the general and the specific, the finished and the unfinished, the individual and the collective, the public and the private, first-person autonomy and social dependence, authority and equality, between what is (being, space) and what might be (becoming, time), and between what is (science) and what should be (morality), as well as many other such two-sided topics besides, all of which exist as symbolic resources in the common sense of our culture. If we apply this kind of approach reflexively to our own thinking about personal relationships, as well as to our own conduct and reporting of our investigations, then we can perhaps see that theory in the understanding and study of personal relationships and theory in the natural sciences must differ in a number of fundamental ways. Not least, let it be said immediately, we come up against the impossibility (if we take Duck's advice and think of personal relationships as "unfinished business," as I think we must) of defining our objects of study in any general terms, ahead of time, irrespective of their situation, irrespective of the different particular resource topics located in the different time-spaces (Giddens, 1980) or chronotopes in which they are conducted.

Conclusions

For Personal Relationships

What I have argued above, then, is that for the most part people relate themselves to one another not only within certain (argumentatively structured) traditions but also within certain speech genres constructed from resources made available within such traditions. Hence, the forms of personal relationships within the different regions of (especially a modern) society are clearly many and varied. Indeed, to return to our point of departure—that personal relationships are both constituted and mediated by talk—we can now begin to see the complexity that claim. Society seems to contain a whole ecology of different interdependent regions and moments, containing different forms of social life sustained by different speech genres, constituting different forms of social and personal relationships. But there do seem to be some common features of all personal or intimate relationships: They all have a conversational character, that is, the participants' position in public life plays no part in the responsive nature of their exchanges. Indeed, as Bakhtin (1986) notes, the speech genres created for use in genuinely intimate exchanges not only operate in a private sphere, removed from public life, but they also open up a special inner, self-conscious aspect of life, separate and different from the genres used in public life.

But these two realms—the private and the public—are related to one another, and people can move from the intimate interpersonal realm into the realm of public affairs in a (careless) instant. The move occurs when the interpersonal flow of activity between them breaks down to such an extent that they feel they must account for (i.e., justify) their conduct to one another as properly socially competent individuals, instead of finding the resources required from within their relationship: "Oops, there we go again. We've gotten overtired again. Let's talk about it in the morning when we're not so tired." It is when such resources are lacking that appeals to larger, more public schemes of accountability become apparent. We can see now why it is that within an intimate, personal (love) relationship that, irrespective of whether the participants have been able to establish an approprate narrative or not, the transition from an "us" to a "you-and-I" way of talking indicates a fading of intimacy. From having been merged in their love (in pure joint action) into an "us," the participants reemerge into their separate individualities, into still a personal relationship but now one of a more publicly accountable kind.

For Relationships Research

My claim in this chapter, then, is that the unsatisfactory state of theory in the understanding of what a personal relationship is, does not arise out of a continual failure yet to formulate "the correct" theory, but that it arises out of a failure to understand what theory in this area should be like. It is still thought that it should copy natural scientific theory, as this is the only sort which is respectable. Whereas, if we apply Billig's (1987) proposals—to do with the rhetorical, argumentative, two-sided nature of thought, as well as to do with the oscillation between the general and the particular, the decontexted and the contexted—reflexively to our thinking about personal relationships, then we can perhaps see that theory in the natural sciences and theory in the understanding and study of personal relationships must differ fundamentally.

In fact, what we should note, I think, is Aristotle's division of the sciences into the theoretical (e.g., mathematics, physics, and psychology), productive (arts and crafts, medicine, engineering, etc.), and practical (ethics and politics) sciences (see Bernstein, 1983, pp. 38–44; Shotter, 1984, Chap. 2)—where our concern is not so much with theoretical science but with practical science or reasoning; where practical reasoning is concerned with living with indeterminacy *in practice*; and where, in practice, it is not a case of choosing between *incommensurate* moral premises or of facing *incompatible* "goods," nor of following an already determined good, because one does not have to choose in general, ahead of time. In practice, one must choose in particular, in different ways in different local circumstances—and if one is rooted in one's circumstances and has grounds at the time for one's choice—there is always a best choice in the circumstances, one which one can justify to others and feel to have manifested some honor and virtue in having chosen it. Indeed, as MacIntyre (1981) points out, this is why the manifestation of a virtue in the solution of a moral problem is not at all like the practice of a professional skill, making use of the techniques of the productive sciences—in which one can be judged against the standards of the profession.

In science, our task is to reason from grounds (empirically warranted, theoretical premises) to conclusions, in order to explain people's behavior. Thus, what we want from our theories (at least) is explicitness, abstractness (generality), systematicity, and the power of predicting—thus to enable us to control—what is in fact the case. Is this what we want here in the sphere of personal relationships research? In politics and ethics in everyday life, our task is to reason from people's (and our own) actions to their grounds, in order to justify their (or our) behavior—a movement in the opposite direction from scientific reasoning. Thus, what we want from our theoretical resources is not so much explicitness as open-texturedness (adaptability to a specific context), not abstractness but specifiability (of their significance in the context), not systematicity but a meaningful coherence, for we do not want to predict behavior but to understand what we ought in the circumstances to do. In science, we are already in touch with the grounds of our reasoning and we wish to extend its scope. In politics and ethics, we know what we would like to do, but we are not in immediate touch (or have lost touch) with the grounds of our reasoning—we are unsure as to how our actions should be evaluated, we are puzzled as to their *normative accountability*. This, I think, is the kind of puzzle we face in trying to understand what the nature of a personal relationship "is."

References

Alberoni, F. (1984). *Falling in love*. New York: Random House.

Bacon, F. (1858). *Of the dignity and advancement of learning*. London: Longman. (Original work published 1605).

Bakhtin, M.M. (1981). *The dialogical imagination*. (C. Emerson & M. Holquist, Trans.) Austin, TX: University of Texas Press.

Bakhtin, M.M. (1986). *Speech genres and other late essays*. (Vern W. McGee, Trans.). Austin, TX: University of Texas Press.

Barthes, R. (1983). *A lover's discourse*. New York: Hill and Wang.

Baxter, L.A. (1988). A dialectical perspective on communicational strategies in relationship development. In S.W. Duck, D.F. Day, S.E. Hobfall, W. Iches & B. Montgomery (Eds.), *Handbook of Personal Relationships*. London: Wiley.

Baxter, L.A. (1990). Dialectical contradictions in relationship development. *Journal of Social and Personal Relations, 7*, 69–88.

Bellah, R.N., Madsen, R., Sullivan, W.M., Swidler, A. & Tipton, S.M. (1985). *Habits of the heart: Individualism and commitment in american life*. Berkeley, CA: University of California Press.

Bernstein, R.J. (1983). *Beyond objectivism and relativism*. Oxford: Blackwell.

Billig, M. (1985). Prejudice, categorization and particularization: From a perceptual to a rhetorical approach. *European Journal of Social Psychology, 15*, 79–103.

Billig, M. (1987). *Arguing and thinking: A rhetorical approach to social psychology*. Cambridge: Cambridge University Press.

Billig, M., Condor, S., Edwards, D., Gane, M., Middleton, D., & Radley, R. (1988). *Ideological Dilemmas*. London: Sage Publications.

Chomsky, N. (1965). *Aspects of the theory of syntax*. Cambridge, MA: M.I.T. Press.

Duck, S.W. (1990). Relationships as unfinished business: Out of the frying pan and into the 1990's. *Journal of Social and Personal Relationships, 7*, 5–28.

Gauld, A.O. & Shotter, J. (1977) *Human action and its psychological investigation*. London: Routledge and Kegan Paul.

Gergen, K.J. & Gergen, M. (1987) Narratives of relationship. In R. Burnett, P. McGee, & D. Clarke (Eds.), *Accounting for personal relationships: Social representations of interpersonal links*. London: Methuen.

Giddens, A. (1980). *The constitution of society*. Cambridge: Polity Press.

MacIntyre, A. (1981). *After virtue*. London: Duckworth.

MacIntyre, A. (1988). *Whose justice? Which rationality?*. London: Duckworth.

Macpherson, C.B. (1962). *The political theory of possessive individualism: Hobbes to Locke*. Oxford: Oxford University Press.

Menzel, H. (1978). Meaning—Who needs it?. In M. Brenner, P. Marsh, & M. Brenner (Eds.), *The social contexts of method*. London: Croom Helm.

Mulkay, M. (1985). *The word and the world*. London: George Allen and Unwin.

Perelman, C., & Olbrechts-Tyteca, L. (1969). *The new rhetoric: A treatise on argumentation*. Notre Dame, IN: University of Notre Dame Press, 1958.

Potter, J. (1984). Testability, flexibility: Kuhnian values in scientists' discourse concerning theory choice. *Philosophy of the Social Sciences, 14*, 303–330.

Potter, J., & Mulkay, M. (1982). Making theory useful: Utility accounting in social psychologists' discourse. *Fundamenta Scientiae, 34*, 259–278.

Prelli, L.J. (1989). The rhetorical construction of scientific ethos. In H. Simons (Ed.), *Rhetoric in the human sciences*. London: Sage Publications.
Said, E. (1985). *Orientalism*. Harmondsworth, England: Penguin Books.
Sampson, E.E. (1990). social psychology and social control. In I. Parker & J. Shotter (Eds.), *Deconstructing social psychology*. London: Routledge.
Shotter, J. (1984). *Social accountability and selfhood*. Oxford: Blackwell.
Shotter, J. (1986). A sense of place: Vico and the social production of social identities. *British journal of social psychology, 25*, 199–211.
Shotter, J. (1987). The social construction of an "us": Problems of accountability and narratology. In R. Burnett, P. McGee, & D. Clarke (Eds.), *Accounting for personal relationships: Social representations of interpersonal links*. London: Methuen.
Shotter, J. (1989). The social construction of "you". In J. Shotter & K.J. Gergen (Eds.), *Texts of identity*. London: Sage Publications.
Shotter, J. (1990). Social individuality versus possessive individualism: The sounds of silence. In I. Parker & J. Shotter (Eds.), *Deconstructing social psychology*. London: Routledge.
Wittgenstein, L. (1969). *On certainty*. Oxford: Blackwell.

3
Interactions of Process and Moderator Variables in Account Episodes

PETER SCHÖNBACH

Imagine a babysitter who fails to notice that his or her charge, a 3-year-old boy, sneaks out of bed and into the kitchen, and drinks from a bottle of cleaning fluid. Alerted by the boy's screaming, the babysitter rushes into the kitchen, sees what has happened, and calls the emergency ambulance. The boy is whisked to the hospital, where his stomach is pumped out, and no permanent damage is to be feared. When the boy's parents return from their outing they learn already on the staircase from a neighbor what has happened before they approach the waiting babysitter. What will the parents say to the babysitter? How will she or he respond? And what will be the parents' reaction to all of this?

The vignette just described and the three appended questions exemplify an interaction process that I call an *account episode*. Account episodes may take on various forms, but most of them reveal the same basic pattern (see Figure 3.1).

Structure and Functions of Account Episodes

The basic pattern of an account episode contains its minimal ingredients: two agents, an "actor" and an "opponent," who engage in an interaction across the following four phases.

1. *Failure event*. The actor is, rightly or wrongly, held at least partly responsible by the opponent for the violation of a normative expectation held by the opponent. This can either be an acted offense or the omission of an obligation.
2. *Reproach phase*. Frequently the opponent reacts to the failure event with some kind of a reproach, mild or severe, hence the name of this

---

Paper presented at the Symposium on Attribution, Accounts and Close Relationships, International Conference on Personal Relationships, Oxford, July 1990.

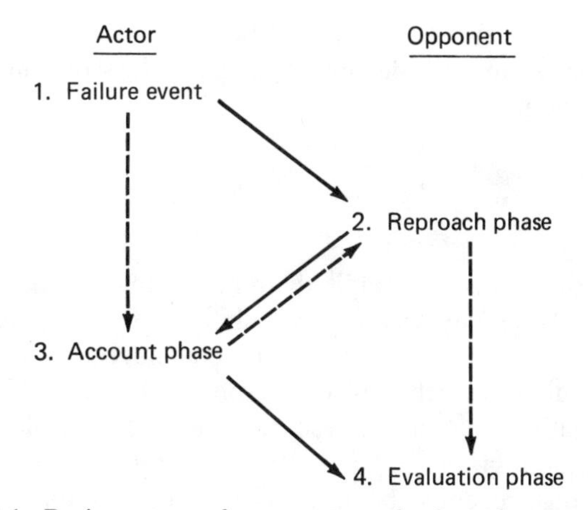

FIGURE 3.1. Basic pattern of an account episode and some variants.

phase. However, the opponent may also respond with a neutral why question or an expression of sympathy or compassion, instead of, or in addition to, a reproach.

3. *Account phase*. The actor, called upon to respond to the opponent's challenge, may react with an account in the narrow sense—an excuse or a justification. Alternative or supplementary reactions of the actor during this phase may be concessions of responsibility or guilt, or else some explicit or covert refusal to offer an account or to admit one's own involvement in the failure event.
4. *Evaluation phase*. Eventually—either right after the actor's account, concession, or refusal, or after some more interchanges between the two agents—the opponent will come to an evaluation of any or all of the following: the account or account substitute, the failure event in the light of the account, and the actor's personality in the light of both failure event and account.

Account episodes are ubiquitous components of social processes at all levels of complexity, from mild collisions of marital partners to the intricacies of negotiations at disarmament conferences. They derive from the time-honored judicial principle *audiatur et altera pars* (the other side should also be heard) and thus ultimately from the basic desire to avoid or minimize uncontrolled intrasocietal strife. Prevailing norms impose negative sanctions upon unmitigated forms of retribution such as the blood feud, and indeed, such raw forms of retribution have become the exception almost everywhere in the light of those sanctions as well as the social benefits of account episodes in and out of court. Conflicts engendered by a failure event and leading to the negotiations across phases of reproach, account, and evaluation may be resolved or diminished in the very course of such an episode. This is their main social purpose. There may also be individual benefits for the participants if in the course of such an episode hurt feelings of loss of control and self-esteem are soothed.

Basic Question

As a rule, account episodes fulfill their mitigating functions fairly well, but there are also many cases in which they founder, leading to an escalation rather than a diminution of the engendered conflict. What are the conditions under which this will happen? This has been the basic question stimulating my central research efforts for the last 15 years. I have written a monograph under the title *Account Episodes* (Schönbach, 1990), which has recently been published by Cambridge University Press.[1] This book presents the fruits of our research program so far: theory, methods, and the results of a dozen interconnected studies. Obviously, it would be foolish to try to compress all this into this chapter. Instead I shall select two or three remarkable examples of rather complex yet meaningful interplays of situational, procedural, and dispositional variables that seem to contribute to the accomplishment or else the foundering of account episodes. Let me first briefly introduce my theoretical frame so that those data constellations will become transparent.

A Theory of Conflict Escalation

The basic assumption is that both participants in an account episode, the actor as well as the opponent, are particularly vulnerable in their needs for control and positive self-evaluation. If under these conditions at least one of the participants tries to maintain or regain a sense of control and self-esteem in a way that disregards the corresponding needs of the other participant, then the probability of the conflict to escalate and the account episode to founder is relatively high. This basic assumption led to a network of specific hypotheses, presented in Figure 3.2.

One example may help to explain the meaning of the symbols in Figure 3.2. The more severe the reproach (Sev Rep) uttered by the opponent, the stronger will be the feeling of lack or loss of control and hence also the need to assert or reassert control on the part of the actor, and this will increase his or her tendency to react with a defensive account (Def Acc). The more defensive an actor's account, the greater will be the opponent's

[1] In this book I duly acknowledge the splendid contributions of my co-workers and students, and refer to the relevant literature from other quarters. The publisher kindly granted permission to reproduce here five figures from this book.

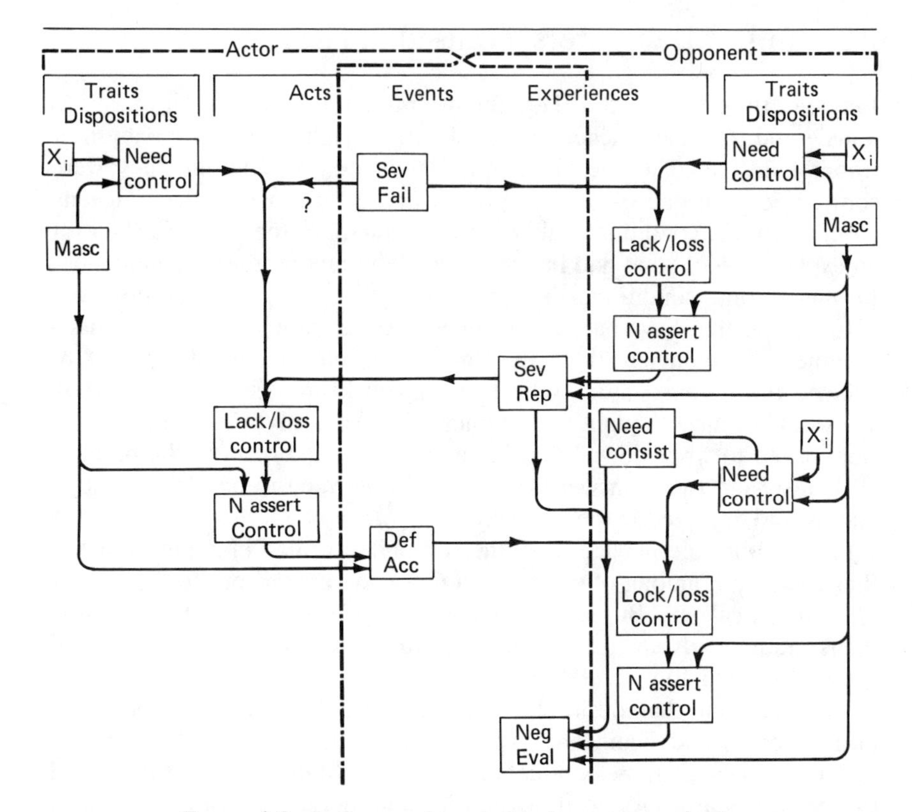

FIGURE 3.2. A theory of escalation in account episodes.

feelings of lack or loss of control, feelings that had already been created in accordance with the severity of the failure event (Sev Fail). Consequently, the need to (re)assert control on the part of the opponent may be particularly high in such a case and induce in him or her markedly negative evaluations, with corresponding bleak aspects for the future of the relationship between actor and opponent.

A further set of hypotheses implies that males (Masc) as compared to females have higher needs for control as well as higher needs to assert or reassert control, given a certain amount of loss of control feelings, and also stronger tendencies, with control aspects held constant, to react with severe reproaches and negative evaluations in the role of opponents, and with defensive accounts in the role of actors.

The various hypotheses may be seen as representing additive components on the route of escalation toward negative evaluation and disruption. However, from the very beginning it seemed possible that some or all of the factors involved would interact in ways that could either dampen or enhance the conflict escalation beyond any additive effects. This indeed proved to be the case, and I turn now to some demonstrations.

Accounts of Babysitters Accused of Negligence

In one of the studies (APS II) that concentrated on the account phase, 93 female and 92 male teachers were asked to imagine being the babysitter whom I described at the beginning of my talk. In addition they were confronted with one of three reproach phase reactions of the returning parents. In one condition, dubbed *neutral question*, the parents asked for an explanation of what had happened, without any reproachful innuendo. In the second condition, *derogation of self-esteem*, the parents said: "How could that have happened to you? Apparently you were too much occupied with yourself!?" In the third condition, *derogation of sense of control*, the parents said: "Why haven't you been able to prevent this? We wouldn't have thought that you lose sight so easily!" The respondents were asked to write down verbatim how they would react to the parents' challenge, and these answers were coded according to an elaborate taxonomy and analyzed in various ways.

Prior to the role-playing task, the respondents filled in a questionnaire that contained, among other items, a German version[2] of the *desirability of control* scale by Burger and Cooper (1979) and six self-satisfaction items adopted from the scales of Hormuth and Lalli (1986) and Bergemann and Johann (1985).

It turned out that desire for control and self-satisfaction correlated fairly strongly and significantly ($p < .01$) among both, female ($r = .54$) and male ($r = .45$) respondents of APS II. Many of the Burger and Cooper items are phrased in a way that the measured desire for control might also be called "self-confident claim on control." For one of the analyses, to be presented in a moment, we decided to combine the control and the self-satisfaction measure as quasi-independent variables in order to contrast respondents with high desires for control *and* high degrees of self-satisfaction, according to median split criteria, with respondents low on both dimensions.

The babysitter vignette proved to be useful in several of our studies because it stimulated a variety of account phase reactions, ranging from unreserved concessions of guilt feelings and responsibility for the mishap via all sorts of excuses and/or justifications to outright refusals to accept any blame, sometimes coupled with sarcastic remarks about the negligent parents who had left the cleaning fluid bottle within reach of the child. This wide range of reactions encouraged us to construct a summary index of account phase defensiveness by summing for each respondent twice the number of refusal categories in the respondent's account plus the number

---

[2] I am grateful to Delia Nixdorf and Ilona Prystav for having provided a first draft of the German translation of the Desirability of Control Scale, and to Petra Kleibaumhüter, who was in charge of the APS II investigation.

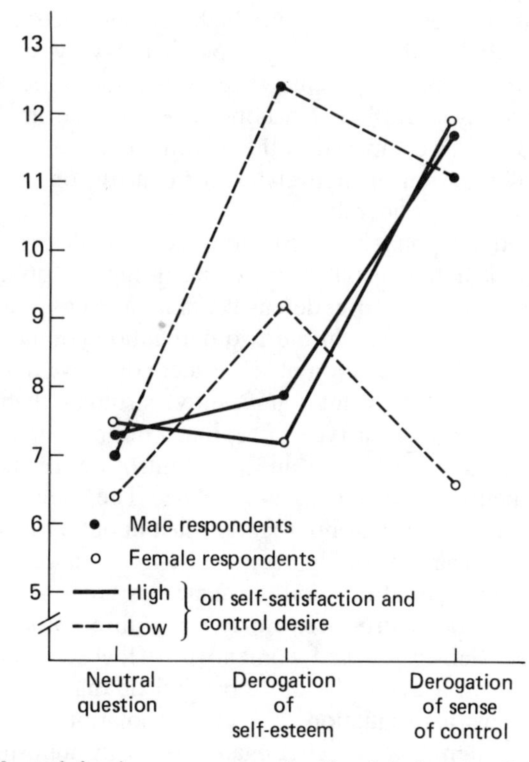

FIGURE 3.3. Mean defensiveness scores of self-satisfied and self-dissatisfied male and female respondents with high and low desire for control, within three reproach conditions of APS II.

of justification categories, minus the number of excuse categories, minus twice the number of concession categories, plus a constant of 10 to avoid negative values. The higher the score, the more marked the respondent's defensiveness in the face of the parents' question or reproach.

According to the escalation theory, I expected the respondents in the two derogation conditions to react more defensively than those confronted with a neutral question. No prediction was made as to which of the two derogations, if at all, would generally have more severe effects on the actors' reactions. Males were, of course, expected to offer more defensive accounts than females, and respondents with high desire for control were expected to be more defensive than respondents with low control desire. Finally, I expected that self-dissatisfied respondents would show more defensiveness than the self-satisfied ones and that this might show up most clearly in the condition derogation of self-esteem, whereas the respondents with marked control desires might be particularly vulnerable to the reproach in the condition derogation of sense of control. Figure 3.3 shows the data constellation we obtained.

Look first at the respondents with high self-satisfaction and control desire. Males and females in this group reacted very similarly to the various challenges from the parents. The derogation directed at the self left them apparently unruffled. No noticeable increase in defensiveness under this condition as compared to the neutral question condition can be detected. The derogation of their claims for control, on the other hand, raised their defenses considerably.[3]

Self-dissatisfied respondents with low control desire produced a markedly different data constellation. In this group the predicted gender difference—males to be more defensive than females—appeared, but strongly and significantly only in the two derogation conditions. Furthermore, in this group the derogation of self-esteem did have a defensiveness-raising effect, even (though not significantly) stronger than the control derogation. Finally, the latter type of reproach did not seem to affect the women with little self-satisfaction and low control desire, if we take the effects of the neutral question as a baseline. The men in this group, however, reacted to the control derogation just about as strongly as their self-satisfied counterparts with high control desire. This gender difference suggests the possibility that one and the same position on a scale measuring self-satisfaction or control desire may carry different implications for men and women. Self-dissatisfied women with a low score on the control desire scale may, on average, be more pessimistic than men with similar scores and react with resignation to a direct violation of their sense of control, whereas men tend to rebel against such an imposition, because indicating "low desire for control" does not at all imply that they are willing to abdicate whatever control they have.

What are we to learn from the data pattern in Figure 3.3? There is encouragement for the escalation theory, especially for its heuristic version, which allows and looks for interaction effects. The basic prediction that links severity of reproach to defensiveness of account receives strong support, but this main effect should be considered in the light of the demonstrated interactions. Gender characteristics, in conjunction with a specific combination of self-esteem and control dispositions, may sensitize a person to react to a particular type of reproach either with a markedly low or a markedly high degree of defensiveness.

Specifications of the Desire for Control

Desire for control can be differentiated into two components according to a factor analysis with the data from APS II. I call these two components *desire for competence* and *desire for constancy*; they are represented by

[3] All contrastive statements of this kind are supported by significant ($p < .05$) F-tests, if not indicated otherwise.

two subscales, each containing nine items. A typical item of the first subscale reads: "I would prefer to be a leader rather than a follower." This scale measures the desire for influencing the environment and for the assertion of competence. A typical item of the second subscale reads: "I try to avoid situations where someone tells me what to do." A high score on this subscale indicates a need for constancy in the social environment and for shielding against any environmental variations that seem unmanageable or threatening.

Desire for competence and desire for constancy correlate positively, but at best at moderate, though significant ($p > .01$), levels, namely $r = .45$ among males, and $r = .41$ among females in the APS II sample. This left sufficient degrees of freedom for introducing desire for competence and desire for constancy as separate moderator variables into some of our analyses, and indeed, they led to further differentiations. As a demonstration example, I chose a data pattern from one of the studies (EPS III) directed at the evaluation phase.

Assault and Robbery Victims Evaluating the Assailant's Account

In this study, 67 women and 56 men, adult citizens of various urban communities, took part as respondents. Roughly equal quotas from three age brackets were envisaged and obtained for each gender. The respondents received a typed vignette of a case of assault and robbery by an adolescent and were requested to take the victim's role. First they had to write down verbatim what they would say to the assailant, who had been caught by a sturdy man a few seconds after the assault and attempt to run away with the victim's bag. After that the instruction continued with an account offered by the adolescent and the further request to the respondent to write down his or her reply to this account. A number of items with answer scales, including the desire for control and self-satisfaction measures, followed and concluded the questionnaire.

Two accounts were used in this study; they formed one of the independent variables. The *concessive account* showed little defensiveness; it was composed of concessive and excusatory themes. The *refutational account* consisted of highly defensive justificative and refutational arguments. This account variation also entered into intriguing interactions, but I shall bypass further details here because the one data pattern I want to present from this study holds for both account conditions.

Figure 3.4 shows a significant ($p < .03$) three-way interaction of the respondents' gender, desire for competence, and desire for constancy as factors and the account's evaluations, obtained with a scale, as dependent variable. The higher the score, the more negative the evaluation.

FIGURE 3.4. Mean negative evaluations of the accounts in EPS III by men and women with various combinations of desires for competence and for constancy.

The highest degree of negativity was produced by the male group with high desire for competence and low desire for constancy. The lowest degree of negativity appeared in the most opposite group: among the females with low desire for competence and high desire for constancy. This pattern fits well into the theoretical frame. Men who are mainly intent on asserting themselves and who show little concern with the stability of their environment are those persons in the opponent role we would expect to be most outspoken and aggressive in their evaluation of a misdeed and its culprit. Women who mainly desire that their environment remains nonthreateningly constant, rather than wishing to assert their competence, may well be expected to be notably restrained in their evaluative reactions.

The data constellation in Figure 3.4 suggests that the two aspects of control—desire for competence and desire for constancy—may acquire widely different functional meanings for various participants in an account episode. This conclusion is most clearly supported by the four data points of the respondents with high desire for competence. Men who also showed high desire for constancy reacted less negatively to the account than the competence-prone men who cared little about constancy. With the women the reverse pattern appeared. It seems that among the female respondents only the joint force of high need for competence *and* constancy produced markedly negative reactions.

The Chances of Excuses and Justifications in a Case of Dubious Self-Defense

My third and last example concerns the question of whether, in general, justifications or excuses stand a better chance to be evaluated positively by the opponent in an account episode. Presumably, in each individual case the chances of a particular account will very much depend on its specific content and wording and on the situational context. One may nevertheless look for main effects of category memberships of accounts as excuses versus justifications, despite those individual variations, and one may argue for two contradictory hypotheses in this respect:

1. According to the escalation theory, a justification, with which an actor asserts the full or partial legitimacy of his or her behavior under the circumstances of the event in question, is considered as more defensive than an excuse, which does at least admit the failure aspect of the event. Consequently, justifications are considered to meet with more negative evaluations, on average, than excuses do.
2. On the other hand, a halfway plausible justification may stand a better chance than an excuse to be accepted with some relief, because it can more convincingly maintain or recreate the impression (or illusion) of a just and orderly world.

We[4] approached this issue in our first, mainly exploratory evaluation phase study (EPS I) with a case of dubious self-defense presented in a vignette to 64 male students with fields of study other than psychology or law. The actor presented in this vignette, after having been accosted by a drunkard, had thrown a beer bottle at the drunkard's head, thereby causing a head injury. The self-defender, called in for an investigation, offered an account that, among other things, had to be judged on several scales.

Four accounts were used in this study as independent variables, two excuses and two justifications—in each of these two categories one account with an internal and the other one with an external locus of argument. Because the locus dimension did not produce any significant differences, I shall illustrate the excuses and justifications by just one, the "internal" pair:

Excuse: "I am sorry, but I felt threatened, and I did not know how to help myself otherwise. If one is frightened like that one acts in a way instinctively. The beer bottle was the only thing at hand at that moment."

[4] Gunter Damerow was in charge of this study under my supervision.

Justification: "I felt threatened, and therefore I defended myself. I was entitled to protect my health and possibly even my life. The beer bottle was the only usable thing at hand at that moment."

During the first part of the interview each respondent was confronted with just one of the four accounts. For this part each cell of the 2 × 2 design contains 16 cases. I shall call the evaluations during this phase "separate judgments." In the final part of the interview all 64 respondents received all four accounts with the request to read them and then judge each one with respect to its acceptability. The data from this part will be labeled "comparative judgments."

The data from the separate judgments show that the justifications performed somewhat better than the excuses in eliciting positive evaluations. On several scales, for instance on the dimension "acceptability of the account," the differences were not significant. But with respect to the justifiability of the self-defensive act the ratings were significantly ($p < .02$) higher after a justification than after an excuse. This, however, was not the final word, as Figure 3.5 shows.

Please note: The higher the score in this diagram, the more *unacceptable* the account was judged to be. Although the separate and the comparative judgments are not strictly comparable, it seems that the chances of the justifications worsened, whereas the chances of the excuses improved. A

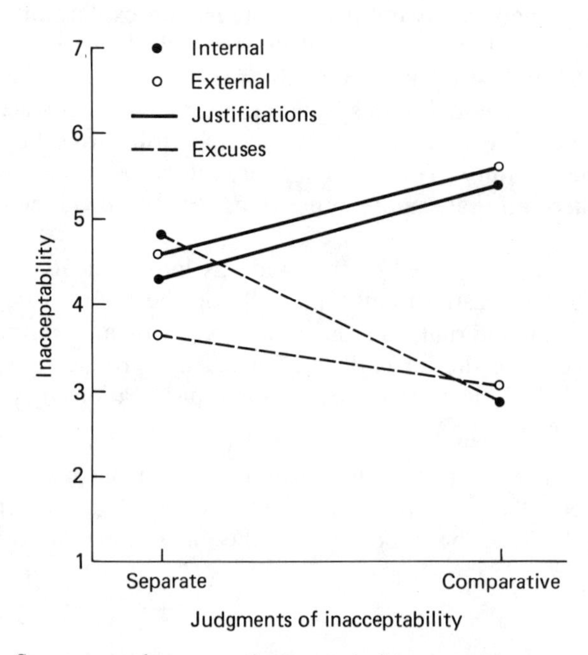

FIGURE 3.5. Separate and comparative mean judgments of inacceptability of four types of accounts in EPS I.

repeated-measures ANOVA with the comparative judgments resulted in a highly significant ($p < .001$) main effect of excuses versus justifications. When compared directly with the excuses, the two justifications appeared clearly less acceptable, perhaps because the lack of an apologetic note in the justifications became salient through the comparisons.

The data from the comparative judgments strongly favor the corresponding hypothesis of the escalation theory; the data from the separate judgments do not. Together, the two data constellations suggest that postaccount evaluations formed by opponents are likely to be highly context-dependent.

Conclusion

The illustrations offered and many other results from our studies suggest for further studies the hypothesis that the interaction processes started by failure events and forming account episodes are likely to create particularly brittle structures. Brittle they seem to be for two reasons: (a) There are many variables that enter into, and may alter the course of, account episodes, and (b) the participants, actors as well as opponents, are likely to be especially sensitive in their reactions to the events of such an episode. And they are so sensitive mainly because an account episode is rarely just concerned with resolving a specific issue. As Scott and Lyman (1968) already pointed out in their seminal article, the interactants' attempts to cope with the specific conflict at hand implies a negotiation of identities in the service of preserving, restoring, or enhancing self-esteem, and—may I add—feelings of being in control! The basic rub may be that in these very attempts at maintaining or regaining control and self-esteem, both actor and opponent often fail to pay sufficient attention to the corresponding needs of the other participant. A foundering account episode, according to the escalation theory, is a likely outcome.

References

Bergemann, N., & Johann, G.K. (1985). Zur Erfassung der Selbstakzeptanz und Akzeptanz anderer: Eine deutschsprachige Version der Berger-Skalen. *Diagnostica, 31*, 119–129.

Burger, J.M., & Cooper, H.M. (1979). The desirability of control. *Motivation and Emotion, 3*, 381–393.

Hormuth, S.E., & Lalli, M. (1986). Eine Skala zur Erfassung der bereichsspezischen Selbstzufriedenheit. Unpublished manuscript. University of Heidelberg.

Schönbach, P. (1990). Account episodes: The management or escalation of conflict. Cambridge: Cambridge University Press.

Scott, M.B., & Lyman, S.M. (1968). Accounts. *American Sociological Review, 33*, 46–62.

4
Autobiographical Accounts, Situational Roles, and Motivated Biases: When Stories Don't Match Up

ROY F. BAUMEISTER and ARLENE M. STILLWELL

Much of people's knowledge about themselves is stored in the form of personal narratives or stories rather than in terms of abstract generalizations such as trait terms or broad principles (Gergen & Gergen, 1988). These narratives, also known as autobiographical accounts, offer a valuable tool for understanding people's subjective experience of important life events. The narratives are of great interest in their own right, because they indicate how people reconstruct their experiences and make sense of the major events that happen to them. The narratives are also a useful means of learning about many phenomena that are not amenable to other methods of research. The difficulty of studying relationships with traditional methods makes them a prime candidate for the autobiographical methods (e.g., Harvey, Flanary, & Morgan, 1988; Harvey, Weber, Galvin, Huszti, & Garnick, 1986).

This chapter will provide an overview of a current research program that has used such autobiographical narratives to explore a variety of important patterns—including masochism, conflict, guilt, anger, and unrequited love. This research program has sought to compare accounts that differ by a well-defined dimension, such as comparing the accounts told from the perspective of two situationally defined roles. A second goal of this chapter will be to present implications of our various findings for the general problem of understanding intimate relationships.

Autobiographical Methods

Before presenting the findings themselves, it is useful to review briefly some issues concerning the methodology of using autobiographical accounts. This methodology, after all, is rather new, and it encounters a unique set of problems. If researchers can share their solutions to these various problems, the entire field of study may benefit.

Our own approach uses what Gergen and Gergen (1988) have termed micronarratives, that is, brief stories focused on a specific experience or incident—as opposed to collecting broadly focused life stories that integrate an entire autobiography (e.g., McAdams, 1985). Our approach is to collect a sample of written stories on a well-defined theme and then to code these stories on a set of dimensions. We favor dichotomous codings—that is, the coder simply judges whether each feature is present or absent in the story. Occasionally, it is necessary to use continuous scales to rate stories on some dimension, but the dichotomous codings are more objective and yield higher interrater agreement.

Like other researchers in this area, we found people ready and willing to tell the stories. People do seem to have the experiences available in story form, and they find the exercise of relating these stories to be easy (and sometimes enjoyable). Collecting data is thus rather easy, although this advantage can be offset by the laborious and time-consuming process of content coding. Obtaining written accounts simplifies this process considerably, for one does not have to begin by transcribing tape-recorded material. Written accounts also have the advantage of greater standardization of format, which may help to remove demand characteristics and other troubling features than can reduce the validity of stories obtained in an interview. In simple terms, obtaining stories orally may run the risk that the interviewer is induced to make comments, probe with further questions, or provide nonverbal signals that could affect the stories.

The major disadvantage of written stories is that not everyone is equally skilled and comfortable at writing. With illiterate populations, obviously, only oral methods are possible. It is also possible that people may be more thorough when speaking than when writing. Thus, some researchers favor spoken accounts (e.g., Ross & Holmberg, 1990), although on balance we favor written methods when they are feasible.

We have found it advisable to make the instructions narrow and explicit. If the instructions are too general, the stories end up being too heterogeneous, and so coding becomes impractical.

A large sample of stories is very helpful. Dichotomous coding entails that one's statistical analyses are going to rely on Chi-squared or some such statistic, and these are not necessarily sensitive to small differences in small samples. In this research, conclusions are based on comparing two sets of stories to determine which set has a higher percentage of some feature. One wants one's research to be able to detect a difference of 15 or 20 percentage points as significant, and it is typically necessary to have a sample of more than 100 stories to be able to accomplish that.

Optimal results may require careful advance thought about research design. Our work with this method, probably like that of many researchers, began with an interest in a phenomenon that led us to collect personal accounts about it. Without an adequate comparison group, however, it is difficult to know what use to make of these stories, and so one's analysis may be limited to analyzing sex differences or some other easily available independent variable. To avoid this dilemma, we have learned to place greater emphasis on the independent variable(s) when planning a project. Instead of conceptualizing a research project as collecting stories on some interesting theme, one conceptualizes it as collecting sets of stories that differ on some key dimension. Independent variables may include situational role, personality traits, alleged purpose or use of the stories, and other factors.

Because our access to human subjects is limited, we have often resorted to asking each subject to furnish two stories (typically one on each of the two themes in the research design). Originally, we worried about sequence effects and other such problems, but these have not materialized. On the other hand, this procedure does raise the question of the appropriate unit of analysis. The two stories each subject furnishes are not necessarily independent, and one could argue that the subject rather than the story should be the unit of analysis. Any within-subject effects would be likely to work against one's chances of finding significant results, so this problem is not likely to be severe, but it is something that is worth considering, especially if an attractive long-term solution can be found.

Another technical problem for the autobiographical methodology is to ensure comparability of stories on all dimensions other than the independent variables. For example, people may choose stories from the distant past as opposed to the recent past, and differences may be found because recent events are recalled better than long-ago ones, which could confound the independent variable. One partial solution is to specify that the events should have occurred within the past 2 years (or 2 months, or weeks!). Still, this sort of problem may continue to raise interpretive issues for researchers.

It is worth noting that the content of stories does seem to be influenced both by the immediate situational context and by the storyteller's personality. Baumeister and Ilko (1990) found that self-esteem had significant effects on the content of stories, indicating that there are individual differences that can affect the nature of accounts. In that same study, stories also differed as a function of whether the story was public or private. This underscores the point made by Gergen and Gergen (1988) that an account is a performance in the present rather than simply a recounting from memory. Thus, researchers may want to be sensitive to issues of individual differences and situational causes.

In conclusion, the autobiographical method has both strengths and weaknesses when compared with traditional laboratory and survey methods. Its advantages include high external validity (after all, these are real events from actual lives, not laboratory simulations or hypothetical scenarios or other artificial experiences), flexibility in allowing the individual to shape the story according to biases and motivations, and the capacity to learn about issues that other methods cannot easily study. Its weaknesses include a loss of experimental control and standardization, and a difficulty in establishing the mechanism that is responsible for the effects found. (For example, if two sets of stories differ on some dimension, that difference could be due to differential selection of story, biased interpretation and encoding that occurred during the experience, or distortions arising during the retrieval from memory.) It is an extremely valuable method for learning about the subjective aspect of important life experiences, but it must be considered inferior to laboratory methods for isolating variables and testing hypotheses about causal processes.

Sexual Masochism

The first project in this program was concerned with sexual masochism (see Baumeister, 1988a, 1988b, 1989). As one of psychology's oldest puzzles and a phenomenon that centers on a seemingly incomprehensible desire for pain and humiliation, masochism holds great interest. Masochism had remained enigmatic partly because of the difficulty of obtaining data to shed light on it. Masochists are reluctant to participate in interviews or surveys, and laboratory methods proved almost completely useless.

The Research

Use of personal narratives was able to shed valuable light on the nature of masochism. A sample of more than 200 first-person narratives was collected from letters to a specialty magazine that regularly featured such letters. Using popular magazines as a source of accounts raises several problems, such as the risk of bias through editorial selection or through editorial alteration of the letters, but in view of the difficulty of obtaining data about masochism the use of this source seemed warranted (see Baumeister, 1989). Another problem is that there was no way to verify whether the letters reported actual experiences, mere fantasies, or some blend of fantasy and actual experience. In other words, the cognitive and behavioral processes behind the account remained unclear. But the important question about masochism is the nature of the motivation, and the motivation is presumably the same regardless of whether the person is describing a favorite experience or a favorite fantasy.

Content analysis of these accounts was able to shed substantial light on the nature of sexual masochism. It appears that these individuals are motivated not by guilt, self-dislike, or sexual inadequacy, as various past theories had proposed. Rather (and consistent with recent behavioral data; e.g., Scott, 1983), the appeal of masochism is apparently that of offering an opportunity to play out extended sexual fantasies in ways that produce drastic escapes from the concerns of normal, everyday life.

Masochism removes the person's normal identity and allows the individual to become someone else for a brief period of time (Baumeister, 1988a, 1988b).

Comparison of letters by dominants as opposed to submissives furnished some insight into the respective S & M roles. Some features, such as having the submissive do housework or perform oral sex, were most strongly associated with the dominant role accounts, indicating that these activities may especially appeal to the dominant. Other features were more common in the submissive role accounts, suggesting that masochists themselves may be especially drawn to having an audience, being symbolically transformed into a member of the opposite sex, or being humiliated in various ways.

Gender differences in masochism have long been a topic of controversy (e.g., Caplan, 1984; Franklin, 1987). By comparing male and female accounts, it was possible to shed new light on the differences between male and female masochism (see Baumeister, 1988b, 1989). Female masochists apparently were able to shed their normal identities more readily than the male masochists, so their desires focused on elaborating new fantasy selves. The female accounts placed greater emphasis on context, implication, and suggestion. In contrast, the male masochists emphasized techniques to accomplish the removal of the self, such as strong doses of pain and intense humiliations. Patterns of intercourse were also different. Male masochists apparently desire to be treated as nonsexual beings, and their humiliations often extended to a repudiation of their sexuality. Such patterns were almost completely absent from the activities of female masochists, who retained strong claims on the sexual interest and fidelity of their partners.

Implications for Relationships

This first project was not concerned with elucidating normal relationships, and indeed it was necessary to reject the notion that masochistic patterns were typical of normal men or women. Still, masochism involves one unusual and intense form of intimate contact, so some implications are worth mentioning.

First, it appears that masochism is a form of intimacy that is not love but may be compatible with love. Perhaps the best conclusion is that it is an "alternative intimacy" (Baumeister, 1989). By fostering a merger of selves, it accomplishes some of the emotional power and satisfaction that love offers, although of course the merging of selves in masochism is more one-sided than in love. When one considers both love and masochism, it is necessary to conclude that loss of individual selfhood through merger with another human being is a powerful source of positive affect.

Second, it is noteworthy that masochists have an unusually strong orientation toward relationships. Masochistic accounts were much more likely to feature episodes involving long-term relationship partners than an otherwise comparable sample of magazine letters dealing with conventional sexual experiences (Baumeister, 1989). The masochist's preference for long-term relationship contexts is partly attributable to the necessity for trust and the difficulty of finding partners; still, this preference was apparent even in letters that were explicitly described as fantasies, and fantasies are by definition free of practial constraints. Thus, it appears that masochists do have a strong attraction to a relationship context for their activities. This suggests, again, that the masochist seeks to escape from self by means of a strong intimate bond with another human being.

Finally, masochistic practices have several parallels to common practices used by sex therapists to enhance sexual responses, and this makes plausible the claim that S&M enhances sexual pleasure (see Baumeister, 1989, chap. 6). The broader suggestion that egotism and self-awareness are detrimental to sexual performance and pleasure (e.g., Masters & Johnson, 1970) is consistent with this claim, although further research is needed. In short, there may be costs to the excessive modern preoccupation with self, and an occasionally reduced capacity for sexual enjoyment may be one of these costs.

Interpersonal Conflict and Anger

A second project was centrally concerned with anger (Baumeister, Stillwell, & Wotman, 1990). Anger is a common experience, but it has resisted laboratory research for various reasons (see Averill, 1982; Tavris, 1982). In particular, it has been particularly difficult to induce laboratory subjects to make someone else angry, so the role of offender has remained unstudied. Some studies have involved making subjects angry, usually with arbitrary provocations and gratuitous frustrations, but one may question how closely these correspond to the genesis of anger in everyday life. After all, how often does one go out of one's way to deliver a gratuitous insult to a total stranger?

The Research

The design for this project focused on comparing the two roles involved in a conflict: specifically, the offender (or perpetrator), and the victim. Participants in this work were college students, and they were each asked to furnish one account in which they made someone angry and another in which someone made them angry. The instructions specifically asked for especially strong or memorable incidents.

We found a host of differences between the perpetrators' and victims' accounts (see Baumeister, Stillwell, & Wotman, 1990). The perpetrators tended to present the incidents as isolated episodes that had occurred in the past but were now long over and done, and that had few or no lasting harmful consequences. The victims, in contrast, tended to feature a longer time frame, with relationship damage and other harmful consequences that often continued in the present. This finding is consistent with other suggestive evidence about interpersonal transgressions: Victims continue to suffer and to keep the memory alive, whereas perpetrators soon manage to bury the event in the past. Anyone familiar with the contrast between Northern and Southern recollections of the Civil War, or black and white recollections of Negro slavery, can probably appreciate this difference.

Consistent with the general strategy of minimizing the incident, perpetrator accounts tended to cite external causes for their actions, to present what they did as impulsive, and so forth. In contrast, victim accounts were generally strong and explicit about portraying the perpetrators as acting in an immoral and unacceptable fashion, without any excuses.

Of particular interest was the finding that the victim accounts often seemed to convey a complete lack of understanding of why the perpetrators acted the way they did. A few perpetrator accounts had this characteristic (e.g., "I don't know why I did it"), but most perpetrators were able to furnish a reasonably clear and understandable explanation for their actions. These reasons were often not seen by the victims, however, who therefore tended to see the perpetrator's actions as gratuitous, inexplicable, arbitrary, or motivated by sheer malice. And, indeed, the anger sometimes seemed especially focused on this feature of the story. The inability to understand the reasons for another person's action appears to be a central factor in the genesis of interpersonal conflict and anger.

One further set of findings is of particular relevance to relationship issues. Victim accounts tended to describe multiple, accumulating provocations, whereas perpetrator accounts usually described just a single incident. Victim accounts often mentioned suppressing one's anger, whereas perpetrator accounts were (understandably) almost devoid of references to anger that was stifled, other than the occasional cold shoulder. And perpetrators were more likely than victims to portray the anger itself as an unreasonable overreaction. Taken together, these findings suggest that victims may sometimes stifle their anger until several grievances accumulate, at which point they may express their anger in response to the entire sequence; perpetrators, however, see only the single most recent incident, and hence they regard the angry outburst as excessive.

Implications for Relationships

The two partners involved in relationships have different perspectives on events, and these discrepant perspectives can contribute to the genesis of interpersonal conflict and anger, with potentially destructive consequences.

The results of this study suggest one common process by which this may occur. Inevitably, relationship partners will occasionally offend or provoke each other. A minor offense or grievance may cause one partner to feel angry, but in many cases these victims will stifle their anger rather than express it. Although the suppression of angry responses may in itself be a relationship-enhancing strategy, it can prevent the offender from realizing what he or she has done. As a result, the victim leaves the first incident of this type with some anger or resentment, while the offender has no idea that any problem or conflict existed. The perpetrator may therefore be likely to repeat the incident or do other, similar things.

Over time, then, the victim's sense of grievance accumulates, whereas the perpetrator is blithely ignorant of this accumulation. Eventually, the totality of grievance may become too much for the victim to tolerate, particularly as he or she now begins to realize that each act of tacit forgiveness seems only to encourage further misdeeds. Alternatively, the perpetrator's offenses may escalate, and at some point the degree of severity crosses a threshold and becomes intolerable to the victim.

At this point, then, the victim finally expresses anger in forceful terms. Freudian interpretations of such responses might suggest that the unexpressed anger built up over time and finally burst forth in excess (but see Tavris, 1982, for critique of this view). Our results suggest a different perspective, however. The victim is simply responding to an accumulated series of offenses, and the combination of offenses is aggravated by the fact that the victim's past forbearance has not only been unappreciated but positively abused—at least, from the victim's point of view. In other words, the victim may feel that he or she has gone to the trouble of swallowing anger and thus made a martyr-like sacrifice for the sake of the relationship, only to get taken advantage of as a reward. The offenses have continued and even perhaps escalated, and the victim's severe anger represents a response to the accumulated pattern and the troublesome trend. A severe display of anger seems quite warranted and justified in response to that pattern, from the victim's point of view, and the latest offense is perhaps only an occasion for expressing one's displeasure over the entire series of incidents.

But things look quite different to the offender. The offender sees only the immediate incident that is taking place, and the angry outburst seems wholly out of proportion. If the offender does realize that he or she has acted in similar ways in the past, this will only make the angry response seem that much more inappropriate, because no anger was displayed on previous occasions (presumably because the victim was swallowing his or her anger). The offender thinks, "I've acted this way before, and you never objected, but now all of a sudden you change and express these strenuous objections." Under such circumstances, the offender may well leave the episode feeling unjustly persecuted, and so in a sense the offender is transformed into a victim. Indeed, several accounts in our sample explicitly captured this feeling of indignation on the part of the perpetrators.

Other findings from this study also have relationship implications. The failure of victims to comprehend the motives and intentions of perpetrators is significant. Victims are especially angered when they think someone has no comprehensible reason for acting the way he or she did. This hypothesis would suggest that the greater the empathy that exists between relationship partners, the less they will be prone to anger and conflict of this kind. Being able to understand the partner's viewpoint may encourage people to make excuses for the partner and sympathize with the external causes or mitigating circumstances that can cause such a transgression. Of course, ability alone may not be sufficient; it may be that people may not always want to see their partner's viewpoint.

Finally, the different time spans of victims and offenders should be kept in mind for analyzing relationship dynamics. The two partners may agree that a certain offense occurred and may even agree on the extent of the fault and responsibility, but they may still feel quite differently about it. The perpetrator may soon come to feel that the incident is over and done and that the couple is now putting it behind them; the perpetrator may also be inclined to see that there are no lasting harmful consequences of his or her actions and no relationship damage. In contrast, the victim may continue to see harmful effects of the incident, may feel reluctant to trust the partner in various ways, and generally may keep the memory alive for a longer period of time. As a result, the victim may end up feeling that he or she is entitled to some consideration on the partner's part, whereas the offender may not feel that he or she owes any special consideration now that the incident is closed.

Guilt

We (along with Baumeister, Stillwell & Heatherton, 1991) have conducted several studies dealing with guilt. Guilt is of special interest because it reflects subjective interpretations of actions including comparing them with standards of appropriate behavior. Yet guilt, too, has proven elusive in laboratory research. Other than leading subjects to think that they have actually done some damage or harm, laboratory methods for studying guilt have been rare.

The Research

Our first project in this connection asked subjects to write about incidents in which they angered another. Half the stories were to refer to cases in which the subject felt guilty; the others were to refer to incidents in which the subject did not feel guilty. In this way, we sought to compare incidents involving interpersonal transgressions as a function of residual guilt feelings.

One big difference between the two sets of stories was how highly the subject regarded the other person (who was usually the victim of the subject's transgression). High esteem for this person was associated with feelings of guilt, whereas the absence of guilt feelings was associated with holding the other person in low regard. Thus, the difference between guilt-producing transgressions and guiltless transgressions was less in the content of the action than in the esteem one had for the other person.

Second, people learned lessons from the guilt stories. That is, they were more likely to say that they had learned something, such as by giving the story a moral or indicating that an insight had occurred to them at the time. In contrast, if the subject did not feel guilty afterward, the likelihood of having learned anything was minimal. Knowledge is acquired at the price of guilt, it seems. Innocence means ignorance. Insights into people and self come painfully, each lesson the consequence of an event that leaves one with a burden of guilt.

The third finding was that there was more behavior change following the guilt incidents than the not-guilty ones. Apparently, the lessons learned in connection with guilt are often translated into action. Guilt makes people change their behavior.

The second study dealt with people making each other feel guilty. We asked for incidents in which the subjects had done something to make someone feel guilty and for incidents in which another person had done something to make the subject feel guilty. These stories offered a variety of insights into guilt as an interpersonal transaction.

First, the slight majority of stories involved guilt being administered for not doing something rather than for actually doing it. The biggest single subcategory of these was neglecting to pay someone attention. But there were many others. It seems that guilt is one thing people use to motivate each other to do what one wants them to do. People reveal that they suffer because of you, or are disappointed in you, or feel betrayed that you ignore your commitments and obligations, and so you do what they want.

Second, the reproachers often referred to exaggerating their suffering as a technique, although this was never mentioned by the targets of the guilt induction. Sometimes reproachers seemed quite explicit about using this technique to manipulate someone. "Ohh, the benefits of guilt," gloated one very high self-esteem individual in describing how he had manipulated his mother into feeling guilty for a pattern of unjust punishment in the past, making her too uncertain to punish him for anything he did now. Another kept reminding his parents that his siblings had been treated to a European vacation but he hadn't, thereby making the parents feel that they owed him an unspecified amount of money as well, and so he was now able to ask his mother for money any time, in small amounts, as needed. He concluded, "Thus, this guilt trip bit should work fine for at least 5–6 months; then it will be business as usual".

On the other hand, many people often felt guilty about inducing guilt. One woman received the instruction to write a story about an important incident in which she did something to make someone else feel guilty. She gave us only four sentences. She began her account with a protest and then proceeded to explain (using the subjunctive, which is to say the hypothetical, tense) why she had no significant or important incidents to relate:

> I am the one who takes on everyone else's guilt. The only people who would feel guilt caused by me would be my children. The guilt would be short lived and would involve undone tasks, such as cleaning their rooms, picking up after themselves, being late, etc. As soon as the task is done the guilt disappears.

Other subjects likewise described feeling bad about making someone feel guilty. In fact, sometimes the target figures this out and feigns guilt to induce guilt in someone else. Listen to how this low self-esteem person has developed this interpersonal strategy to a fine art:

> If I do poorly at some task (in this case exams) and I sense disappointment from my peers or parents I will show them by my behavior that I am at least equally disappointed. If they (parents, peers) had intended in punishing me they will as a result feel guilty, because I am obviously punishing myself intensively. Their desire to punish or chastise me now becomes a desire to console me and an attempt to raise my spirits.

Still, subjects generally felt bad about inducing guilt only if their efforts had been too successful. For the most part, guilt-inducing subjects felt that the partner was somehow oblivious to his or her misbehavior, and so it was necessary to use guilt to bring insight to this person. In contrast, the objects of the guilt-inducing strategies of others often simply regarded the reproacher as self-righteous or manipulative. They also frequently expressed resentment at being made to feel guilty.

Implications for Relationships

Guilt is a potentially powerful and currently operative mechanism for exerting control over relationship partners. People use guilt to get an individual to conform to their expectations and to do what they want him or her to do. In many cases the person privately feels that he or she has done nothing wrong—but still feels guilty and conforms to what the other person wants. In these cases, the guilt may be mixed with stifled anger or resentment, which can be the beginning of a long-term grudge. The potential relationship damage caused by such patterns could be seen in several stories that expressed strongly negative feelings about someone (typically an older female relative) who repeatedly induced guilt.

These findings suggest that guilt may be a relationship strategy that can be successful but at a hidden cost to the relationship. If you make someone feel guilty, the person may do what you want but may also begin to resent you. And from our stories it appears that people are largely unaware that others resent them for making them feel guilty.

A second important implication is that guilt appears to be crucially linked to the bond that holds people together. If one person feels neglected, she or he will sometimes resort to inducing guilt in the other about this. A large category of induced guilt feelings is linked to the recognition that one has not spent time with or paid attention to particular other people with whom one has a close relationship. People use guilt to bind others to them.

A general pattern that pervaded these stories was that the guilt inducer felt distressed at the beginning of the episode because of something the other had done (or failed to do). Reproachers ended up feeling better, especially in their own accounts, whereas of course the target ended up feeling guilty.

Guilt can thus be regarded as a mechanism for the redistribution of negative affect within a relationship. One feels guilty for making another feel bad, and as a result of one's guilt the other feels better. Guilt induction thus transfers negative affect to its (presumably) rightful owner.

Success, Failure, and Self-Esteem

Major successes and failures are centrally important events on which the self-concept is based. People's self-esteem and claims on public respect depend heavily on how well they have managed to achieve success and avoid failure. A study by Baumeister and Ilko (1990) examined the relation between self-esteem and accounts of major success and failure experiences.

The Research

For this project, subjects were run in groups of four to seven. They were each asked to furnish an account of a major, recent success experience and a major, recent failure experience. Self-esteem was also measured. In addition, one half of the subjects were told that they would read their stories aloud to the group, but the rest were told that the stories would remain completely anonymous.

Two findings of particular interest emerged from this study. The first pertained to the references to the contributions of other people, particularly in the success stories. There are of course norms requiring that people thank others and assign credit where it is due. They should therefore feel some obligation to mention the role others played in helping them succeed. On the other hand, the tendency to make self-flattering illusions in order to sustain maximally positive views of self (e.g., Taylor & Brown, 1988) would predict that people would want to claim all the credit for themselves and downplay any contributions made by other people.

In the accounts of success, we found evidence that people were affected by both motivations. The balance between the two motivations depended on self-presentational factors. When subjects expected to read their stories aloud to the group, they thanked people—that is, they included ample references to the material aid and emotional support provided by other people. But when they did not expect to read their stories aloud, all of those grateful acknowledgments disappeared, and people simply featured their own activities. Apparently, in public they felt it necessary to conform to norms of modesty and appropriate gratitude, but in the privacy of their own mind they recalled their major successes as chiefly due to their own efforts. Public expressions of gratitude, in other words, may often be shallow concessions to self-presentational norms.

The second finding concerned the time perspective of the failure accounts. People may desire to bury their major failures in the past, so they might be inclined to furnish failure accounts that are entirely in the past tense. Alternatively, if people are not too threatened by the past failures, they may keep the memory alive in the present as a way of learning from their mistakes and perhaps of motivating themselves to perform better in the future. This was studied by examining whether the story made reference to the present or not, and as a separate confirmation the number of sentences in the present tense was counted.

On both measures, people with high self-esteem appeared to link their past failures up to the present more strongly than did people with low self-esteem. This effect was particularly strong in the private, anonymous accounts. Apparently, people with high self-esteem maintain a clear memory of a major past failure experience and relate it to the present, whereas people with low self-esteem are more likely to bury such failures in the past. Part of the reason for this difference may be that people with high self-esteem are less threatened by past failures; their self-esteem is strong enough to survive the implications of a failure. A related reason involves the invocation of emotional distress associated with failure. People with high self-esteem appeared to divest these failures of their emotional ramifications, which would obviously make it much more tolerable to recall them in the present. In contrast, the failure accounts of people with low self-esteem were relatively full of emotional distress, and so these people may be especially motivated to bury such incidents in the past rather than relating them to the present (in order to avoid having to recall and reexperience the emotional distress).

Implications for Relationships

This study was not centrally concerned with relationship issues, but the gratitude findings do have some implications. An important aspect of a good relationship may be that people help each other and offer emotional support for major personal efforts. Although people will not necessarily expect payment in kind, they probably do expect to be thanked and appreciated for the help and support they give. Apparently, most adults have learned this obligation to express gratitude and appreciation, and public celebrations of major successes do indeed tend to feature thorough, grateful acknowledgments of all the significant others who helped out and contributed in various ways.

On the other hand, this study's findings suggest that these acknowledgments may be rather superficial. People's own private recollections downplay the contributions of others. The reason for this is presumably that people want to claim all the credit for themselves. Regardless of what they may say in public, their own belief may be that they achieved success largely on their own. There is thus the potential for conflict if the relationship partner comes to understand the person's viewpoint too well. The findings from the anger study described earlier in this chapter (Baumeister, Stillwell, & Wotman, 1990) pointed to the value of communication and empathy, but the shallow gratitude findings suggest potential problems that could arise from understanding one's partner too well. You might find out that your partner doesn't really appreciate you as much as he says he does.

Unrequited Love

Unrequited love is an extremely pervasive phenomenon. It causes substantial sadness, heartbreak, frustration, annoyance, and general emotional distress, which are distributed to both parties involved (i.e., the would-be lover and the love object). Yet relatively little is known about this phenomenon. One reason for psychology's seeming ignorance is that unrequited love resists traditional research methods. Laboratory experiments probably cannot simulate unrequited love effectively; after all, a romantic rejection by a stranger may not have the same impact as a rejection by someone you have been yearning for and dreaming about. Clinical studies will not generally have much to offer on this phenomenon, for unrequited love is not a pathological pattern. And of course unrequited love does not make a couple, so the recent surge of studies of couples and relationships will not find these noncouples. On the other hand, autobiographical narratives may be a valuable way to learn about unrequited love.

The Research

Baumeister and Wotman (in press) recently conducted a study of unrequited love. Subjects were advanced undergraduates, and they were asked to furnish two accounts of unrequited love. One was to involve a case in which they felt a strong romantic attraction to someone who was not interested in them. The other involved someone else being romantically attracted to the subject, without the subject's having a comparable interest in that person.

The power of these stories was immediately obvious. Indeed, these were the longest accounts we have obtained in any of our studies using this methodology, including all of the ones described in this chapter and several others. Also, the majority of these stories made reference to the present, indicating that these experiences were remembered in ways that linked them to present circumstances.

As usual, our investigation was based on comparing the two roles involved in the incident—in this case, the would-be lover and the love object (or "heartbreaker"). These were found to differ on a large number of dimensions. Some of the main findings are as follows.

First, it is clear that unrequited love raises the self-esteem of the heartbreaker and lowers that of the would-be lover. (Keep in mind that the heartbreaker is often a reluctant one, an innocent bystander, especially in his or her own eyes). It is flattering to be loved and degrading to be spurned. The would-be lover, however, seemed typically to be unaware that the love object found the interest flattering.

Second, the emotional patterns were quite different. Predictably, the would-be lovers went through the spectrum of feelings, including both positive and negative feelings. The stories by the love objects held perhaps greater interest, for our culture has paid less attention to that side of the experience. These heartbreakers expressed a range of negative affects and emotional distress, including anger, annoyance, and guilt. In retrospect, they expressed more negative affect than did the would-be lovers, which may seem surprising. Rejected lovers often seem to maintain a soft spot in their heart for the elusive love object, and despite their frustration and humiliation they rarely express any wish that the incident had never occurred. The love objects, despite the boost in self-esteem, go away with plenty of negative affect and often seem to wish that the episode had not occurred.

It is noteworthy that the rejected lovers' stories contained almost no reference to the emotional distress of the heartbreaker. Would-be lovers are apparently oblivious to the annoyance, guilt, and other negative affect that their love object feels as a result of their attentions. In contrast, the love objects are much more aware of the distress felt by the rejected lovers, which is presumably one reason that they feel guilty.

The guilt is perhaps especially ironic. The love objects generally presented themselves as not having done anything to encourage the would-be lover. In their view, they are blameless, and in fact they never wanted the episode to occur, but they end up with a load of guilt anyway. Love objects were much more likely than would-be lovers to make statements justifying their actions and feelings. These justificatory statements reflect the guilt felt by these individuals. In contrast, the would-be lovers did not seem to feel that their acts and feelings needed justification. Even when they acknowledged having acted out of character, they did not generally offer justifications Apparently, they feel that love is sufficient justification for their actions. Moreover, they are often unaware that they caused the other person distress.

The two sets of accounts tended to differ as to what had actually happened, which may well reflect the ambiguity of interpersonal communication of love interest. The would-be lovers' accounts often made reference to being encouraged or led on by the love object, but from the love object's perspective nothing of the sort had happened. Indeed, the would-be lovers were much more likely than the love objects to indicate that the feelings had been reciprocated at some point. The love objects often indicated that they had overtly rejected the would-be lover, but the would-be lovers' accounts reported far fewer overt rejections. The love objects thought the would-be lovers engaged in self-deception and denial and that they were extremely persistent; the would-be lovers did not see their actions that way.

Thus, would-be lovers think that their feelings are reciprocated and that they are receiving encouragement from the love object. They persist, not realizing that they are being annoying or obnoxious to the love object, and they end up thinking that the love object changed abruptly for some mysterious, incomprehensible reason. The love object, on the other hand, is not aware of encouraging the would-be lover or reciprocating feelings. Instead, the love objects think that they express their rejections overtly (despite the inner struggles and difficulties in getting themselves to do this)—but their clear signals are ignored by the love object, who persists in his or her unwanted attentions rather than facing the facts, thereby prolonging the unpleasantness for everyone.

Implications for Relationships

Unrequited love, for the most part, is a nonrelationship, but these findings are of general interest to researchers who are concerned with relationships for several reasons. A good relationship may depend on mutual attraction; episodes of unrequited love reveal what happens when the attraction is decidedly not mutual. A divorce is a failure of a relationship to continue, whereas unrequited love is, in a sense, a failure of a relationship to begin.

The findings described above shed considerable light on the experience of unrequited love, and we shall not reiterate them. One general point, however, is the suggestion that the communication of romantic interest *and* disinterest is difficult. The would-be lovers experienced fear of rejection; the love objects experienced reluctance to say they were not interested. Not only did people have difficulty expressing their feelings, but the partner had difficulty getting the message. Would-be lovers thought they had been encouraged but failed to see rejecting messages; love objects failed to note encouragement but thought they had been clear about expressing their lack of interest.

The experience of the love object is perhaps especially illuminating. These people denied responsibility for the episode, did not want it to happen, and yet ended up feeling guilty. They felt both flattered and annoyed, and they ended up often wishing that the incident had never occurred. To deal with the guilt, they often felt it necessary to justify their actions or to derogate the partner—indeed, derogating the very person who was idealizing them. And although Western culture typically portrays a broken heart as one of life's great tragedies, in the end it was the love objects who were the victims. The rejected lovers ended up with largely positive feelings about the incident, despite their disappointment, whereas the accounts of the love objects were much more full of negative affect.

Conclusion

This series of studies reveals that autobiographical accounts form an extremely valuable methodology for learning about a range of important phenomena, especially ones that resist more traditional methods. It seems safe to conclude that accounts will continue to be a useful methodology for the study of close relationships.

Autobiographical accounts are especially useful for elucidating subjective processes and motivations. These accounts allow people to tell their own stories in their own words, thereby enabling them to include, delete, or distort material as they see fit. Systematic patterns in stories thereby constitute revealing clues as to the motivations that underlie how people make sense of their lives.

Several themes came up repeatedly, and future studies with personal accounts may want to attend to these. One is the use of time. Some accounts narrate isolated, brief episodes, whereas others cover long-term series of events and relate outcomes to present circumstances. References to the present constitute one indication of the importance of past events, but isolating an incident in the past may be a defensive strategy to avoid its possible implications.

A second theme is self-esteem. People are greatly concerned about their esteem, and important events can be defined as ones having implications for one's self-esteem. The use of individual differences in self-esteem is one approach to understanding this pattern of motivation, and the coding of overt references to gains and losses of esteem is a useful way to examine people's own spontaneous linking of past events to their esteem.

A third theme is the broad tendency to neglect the emotions of others. It is not surprising that people are generally more aware of their own emotions than of other people's emotions. But insensitivity to the emotions of others may be a common source of misunderstandings, conflicts, and other discrepancies in subjective processes.

A last theme is guilt and justification. It is clear that people feel guilty about some things they have done, and their efforts to deal with guilt come through in their autobiographical accounts. Social psychology has lacked effective research methods for dealing with guilt, and currently the field does not treat guilt as an important factor in human psychology. Indeed, many textbooks dealing with motivation and emotion have few or no references to guilt. Guilt may be a more pervasive and powerful motivation than is currently acknowledged, and autobiographical accounts may offer a useful way to understand it.

References

Averill, J. (1982). *Anger and aggression: An essay on emotion.* New York: Springer-Verlag.

Baumeister, R.F. (1988a). Masochism as escape from self. *Journal of Sex Research, 25*, 28–59.

Baumeister, R.F. (1988b). Gender differences in masochistic scripts. *Journal of Sex Research, 25*, 478–499.

Baumeister, R.F. (1989). *Masochism and the self.* Hillsdale, NJ: Lawrence Erlbaum Associates.

Baumeister, R.F., & Ilko, S. (1990). Shallow gratitude and still-smarting wounds: Self-presentation, self-esteem, and autobiographical accounts of success and failure. Manuscript submitted for publication.

Baumeister, R.F., Stillwell, A.M., & Heatherton, T.F. (1990). The interpersonal dimension of guilt: Subjective accounts of guilt experiences. Manuscript in preparation, Case Western Reserve University, Cleveland, OH.

Baumeister, R.F., Stillwell, A.M., & Wotman, S.R. (1990). Victim and perpetrator accounts of interpersonal conflict: Autobiographical narratives about anger. *Journal of Personality and Social Psychology*, 59, 994–1005.

Baumeister, R.F., & Wotman, S.R. (in press). *Breaking hearts: The two sides of unrequited love*. New York: Guilford Press.

Caplan, P. (1984). The myth of women's masochism. *American Psychologist, 39*, 130–139.

Franklin, D. (1987). The politics of masochism. *Psychology Today, 21* (1), 52–57.

Gergen, K.J., & Gergen, M. (1988). Narrative and the self as relationship In L. Berkowitz (Ed.), *Advances in experimental social psychology* (Vol. 21, pp. 17–56). San Diego, CA: Academic Press.

Harvey, J.H., Flanary, R., & Morgan, M. (1988). Vivid memories of vivid loves gone by. *Journal of Social and Personal Relationships, 3*, 359–373.

Harvey, J.H., Weber, A.L., Galvin, K.S., Huszti, H.C., & Garnick, N.N. (1986). Attribution in the termination of close relationships: A special focus on the account. In R. Gilmour & S. Duck (Eds.), *The emerging field of personal relationships* (pp. 189–201). Hillsdale, NJ: Erlbaurm.

Masters, W.H., & Johnson, V.E. (1970). *Human sexual inadequacy*. Boston, MA: Little Brown.

McAdams, D.P. (1985). *Power, intimacy and the life story: Personological inquiries into identity*. Homewood, IL: Dorsey.

Ross, M., & Holmberg, D. (1990). Recounting the past: Gender differences in the recall of events in the history of a close relationship. In J.M. Olson & M.P. Zanna (Eds.), *Self-inference processes: The Ontario symposium (Vol 6)*. Hillsdale, NJ: Erlbaum.

Scott, G.G. (1983). *Erotic power*. Secaucus, NJ: Citadel Press.

Tavris, C. (1982). *Anger: The misunderstood emotion*. New York: Simon & Schuster.

Taylor, S.E., & Brown, J.D. (1988). Illusion and well-being: A social psychological perspective on mental health. *Psychological Bulletin, 103*, 193–210.

5
The Role of Account-Making in the Growth and Deterioration of Close Relationships

SALLY PLANALP and CATHERINE A. SURRA

A relationship changes and becomes closer or less close primarily because one or both partners let it change. To one person, a disagreement about politics might be a sign of serious incompatibility; to someone else, it might mean nothing. To one person, breaking a confidence might be a small mistake to be overlooked; to another person, it might signal a gross violation of trust. Each person must decide what events are relevant to the relationship, why the events occurred, and what implications they have for the relationship. In this way, people's perceptions and interpretations of events affect their judgments and beliefs about the relationship, and ultimately what actions they take. This chapter concerns the types of events that partners believe are responsible for important changes in their relationships, the processes through which they account for the events, and the effects on relational assessments. By *relational assessments* we mean the qualities people ascribe to a particular close relationship, such as love, commitment, trust, satisfaction, and the like (Surra & Bohman, in press).

The ideas we present are drawn from our respective programs of research on accounts of why relationships change. Surra's research has focused on accounts of changes in commitment, measured as newlyweds' and daters' estimates of changes in the likelihood of marriage over the course of their romance. Planalp's research has concentrated on accounts of events that increase uncertainty about or change prior knowledge about an already established close relationship. Both of us have examined how accounts affect beliefs about relationships, such as how trusting, close, or satisfying they are and whether they are likely to endure.

This chapter is divided into three major sections. First, we describe the methods that we used to study accounts and how similarities and differences in the methods might have influenced the accounts we obtained. Second, we analyze the accounts in terms of three essential components—precipitating events, interpretations, and changes in beliefs and assessments about the relationship. Third, we reflect on why the work is important and what general conclusions may be drawn from it.

Methods for Studying Accounts and the Nature of Accounts

In analyzing accounts of relationship change, we draw on published and unpublished analyses of four data sets. Planalp and colleagues (Planalp & Honeycutt, 1985; Planalp & Rivers, 1988; Planalp, Rutherford, & Honeycutt, 1988) studied events that undermined people's knowledge of their relationships. In the first study (Planalp & Honeycutt, 1985), college-student volunteers were asked to report retrospectively on an experience in which they "learned some surprising information about a friend, spouse or romantic partner" that led them to question something basic to the relationship (p. 595). The volunteers were asked to provide written descriptions of the events and their outcomes and to rate how much the events affected 12 beliefs about the relationship, including supportiveness, trust, fairness, companionship, and the like. In the second study, Planalp and her co-workers (Planalp et al., 1988; Planalp & Rivers, 1988) followed a sample of college students for 12 weeks and had them fill out a semistructured questionnaire whenever they experienced an event that challenged their beliefs about a close relationship. Although some people experienced more than one such event over the course of the study (18%), the analyses focused on those who reported only one event. At the time of the event, each volunteer filled out an extensive questionnaire concerning the nature of the event, interpretations of it, and its effects on beliefs. At the end of the monitoring period, each person also filled out a brief follow-up questionnaire.

Surra and colleagues conducted three studies on accounts of changes in commitment in romantic relationships. In the first two, samples of newlywed couples were asked to recall the events and processes that led to the decision to wed (Surra, 1987a; Surra & Huston, 1987; Surra, Arizzi, & Asmussen, 1988). Spouses were interviewed separately, and each plotted a graph of changes in the chance of marrying the partner over the course of the courtship. Each time a turning point in commitment (an upturn or downturn in the graph) was reported, the respondent was asked, "Tell me in as specific terms as possible what happened from (date of beginning of turning point) to (date at end of turning point) that made the chance of marriage go (up/down) ____%." Interviews were tape-recorded, and accounts of changes in commitment were transcribed from the recordings.

Each sample of newlyweds was recruited from the marriage license records. The first sample (Surra, 1987a; Surra & Huston, 1987) consisted of rural Pennsylvanians married 10 months or less who came from a mix of social classes and religious denominations. The second sample (Surra et al., 1988) consisted of Utah residents, mostly Mormons (96%), who had been married 19 months or less. Data from the second study essentially corroborated those from the first (Surra et al., 1988), suggesting that the length of marriage at the time of the interview did not seriously affect the nature of retrospections and that the decision to wed among Mormons is similar to that in other populations (also see Surra, Chandler, Asmussen, & Wareham, 1987). After about 4 years of marriage, respondents in the Utah study completed mailed questionnaires to ascertain their degree of satisfaction with the marriage.

In a more recent longitudinal study (Surra & Planalp, 1990), the method used to study newlyweds' retrospective accounts of changes in commitment was adapted for investigating concurrent changes in commitment among daters. During the first phase of the study, a sample of 120 college students and their primary dating partners graphed changes in the chance of marriage to their partners from the day they met to the present (i.e., the time they drew the graph). During the second phase, respondents were interviewed over the telephone about once a month to update their graphs. After 11 months, they once again graphed the entire course of their relationship from memory.

Similarities in Methods

Planalp and colleagues' and Surra and colleagues' methods were similar in several important respects. In both, the target of investigation was partners' perceptions of changes in their beliefs about their relationship. Both provided data about the dynamic processes by which relationships evolved and addressed both positive and negative changes. In addition, in both sets of studies open-ended questions were used to elicit accounts of changes in relationship beliefs. Thus, respondents had a relatively free rein in giving an account of why the changes occurred. In both case, respondents were asked to describe specific time periods and events. This approach tended to yield specific, constrained descriptions of what happened, and events were ordered logically, sequentially, or temporally within accounts (Surra & Planalp, 1990). This method was in contrast to that utilized by those researchers who have studied accounts by asking respondents to tell, for example, "why your relationship ended or broke up" (see, e.g., Cupach & Metts, 1986; Fletcher, 1983; Harvey, Wells, & Alvarez, 1978). The latter technique placed no limits on the types of events or when they occurred and therefore tended to yield descriptions that were story-like and that had plot structures that lent coherence to accounts (see Harvey, Weber, Galvin, Huszti, & Garnic, 1986).

Surra's and Planalp's approaches were similar in another important respect: Each researcher first began by gathering recollections of accounts of past events and, in subsequent investigations, studied accounts concurrently with events. Both researchers devised schemes for coding accounts based on content analyses of the retrospective data and then used similar codes to describe accounts gathered concurrently. Surra's

(1987b) scheme had 21 codes that were refined subcategories of four major categories: intrapersonal/normative reasons, which concerned normative beliefs and standards for suitable partners and relationships; dyadic reasons, which included interaction with and attributions about the partner and the relationship; social network reasons, which involved interaction with and attributions about third parties; and circumstantial reasons, which were forces and institutional events that were relatively uncontrollable. Planalp's (Planalp & Honeycutt, 1985; Planalp et al., 1988) accounts were classified into such categories as competing relationships, unexplained loss of contact or closeness, sexual behavior, deception, and the like. In Surra's studies, accounts were first divided into separate reasons or thought units and then categorized into one of the 21 codes, whereas in Planalp's research the entire account was classified into one category. In their first study, Planalp & Honeycutt (1985) had independent coders categorize the accounts, but in the second, concurrent study, respondents themselves categorized their reports using the same coding scheme. These procedures, in which accounts were studied both retrospectively and concurrently, and from the points of views of coders and participants, support the validity of the content of accounts, which we describe more fully later in this chapter.

Differences in Methods

Several differences in the methods employed by Planalp and by Surra also affected the kinds of accounts that were obtained. The most important of these was that the researchers studied changes in different beliefs about relationships, thereby focusing respondents' attention on different types of events. By asking respondents to note events that increased uncertainty (i.e., led to something surprising about the relationship and that changed basic beliefs), Planalp's question elicited accounts of occurrences that resulted in relatively dramatic changes. In contrast, Surra studied all perceived changes in commitment, which elicited moderate or negligible changes in addition to large changes.

Although both methods provided information about both positive and negative changes, the changes tapped by the Planalp method were primarily negative, even when both positive and negative examples of events were used as stimuli in the questionnaires. This was probably due to the fact that increases in uncertainty are, in fact, costly and usually have a negative impact (Planalp et al., 1988). Surra's method yielded data on mostly positive changes in commitment, particularly when it was utilized with relationships that progressed to marriage.

Another important difference between the methods used by Surra and those used by Planalp is that they sampled different types of close relationships. Surra's work only included heterosexual romantic relationships, whereas Planalp's work also included same- and opposite-sex friendships.

The two methods also differ with respect to the techniques used to record accounts. Planalp had respondents write out their accounts, whereas Surra had them describe their accounts verbally. The verbal accounts typically were longer than the written, and the variation in length had implications for the content of the accounts. When writing down their accounts, respondents were inclined to focus on the event itself. When describing their accounts verbally, participants were more apt to report the event and then go on to say how it affected their beliefs about the relationship and their assessments of it. As described below, the accounts obtained by each of the two methods tapped into different parts of the account-making process. As a result, the two data sets in combination provide especially solid grounds for theorizing about account-making and changes in relationship beliefs.

The Three Components of Account-Making

The linkage between accounts and assessments of the relationship can best be understood by dissecting account-making into three components. The first is the precipitating event or events, which are usually behaviors perceived by one partner, both partners, or third parties. Next is the account-maker's interpretation of the event, which is guided by basic attributional and emotional considerations. Third is a change in the individual's relational schema (the organized set of traits, beliefs, actions, and action sequences that are relevant to the partner and the relationship; see Planalp, 1985; Surra & Bohman, in press) and in subjective assessments of the relationship such as satisfaction.

The idea that account-making has these three components was suggested to us by the results of our research on the networks of inferences apparent in accounts (Surra & Planalp, 1990). The goal of that research was to describe the patterns of reasons found in accounts of changes in commitment. In the past, research on accounts of commitment has concerned the frequency of occurrence of separate reasons (i.e., the frequency or proportion of reasons in each coding category; see Surra, 1987a; Surra et al., 1988; Surra & Huston, 1987). This procedure, however, failed to capture the thematic, coherent nature of accounts. Typically, accounts of changes in commitment are in the form of an interconnected set of reasons rather than single reasons or a series of unrelated reasons. The following example, coded by means of Surra's (1987b) Turning Point Coding Scheme, illustrates the interconnectedness of reasons: "High school started [circumstance]. He started hanging around with his wild crowd of friends [one partner's behavior with the network]. I got jealous [negative dyadic attribution], so I told him about it [self-disclosure], and we had a big fight [conflict]."

In order to describe the patterns of reasons apparent in accounts, we utilized data gathered from the first phase of Surra's study of dating couples. Accounts of why commitment changed at each turning point were first divided into thought units, and then each reason was coded into one of 21 categories (Surra, 1987b). We then examined the co-occurrence of different reasons within each turning point by cluster analyzing the co-occurrence matrix of every reason with every other reason, after controlling for such factors as differences in numbers of reasons and in number of turning points reported. (For details of the study, see Surra & Planalp, 1990.)

Four patterns of reasons emerged from the analysis. In three of four of the patterns, behaviroal occurrences were at the heart of a complex of reasons that also contained beliefs about the partnership or third parties. In one pattern, for example, various codes that include references to dyadic interaction or to the partner's independent behavior co-occurred with positive beliefs about the partnership and with beliefs that the relationship measured up to what is desirable. This example illustrates how dyadic interaction triggered changes in positive schematic content: "Before we went home for Christmas break, Carol and I had a talk, and Carol thought she would like to get back together and so I told her I'd think about it over break and then when we got back we talked and we both realized it was a mistake that we were apart for a while and that we're glad we're back together." Interaction with the network can combine with dyadic interaction to have similarly positive effects: "There was a time when we would specifically write down what we learned about each other during the year. . . . I shared that with some of my friends who are counseling majors and they were really impressed. They gave us excellent suggestions as to what to write down. We went camping and we talked about that so it was really exciting because it was almost all positive that was coming up."

Behavioral events can also result in negative changes in relational schemata. This pattern was evident in a cluster in which reasons that concerned one partner's interaction with the network co-occurred with negative network attributions, with negative dyadic attributions, and with standards for relationships not being met. In one case, for example, a woman told her parents about her engagement, and, though her father approved, her mother did not. The woman concluded that even though her partner was not Mr. Right—there were a lot of things he didn't have that she wanted—it really didn't matter. A third pattern consisted of problematic dyadic interaction (e.g., conflict and lack of disclosure) combining with negative beliefs about the relationship and negative inclinations about getting involved.

The fourth pattern was the only one in which behavioral reasons were not included in the general pattern. This cluster consisted of two types of reasons, alternative partner involvements and positive social comparison, as in this example: "We can go out with other people. . . . After I went out with somebody else, I really don't like him as much as I like Robbie and care about him." In the example, interaction with a competing partner was a boost to beliefs about the relationship via social comparison. Alternative partner involvements, however, did not necessarily involve interacting with other partners; they could also include simply monitoring alternatives or thinking about dating others. Thus, behavioral events were not always central to this pattern.

The results of our analyses of co-occurrences of reasons, combined with qualitative analyses (also see Planalp & Rivers, 1988), support our argument that the process of account-making has three components. Usually they occur in chronological order, such that a behavioral event occurs that stimulates a cognitive and affective interpretation; the interpretation alters a midlevel relationship belief and may ricochet to affect different but related beliefs (the relational schema) and assessments of the relationship such as satisfaction. We wish to emphasize, however, that ours is not a chronological stage-model of account-making. This is because the three components are closely related and can occur simultaneously, as in the case where the objective event of a "temper tantrum" is difficult to separate from the respondent's interpretation of it. Moreover, one or more components may be left out or may be hard to identify. In some cases, for instance, the impact of the event is so clear that the interpretation is readily inferred (e.g., your infidelity ends our engagement). Finally, not all events will result in changes in beliefs about or assessments of the relationship. In our research, we tended to get information about all three stages of the process because we asked questions about why assessments of relationships changed. In many cases, however, especially when relationships are stable, events may be interpreted in ways that reinforce preexisting beliefs about the relationship, such that the impact on relational schemata and assessments is minimal (see Surra & Bohman, in press). In the next sections, we discuss each component of account-making in greater detail.

Precipitating Events

What elements are needed to constitute a change-producing event? The results of our research suggest that three elements of events are important. The first is the extent to which the behavioral event provides information that is inconsistent with prior knowledge about the self, the partner, the relationship, or relationships in general. The second concerns the behavioral content of events, and the third, the pattern or form of behavioral events.

INCONSISTENCY OF EVENTS

Events have the potential to precipitate change when they are inconsistent with beliefs about how the relationship is or should be (Fiske & Linville,

1980; Planalp, 1987; Surra & Bohman, in press). The inconsistency brings the event to conscious awareness and invites an interpretation that may (a) make the event irrelevant to the relationship (e.g., my opposite-sex friend was just moved by the romantic setting and he'll never kiss me again); (b) accommodate the event within the existing relational schema by interpreting it as consistent with the schema (e.g., he loves me, but not in a romantic way, and it wasn't a romantic kiss); (c) reconcile the event with beliefs by changing the beliefs (e.g., there is often sexual tension between opposite-sex friends); or (d) reinforce the discrepancy between what is and what should be (e.g., it was a romantic kiss and so maybe he's not just a friend). The latter option sets the stage for changes in the schema.

Inconsistencies arise when information contained in behavioral events is compared with preexisting knowledge (see Planalp & Rivers, 1988; Surra & Bohman, in press). Some of this knowledge concerns beliefs about the nature of particular types of close relationships, such as romantic relationships, friendships, and marriages (Argyle, 1986; Davis & Todd, 1985; La Gaipa, 1987). In the example just described, the kiss was inconsistent with beliefs about friendships. Events may also be inconsistent with beliefs about close relationships in general (Argyle, 1986), such as beliefs that partners should not betray confidences (Planalp et al., 1988). In addition, events may be interpreted as inconsistent if they are incompatible with beliefs about other close relationships the individual has experienced (Surra & Bohman, in press; Surra & Milardo, in press). Thus, an individual may use information about her relationship with her sister to evaluate her newly forming relationship with a friend.

Events may also be inconsistent with partners' beliefs about the character of the self, the other, and their relationship. If a partner believes that his or her relationship is placid and conflict-free, an argument might provoke a change in beliefs. In a conflict-habituated relationship, however, arguments are consistent with beliefs about the relationship. Similarly, knowledge about the self frequently is used to make assessments of the other's personality and the degree of match between self and other (Wilkinson, 1987).

CONTENT OF PRECIPITATING EVENTS

Typically, the account is precipitated by a behavioral occurrence observed by the person. The behavior can occur within the context of dyadic interaction, or it may involve an independent behavior by the partner, sometimes in the presence of others. It may also stem from interaction with third parties.

Both Surra's data and Planalp's data indicate that dyadic interaction is the most common precipitating event. An event may simply involve a particular behavior performed by the partners, such as talking for hours or making love; spending time together; or doing a variety of activities together (e.g., we studied together, went bowling, went to the movies, and did dating kinds of things). Reasons for commitment were replete with references to interaction between partners—22% of all reasons given for changes in commitment in one study (Surra et al., 1988). Likewise, Planalp's data included several references to interaction, such as when the partner hinted at marriage the first time or when a date "ended up quite nicely."

In dyadic interaction, negative behaviors and conflict were frequent precipitating events. Surra coded overt disagreements, tension, and the exchange of negative behaviors between partners as "conflict." In the study of daters (Surra & Planalp, 1990), for instance, a male partner described a conflict in which his partner threw a "tantrum" and he had to "smack" her to get her out of it. In the study by Planalp et al. (1988), the categories of deception and betrayal of confidences were common negative behaviors. In addition, some people reported inadequate patterns of interaction, such as having trouble communicating or frequent fights.

Self-disclosure is a specific kind of positive interaction that is a common triggering event (7.5% of all 1,763 reasons in the study by Surra et al., 1988). For instance, Surra found people who reported that the chance of marriage increased when they "talked about marriage for the first time" or when one person said "I love you." Although self-disclosure was not coded separately by Planalp and her colleagues, several cases did involve increasing self-disclosure (e.g., the other person "has been disclosing deeply and on a regular basis").

The lack or absence of particular dyadic interactions can also precipitate accounts. Surra's data indicated that two types of behavioral deficits are especially important in this regard: lack of interaction, such as "not spending time together," or "He didn't call me"; and an absence of self-disclosure (e.g., "He didn't say he loved me"). Planalp's data also showed that reduced contact and lack of self-disclosure were common precipitating events, as when a friend stopped calling and another friend wouldn't talk about her mother who was dying of cancer.

A final type of dyadic behavioral event is what Surra (1987b) calls "behavioral-response interdependence." In these cases, one partner's behavior independent of other people was the triggering event. Thus, a partner's "giving up a vacation to be with me," or "getting drunk and ignoring me," can stimulate changes in relational beliefs. Although these types of events were relatively infrequent (2.8% of all reasons in Surra et al., 1988), they often had strong effects on beliefs about relationships and were reported at least once by nearly one half (43%) of the sample (Surra et al., 1988). Planalp and colleagues also coded similar triggering events as personality changes in the partner, representing 25% of the events in the two studies (Planalp et al., 1988, p. 529).

Interaction with third parties were precipitating events observed in both Surra's and Planalp's data. In both data sets, third parties included friends and other dating partners; in Surra's data they also included kin and significant others such as ministers and co-workers. In the Planalp et al. data, events involving other people produced change primarily when the third party was in competition for the partner's affections, either as a friend or as a romantic partner. In Surra's data, the behaviors and targets were more varied, including cases in which parents expressed approval or disapproval of the partner or the couple spent time with another couple. Network-related events need not involve direct interaction. Sometimes passively observing the other in a social context stimulated changes in relational beliefs, as in the instance where watching a girlfriend babysit led a boyfriend to conclude that she would be a good mother. (For further discussion see Surra & Milardo, in press.)

Although changes in life circumstances are not directly responsible for accounts, they often set the stage for changes in behavior that do stimulate account-making. Such circumstances might include getting a job in a city that permitted the partners to be together or a father's sudden illness, which provided an opportunity for the partner to show support. In Planalp's study (Planalp & Rivers, 1988), one person was accepted to study in Vienna, which prompted her romantic partner to start crying and to tell her that he had always thought of her as an important part of his future. Thus, circumstances per se rarely produced a change in beliefs, but they often kindled behaviors that did.

FORM OF PRECIPITATING EVENTS

The accounts of changes in relationships that respondents have provided suggest that precipitating events take four different forms, depending upon the number and confluence of events that stimulate the change. The first form that precipitating events take is when a *single event* provoked change, as when one woman and her partner asked other people to a dance in order to get back at one another (Surra & Planalp, 1990) or when a friend betrayed a confidence (Planalp et al., 1988). These singular occurrences were enough to stimulate change because they were glaringly inconsistent with the way relationships are or should be.

The second form that precipitating events take is a *gradual build-up* of the same or similar events over time. In accounts gathered by Surra and colleagues (1988), a common event that occurred through gradual build-up was behavioral interdependence. People spent an increasing amount of time together and did increasingly more varied things together. Such changes are incremental and unidirectional, and it is the pattern of events rather than any particular occurrence that stimulates a change in beliefs about closeness. In the case of gradual build-up, the pattern of change is assessed by comparing it to beliefs about how other relationships changed or how the person expects this particular relationship to change. For example, a person might decide that the relationship is progressing too slowly compared to beliefs about how courtship typically progresses (Baxter, 1987; Honeycutt, Cantrill, & Greene, 1989) or that it is progressing faster than he or she would like.

Precipitating events may also consist of a *confluence of events* (either over time or concurrently) that point to the same interpretation. One example from the Planalp et al. (1988) data was a woman whose male friend became very interested in her life and promised many times to come to her party; then she heard from someone else that he had a crush on her. This confluence of events prompted interpretation that he was interested in her romantically rather than as a friend. In another case, a man reported a recurrent pattern in which he and his girlfriend broke up because she belittled him, got back together, then broke up again. This pattern led to the interpretation that "it was like a power trip for her." As in the case of gradual build-up, confluent events provide a pattern of inconsistent information that leads to the same interpretation.

The final form that the precipitating event can take is a sudden *realization* of the relational significance of previous events or patterns of events. One woman, for example, realized that her friend called her only when he wanted to get homework. Another woman was surprised to learn of her opposite-sex friend's engagement but recognized in retrospect that they had been seeing each other less often since he had started dating his fiancée (Planalp & Rivers, 1988). In these cases, the change results from the partner's reflections on past happenings and the inconsistent information that retrospection provides rather than from an overt occurrence. One of Surra's respondents attributed a decrease in likelihood of marriage to "my own realization [that she isn't the girl I'm looking for], not anything she's done."

Interpretation of the Event(s)

After an inconsistency has been noted between events occurring in the relationship and existing beliefs about relationships, the connection between the two must be worked out. This involves reasoning that relies heavily on both straightforward and complex attributional processes and on emotional reactions to the event(s).

Interpretations Irrelevant to the Relationship

The first possibility, as stated earlier, is that the connection between the event(s) and the relationship is broken because the precipitating event is attributed to a temporary situation or to causes that are irrelevant to the relationship (Surra & Bohman, in press). This was not a common occurrence in our data because we specifically asked for events that were relevant to the relationship. Nevertheless, there were cases in which the event appeared relevant at first but was later attributed to causes that were irrelevant to the relationship. For example, one woman was at first angry because she thought her friend was just using their relationship to get homework. Later she found out that he dropped out of school, disappeared for a time, and moved to Hawaii. With this additional information, she attributed the problem to his desperate situation rather than to disrespect for her or for their relationship.

Straightforward Interpretations

In many cases, an event is interpreted as relevant to the relationship in a relatively simple and straightforward way, seemingly without conscious awareness of the interpretive process and without conscious consideration of alternative interpretations. This seems most likely when all of the information available about the precipitating event points to one plausible cause and when the effects on the relationship are easily understood. For example, Surra et al.'s (1988) respondents cited the discovery that they had similar interests with their partners, deciding they were compatible or deciding that the partner did or did not have suitable characteristics. In these cases, the respondents seemed to have no trouble interpreting events (e.g., attributing behaviors to similar interests, compatibility, or certain characteristics of the partner) or recognizing their links to implicit beliefs that similar interests, compatibility, or certain characteristics were important for relationships.

Motivational factors also seemed to influence how events were interpreted. Some changes were so desirable and others so objectionable that questions of why they occurred or whether they had implications for the relationship were never considered consciously. Examples from Planalp et al.'s (1988) data are a proposal of engagement and finding the partner engaged in an illegal act. The respondents did not seem to care why the events occurred or to question their relevance to the relationship.

Other interpretations were straightforward because respondents were able to make unequivocal attributions following classic attribution principles. For example, Kelley (1972) states that "an effect is attributed to the one of its possible causes with which, over time, it covaries" (p. 3). One respondent reported an almost textbook example of this type of attribution when her roommate yelled at her to clean up the room. Because the roommate had just been elected president of their sorority and because she never cared how the room looked before, the respondent concluded that "her new position has made her power-hungry."

Another type of attribution followed distinctiveness, consistency, and consensus criteria (Kelley, 1967; Surra & Milardo, in press). Distinctiveness refers to whether the effect occurs when the cause is or is not present; consistency refers to whether or not the effect occurs across contexts; consensus refers to whether the effect occurs across people. A textbook example of this type of attribution occurred when a friend called when he needed homework but didn't call when he didn't (distinctiveness), always called when he needed homework (consistency), and called other people when he needed homework (consensus), leading to the conclusion that needing homework caused the calls. Although few accounts give as complete a rendering of attributional cases as this one does, the same type of reasoning may have led to the large number of dispositional attributions that were found in the data. Partners were rejected as being inconsiderate, immature, self-centered, or rude, or accepted for being nice, heterosexual, or "not repulsive in any way."

Making a clear attribution depends, at least in part, on having enough information to pin down one cause and rule out others. Several respondents found the event hard to interpret at first due to lack of information but were able to gather more information from their partners or other people, which resolved the problem fairly easily. For example, one woman whose friend had betrayed a confidence confronted the friend, who responded with the explanation that someone had "twisted her arm" to tell. She did not believe that explanation because other friends said the friend had done the same thing to them. In other cases, the attribution itself changed when new information became available. For example, a "fitness nut's" smoking a cigarette was interpreted at first as a bid for attention, then later as his being in a phase of experimenting with different things.

Complex Interpretations

Many cases of interpretation, however, engage people in complex and difficult interpretive struggles. These cases occur most often under two conditions. First, when the cause of the event is difficult to determine, it is difficult to determine the effects. For example, if a person cannot tell whether her partner lied to save her feelings or to make himself look good, it is difficult to assess the effects on the relationship. Second, regardless of the cause(s), the effects on the relationship may be so complex that simply to understand them is a difficult feat. Divorce is a good example. Regardless of the reason for divorce, understanding its possible effects is a major task.

To return to the first type of problematic interpretation, problems may arise due to indeterminant causes. One reason that the cause(s) of events may be indeterminant is that the events themselves were sometimes vague or ambiguous (Sillars & Weisberg, 1987). An example was a case in which a woman's friend "seemed as though he had no time for her." Whether or not any objective event even occurred was questionable because her friend said it was only her imagination. It is impossible to figure out why the event occurred until one knows whether or not the event has occurred at all.

More often, however, the occurrence of the event was undeniable, but it had several plausible causes. In their accounts, respondents in the Planalp et al. (1988) studies very often described the difficulties they had in sorting out causes, including what possibilities they considered, what information they gathered, to whom they talked, and what they finally concluded.

Alternative causes often came out in discussing the event with their partners, leading to attributional conflict, that is, conflict between partners over the causes of the event (Orvis, Kelley, & Butler, 1976). Some partners were able to work through the problems productively; others were not. Certain findings from the Planalp, Rutherford, and Honeycutt study (1988) helped to clarify the role of partners' attributional conflict in determining the causes of events. Although some of the findings were of marginal statistical significance, they suggested that insufficient or incomplete information is one reason that attributional conflicts occur (Table 9, p. 536). Engaging in communication with the partner (especially exchanging information, explaining feelings, or negotiating rules for the relationship) was more likely to lead to positive relationship outcomes than was avoiding the partner or the issue or engaging in communication in unproductive ways (blaming or making demands). Many people (15%) also said that in retrospect they wish they had talked to their partners more or more openly (Planalp, Rutherford, & Honeycutt, 1988, p. 543).

Of the four forms of events—single events, gradual build-ups, confluence of events, and realization—single events are often the most difficult to interpret because they are the least informative. Because a single event occurs in a specific situation, no information is available about its consistency across a variety of situations. In addition, a person experiencing gradual build-up or a confluence of events may be in a position to rule out alternative explanations by actively manipulating the situation to get the information he or she needs. For example, a man suspected that his partner wanted to break up when they were together and wanted to get together after they had broken up, so went about "testing his theory by rejecting her and letting her come back to [him]."

The second reason that events may be difficult to interpret is that there are so many possible links between the event and different beliefs about the relationship that simply thinking through the implications is difficult. One example speaks for itself. This was a case in which a man's long-term same-sex friend made a sexual advance toward him. The event challenged his beliefs about himself (questioned what had he done to make the friend think he might be responsive), fundamental beliefs about the friend (doesn't feel like he knows him and never did), beliefs about their previous relationships (8 years together, including double dating with women and talking about sexual exploits), and their future relationship (leery of being alone with him).

EMOTIONAL PROCESSES

One of the most direct and immediate types of interpretation was a simple emotional reaction. Surra et al.'s respondents often reported "having a good time together" as increasing the likelihood of marriage or "I just don't feel close" as decreasing it. Emotional reactions may sometimes be diffuse and unrelated to particular events, such as one man's statement that he "just didn't feel that zing." In these cases, the feelings *are* the events and they are either consistent or inconsistent with the belief that relationships should make the people in them feel good, feel close, or feel "that zing."

Seldom, however, are interpretations either purely emotional or totally rational; they are almost always both. For example, one man's estimates of his chances of marrying dropped when he found out that his girlfriend was bulimic. His reaction was both reasoned ("In my family, you know, it's always you eat what's on the table and you don't waste food and stuff") and emotional ("It just made me so mad" and "It just revolted me"). It is not surprising to find emotional and attributional processes going hand-in-hand because emotions and attributions are both prompted by unexpected events, especially those that facilitate or impede important goals (Berscheid, 1988; Frijda, 1986; Wong & Weiner, 1981).

Not only do attributions and emotions occur together, but they also influence each other in specifiable ways. One way is that certain attributions are more likely to produce strong emotions than others. For example, an event that is attributed to causes that are more relevant to the relationship (such as love) are likely to produce stronger emotions than events that are less relevant (being drunk). Another way in which attributions influence emotions is that different attributions about the situation lead to different emotions. (See Scherer, 1988, for a recent review of several such theories.) For example, events that are seen as controllable (such as an illegal act) are more likely to result in anger than sadness, whereas events that are less controllable (such as a friend having less time after getting engaged) are more likely to result in sadness than anger (Frijda, 1986). Similarly, an attribution that focuses on the event (such as a betrayal of confidence) may produce anger, but if the attribution is globalized to the person (such as an untrustworthy person), the emotion may become hatred (Frijda, Mesquita, Sonnemans, & Van Goozen, in press).

Emotions also affect attributions. Emotion has been found to influence several cognitive processes that are strongly linked to attribution. Bower and Cohen (1982) demonstrated that people in good moods are more likely to remember positive than negative events, with the reverse true for people in bad moods. Mood had similar effects on estimated probabilities of future events and on interpretations of ongoing events, especially if they are ambiguous (Moore & Isen, 1990). Thought also tends to intensify feelings (Tesser, 1978). To see these effects, consider a case in which one partner lied to the other. This is likely to make the partner who was lied to feel bad. Because of feeling bad, he is likely to remember primarily bad things that she has done in the past, forecast primarily bad behavior in the future, and interpret ambiguous events as bad. And the more he thinks about it, the worse it seems. These kinds of thoughts point to the global bad-person attribution discussed earlier, rather than an attribution that stays limited to the event.

Emotions can also be data on which attributions are based. A woman who is trying to determine if she loves someone would compare how she feels with him to how she feels without him, as illustrated earlier with the distinctiveness criterion for attributions. Expressions of feelings can also provide direct support for attributions (an "I love you" note on flowers indicates that she sent the flowers because she loves him). Other people's feelings about the partner, such as parents' like or dislike, can provide additional support for attributions ("If my mother likes him, he must be nice").

Some or all of these factors may help to explain the phenomenon of "sentiment override," or more specifically, why distressed or depressed couples tend to make negative attributions and nondistressed or happy couples tend to make positive attributions (Fincham, Bradbury, & Scott, 1990; Fletcher, Fitness, & Blampied, 1990; Holtzworth-Munroe & Jacobson, 1985). Distressed or unhappy partners may have attributional patterns that are conducive to producing and perpetuating negative emotions, and those negative emotions, in turn, are fodder for more negative attributions. For happy partners, the cycle may be the same, but the content is benevolent.

Changes in Relational Schemas and Assessments of the Relationship

The third component of the accounts that we studied is change in the relationship schema (organized sets of beliefs about the relationship). This component is linked to the two earlier components in the following way: When an event that is inconsistent with the schema is noticed, interpretive processes are triggered to determine the nature of the inconsistency. If, upon closer scrutiny, the event is still determined to be both relevant to and inconsistent with the schema, the schema changes. There is reason to believe that schemata are very resistant to change. People prefer instead to discount the event rather than to change the schema (Nisbett & Ross, 1980), especially if the change is undesirable. But sometimes the evidence is inescapable, the schema is untenable, and it changes.

In their discussion of schema change, Crocker, Fiske, and Taylor (1984), following Rothbart (1981), refer to three basic models of schema change—subtyping, bookkeeping, and conversion. Subtyping refers to developing a new subschema that deviates from the general pattern but shows a consistent pattern within the subtype (Planalp, 1987). Even though examples of subtypes of relationships come to mind (commuter marriages, opposite-sex friends who have sex), we found no evidence of this type of change in the accounts that were analyzed.

Bookkeeping refers to change that occurs gradually and the schema is updated whenever new information becomes available. Although this type of change was rare in Planalp's data (probably because of how the question was posed), it was common in Surra's data. Surra and colleagues (Surra & Bohman, in press; Surra et al., 1988) distinguished between relationship-driven and event-driven commitment processes. Relationship-driven commitments were similar to bookkeeping changes. These were based on dyadic processes such as spending time together, engaging in particular activities, disclosing information, or failing to do those things. They were also associated with moderate changes in commitment, tended to occur over longer periods of time, and were associated with higher marital satisfaction four years later.

Conversion refers to change that is sudden and "all-or-none." Surra's (Surra & Bohman, in press; Surra et al., 1988) event-driven changes were consistent with the conversion model. These were based on dramatic or salient events that seemed to provide immediate, undeniable information about commitment. Event-driven changes often involved the social network but also included certain types of dyadic occurrences such as partners deciding on a new stage of involvement or one partner independently and voluntarily doing something that altered the other's conception of the relationship. These changes tended to produce large changes in commitment, tended to occur more suddenly, and were associated with lower marital satisfaction 4 years later.

Nearly all of the changes studied by Planalp and colleagues were consistent with the conversion model (Planalp et al., 1988; Planalp & Rivers, 1988). Not only were they sudden and dramatic, but they also resulted in large, primarily negative changes in beliefs about the relationship. Only 25% of their respondents indicated that their relationship remained the same after the event; another 25% said that it became closer, and the remaining 50% said it became less close or terminated (Planalp et al., 1988, pp. 530–531). Crocker et al. suggested that when conversion occurs, the old schema is tossed out only when there is a new one to replace it. Although there were many cases of conversion from one belief to another (from trust to distrust, uncommitted to committed), there were also cases in which the conversion was never made and respondents hung in limbo for some time, if not indefinitely, trying to come up with a interpretation in which they could have confidence and that would reconcile events with beliefs.

The Surra and Planalp data sets also differed in how likely respondents were to volunteer information in their accounts about what parts of the schema changed and how the changed schema measured up to standards for what relationships should be like. When respondents explained why the chance of marriage changed (Surra et al., 1988), they often stated explicitly and specifically what beliefs changed. In addition, they often explained how their new views of the relationship measured up to internal standards for what a relationship should be like or to comparisons to their previous relationships. For example, one man said he "got a different perception of" his current girlfriend, compared her with his former girlfriend, and realized he felt closer to his former girlfriend than to his current one. Another man said that they spent more and more time together, they got along better, and "kinda figured out that we were a lot more compatible." Several of Surra's (1987b) codes for reasons for marrying reflect these explicit statements about changes in the current relationship and how it measures up (e.g., standards for partnership met/unmet, positive/negative social comparison, positive/negative attribution about the partnership).

On the other hand, when the respondents in Planalp's studies (Planalp & Honeycutt, 1985; Planalp et al., 1988) explained why their uncertainty about their relationships increased, they rarely volunteered what the change was and how the changed relationship measured up to standards. This was probably because the types of changes reported were almost self-explanatory. When a partner lied or cheated, it was usually easy to infer the effects on beliefs. Indeed, when they were asked later in the questionnaire to judge what beliefs were affected, respondents indicated that deception affected beliefs about trust, competing relationships had strong effects on beliefs about exclusiveness, and so on.

One of the goals of the Planalp studies (Planalp & Honeycutt, 1985; Planalp et al., 1988), however, was to trace how changes spread among different beliefs about the relationship. Respondents were asked to estimate the effects of the event on 12 different beliefs about the relationship (closeness, companionship, emotional involvement, honesty, confiding, duties and responsibilities, exclusiveness, support, freedom and autonomy, fairness, trust, and rewards). The responses were then factor analyzed to determine if there were underlying sets of beliefs that were affected by the events. Although confirmatory factor analyses of two data sets yielded slightly different results, the basic factor structure was the same in both. Three factors were found—trust, involvement, and rules—with correlations among the factors ranging from .40 to .52 (Planalp et al., 1988, pp. 531–533). These findings indicate that changes in beliefs spread substantially within the three factors but also spread throughout the entire set of beliefs to a marked degree. For example, deception affected the factor "trust" most strongly, but it also affected the respondent's involvement and perceptions that rules of the relationship were being followed. Whether this is due to connections among beliefs or to sentiment override is unclear. That is, the event may have affected a large number of beliefs, or the emotional reaction may have produced a "halo" or "horn" effect, which made all beliefs about the relationship more positive or more negative.

Conclusions

In this chapter, account-making is described as having three components: the precipitating behavioral event(s), the interpretation of the event(s), and the impact on relational schemata and assessments. Based on the results of our research on accounts of changes in close relationships, we identified the content and form of precipitating events. The cognitive and affective processes central to interpreting events were examined, and the impact of accounts on changes in relational beliefs and assessments was described.

The approach taken in this chapter highlights the role of accounts in developmental change in relationships and in the acquisition and transformation of relational knowledge. Researchers have given increasing attention to how behaviors exchanged during interaction shape partners' momentary cognitive and affective experiences (see Fletcher & Fincham, in press). This work informs us about microscopic events in relationships and why they are significant in partners' lives. Our research builds on this work by focusing attention on the singular events that result in wholesale changes in relationships. In addition, our research takes the emphasis off behaviors exchanged dyadically and underscores the fact that a wide array of events and behaviors are responsible for changes in relationships. Events that precipitate change include partners' independent behaviors, their interactions with third parties, and passive observations of partners with others. Change-producing events can occur in isolation and in combination, in the present and past, for better and for worse.

Contrary to the study of momentary subjective changes, the study of accounts emphasizes that certain occurrences effect drastic shifts in relational knowledge and in individuals' feelings about their partners. The changes that result may be localized, focused on one or two relationship beliefs. More often, however, the implications of events permeate the most central characterization of the relationship and affect a variety of interrelated beliefs. In this way, studying accounts enlightens us about how relational knowledge forms and, once in place, how and why it changes.

References

Argyle, M. (1986). The skills, rules and goals of relationships. In R. Gilmour & S. Duck (Eds.), *The emerging field of personal relationships* (pp. 23–29). Hillsdale, NJ: Erlbaum.

Argyle, M., & Henderson, M. (1984). The rules of friendship. *Journal of Social and Personal Relationships, 1*, 211–237.

Baxter, L.A. (1987). Cognition and communication in the relationship process. In R. Burnett, P. McGhee, & D.D. Clarke (Eds.), *Accounting for relationships: Explanation, representation, and knowledge* (pp. 192–212). London: Methuen.

Berscheid, E. (1988). Emotion. In H.H. Kelley, E. Berscheid, A. Christensen, J. Harvey, T.L. Huston, G. Levinger, E. McClintock, L.A. Peplau, & D.R. Peterson (Eds.), *Close relationships*. (pp. 110–168). San Francisco: W.H. Freeman.

Bower, G.H., & Cohen, P.R. (1982). Emotional influences in memory and thinking: Data and theory. In M.S. Clark & S.T. Fiske (Eds.), *Affect and cognition* (pp. 291–331). Hillsdale, NJ: Erlbaum.

Crocker, J., Fiske, S.T., & Taylor, S.E. (1984). Schematic bases of belief change. In J.R. Eiser (Ed.), *Attitudinal judgment* (pp. 197–226). New York: Springer-Verlag.

Cupach, W.R., & Metts, S. (1986). Accounts of relational dissolution: A comparison of marital and non-marital relationships. *Communication Monographs, 53*, 311–334.

Davis, K.E., & Todd, M.J. (1985). Assessing friendship: Prototypes, paradigm cases and relationship description. In S. Duck & D. Perlman (Eds.), *Understanding personal relationships: An introductory approach* (pp. 17–38). Beverly Hills, CA: Sage.

Fincham, F.D., Bradbury, T.N., & Scott, C.K. (1990). Cognition in marriage. In F.D. Fincham & T.N. Bradbury, *The psychology of marriage* (pp. 118–149). New York: Guilford.

Fiske, S.T., & Linville, P. (1980). What does the schema concept buy us? *Personality and Social Psychology Bulletin, 6*, 543–557.

Fletcher, G.J.O. (1983). The analysis of verbal explanations for marital separation: Implications for attribution theory. *Journal of Applied Social Psychology, 13*, 245–258.

Fletcher, G.J.O., & Fincham, F. (Eds.). (in press). *Cognition in close relationships*. Hillsdale, NJ: Erlbaum.

Fletcher, G.J.O., Fitness, J., & Blampied, N.M. (1990). The link between attributions and happiness in close relationships: The roles of depression and explanatory style. *Journal of Social and Clinical Psychology, 9*, 243–255.

Frijda, N. (1986). *The emotions*. Cambridge: Cambridge University Press.

Frijda, N., Mesquita, B., Sonnemans, J., & Van Goozen, S. (1991). The duration of affective phenomena: Emotions, sentiments, and passions. In K. Strongman (Ed.), *International Review of Emotion*, Vol. 1. New York: Wiley. pp. 187–225.

Harvey, J.H., Weber, A.L., Galvin, K.S., Huszti, H.C., & Garnick, N.N. (1986). Attribution and termination of close relationships: A special focus on the account. In R. Gilmour & S. Duck (Eds.), *The emerging field of personal relationships* (pp. 189–201). Hillsdale, NJ: Erlbaum.

Harvey, J.H., Wells, G.L., & Alvarez, M.D. (1978). Attribution in the context of conflict and separation in close relationships. In J. Harvey, W. Ickes, & R. Kidd (Eds.), *New directions in attribution research* (Vol. 2) (pp. 235–259). Hillsdale, NJ: Erlbaum.

Holtzworth-Munroe, A., & Jacobson, N.S. (1985). Causal attributions of married couples: When do they search for causes? What do they conclude when they do? *Journal of Personality and Social Psychology, 48*, 1398–1412.

Honeycutt, J.M., Cantrill, J.G., & Greene, R.W. (1989). Memory Structure for relational escalation: A cognitive test of the sequencing of relational actions and stages. *Human Communication Research, 16*, 62–90.

Kelley, H.H. (1967). Attribution theory in social psychology. In D. Levine (Ed.), *Nebraska Symposium on Motivation: Vol. 15* (pp. 192–238). Lincoln, NE: University of Nebraska Press.

Kelley, H.H. (1972). Attribution in social interaction. In E.E. Jones, D.E. Kanouse, H.H. Kelley, R.E. Nisbett, S. Valins, & B. Weiner (Eds.), *Attribution: Perceiving the causes of behavior* (pp. 1–26). Morristown, NJ: General Learning Press.

La Gaipa, J.J. (1987). Friendship expectations. In R. Burnett, P. McGhee, & D.D. Clarke (Eds.), *Accounting for relationships: Explanation, representation, and knowledge* (pp. 134–157). London: Methuen.

Moore, B.S., & Isen, A.M. (1990). Affect and social behavior. In B.S. Moore & A.M. Isen (Eds.), *Affect and social behavior* (pp. 1–21). Cambridge: Cambridge University Press.

Nisbett, R. & Ross, L. (1980). *Human inference: Strategies and shortcomings of social judgment*. Englewood Cliffs, NJ: Prentice-Hall.

Orvis, B.R., Kelley, H.H., & Butler, D. (1976). Attributional conflict in young couples. In J.H. Harvey, W.J. Ickes, & R.F. Kidd (Eds.), *New directions in attribution research (Vol. 1)*. Hillsdale, NJ: Erlbaum, pp. 353–386.

Planalp, S. (1985). Relational schemata: A test of alternative forms of relational knowledge as guide to communication. *Human Communication Research, 12*, 3–29.

Planalp, S. (1987). Interplay between relational knowledge and events. In R. Burnett, P. McGhee, & D.D. Clarke (Eds.), *Accounting for relationships: Explanation, representation, and knowledge* (pp. 175–191). London: Methuen.

Planalp, S., & Honeycutt, J.M. (1985). Events that increase uncertainty in personal relationships. *Human Communication Research, 11*, 593–604.

Planalp, S., & Rivers, M. (May, 1988). Changes in knowledge of relationships. Paper presented to the International Communication Association, New Orleans, LA.

Planalp, S., Rutherford, D.K., & Honeycutt, J.M. (1988). Events that increase uncertainty in personal relationships II: Replication and extension. *Human Communication Research, 14*, 516–547.

Rothbart, M. (1981). Memory processes and social beliefs. In D. Hamilton (Ed.), *Cognitive processes in stereotyping and intergroup behavior* (pp. 145–181). Hillsdale, NJ: Erlbaum.

Scherer, K. (1988). Criteria for emotion-antecedent appraisal: A review. In V. Hamilton, G.H. Bower, & N.H. Frijda (Eds.), *Cognitive perspectives on emotion and motivation* (pp. 89–126). Dordrecht, The Netherlands: Kluwer Academic Publishers.

Sillars, A.L., & Weisberg, J. (1987). Conflict as a social skill. In M.E. Roloff & G.R. Miller (Eds.), *Interpersonal processes: New directions in communication research* (pp. 140–171). Newbury Park, CA: Sage.

Surra, C.A. (1987a). Turning point coding manual: A scheme for classifying subjective reasons for commitment. *Social and Behavioral Sciences Documents, 17*, 52–53.

Surra, C.A. (1987b). Reasons for changes in commitment: Variations by courtship type. *Journal of Social and Personal Relationships, 4*, 17–33.

Surra, C.A., Arizzi, P., & Asmussen, L.A. (1988). The association between reasons for commitment and the development and outcome of marital relationships. *Journal of Social and Personal Relationships, 5*, 47–63.

Surra, C.A., & Bohman, T. (in press). The development of close relationships: A cognitive perspective. In G.J.O. Fletcher & F.D. Fincham (Eds.), *Cognition in close relationships*. Hillsdale, NJ: Erlbaum.

Surra, C.A., Chandler, M., Asmussen, L. & Wareham, J. (1987). Effects of premarital pregnancy on the development of interdependence in relationships. *Journal of Social and Clinical Psychology, 5*, 123–139.

Surra, C.A., & Huston, T.L. (1987). Mate selection as a social transition. In D. Perlman & S. Duck (Eds.), *Intimate relationships: Development, dynamics, and deterioration*. (pp. 88–120). Newbury Park, CA: Sage.

Surra, C.A., & Milardo, R.M. (in press). The social psychological context of developing relationships: Interactive and psychological networks. In W.H. Jones & D. Perlman (Eds.), *Advances in personal relationships: Vol. 3*. London: Jessica Kingsley Publishers.

Surra, C.A., & Planalp, S. (July, 1990). The structure of causal accounts of commitment. Paper presented to the International Society for the Study of Personal Relationships, Oxford.

Tesser, A. (1978). Self-generated attitude change. In L. Berkowitz (Ed.), *Advances in experimental social psychology* (Vol. 11) (pp. 289–338). New York: Academic Press.

Wilkinson, S. (1987). Explorations of self and other in a developing relationship. In R. Burnett, P. McGhee, & D.D. Clarke (Eds.), *Accounting for relationships: Explanation, representation, and knowledge* (pp. 40–59). London: Methuen.

Wong, P.T.P., & Weiner, B. (1981). When people ask "why" questions, and the heuristics of attributional search. *Journal of Personality and Social Psychology, 40*, 650–663.

6
Coping with Relational Dissolutions: Attributions, Account Credibility, and Plans for Resolving Conflicts

MICHAEL J. CODY, LARRY KERSTEN, DAVID O. BRAATEN, and RISA DICKSON

In this chapter we will review the different types of studies we have completed concerning how people cope with deteriorating relationships. First, we will review research on the communication and evaluation of *accounts*. Our research in this area focuses attention on basic issues concerning why people communicate apologies, excuses, justifications, and denials, and the consequences of using such oral arguments in performing needed remedial work or in promoting a particular public image. The second line of research to be reviewed focuses attention on *relational break-ups* and deals with basic issues concerning why dating partners disengage, the tactics used either to resolve relational problems or to disengage, and the consequences that follow.

The research reviewed here focuses attention on how social actors cope with relational problems. First, during an "intrapsychic" phase of potential disengagement (Duck, 1983), a partner may offer some type of an account for the problem he or she sees as responsible for the deteriorating relationship. Presumably, a relationship may be saved if the account-giver provides a credible accounting. If the account-receiver does not find the account credible, he or she may devise some plan for resolving the relational problem or may move toward deescalating the relationship (i.e., redefining the relationship so that it is a less intimate one) or terminating the relationship. Research confirms basic expectations concerning the determinants of message strategies: Relational problems (e.g., jealousy or possessiveness) are related to attributions of causality and to beliefs concerning whether a relational partner can change the undesirable behavior. Both attributions and beliefs, coupled with a partner's motivation to perform needed relational work, are significantly related to the perceptions that accounts are helpful in resolving the problem, the plans social actors possess for solving the problem, and the decision to terminate the relationship.

Considerable research has focused on attributions and relational dissolutions in the 1980s (see other contributions in this book). Our contribution focuses attention on strategic communication between the disengager and the disengagee. We view the individual communicator as a problem solver who utilizes perceptions of causality and beliefs about everyday problems as a road map for knowing how to navigate around inexcusable relational problems, to implement plans concerning how "solvable" problems can be remedied, and to withdraw from relationships that are too costly (or when plans to solve relational problems fail).

The Accounts Literature

Impression management scholars employ the term *Social predicament* to denote "any event that casts undesired aspersions on the lineage, character, conduct, skills, or motives of an actor" (Schlenker, 1980, p. 125; also see Tedeschi & Riess, 1981). Other scholars in this area use the term *failure event* to denote specific (alleged) behaviors or "offenses" that result in an account's being requested, offered, and evaluated. Accounts are messages used to cope with social predicaments or failure events. (For historical references and reviews, see Cody & McLaughlin, 1985, 1990; Semin & Manstead, 1983; Snyder, Higgins, & Stucky, 1983.) Failure events involve either the perception that the account-giver has engaged in an inappropriate or unexpected behavior (e.g., Roommate: "Why were you flirting with Lesley at the party?"), or the *failure* on the account-giver's part to engage in an appropriate or expected behavior (e.g., Roommate: "Why didn't you pay the phone bill on time?").

Considerable attention has focused on *account episodes* (see Schönbach, 1990). Following the recognition that a failure event has occurred (or is alleged to have occurred), an account episode unfolds in three phases. First, a reproacher employs some type of a *reproach*—a question, assertion, rebuke, or sign (such as a frown or look of disgust)—is employed in order to elicit an explanation. Second, an *account* is communicated. Third, a receiver (usually the reproacher) offers an *evaluation* of the account. An account that is found acceptable by receivers is said to be honored, and receivers reject the accounts when asserting that the explanation is not sufficient or believable. Accounts may also elicit partial honoring (i.e., the receiver accepts the explanation for the present failure event but warns the account-giver not to engage in the failure event again). A number of different types of consequences may follow from the account episode. If remedial work is effective, then the status quo of the reproacher/account-giver's relationship will be maintained, no negative changes will occur in the relationship, and no negative reevaluation of identities will follow. On the other hand, episodes can escalate to conflict, the filing of formal complaints in organizations, ticketing by traffic officers, penalties by judges and parole boards, and so forth (see review by Cody & McLaughlin, 1990).

A brief overview of the nature of tactical or strategic account-giving would include the following four topics: (a) a typology of accounts and the functions served by accounts; (b) a discussion of the determinants of accounts, plus comments on the credibility of accounts; (c) the nature of reproach forms and the effect reproach forms have on accounts and their evaluations; and (d) the consequences of the account episode.

Accounts and Functions

The classic work by Scott and Lyman (1968) presented two forms of accounts: *excuses* and *justifications*. An excuse was said to involve the offender's admitting that the failure event occurred but denying that he or she was fully responsible for the act's occurrence. Scott and Lyman speculated that there were certain forms of excuses: appeal to accidents, biological drives, appeal to defeasibility, and scapegoating. When using a justification, the account-giver accepts responsibility for the failure event but denies that it was harmful or claims that there were positive consequences associated with the action. Six common forms of justifications included denial of injury, denial of victim, appeal to loyalties, condemnation of condemners, self-fullfilment, and sad tale (Scott & Lyman, 1968).

When confronted with a failure-event situation, account-givers in reality have more options than merely excusing or justifying actions. Schönbach (1980) was one of the first (also see Tedeschi & Riess, 1981) to propose that there are certain basic strategic moves available to account-givers beyond excuses and justifications. A four-part typology of accounts would include *concessions/apologies*, *excuses*, *justifications*, and *refusals/denials* (see Cody & McLaughlin, 1990). *Concessions/apologies* include the account-giver's admissions of guilt for the occurrence of the failure event including any statements of remorse. Refusals/denials, on the other hand, include statements in which the account-giver asserts or attempts to prove that he or she is innocent of having caused the failure event.

The four forms of accounting serve specific functions in interaction. By definition, an excuse attempts to exonerate the account-giver from being held personally responsible for an offense, whereas a justification serves the function of making the action seem less negative (or even positive). The use of a concession communicates that the account-giver agrees with a reproacher's assessment of responsibility and consequence and that, if appropriate forms of an apology are used, the account-giver will not engage in the act again and/or will make restitution (or compensation) for the failure event. In the use of a refusal, however, the account-giver asserts (or proves) his or her innocence of the accusation or refuses to grant the reproacher the right to ask about a questionable behavior (e.g., "You are not my supervisor. I don't have to answer to you.").

In our earlier work, we argued that the four basic types of accounts can be arrayed on a "mitigating-aggravating" continuum of politeness, with a concession or an apology representing the most polite (mitigating) form of argument, followed by excuses and justifications, and with refusals/denials representing the least polite (aggravating) forms of accounting (McLaughlin, Cody, & O'Hair, 1983; McLaughlin, Cody, & Rosenstein, 1983). Research evidence to date supports the claim that apologies and excuses are more mitigating than justifications and refusals/denials, with apologies and excuses eliciting more honoring than justifications and refusals/denials (see Cody & McLaughlin, 1990; Holtgraves, 1989). However, the four-part breakdown of accounts arrayed on a single continuum is an obvious oversimplification. First, certain subcategories of each type of account are significantly more effective in eliciting a desired outcome than other subcategories. Second, the ranking of accounts on the basis of politeness is a primary concern if the account-giver focuses attention on maintaining cordial relations and desires to be liked. If account-givers emphasize some other aspect of impression management, such as being perceived as competent, intimidating, dedicated, and so forth, then the four-part ordering on the basis of politeness is useless—account-givers should employ justifications and some forms of refusals and should avoid most forms of apologies and excuses (see below).

We should comment briefly on each of three topics: (a) the evidence that apologies and excuses are more mitigating and result in more frequent honoring than justifications and refusals; (b) the evidence that certain subcategories of accounts are more effective than other subcategories; and (c) the evidence that certain subcategories are significantly related to the creation and maintenance of particular public images of competence, dedication, and so forth.

Mitigation

In earlier studies (Cody & McLaughlin, 1985; McLaughlin, Cody, & O'Hair, 1983; McLaughlin, Cody, & Rosenstein, 1983), we simply compared how frequently apologies and excuses were honored relative to justifications and refusals/denials. We did not have participants actually rate the accounts on perceived politeness, hearer satisfaction, difficulty of communication, or helpfulness in solving the problem. Fortunately, Holtgraves (1989) provided such a direct assessment. Holtgraves had college students read a scenario in which a man named James arrived late to take his friend Paul to a concert. The students read one of several accounts that James could have used: a full-blown apology, a standard apology, a regret, a hybrid regret + excuse, an excuse, a hybrid regret + justification, and a simple justification ("It's not that big a deal; it wasn't going to be that good a concert anyway.") The latter, specific form of a justification is called a "minimize harm" argument. (Holtgraves did not include refusals or denials.)

Holtgraves (1989) found that students rated the simple justification as less satisfying to hear and less helpful in solving the problem/conflict. Further, the justification + regret did not fare much better. Effective accounts (in descending order) included full-blown apology, standard apology, excuse + regret, and regret. An excuse without a statement of regret was rated fairly low in helpfulness, and both forms of justifications were rated extremely low in helpfulness. A full-blown apology was rated as more difficult to communicate than other forms of accounts.

Apologies and excuses that contain elements of regret are more satisfying to hear and more helpful in solving problems than justifications (in interpersonal settings).

Relevant Subcategories of Accounts

Both Holtgraves's (1989) project and a recent project in an organizational setting (Braaten, Cody, & Bell, 1990) distinguished between two types of apologies: *full-blown* (or compensation), and *standard apology* (a perfunctory "I'm sorry"). Both projects concluded that the extreme form of apology was more effective or helpful than a simple expression of regret. Apologies may in fact include as many as five specific components: (a) an expression of guilt, remorse, or embarrassment; (b) a clarification in which one recognizes what the appropriate conduct should have been and expresses acknowledgment that negative sanctions apply for having committed the failure event; (c) a rejection of the inappropriate conduct and disparagement of the "bad" self that misbehaved; (d) an acknowledgment of the appropriate conduct and a promise to behave accordingly in the future; and (e) the performance of penance, restitution, and/or an offer to compensate the victim(s) (see Goffman, 1971; Schlenker, 1980). As a general rule, a guilty account-giver will benefit from employing more elements of apologies when attempting to seek forgiveness (also see Ohbuchi, Kameda, & Agarie, 1989).

One useful form of excuse is the *appeal to accident*. Because accidents do occur randomly and can befall anyone, the claim that the account-giver was victimized by traffic snarls, flat tires, and so forth are often accepted as valid by reproachers. However, one problem with the credibility of excuses stems from the fact that excuses are lies. In a recent survey we asked students to recall account episodes that involved professors, and 26% of the students reported having used lies (Cody & Braaten, 1990). Students would claim an accident or an illness in order to account for missed exams, missed meetings, and late papers. A second popular form of excuse is *denial of intent*. In the Braaten et al. (1990) study of accounts in organizations, the appeal to accident claim was honored more frequently than the denial of intent claim.

Two popular types of justifications include the *minimize harm* claim (used by Holtgraves, 1989), and the *higher involvement* (or, to use the original typology of Scott & Lyman, 1968, *appeal to loyalties*) claim (used by Hale, 1987). The claim that the missed concert "wasn't going to be good anyway" was judged as unhelpful in resolving a conflict (Holtgraves, 1989). Hale's (1987) use of "higher involvement" involved the claim that a student was going to be late with a term paper assignment because a job interview trip interfered with completing the assignment on time. The higher involvement justification was rated as effective by students in Hale's study. Braaten et al. (1990) also found that the higher involvement claim was more effective than the minimize harm claim in an organizational setting. At issue here is whether the reproacher and the account-giver are in agreement concerning priorities as to who or what is a more important goal or higher loyalty. For example, a worker may be late in completing a routine computer check on finances because the worker had devoted several hours to helping an important client attend to a crisis. Such a claim to higher involvement (important client) was considered quite credible (see Braaten, et al., 1990), whereas other claims of higher involvement (family constraints) were not evaluated as positively by managers.

Braaten et al. (1990) also assessed the relative contribution of three forms of refusals/denials: denial that offense occurred, a challenge to the authority of the reproacher, and logical proof (using memos, documents, and logic, the account-giver attempts to prove that he or she is innocent of having committed the failure event). Logical proofs were vastly superior in eliciting honoring than both other forms of refusals/denials. Also, the use of logical proof was a superior ploy when drivers made oral arugments in traffic court (Cody & McLaughlin, 1988).

It is regrettable that earlier projects treated all subcategories of apologies, excuses, justifications, and refusals as equal. Within each form of argument, particular forms are superior (in eliciting honoring) to others.

Impression Management Function

Many studies on accounts focus on the ability of oral argument to perform a needed or desired "remedial" work—to repair a disrupted conversation, to reestablish the status quo of a relationship. However, specific forms of accounts are also significantly related to the public images of account-givers. Although impression management scholars frequently discuss accounts as important elements in managing images, few studies actually demonstrate the relationship between specific forms of oral argument and impressions. Braaten et al. (1990, Study II) found that account-givers received higher ratings on ingratiation (being perceived as likable) if they used a *compensation apology*, a *perfunctory apology*, or a *higher involvement justification*; unlikable accounters used *challenge authority* and *deny offense* forms of refuals/denials. Account-givers who employed the compensation apology, justifications, and logical proofs were perceived as more competent and as more dedicated (Jones & Pittman's [1982] "self-promotion" and "exemplification" impressions, respectfully). Account-givers were rated as weak and indecisive (i.e., "supplicators") if they used excuses (especially the "appeal to accident" form) and if they used the mere perfunctory apology, Finally, account-givers were rated as intimidating (strong, aggressive) if they used deny offense and challenge authority forms of refusals/denials.

There are a number of important implications stemming from the impression management view of the consequences of accounts. First, an apology (specifically a "compensation apology") is not the only effective claim that can be made in terms of eliciting honoring and likability. The higher involvement form of justification claim was also quite effective. Second, even when a form of excuse was rated as effective in exonerating the account-giver of blame (the appeal to accident), the excuse maker's image is diminished by being perceived relatively low in dedication, intimidation, and competence (and high in supplication, "weak"). Because less competent and less dedicated workers stand little chance of earning promotions, merit raises and so forth, a frequent reliance on excuses could be costly in the long run. Third, although the use of aggravating forms of accounts (challenge authority, deny offense) are infrequently honored, these claims may also result in some long-term benefit. By creating an impression of the self as an aggressive, strong intimidator, the account-giver may ultimately create an environment in which he or she is rarely asked to provide accounts in the future. Intimidators are probably left alone.

Determinants of Accounts

Schlenker (1980) argued that *reality constraints* limit the account-giver's construction of accounts. Specifically, "reality constraint" means that people will select a tactic they believe best fits the situation as it appears to be known to the audience. Schlenker lists three constraints: (a) Account-givers will take into consideration the gravity of the situation, as perceived by audience members; (b) account-givers are likely to take into consideration the facts that are known about the situation by the audience members; and (c) account-givers will take into consideration the prevailing beliefs the audience has about such situations, as represented by the values and beliefs of the particular society or subgroup. The nature of account-giving and evaluation in legal settings highlights (in our opinion) the operation of reality constraints (see Cody & McLaughlin, 1990, review; Felson & Ribner, 1981); for instance, a violent criminal may attempt to claim that he accidently struck a victim once—however, if he struck the victim repeatedly the reality of the crime precludes the use of an excuse (the criminal attempts to justify repeated beatings). Also, because members of our society abhor violence directed toward females, men prone to commit violence attempt to argue that the violence was not intentional, but accidental—they do not want to be perceived as personally responsible for female-related violent actions.

Other research projects have focused on situational variables as determinants of accounts. Cody and McLaughlin (1985) concluded that expressed guilt and severity of the failure event were related to more frequent use of concessions and apologies, and excuses were more frequently employed when the account-giver believed that he or she was not personally responsible for the failure event. Justifications were more frequently used when there was greater relational intimacy, less important instrumental goals, greater perceived responsibility, and perceived rights to persuade—that is, when account-givers accepted responsibility for a course of action they believed was warranted and were explaining their actions to friends and peers who might accept their reasons for justifying what might be a questionable action (or, at least, be more inclined than strangers to accept the explanations). Refusals and denials were more likely to be used when the account-giver believed that he or she was falsely accused of an action and when the account-giver expressed low levels of guilt (see Cody & McLaughlin, 1985).

The severity of the offense is one variable that has obtained considerable attention in the literature. Schlenker (1980) proposed that as severity increases an account-giver will provide more elaborate forms of accounting. Less severe failure events may be handled in a perfunctory fashion, whereas more severe offenses elicit more verbal components and more overall different types of account messages (see Cody & McLaughlin, 1990; Gonzales, Pederson, Manning, & Wetter, 1990). There are, however, two problems with research on severity. First, some scholars use the term *high severity* to denote the kind of situation in which a person apparently dropped a liquid into a tote bag containing a camera and other equipment (Gonzales et al., 1990). Other studies use the term when referring to traffic violations, being fired from employment, being accused of cheating on tests, and so on (Cody & Braaten, in press; Cody & McLaughlin, 1990). Unfortunately, different types of consequences, emotions (embarrassment, anger, regret), and levels of severity have been labeled "high severity."

Second, we are not convinced that severity is related to specific forms of accounting. Gonzales et al. (1990) argue that Schönbach (1980) claims that high levels of severity are associated with more frequent denials, and that we argued (Cody & McLaughlin, 1985; McLaughlin, Cody, & O'Hair, 1983) that high levels of severity are associated with more frequent apologies. Actually, severity is associated with more frequent and more complex forms of accounting, as well as with more keenly experienced emotional reactions (guilt, anger, shame, etc.). Schönbach (1990) more recently noted that increased levels of severity may be related to more frequent and stronger attempts to prove one's innocence, or to more frequent and extreme forms of apologies, depending on other variables (guilt, the belief that one is being accused falsely). When confronting relational problems (see below), severity of relational problems is associated with increased motivation to resolve the problem and the elaboration of a plan to resolve the problem, as well as with an increased probability of withdrawal from the relationship. Causal attributions, guilt, responsibility, and beliefs concerning failure events are related to specific forms of accounting.

The most recent approach to the study of determinants focuses attention on a typology of failure events. Schönbach (1990), in fact, lists the development of a typology of failure events as one of the pressing needs in this area of research. A typology of failure events would specify norms, beliefs, expectations, anticipated values, and attributions of perceived underlying causes (also see Read & Collins, Chap. 7, this volume). Certain types of failure events have been identified; for example, in Braaten et al. (1990) four common types of accusations were made of workers and peers: *tardiness*, *lack of sociability* (i.e., not being a team player), *performance errors*, and *questionable judgment*.

Braaten et al. (1990) argued that the failure events differed from one another in terms of underlying causes and found that the failure events strongly affected the use of accounts. Tardiness included errors in being late for work, and these involved uncontrollable, unintentional, unstable, and external causes (e.g., a truck jackknived on the freeway, causing the worker to be late). Performance errors involved unintentional, unstable, controllable causes that may sometimes be external ("Oh, I got distracted by the noise," "The heat in here is unbearable and I got drowsy"). Claims concerning lack of sociability involved causes that are stable, internal, intentional, and probably characterized by managers as uncontrollable (e.g., that the worker can not control his anger or arrogance). Finally, questionable judgment involved asking others to account for decisions concerning merit, schedules, and assignments—causes that are stable, internal, intentional, and controllable.

Braaten et al. (1990) found that types of failure events significantly influenced the communication of accounts. Workers often *apologized* for the unintentional, unstable, and controllable performance errors and rarely apologized for failure events that involved internal, intentional, and (potentially) controllable causes (judgment and sociability). Almost all *excuses* were communicated for failure events involving tardiness and performance errors, presumably because causes of the events are largey uncontrollable, unstable, and inintentional—the types of situations in which excuses are to be expected (see Weiner, in press). *Justifications* were frequently used to account for questionable judgments, when causes are controllable, internal, and intentional. *Denials* of wrongdoing were rarely attempted when the worker was accused of being tardy—most likely because reality constraints operate to prohibit the worker from attempting such a claim; that is, it should be obvious in most cases when a worker arrives late that the attempt to deny it violates perceptions of reality.

A limitation of the Braaten et al. (1990) study is that we did not directly assess the underlying attributed causes, nor did we assess any number of relevant beliefs about the failure events. In our most recent project on coping with relational problems (Kersten, Braaten, Dickson, & Cody, 1990), we asked college students a series of questions concerning their beliefs about the following six problems: A person failed to *confide* his or her feelings and thoughts to a dating partner, a person failed to *share quality time* with a dating partner, a person was *rude* in public and embarrassed a dating partner, a person failed to make him or herself *presentable* in public, a person was *possessive*, and a person was *jealous*. Kersten et al. had the students rate the perceived underlying cause of each relational problem and indicate the extent to which they believed each relational problem was serious (harmful), forgivable, and solvable. They also indicated the extent to which they would be motivated to solve the problem and the extent to which they would withdraw from the relationship. The students also rated a full-blown apology (e.g., "I'm sorry. I regret that this happened. I promise not to do this again.") in terms of credibility and helpfulness (in resolving the problem). Finally, students wrote essays detailing their plans to solve each problem (see section below, "Attributions and Disengagement").

Table 6.1 presents data concerning how relational problems were evaluated in regard to underlying causes. Lack of confiding and problems in presentability were rated as significantly less intentionally caused than all other problems, and rudeness was rated as more intentionally caused than all other problems. Possessiveness and jealousy were rated as significantly less controllable than other problems, whereas problems in

TABLE 6.1. Perceived causes as a function of type of relational problem.[a]

	Attributed causes			
Relational problem	Intent	Control	Internal	Stable
Lack of confiding	4.89	3.43	2.76	3.57
Lack of shared time	4.13	2.87	4.23	3.39
Rudeness	3.20	2.55	2.92	3.26
Presentability	4.69	2.18	3.31	3.33
Possessiveness	3.83	3.66	2.64	3.20
Jealousy	4.32	3.66	2.84	3.36

[a] From Kersten, Braaten, Dickson, and Cody (1990, unpublished source). Smaller numbers denote higher ratings of perceived causality.

presentability and rudeness were rated as more controllable than other problems. Lack of shared time and problems in presentability were considered as less internally caused than other problems. The relational problems did not vary significantly in perceived stability.

Relational problems were similarly related to beliefs concerning the extent to which the problem posed serious harm to the relationship, whether the partner could be forgiven, whether the problem is difficult to resolve, the extent to which the respondent would be motivated to resolve the problem, and the likelihood that the respondent would withdraw from the relationship (see Table 6.2). Rudeness and possessiveress were rated as significantly more serious than other problems, and problems in presentability rated least serious. Lack of confiding and problems in presentability were rated as more easily forgivable than rudeness, possessiveness, jealousy, or lack of shared time. Rudeness, possessiveness, and jealousy were rated as more difficult to solve that lack of confiding, lack of shared time, and problems in presentability. Motivation to work on the relational problem was generally high (see Table 6.2), and motivation was rated highest for lack of confiding, followed by lack of shared time. Finally, students were less likely to withdraw from the relationship if the problem dealt with lack of confiding, problems in presentability, jealousy, and lack of shared time, but they rated withdrawing from the relationship more likely when the problems dealt with rudeness and possessiveness.

As indicated in Table 6.2, men and women differed in their beliefs concerning the relational problems. There is very strong evidence in support of gender effects in managing relational problems (see, for example, Cody, Canary, & Smith, in press), and gender effects were

TABLE 6.2. Beliefs concerning relational problems.[a]

Relational problem		Beliefs				
		Serious	Forgive	Solve	Motivated	Withdraw
Confide	M	3.24*	2.86	2.93	2.68*	4.35
	F	2.74	2.60	3.14	1.90	4.26
Share time	M	2.86	2.95	2.83	2.49	3.68
	F	2.69	3.13	2.68	2.26	3.80
Rudeness	M	2.36*	4.17*	3.46	2.81	3.33*
	F	1.94	4.52	3.49	2.49	2.81
Presentability	M	3.70	2.69	2.57*	3.02*	4.69
	F	3.66	2.50	2.02	2.36	4.86
Possessiveness	M	2.18	3.39	3.68	2.84*	3.36*
	F	1.94	3.62	3.69	2.44	2.82
Jealousy	M	2.66	3.37	3.43	2.69	3.74
	F	2.44	3.31	3.54	2.37	3.79

[a] From Kersten, Braaten, Dickson, and Cody (1990, unpublished source).
Smaller numbers denote higher ratings on the beliefs.
* Denotes a significant difference between men and women.

TABLE 6.3. Credibility and effectiveness of an apology as a function of type of relational problem.[a]

	Reactions to apology	
Relational problem	Credibility	Helpfulness
Lack of confiding	4.11	3.84
Lack of shared time	3.89	3.42
Rudeness	4.17	3.81
Presentability	3.54	3.21
Possessiveness	4.48	3.99
Jealousy	4.33	4.03

[a] Adapted from data reported in Kersten, Braaten, Dickson, and Cody (1990).
Smaller numbers denote higher levels of credibility and helpfulness.

significant here as well. Women (compared to men) rated lack of confiding as a more serious problem and indicated that they would be more motivated to solve the problem. Women rated rudeness as a more serious problem, one they are less likely to forgive, and a problem that would result in withdrawing from the relationship. Women rated problems in presentability as easier to solve, and they rated motivation to solve the problem higher. Finally, when confronted with possessiveness, women rated motivation to solve the problem higher and indicated a greater likelihood of withdrawing from the relationship.

Table 6.3 presents the means concerning the perceived credibility of an apology and perceived helpfulness of an apology. Students rated a full-blown apology as more credible and as more helpful for problems in presentability and lack of shared time, problems in which intention to commit the failure event is low and controllability is high. Indeed, Figure 6.1 diagrams the significant relationships between variables pertaining to the decision to withdraw from the relationship. As the figure indicates, there is no direct relationship between controllability of the relational problem and the decision to withdraw; rather, controllability is related to credibility of an apology, solvability of a problem, and seriousness of the problem, and these are related to withdrawing. There is no direct relationship between either stability and internality with the perceived credibility of an apology. Both stability and internality are related to perceived seriousness of the problem and to withdrawing.

The credibility of an apology is high when students believed the cause to be controllable and the problem solvable, and it was low when they believed the cause was intentional (in this study, rude public behavior). The credibility of an apology was weakly but significantly related to the decision to not withdraw from the relationship ($r = -.19$), as was the

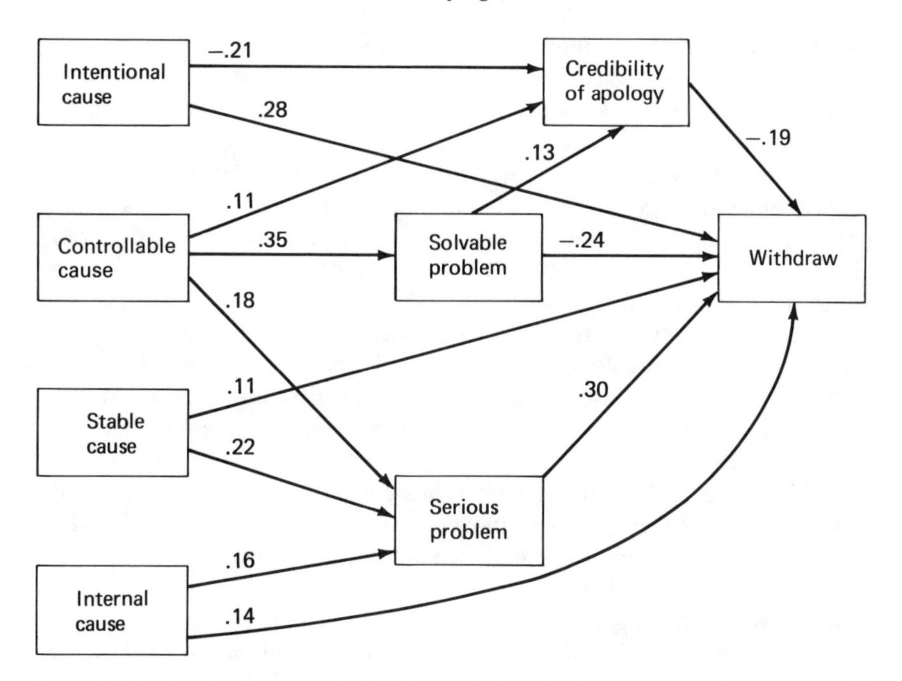

FIGURE 6.1. Attributions and beliefs in the decision to withdraw from a relationship.

belief that the problem is solvable ($r = -.24$). The decision to withdraw from the relationship was related positively to the belief that the problem is serious and to intentional, stable, and internal causes. In sum, attributed causes and beliefs concerning relational problems are related to the perceived credibility of apologies, and an apology is weakly associated with remaining in a relationship (at least one in which the problem is perceived to be solvable).

The Account Episode and Severity of Reproach

Cody and McLaughlin (1985) have reviewed earlier research on the "interactional constraint" that operates as the three-step communication sequence (reproach, account, and evaluation) unfolds. Originally, we expected that specific forms of reproaches and specific forms of accounts would be matched, in that polite requests for accounts would result in polite (mitigating) accounts, whereas rude or hostile forms of reproaches would result in aggravating forms of accounts. Actually, the first half of this expectation was not consistently supported: a polite form of a reproach (e.g., "Will you please tell me why your grade in history went down?") may be followed by any form of an account. However, a rude or harshly phrased reproach restricts the account-giver's freedom to use any desirable form of an account; harshly phrased reproaches elicit defensive reactions from account-givers.

Schönbach (1986, 1990; Schönbach & Kleibaumhuter, 1990) specifically relied on psychological reactance theory to argue that severely phrased reproaches pose a threat to the freedom of the account-giver and that as a consequence the account-giver communicates more defensive accounts (denials/refusals, justifications) and fewer conciliatory accounts (apologies, excuses). Schönbach (1990) more recently made a second claim concerning severely phrased reproaches: Not only are severely phrases reproach forms related to more defensive accounts, but they are also related to negative evaluations. A need to be consistent (see Schönbach, 1990) would lead the user of a severely phrased reproach form to continue to be harsh and to later reject the account, no matter what was communicated. In fact, Braaten et al. (1990) found support for both hypotheses: Severely phrased reproaches elicited more denials and justifications, and managers who employed severely phrased reproaches were significantly more likely to reject accounts than managers who relied on other forms of reproaches.

When would managers (or any reproacher) employ severely phrased reproach forms? The Braaten et al. (1990) data could only provide a few details to answer this question: (a) when there already existed a relatively poor manager-worker relationship and (b) when the failure event was severe or its occurrence was a negative reflection on the manager. However, it is also possible that severely phrased reproaches may be used by managers as an attempt to create and maintain an intimidating style so that workers would fall into line and think twice about making errors and being tardy.

What, precisely, are "severely phrased reproaches"? Schönbach and Kleibaumhuter (1990) employed two forms of severe reproaches (derogation of self-esteem and derogation of sense of control) but admitted that they had no typology of reproach forms. Cody and Braaten (in press) performed an open-ended coding of severely phrased reproaches in the Braaten et al. (1990) data and identified four subcategories: *threat* ("One more time and you can pack your bags!"); *pre-judged guilt* ("You will stay after work to solve this" [i.e., the reproacher has predetermined that the account-giver is the one who is responsible for the error and assesses a penalty prior to hearing an account]); *attack on commitment* ("You! Why are *you* always the last one?"); and *assertive/hostile* ("Why the #%@@ is this still wrong?").

The fact that severely phrased reproaches occur and influence the accounting process has obvious implications concerning the management of conflict (see below). Unfortunately, most of the research on the issue of reproach severity ivolves scenario research with parents and children (see Schönbach, 1990) or conversations among strangers and organizational settings (see Cody & McLaughlin, 1990). It is obvious, however, that relational partners limit their ability to resolve interpersonal problems and disputes by using severely phrased reproaches, although we know of no research that addresses this particular issue.

Consequences and Conflict

Rejected accounts result in ticketing by traffic officers (Cody & McLaughlin, 1985), penalties assessed in traffic grievance court (Cody & McLaughlin, 1988), and any number of conversational disagreements and displays of disappointment (McLaughlin, Cody, & O'Hair, 1983; McLaughlin, Cody, & Rosenstein, 1983). More dramatic instances of escalating conflict are observed during child custody cases (Manusov, Zappa, Cody, & Donohue, in press) and in organizations (Braaten et al., 1990).

Conflict may result from the account episode in several ways: An account-giver may perceive that he or she is being falsely accused of a highly personal matter (sociability or personal habit), an account-giver may be the recipient of a severely phrased reproach form, and the account-giver may believe that his or her communicated account was unjustifiably rejected by the reproacher.

Manusov, Zappa, Cody, and Donohue (in press) assessed account episodes in child custody mediation sessions, a setting in which former intimates expressed unmonitored loathing for one another—in some cases the two former intimates had not talked to each other in more than a year. In settings such as these, there are remarkably few mitigating reproaches or mitigating accounts, and most evaluations of social explanations were rejected. Destructive forms of conflict involve spirals in which former intimates engage in a series of severely phrased reproaches (rebukes), and issues pertaining to the custody matter are not resolved. One of the important findings in this study is that mediators were more likely to exert control over the session, and sessions were more likely to end in agreement, if the mediator intervened between the reproach phase and the account phase—that is, after a severely phrased reproach was given, the mediator who stopped the sequence prior to the account-giver's communication of a denial or justification was more likely to elicit a custody agreement between the two parties than if the mediator did not intervene. Also, waiting to intervene between the account phase and the evaluation phase was unrelated to resolving the sessions; early intervention was preferable.

Braaten et al. (1990) found that workers filed complaints when accused of engaging in performance errors, or questionable judgments, when severely phrased reproaches (rebukes and direct requests) had been used and when accounts had been rejected.

Attributions and Disengagement

Although considerable attention has been focused on the topic of relational disengagement during the 1980s—and a separate chapter could easily be prepared on the topic—we include a section on this issue in this chapter in order to extend the analysis of coping with relational problems. If accounting for a violation of expectations pertaining to the relationship (a failure event) is not accepted by a relational partner, then one or both of the parties may select to (a) stay in the relationship and devise a plan to change the partner, the self, or the relationship; (b) deescalate the relationship by proposing a reduction in intimacy in order to reassess the relationship, in order to see if changes develop, or as a precursor to termination; or (c) move toward terminating (severing) the relationship. Attributions and beliefs concerning the nature of relational problems are related to these choices and to the tactics that are used to pursue the goals of problem solving, deescalating, and terminating.

Although it is admittedly an oversimplification, classic works in relational dissolution argue that costs, inequity, or lack of equal involvement are related to relational decay (Banks, Altendorf, Greene, & Cody, 1987; Baxter, 1982; Cody, 1982; Hill, Rubin, & Peplau, 1976; Smith, Cody, LoVette, & Canary, 1990, Study 3). However although a general measure of the perception of inequity is associated with breaking off relationships, such a general or global perception was not found to be related to specific tactics used to control the level of intimacy in the relationship (see Cody, 1982). Rather, specific relational problems were related to tactical preferences.

Cody (1982) assessed a number of relational complaints from literature published at the time and identified three types of problems: *faults*, *failure to compromise*, and *constraint*. The faults construct included the complaints that the partner had too many personal faults, embarrassed the disengager, possessed a personality that was incompatible with that of the disengager, and was otherwise personally responsible for the disengagement. The failure to compromise construct incorporated the complaints that the partner no longer behaved romantically toward the disengager and was unwilling to make contributions and compromises for the good of the relationship. The constraint construct incorporated the complaints that the partner was suffocating the disengager, that the partner wanted the relationship to be a more serious and intimate one than that desired by the disengager, and that the disengager was getting bored (with what allegedly appeared to be a highly structured situation involving little spontaneity).

The Cody (1982) study specifically asked college students to recall and report on a real relationship that resulted in disengagement. Few of these students then wrote essays on plans they had in mind for solving the problems. Instead, the students wrote essays on how they would disengage or terminate the relationship. Six basic ways of coping with the problems were identified (but see Cody, 1982, for details):

Positive tone: I would say that it is unfair on my part and would be unfair to you to continue our relationship if one of us had to fake it. I care a great deal about you but I don't feel as strongly toward you as you toward me. It would be cheating you if I were to pretend I felt this way and would cause more heartache if I continue to do so. I think it would be wise if we stopped seeing so much of each other.

Deescalation: I would say that we are becoming too dependent upon each other so we have nothing individual to bring to the relationship at this point. If we take time to do things on our own and make discoveries about ourselves and others, then we will be capable of continuing or beginning a new relationship.

Negative identity management: I would tell him or her that life is too short and we should date other people in order to enjoy life.

Justification: I would say that a good relationship meets the needs of both people and ours isn't meeting my needs. I don't want to change you and I would have to if you are going to meet my needs. So I don't think we should see each other any more.

Withdrawal/avoidance: I'd simply refuse to take any phone calls from him or her, and I'd keep our meetings brief. (This approach to coping with disengagement was used primarily by the less intimate, who felt less of an obligation to discuss directly reasons for the disengagement with the partner. We will spend no further time discussing this as a 'tactic' in this chapter.)

Differences among these basic messages are as follows: Both a positive tone message and a deescalation message ask for a change in the definition of the level of intimacy in the relationship; both ask to reduce the relationship to a less intimate one. In the use of a positive tone, however, the disengager expends more effort in dealing with the disengagee's feelings of hurt, disappointment, and rejection (hence, the disengager tones down the rejection with emotionally supportive material). A justification message differs from all others in that it asks for severing the relationship entirely; the disengager justifies terminating the relationship. Justification tactics contain some claim as to why the relationship was deteriorating or changing (external causes [job moves], self-responsible, target responsible, relationship responsible). The negative identity management tactics are different from all other ones in that they reflect a callous attitude toward the dating partner, and they reflect a unilaterial attempt on the part of the disengager to be in control and dictate what will happen to the relationship. Not only do these tactics fail to take into consideration a partner's potentially hurt feelings, but they are also phrased in a way to reduce any attempt on the part of the disengagee to counterargue and help solve a problem.

Cody (1982) found:

1. Positive tone tactics were more likely to be used when the dating relationship was highly intimate, the partner constrained the disengager, the partner did not fail to compromise and the partner was not guilty of faults;
2. Deescalation tactics were more likely to be used when the dating relationship was highly intimate, the partner constrained the disengager, and the partner was not guilty of faults;
3. Justification tactics were more likey to be used when the dating relationship was intimate, the partner was guilty of faults, and the partner constrained the disengager; and
4. Negative identity management tactics were more likely to be used when the dating relationship was intimate, the partner constrained the disengager, the disengager believed he or she was underbenefited, and the disengager felt angry over the allocation of rewards/benefits in the relationship.

Much like the more recent study by Kersten et al. (1990), attributions, beliefs concerning solving the problem, changing the target, and so forth are related to tactical choices. When a partner was only guilty of constraining the disengager, the disengager employed a tactic (either positive tone or deescalation) that was aimed at reducing the level of intimacy of the relationship—but not aimed at terminating the relationship. In cases where one partner was more in love than the other partner, the communication strategy was merely to control the definition of the relationship and hope to stay friends. However, when the partner both constrained the disengager and was guilty of faults, the disengager moved directly toward terminating the relationship via the use of a justification message. There are any number of reasons for such an outcome—potential disengagers may believe that personality faults are less excusable, solvable, less controllable, more stable, and so forth. Finally, in regard to the use of negative identity management tactics, it would seem that certain disengagers have little tolerance for being constrained (there was a correlation of .41 between constraint and the use of these tactics) and would use the manipulative types of tactics when angry over being treated inequitably. A number of scholars (Banks, Altendorf, Greene, & Cody, 1987; Duck, 1983) have called for the study of the *process* of relational decay and dissolution. When process-oriented studies are conducted, we probably will find that negative identity management tactics are used as second-or third-attempt tactics.

Banks et al. (1987) more recently found that deescalation tactics were used when constraint was high, the disengager believed that the two scored highly on a dyadic adjustment scale, the disengager believed that the two were intimate, and "network overlap" was high (i.e., the two shared many friends). Positive tone tactics were used when the partners were intimate, the partner was not guilty of faults, network overlap was high, and the partner constrained the disengager. In both sets of relationships, there are reasons for intending to stay friends (but less intimate ones) within communication networks, and because (a) the two are intimate and adjusted, and (b) the problem of dating someone who likes the disengager more than the disengager currently reciprocates is a gratifying position that does not require an immedite termination of the relationship. Banks et al. also confirmed Cody's (1982) results in terms of the use of justification tactics: Severing the relationship was attempted when both constraint and faults were high (among other things). The Banks et al. study also provides some interesting findings concerning consequences of disengaging. Depression, anger, "felt freedom," and the ability to stay friends after the disengagement were assessed.

In the Kersten et al. (1990) project discussed above, respondents wrote essays on "How (if at all) I'd Solve this Problem." Essays were coded for specific instances of five ways of handling the problem: (1) *Integrative* tactics included problem-solving tactics that proposed some method in which a change in the relationship, partner, or respondent's behavior was proposed. (2) *Implicit solution*, tactics included ways in which the respondent attempted to resolve the problem by either setting an example (e.g., confiding more in order to prompt the partner to confide more) or invoking greater trust (e.g., telling the partner a secret so that he or she will trust you more). (3) *Negative identity* tactics included the use of ultimata (threatening the partner if he or she didn't change); retaliation (e.g., acting possessive in order to give him or her a taste of what it is like); and general manipulation (making scarcastic comments). (4) *Supportive/information-gathering* tactics included holding open discussions with the partner either in order to verify that the partner is aware of his or her actions or to come to an understanding of why the partner engaged in the behaviors. (5) *Disengagement* tactics included (a) terminating the relationship immediately, (b) diminishing the relationship (withdrawing or becoming emotionally detached from the partner), and (c) avoiding the partner (in order to initiate a disengagement or to let the partner know, indirectly, of the disengager's dissatisfaction). Kersten et al. also coded essays in terms of a general level of elaboration of the plans the students had devised for solving the problem.

Not surprisingly, more elaborate plans were constructed for problems that could be considered more easily solvable, where motivation was high, and where greater closeness or intimacy might follow (e.g., persuading the partner to confide more and to share more time with the agent). These problems also elicited more supportive tactics. Integrative tactics were also used frequently when the goals involved easy-to-solve problems that, interestingly, were rated as less serious but solvable (presentability, confide, and share time). Less elaborate plans were constructed for problems considered more internal and more difficult to solve (possessiveness, jealousy, and public rudeness). More-difficult-to-solve problems that stemmed from internal causes and that were rated as serious (public rudeness and possessiveness) elicited more disengagement tactics, as well as more negative identity management tactics. Implicit solution tactics were used more frequently for two behaviors that may be changed slowly over time (confide and jealousy).

Summary and Future Needs

We have chronicled several lines of research that explore the layperson's logic or implicit theory of influence and relational adjustment. As our programs of research have advanced, we have moved from purely descriptive research concerning how communicators attempt to solve specific problems, to incorporating interactional contraints (in the accounts literature) and more complete models of tactical selection based on attributions, beliefs, and expectations. In regard to the literature on interpersonal accounting, our knowledge of how accounts are used to cope with relational problems over the course of long-term relationships is far from complete. Apologies, excuses, and justifications may be employed by account-givers for particular types of relational problems, and repair may be adequately effected. To date, however, there is consistent evidence demonstrating that *how* the reproacher initiates the explantion processes is a critical factor. We also agree with Schönbach (1990) that additional work needs to focus on a fully elaborated typology of failure events that includes attributions of underlying causes, beliefs, expectations, and values (important in the honoring of justifications).

Further, we have become more and more convinced in our research programs that individual differences in both the accounts literature and the relational coping/decay literature are pervasive. Some earlier projects clearly indicated that females (relative to males) are more motivated to solve a number of problems and construct more elaborate plans in order to solve the problems (See Cody, Canary, & Smith, Smith et al., 1990). Also, low self-monitoring individuals display a greater sense of commitment to a relationship (Smith et al., 1990). However, one of the more recent promising approaches to understanding who breaks away from a relationship with comparative ease is the recent project that stems from the literature on learned helplessness and self-efficacy literature (Kersten et al., 1990). Kersten identified two types of communicators, the *performer* and the *learner*. The performer believes that a person does not have to expend much effort or work in a relationship; a person should enter into and perform a role as friend and intimate partner. When relational problems surface, the performer prefers merely to exit the relationship. A learner, on the other hand, believes that a person needs to work on relationships nearly every day and that relational work and learning go hand in hand. Performers, according to Kersten et al., construct less elaborate plans for solving relational problems and construct fewer tactics that might be implemented. Learners, however, rated relational problems as more serious and as more solvable. They also rated causes as more controllable and rated motivation to work on resolving problems as higher. Needless to say, learners constructed more elaborate plans and detailed more specific tactics to be included in their plans. Research such as this—which integrates the individual's motivation and relational orientations with attributions, beliefs, plans, and tactical preferences—will improve our understanding of important aspects of relational life.

References

Banks, S.P., Altendorf, D.M., Greene, J.O., & Cody, M.J. (1987). An examination of relational disengagement: Perceptions, breakup strategies and outcomes. *Western Journal of Speech Communication, 51*, 19–41.

Baxter, L.A. (1982). Strategies for ending relationships: Two studies. *Western Journal of Speech Communication, 46*, 223–241.

Braaten, D.O., Cody, M.J., & Bell, K.D. (1990, June). *The role of social explanations in mediating organizational conflict*. Paper presented to the International Communication Association, Dublin, Ireland.

Cody, M.J. (1982). A typology of disengagement strategies and an examination of the role intimacy, reactions to inequity, and relational problems play in strategy selection. *Communication Monographs, 49*, 148–170.

Cody, M.J., & Braaten, D.O. (in press). A social-interactive model of account-making. In M.L. McLaughlin, M.J. Cody, & S. Read (Eds.), *Explaining the self to others*. Hillsdale, NJ: Erlbaum.

Cody, M.J., Canary, D.J., & Smith, S.W. (in press). Compliance-gaining goals: An inductive analysis of goal types, strategies, and successes. In J. Daly & J. Wiemann (Eds.), *Communicating strategically*, Hillsdale, NJ: Erlbaum.

Cody, M.J., & McLaughlin, M.L. (1985). Models for the sequential construction of accounting episodes: Situational and interactional constraints on message selection and evaluation. In R.L. Street & J.N. Cappella (Eds.), *Sequence and pattern in communicative behavior* (pp. 50–69). London: Edward Arnold.

Cody, M.J., & McLaughlin, M.L. (1988). Accounts on trial: Oral arguments in traffic court. In C. Antaki (Ed.), *Analyzing everyday explanation: A casebook of methods* (pp. 113–126). London: Sage.

Cody, M.J., & McLaughlin, M.L. (1990). Interpersonal accounting. In H. Giles & P. Robinson (Eds.), *Handbook of language and social psychology* (pp. 227–225). London: John Wiley and Sons.

Duck, S. (1983). A topography of relationship disengagement and dissolution. In S. Duck (Ed.), *Personal relationships 4: Dissolving personal relationships* (pp. 1–30). London: Academic Press.

Felson, R.B., & Ribner, S.A. (1981). An attributional approach to accounts and sanctions for criminal violence. *Social Psychology Quarterly, 44*, 137–142.

Goffman, E. (1971). *Relations in public*. New York: Basic Books.

Gonzales, M.H., Pederson, J.H., Manning, D.J., & Wetter, D.W. (1990). Pardon my gaffe: Effects of sex, status, and consequence severity on accounts. *Journal of Personality and Social Psychology, 58*, 610–621.

Hale, C.L. (1987). A comparison of accounts: When is a failure not a failure? *Journal of Language and Social Psychology, 6*, 117–132.

Hill, C.T., Rubin, Z., & Peplau, L. (1976). Breakups before marriage: The end of 103 affairs. *Journal of Social Issues, 32*, 147–168.

Holtgraves, T. (1989). The form and function of remedial moves: Reported use, psychological reality, and perceived effectiveness. *Journal of Language and Social Psychology, 8*, 1–16.

Jones, E.E., & Pittman, T.S. (1982). Toward a general theory of strategic self-presentation. In J. Suls (Ed.), *Psychological perspectives on the self* (Vol. 1, pp. 231–262). Hillsdale, NJ: Erlbaum.

Kersten, L., Braaten, D.O., Dickson, R., & Cody, M.J. (1990). *Learned helplessness and solving relational problems*. Unpublished manuscript, Department of Communication Arts and Sciences, University of Southern California, CA.

Manusov, V., Zappa, J., Cody, M.J., & Donohue, W. (in press). Account episodes in child custody mediations. *Journal of Applied Communication*.

McLaughlin, M.L., Cody, M.J., & O'Hair, H.D. (1983). The management of failure events: Some contextual determinants of accounting behavior. *Human Communication Research, 9*, 208–224.

McLaughlin, M.L., Cody, M.J., & Rosenstein, N.E. (1983). Account sequences in conversations between strangers. *Communication Monographs, 50*, 102–125.

Ohbuchi, K., Kameda, M., & Agarie, N. 1989). Apology as aggression control: Its role in mediating appraisal of and response to harm. *Journal of Personality and Social Psychology, 56*, 219–227.

Schlenker, B.R., (1980). *Impression management: The self-concept, social identity, and interpersonal relations*. Monterey, CA: Brooks/Cole.

Schönbach, P. (1980). A category system for account phases. *European Journal of Social Psychology, 10*, 195–200.

Schönbach, P. (1986). *A theory of conflict escalation in account episodes*. Unpublished manuscript, Fakultät für Psychologie, Bochum, West Germany: Ruhr-Universität.

Schönbach, P. (1990). *Account episodes: The management or escalation of conflict*. Cambridge: Cambridge University Press.

Schönbach, P., & Kleibaumhuter, P. (1990). Severity of reproach and defensiveness of accounts. In M.J. Cody & M.L. McLaughlin (Eds.), *The psychology of tactical communication* (pp. 229–243). Clevedon, England: Multilingual Matters, Ltd.

Scott, M.B., & Lyman, S.M. (1968). Accounts. *American Sociological Review, 33*, 46–62.

Semin, R.G., & Manstead, A.S.R. (1983). *The accountability of conduct: A social psychological analysis*. London: Academic Press.

Smith, S.W., Cody, M.J., LoVette, S., & Canary, D.J. (1990). Self-monitoring, gender, and compliance-gaining goals. In M.J. Cody & M.L. McLaughlin (Eds.), *The psychology of tactical communication* (pp. 91–135). Clevedon. England: Multilingual Matters, Ltd.

Snyder, C.R., Higgins, R.L., & Stucky, R.J. (1983). *Excuses: Masquerades in search of grace*. New York: Wiley/Interscience.

Tedeschi, T.T., & Riess, M. (1981). Verbal strategies in impression mangement. In C. Antaki (Ed.), *The psychology of ordinary explanations of social behavior* (pp. 156–187). New York: Academic Press.

Weiner, B. (in press). Excuses in everyday interaction. In M.L. McLaughlin, M.J. Cody, & S. Read (Eds.), *Explaining the self to others*. Hillsdale, NJ: Erlbaum.

7
Accounting for Relationships: A Knowledge Structure Approach

STEPHEN J. READ and NANCY L. COLLINS

How do people construct accounts of what happens in their relationships? Although researchers have studied a variety of attribution and accounting phenomena, such as their roles in relationship formation (e.g., Fletcher, Fincham, Cramer, & Heron, 1987), marital discord (for a review see Bradbury & Fincham, 1990), and relationship termination (e.g., Fletcher, 1983a, 1983b; Harvey, Agostinelli, & Weber, 1989), little attention has been paid to studying *how* people construct attributions and accounts in their relationships. As a result, we have gained insights into the importance of attributions and accounts in relationship functioning, but we have very little understanding of the processes through which they are constructed or of the nature and structure of the knowledge that is necessary for these processes. One reason for this may be that we have not had a general model to suggest how we could even begin to explore these issues.

In the current chapter we argue that the processes of account formation and explanation can be understood in terms of a general model of understanding (Read, 1987; Read & Miller, 1989; Miller & Read, in press), based on Schank and Abelson's (1977) knowledge structure approach and other recent work in text comprehension and cognitive science (Kintsch, 1988; Thagard, 1989). (For related accounts see Abelson & Lalljee, 1988; and Lalljee & Abelson, 1983.) This model can be used not only to integrate existing literature but also to guide continued work in this area.

In presenting this model we begin by discussing the various forms of social knowledge that people use in constructing accounts. Next, we will outline a model of how this knowledge is used, in conjunction with the available stimulus information, to construct accounts. In describing this model we will argue that people are strongly influenced by the desire to construct a coherent account in which everything "fits together." We believe that the coherence of an account is strongly based on a variety of goal-based and causal links among the elements composing the account. Finally, we will discuss some of the implications of this approach for better understanding and studying the nature of accounts in close relationships.

Researchers have examined a number of different functions of accounts (see Antaki, 1987). The current chapter focuses on the understanding and sensemaking functions of accounts rather than on their various self-presentational or excusemaking functions. Thus, in the following we treat accounting and explanation as essentially equivalent terms.

A Knowledge Structure Approach to Accounts

Understanding why people do things is central in everyday life. But arriving at these explanations is surprisingly involved and requires people to make numerous inferences based on detailed social and physical knowledge (e.g., Heider, 1958; Lalljee & Abelson, 1983; Read, 1987). For example, a colleague recently described the following interaction he observed at a meeting:

> At dinner the man sat close to her and said ingratiating things to her in a low and warm voice. At one point he reached over and held her arm—too long. Several of us began to make conversation to cover the intimacies that we thought were being discussed by the couple.
>
> The next morning everyone else who had been at the table commented that both the man and the woman seemed to be walking around with big smiles.

Although no one observed any behaviors more intimate than these, everyone assumed that the couple had had an affair. To understand such social interactions, we must relate the actions in them to one another and create a coherent scenario that reveals their meaning. However, the information necessary to do this is rarely explicit. Instead, people must make inferences about such things as the characters' goals and how their actions would achieve those goals. Moreover, making these inferences requires detailed knowledge about the social and physical worlds (Schank & Abelson, 1977), including knowledge about human goals, the plans necessary to achieve those goals, personal relationships, stereotypes, and the characteristics of physical objects and their role in human goals and plans. Unfortunately, the dominant models of social explanation, such as Kelley (1973) and Jones and Davis (1965), do not provide a sufficient analysis of either the knowledge used or the processes involved in the explanation of such social interactions.

Recently, several authors (e.g., Abelson & Lalljee, 1988; Lalljee & Abelson, 1983; Read, 1987) have presented a knowledge structure theory of explanation as an alternative. This approach provides a detailed analysis of the knowledge needed to understand social interactions and a model of the processes by which that knowledge is used. It emphasizes the role of specific, concrete knowledge in explanation, in contrast to the emphasis on abstract, logical analysis characteristic of the dominant models of attribution. Further, the knowledge structure approach argues that the processes by which people understand interactions are similar to those used to understand stories: Individuals assimilate observed events to knowledge structures and create a mental representation of the sequence of events and the causal and goal-based links among them. This representation encodes people's explanations and can be used to answer questions about the event.

In developing a model of how we account for social interactions, it is useful to first think about the structure of the social interactions for which we are accounting. A number of researchers (e.g., Barker, 1963; Barker & Wright, 1955; Ford, 1987; Forgas, 1979; Miller, Galanter, & Pribram, 1960; Schank & Abelson, 1977) have argued that behavioral episodes have a characteristic general form consisting of the following components: (a) the goals of the actor(s); (b) the factors that instigated those goals, such as the actions of others, environmental occurrences, or personal characteristics of the actor(s); (c) the plans and strategies that are being enacted to achieve those goals; (d) what happened to the goals, (e.g., Are they satisfied or blocked? Are other goals substituted?); and (e) the situation or context in which the actions occurred. This behavioral episode is the basic unit of social behavior, with social interactions typically composed of multiple episodes. Many researchers in text comprehension have noted that stories have the same general form (e.g., Mandler, 1978; Mandler & Johnson, 1977; Rumelhart, 1977; Stein & Glenn, 1979).

Accounts researchers have often noted that accounts are frequently presented in the form of a story. Many researchers seem to assume that the story form is imposed on the events. However, as we argued above, we and others believe that this form is actually the basic form of human behavioral episodes and that the form of stories largely mirrors the form of what is being described. A story, then, is an idealized, cleaned-up version of the actual structure of human behavioral episodes.

The form of behavioral episodes provides a framework for understanding what people must do when they construct accounts for relational events. They must ascertain the goals of the actors, the factors that instigated those goals (such as environmental or personal characteristics), and what happened to those goals. Furthermore, they must figure out how the actors' behaviors fit into plans and strategies that were followed in the pursuit of those goals.

There are several reasons why the form of social episodes is so important to a theory of accounts. First, this form makes it clear that people's goals and plans, and the factors that influence those goals and plans, are central to the construction and representation of accounts. This argues that the analysis of these forms of knowledge should be central to an analysis of the knowledge used in constructing accounts. Second, this form is important because it provides the basic framework for what people are trying to do and what inferences they must make when they construct an account for social interactions.

In the following we first examine the nature of a number of different forms of social knowledge and then outline a model of how that knowledge is used to construct accounts for social behavior. (For a more detailed account of these forms of social knowledge, see Schank & Abelson, 1977; Miller & Read, in press; and Read & Miller, 1989.) We start with the forms of social knowledge that have been so extensively examined by Schank and Abelson (1977)—scripts, plans, goals, and themes—and then examine other forms of social knowledge that may be especially relevant to close relationships. One reason we start with scripts, plans, and goals is that many of the knowledge structures we discuss subsequently are composed of these units.

Scripts and Plans

A script is a stereotyped plan or sequence of actions carried out to achieve goals in a particular situation. Many scripts are culturally shared, but others may be idiosyncratic, developed over the course of a particular relationship. Examples in social interaction might be dating scripts, the scripts surrounding sexual behavior (Miller & Hoffman, 1990), or more mundane scripts, such as doing the dishes. Plans are more general and less stereotyped sequences of behavior for the attainment of goals. They function as general building blocks that can be used to construct a course of action in a variety of situations.

Scripts and plans have a number of components: (a) the goal or goals of the actions composing them, (b) the typical sequence of actions aimed at achieving those goals, (c) the typical actors in the script or plan, (d) the objects that play a role in the actions, and (e) the location in which the script or plan is enacted. In addition, scripts and plans also have information about the conditions that are likely to instigate their performance and the preconditions that must be satisfied for their successful performance. Clearly, knowledge of these components can play an important role in our ability to figure out what someone is doing and why. Considerable empirical work has been done on several types of planning knowledge that are central to social interaction, such as knowledge about persuasive tactics (Cody, Canary, & Smith, in press; Rule, Bisanz, & Kohn, 1985; Schank & Abelson, 1977) and knowledge about conflict management and problem-solving tactics in relationships (Canary, Cunningham, & Cody, 1988).

Resources

Successful enactment of a plan requires that one possess the resources required for the plan. Examples of resources might be money, time, various abilities, or physical objects. Our knowledge of the nature of various kinds of resources and their roles in the enactment of plans is important to our understanding of why people do or do not enact certain plans, and why they succeed or fail when they attempt plans. For example, one explanation for the failure to enact a plan is the lack of a necessary resource. Another possible explanation is that the resource, such as time or money, was limited and someone wanted to save the resource to carry out another plan.

Goals and Goal Relations

Knowledge about the nature of human goals is central in arriving at accounts for behavior. For example, we know what conditions are likely to lead to an individual having a particular goal, and we know that different goals have different instigating conditions. Thus, if we know that an individual has a particular goal (to be rich), we can make some reasonable inferences about why (he or she grew up poor). Conversely, if we know about the existence of the appropriate instigating conditions (discovering a partner's affair), we can often make inferences about an individual's goals (to gain revenge).

Further, we all have extensive knowledge about what types of plans are likely to be used to achieve different goals. Thus, if we see someone enact a particular plan (going to a pickup bar) we can infer what his or her goals are; conversely, if we know that someone has a particular goal (to find a partner for a caring relationship), this may help us understand what plans he or she is carrying out.

In social interaction we are typically concerned with a number of goals. Thus, understanding the relations among goals is important in understanding social behavior (Read & Miller, 1989; Wilensky, 1983). For example, if one's spouse seems anxious and short-tempered all the time, this may be due to a conflict between trying to succeed at work and trying to spend enough time with the family. Or if one's spouse fails to have dinner ready on time, it may be because he or she had to deal with a more important goal, such as tending a sick child.

Themes

Often, knowledge about people's goals and plans comes from knowing the roles they fill. Role themes or schemata provide information about the stereotypical characteristics of someone in a particular role. For example, we know a considerable amount about the stereotypical goals and plans of lovers, husbands and wives, college professors, and so forth. Moreover, we know about the conditions that will lead someone to take on a role.

In addition, knowledge about a role often includes information about the people who interact with individuals in that role, so part of our knowledge about wives includes knowledge about husbands. And because our behavior is often a function of the role of the people with whom we interact, referring to the role of the other, as in "This is my husband," can be an important explanation for a behavior.

Clearly, roles can conflict, as in the oft-discussed conflict between being a successful businessperson and a parent. Such conflicting roles can be the source of different kinds of behavior and of serious dissatisfaction in relationships. Knowledge of this can play an important part in accounting for behavior.

Considerable information about an individual's goals and plans comes from knowledge of his or her interpersonal relationships, such as being someone's friend, lover, or enemy. We know the kinds of behaviors friends and enemies typically engage in with each other, and we know about the stereotypical goals of friends (e.g., to help their friends) and enemies (e.g., to destroy their enemies).

Traits

Traits have been viewed as central to the understanding of others. Recently Miller and Read (1987; Read & Miller, 1989) have argued that traits and other stable individual differences,

> can be conceptualized in terms of chronic configurations of four components: (a) an individual's chronic goals, (b) the plans and strategies for achieving those goals, (c) various resources that are required to successfully carry out the plans and strategies, and (d) beliefs about the world that affect such things as the likelihood of activation of goals and the execution of plans. (Miller and Read, in press)

(For related arguments see Allport, 1937; Alston, 1970, 1975; Carbonnell, 1979; Cattell, 1965; John, 1986; Mischel, 1973; and Pervin, 1983). One major implication of this position is that much of what is true about the characteristics of goals, plans, resources, and beliefs, and the inferences that can be made from them and to them, also applies to the inferences people make concerning traits (see Miller & Read, in press, for more details). Recently, Read, Jones, and Miller (1990) demonstrated that the extent to which behaviors are perceived to achieve the goals associated with a trait strongly predicts trait inferences from those behaviors.

Explanation Patterns or Prototypes

For some kinds of unexpected events, people develop stereotyped explanations that can be retrieved and used to explain the current event (Abelson & Lalljee, 1988; Schank, 1986). For example, if a man murders his wife and children and then commits suicide, we can retrieve possible explanations, such as the breakup of the marriage or depression from chronic unemployment. Although many of these explanations may be shared across people, during the course of a relationship we undoubtedly develop patterns that are specific to that relationship. So if we have a partner who occasionally flies into a rage, we may develop a pattern that helps us explain why he or she does so.

Knowledge About Situations

We have argued that goals and plans are central to our knowledge about people. Argyle, Furnham, and Graham (1981) argue that goals and plans are also central to our knowledge about situations. First, Argyle et al. argue that a central component of people's knowledge of situations is the goals that can be achieved in them. Second, situations have roles associated with them, making the plans associated with those roles salient. Third, situations have resources associated with them that are instrumental to carrying out various plans. Fourth, rules govern appropriate behavior in various situations.

Thus, knowledge of the situation a person is in tells as a great deal about his or her potential goals and plans and the resources that are available to him or her for plan enactment. Moreover, because person and situation are conceptualized in terms of similar structures, when we develop accounts for behavior it becomes relatively easy to think about the interplay between the goals, plans, resources, and beliefs of individuals and the goals, plans, resources, and rules that characterize situations.

Culturally Shared Beliefs

In addition to the forms of knowledge outlined above, we have a variety of beliefs about social reality. For example, we have extensive systems of beliefs about the nature of love: what love is, what we should give to others and what we should receive from them, how we fall in love, and how love ends. We also have beliefs about the variety of relationships that people can have with one another. Also in this category might be various stereotypes related to gender or race and our knowledge of various moral and legal standards.

Individual Differences in Beliefs or Mental Models

In addition to culturally shared knowledge, individuals possess "mental models" of people and relationships in general, based on their own experiences in relationships (Bowlby, 1980, 1982; Bretherton, 1985). Such models are likely to contain a wide range of beliefs and expectations about social behavior; some will be specific to love relationships (such as expectations about the nature and course of romantic love), and some will be more general models of the social world (such as whether people are trustworthy and honest).

Models of the Partner and the Relationship

Over the course of our relationships with others, we develop detailed models of what they are like and of what our relationship with them is like. Included in these models are representations of their goals, their typical actions in pursuing those goals (both with us and with others), and how they respond under a variety of circumstances. Other types of information, such as traits and beliefs, are also represented. Our models of others may include both generalizations abstracted from multiple experiences, as well as specific, individual episodes. Thus, sometimes we may use a general model to interpret another's behavior, such as knowledge of his or her traits and typical goals, and other times we may use an analogy to a specific situation, for instance, "I know why John's so depressed. He's acting just like he did the last time his boss chewed him out for making a mistake."

Models of the Self

Our models of ourselves will also have a major impact on how we view other people. As Markus and Smith (1981) and Higgins and King (1981) have shown, central aspects of our self-concept may be chronically accessible constructs that are used to interpret the behavior of others. Thus, if we think of ourselves as dominant and powerful, we may be particularly likely to think about relationships in terms of who is in control. Or if we view ourselves as warm and friendly, we may be particularly likely to judge others along this dimension.

Model of How Accounts are Constructed

But how do we use all of this information and integrate it into a coherent picture? Interpreting a social interaction requires that we construct a coherent scenario that characterizes the goals and plans of the interactants, the conditions that instigated those goals, and the outcome of the plans. To construct this scenario we must determine whether and how the actions could be part of a plan or causal sequence. We must also identify the goal(s) toward which the actions are directed. Once we have identified the goals we must determine whether achieving a goal is merely a means to the achievement of a larger plan or whether it is an end in itself. If achieving that goal is a means to achieving a larger plan, we try to identify that larger plan. On the other hand, if the goal is an end in itself we try to determine its source, such as an interpersonal role, a personal relationship, or some occurrence that instigated the goal. If we are accounting for an interaction in which we played a role, we may view the goal in the particular interaction as an example or instantiation of a general theme that we see running through our life.

Doing all this requires people to make a large number of inferences and to integrate a tremendous amount of information into a coherent package. Moreover, this process typically extends over time. When we create a coherent scenario for a social interaction, we do not build it all at once, but instead we are continually building a representation as the interaction proceeds. At any given point we are trying to build a coherent representation of the interaction *up to that point*. As the interaction proceeds, we make additional inferences and build a more detailed model. In addition, we receive more information in the form of the behaviors of the individuals (what they do and what they say) that helps us identify the goals, plans, and other characteristics of the interactants. We are continually trying to integrate this new information with the current representation.

Precisely how is this done? We suggest the following model based on work in text comprehension (e.g., Kintsch, 1988; Schank & Abelson, 1977) and connectionist modeling (Rumelhart, McClelland, & the PDP research group, 1986; Thagard, 1989). (See Miller & Read, in press, for further discussion of the model). The model includes the repeated application of two steps. First, sets of concepts related to the input information are activated and organized into a loose, somewhat heterogeneous network. Second, this heterogeneous network is organized into a coherent representation of the input by the application of parallel constraint satisfaction processes that act to evaluate the explanatory coherence of the network.

As additional information is received, these steps are repeated. Highly activated aspects of the current representation remain active as the next cycle starts, and these concepts, in addition to the new input, are important inputs to the next cycle. Among the concepts likely to remain active are the last action or event in the current causal chain (Fletcher & Bloom, 1988) and general themes that characterize the social interaction. Although this process can be understood on its own conceptual merits, aspects of it have been explicitly modeled in various computer simulations (Kintsch, 1988; Thagard, 1989).

Step 1: Activation of Related Concepts

When an individual constructs an account, the available information leads to the activation of related concepts through a spreading activation process (e.g., Anderson, 1983) in which activation spreads from an activated concept to those that are linked to it. The greater the activation of a structure, the more likely it is to be used to interpret information. Structures that are used in comprehension receive additional activation, but those that are not used decay.

Let us consider how different types of information are activated. Visual information about individuals, including such things as their physical appearance (e.g., wavy hair, grey business suit, white, male, tall, middle-aged) may activate stereotypes and concepts concerning race, age, gender, social class, roles, and so forth. And, as we argued earlier, these concepts will have associated with them information about the typical goals and plans of these individuals. Visual cues may also convey information about the mental state of the individual: Is he or she tired, angry, happy, depressed, etc.?

Further, information that someone is functioning in a particular role (e.g., husband or wife, teacher etc.) also activates related information. We may also have knowledge about these individuals based on past history with them and information that others have told us.

The behaviors we observe someone perform also activate a wide range of information. First, a behavior may activate a particular goal that this behavior is known to achieve. An insult will bring to mind the goal of hurting someone. Second, a particular behavior may tell us that someone is functioning in a particular role and bring to mind the information associated with that role. Reading someone his or her Miranda rights is an action that identifies an individual as a police officer. Third, a behavior might activate a script or plan of which it is a part (Galambos, 1986). For example, if a member of the opposite sex asks us to see a movie, we may suspect this is the opening move in the dating script.

Behaviors may also activate related trait concepts. For example, if Bill is always asking Alan for help doing things but never offers any help in return, always talks about his own feelings, but acts bored and disinterested when Jean tries to talk about hers, traits such as "selfish" and "self-centered" may be activated. Further, inferences about the goals achieved by a behavior may also lead to trait inferences (Read, Jones, & Miller, 1990).

Information is also activated by causal connections. For example, if we see Jocelyn trip James, we expect him to fall. In addition, if we think the tripping was deliberate we also expect James to say or do something to Jocelyn.

Various aspects of the physical environment can tell us about the situation we are in, with all its associated knowledge. For example, there are obvious physical cues that identify a place as a bar, a restaurant, a church, or a school.

Information that violates any of the various expectations that are active should also activate information. For example, unexpected events should often bring to mind the explanation patterns or explanation prototypes discussed by Schank (1986) and Abelson and Lalljee (1988).

Our currently active goals may lead directly to the activation of concepts, as in activating associated plans that we hope to achieve. Our goals may also activate information indirectly by affecting our attention to various aspects of the situation and our interaction partner. That is, our goals may make us particularly attentive to characteristics of another that would help us carry out our plans or that would inhibit or block our goals and plans.

Concepts may also differ in their chronic level of activation. Some concepts, because, say, they are used more frequently or are more important, have higher chronic levels of activation than others. Several researchers (e.g., Bargh & Pratto, 1986; Higgins & King, 1981) have demonstrated that there are individual differences in the chronic accessibility of constructs and that these individual differences in accessibility are responsible for individual differences in the interpretation of stimuli. One possible example of individual differences in chronic accessibility may be the beliefs associated with different attachment styles (Collins & Read, 1990; Hazan & Shaver, 1987).

As the interaction proceeds and we start to develop a more extensive representation of it, this representation may also activate other structures. For example, after observing a sequence of behaviors in a bar we may decide that it is best characterized as a pickup script. Moreover, instantiation of the pickup script may activate concepts related to the possible characteristics of the people in such scripts, such as shallow and self-centered. This suggests that as the interaction proceeds, *configurations* of actions and characteristics, rather than single ones, become increasingly important in activating concepts.

Clearly, a large number of different concepts may be activated at any one time during the comprehension of an interaction. Kintsch (1988) suggests that, initially, concepts are activated somewhat promiscuously, with no real check on whether they are consistent with the context or with other activated concepts. The initial input and the activated concepts are linked together into a loose network of concepts that is not yet a coherent representation of the interaction. We assume a strong preference for linking concepts that have causal and goal-based relations to each other (Galambos, Abelson, & Black, 1986) and that items that activate one another will be linked. Concepts that contradict one another will be negatively linked so that the activation of one concept will decrease the activation of the negatively linked concept.

Initially, this network includes a mixture of information that is relevant, irrelevant, or even inconsistent with the eventual representation of the event. Further, this network may include multiple interpretations of the input. For example, contradictory goals for the same behavior may be activated, or the same behavior may be considered as part of several different plans.

Step 2: Arriving at a Coherent Representation

How do we move from this initial loose network to a coherent account? We propose a process in which activation is propagated through the links and concepts in parallel to arrive at the resulting level of activation for the concepts (e.g., Kintsch, 1988; Rumelhart, McClelland, & the PDP research group, 1986; Thagard, 1989). This process determines which of the activated concepts best characterizes the interaction and allows one to arrive at a coherent, consistent representation. The activation of a concept can be thought of as an indication of how strongly supported it is by other concepts as part of the representation. The greater the number of excitatory links to a concept and the greater the strength of the links, the higher the activation of that concept. Conversely, the greater the number of inhibitory links and the greater their strength, the lower the activation of that concept. By this process, concepts that are not supported by other concepts in the network die out and concepts that are supported are strengthened. Concepts that are highly activated are taken as the representation of the interaction. Thus, if an individual originally entertained several alternative goals for an action, the goal that is best supported by other concepts and data will be accepted, or if a behavior was considered as part of several possible plans, the plan that is most coherent with the activated concepts, such as other actions and goals, will be accepted.

This is an example of a parallel constraint satisfaction process that is a fundamental part of recent work on connectionist modeling or parallel distributed processing (Kintsch, 1988; Rumelhart, McClelland, & the PDP research group, 1986; Thagard, 1989). Such a process evaluates the extent to which concepts in the network are consistent with and supported by other concepts in the network. Activated concepts that are consistent with numerous other concepts in the network are viewed as better supported and therefore a better representation.

This characterization of parallel constraint satisfaction processes is quite general. These processes can be (and have been) implemented in a variety of ways, with different implementations having different implications. One particularly useful implementation for a model of accounting and explanation is Thagard's (1989) recent model of explanatory coherence, which seeks to simulate what makes a set of data and the hypotheses that explain the data explanatorily coherent. Thagard's model is particularly applicable, because identifying the goals and plans of individuals is central in building accounts of social behavior. This argues that the most important links among concepts should be goal-based and causal relations and that the evaluation of the causal and explanatory structure of the network of concepts should be central in its evaluation as a reasonable account of behavior.

Thagard proposes several principles for the evaluation of the coherence of the network of data and hypothesized explanations. Although these principles are implemented in a computer simulation, the model is quite useful apart from their connectionist implementation. However, it is important to note that the connectionist implementation allows for the application of all the principles simultaneously, rather than serially, one at a time.

The principles are the following: First, the explanation that requires the fewest assumptions will be the most coherent. This is the well-known principle of *parsimony* or *simplicity*. Second, an explanation that explains more facts, that has greater *breadth*, will be more coherent. Thus, an explanation that explains more facts than an alternative explanation is more coherent. Further, any given explanation becomes more coherent as more facts are introduced that support it. Third, explanations are more coherent if they are *explained by higher order explanations*. Here we can see the importance of high-level knowledge structures such as traits or themes in coherence. Read and Marcus-Newhall (1990) have recently provided experimental evidence for the importance of these principles in people's evaluation of explanations. Fourth, explanations are more coherent if they are *supported by an analogy to another system with the same causal structure* (Read & Cesa, 1991).

The current model assumes that when a person accounts for an interaction there are typically multiple knowledge structures active at the same time and that often interpreting a sequence requires people to integrate these multiple sources of knowledge. Further, there are often multiple interpretations of the same behaviors active at the same time. Thagard's model provides an elegant approach to understanding how people might choose among alternative interpretations of an individual's actions. Which knowledge structures are chosen and which scenario is constructed depends on which is more explanatorily coherent. What makes Thagard's model particularly useful is that it is explicitly based on a set of assumptions about how higher order, causal, and goal-based theories are used to explain "data" and other inferences.

In constructing an account for a sequence of actions in a social interaction, people often seem to arrive at explanations that are not good explanations for any individual action taken in isolation but are viewed as quite good explanations for the entire sequence of actions. The judged applicability of these explanations seem to be driven by their coherence as an explanation for the entire sequence. For instance, consider the following example:

Ellen rushes up to Joanne and breathlessly tells her that she (Ellen) had just seen Bill in the jewelry store and that she had overheard him say that he was buying an engagement ring because he was going to ask Joanne to marry him. Joanne rushes off to plan the wedding.

Several hours later, Ellen tells Bill that she will agree to his earlier marriage proposal if they elope immediately.

From the first sequence alone, we might infer that Ellen (although a bit of a busybody) is trying to be helpful. From the second sequence alone, we might infer that Ellen is trying to get Bill to marry her. However, when we are given both sequences together it is obvious that Ellen is trying to hurt Joanne.

Note several interesting things about this example. First, the last interpretation would be improbable if we were not trying to find a coherent explanation that explains all the facts. Second, the individual behaviors by themselves do not seem prototypical of possible negative traits (e.g., hostile, manipulative, aggressive), yet the whole sequence taken together strongly suggests such traits. This clearly demonstrates that the meaning assigned to a behavior depends on the meaning of the behavior in the context of other behaviors.

An Example

Let us consider an example of the model in action. One night your wife is two hours late coming home from her job as an investment banker. By the time you hear her key in the front door, a variety of different concepts are active. Using your knowledge of various aspects of her job—such as that she drives to work, that she has a boss who is a slavedriver—and using various stereotypes about office affairs, you consider a number of possibilities: She has been in an accident, she had to work late and forgot to call, she is having an affair with a colleague, etc. The judged goodness of these explanations should depend on how coherent they are as explanations of the facts so far, although at this point the facts are sparse and the coherence of any explanation is probably somewhat weak. However, Thagard's model suggests that the coherence of these alternative explanations could be strongly bolstered by several factors. For example, a potential explanation will be viewed as more coherent if it can be explained by other theories or explanations. For instance, an explanation might be more coherent if it can be explained by some aspect of your past relationship history: (a) You think she is a somewhat reckless driver, (b) she has often forgotten to call before when she had to work late, or (c) she had previously had an affair five years ago. An explanation might also be bolstered (or weakened) by your general beliefs about people, such as how trustworthy they are. Further, any of these potential explanations would be viewed as more coherent if it is bolstered by a salient analogy: (a) The day before there was a major accident on the freeway, or (b) you have just spent several hours listening to your best friend talk about his wife's affair. Thus, at this point you have already developed a tentative (or perhaps not so tentative) representation of what is going on.

As she walks in the front door, new input becomes available and a new cycle of processing starts in which you attempt to integrate the new information with the current representation. For instance, a variety of visual cues may become available. Suppose she looks flustered and seems somewhat unsteady, and her clothes look vaguely disarrayed. Looking flustered and unsteady may activate concepts such as guilty or upset, and the disarray of the clothing may activate concepts involving physical activity that can disturb clothing. If the concept of an affair is not already active, these inputs may activate it. Other concepts may be activated as well. You then try to settle on a coherent representation, which at this point may be that she was having an affair.

But you then get additional input as she says, "I'm sorry I'm late. I was in a traffic accident, and the front of the car got pretty well banged up. I'm still pretty shook up about it." Here your wife explicitly raises the concept of traffic accident. The two of you then walk out to the car and look at the mangled front bumper. This evidence obviously bolsters the traffic accident scenario and leads to that explanation being the most coherent.

On the other hand, suppose when she says "I'm sorry I'm late," her words are slightly slurred, and as you walk over to her you smell alcohol and what may be someone's aftershave. These observations suggest that your wife has been drinking and that she has been in close physical contact with another man. At this point you would be certain that she was having an affair, because having an affair would explain the available facts. But then she goes on and says, "Beth got some really outrageous gifts at her bridal shower after work today," and you suddenly remember that she had told you about the shower as you were reading the paper that morning, but you weren't really paying much attention. Here your wife has introduced several new facts that do not really fit with the affair interpretation, and you attempt to come up with an interpretation that handles all the facts. In this case, you can explain the lateness, the slurred speech, and the alcohol by a scenario that involves your wife going to a bridal shower after work where alcohol was served.

Dealing with Unexpected Events

In creating our accounts, we are sensitive to whether new information we receive fits or is discrepant with our current representation of the interaction. One of the most interesting effects of discrepant information is that it may force us to recast our interpretation of the scenario. For instance, in the above example the man had pretty much decided that his wife was having an affair, when she mentioned the traffic accident and showed him the dented front bumper. This information is discrepant with the affair interpretation and leads to a reinterpretation of the scenario as his wife being late because of a traffic accident.

To successfully deal with such discrepant information, it is often necessary to explain it. Although there are a number of possible explanations for such unexpected events there are three particularly important classes of explanations (Lalljee & Abelson, 1983): (a) An individual has different goals than we thought, (b) he or she is having problems enacting the expected plans, or (c) he or she is enacting different plans than we expected. Thus, Lalljee and Abelson (1983) suggest that when something unexpected happens, people will consider the following possibilities (among others):

1. We were mistaken about the others' goals and must identify their actual goals. For instance, you may expect a co-worker to ask you for a date after he goes out of his way to strike up a conversation and flatter you. But then he leaves without asking for a date or your phone number. One possibility is that he didn't want to go out with you but just wanted help with his report. Another possibility is that the individual also possesses additional goals that overrode the first set or that he was trying to achieve other goals in addition to the expected ones. For instance, he became embarrassed about asking for a date.
2. We were correct about others' goals, but we misidentified or misunderstood their plans. Your co-worker does want to ask you out eventually, but this single interaction is part of a longer term plan to get to know you and feel comfortable before asking for a date. As soon as we see what others are doing, it actually fits quite nicely with their goals.
3. The others may possess the expected goal but may not share our beliefs about ways to achieve that goal. For example, your co-worker may want to ask you out, but may think it more appropriate to call you on the phone outside of working hours.
4. The others possess the goals that we attributed to them but cannot carry out the necessary plans. They may lack a necessary resource, may not know how to carry out the plan, or may find that plan enactment is blocked by other people or by environmental factors. So perhaps your co-worker has weak social skills and isn't quite sure how to ask you out (lack of a necessary resource), or he saw the boss watching from his office (blockage by other people). Leddo and Abelson (1986) have extensively analyzed people's typical explanations for the failure to enact expected plans.

Implications of the Model

The current model has a number of implications for understanding various aspects of how people construct accounts and attributions for their relationship experiences.

Explanatory Coherence and Themes in Accounts

A number of researchers have observed that people often construct general accounts of their lives, what one might call "meta-accounts," that are organized in terms of general themes that tie together a number of different events. Further, it has been argued that people tend to see accounts of specific occurrences that are consistent with these themes as being better accounts of those specific events.

These tendencies are quite reasonable, given the various principles of explanatory coherence. First, accounts of specific events that are consistent with a general theme would be predicted to be viewed as better because according to these principles, explanations that are explained by yet other explanations should gain greater activation and thus be viewed as better explanations.

Further, people's tendency to gather a variety of events under a general theme or meta-account makes sense given the principle of breadth. First, the greater the number of events explained by the theme, the stronger the theme is. Second, given that the theme gives activation to the events it explains, the stronger the theme, the stronger the specific accounts that are explained by it.

The principle that analogy supports an explanation may also push people toward using general themes to explain a number of different events. Consider that if we give a tentative explanation to an event and are then reminded of a previous event with the same causal structure, the analogy should bolster the explanation for the current event. If we arrived at the tentative explanation because of an already existing theme, then the analogy, by bolstering the tentative explanation, also bolsters the theme from which it is derived.

Analogy may play another role in the development of themes, aside from their role in explanatory coherence. Various theorists, such as Gick & Holyoak (1983); Holland, Holyoak, Nisbett, & Thagard (1986); and Holyoak (1985) have argued that analogies may play an important role in the abstraction of general schemata from concrete exemplars. When one instance reminds us of another, we may compare the two and try to abstract out their similarities, particularly at the level of similar causal structure. Thus, if an event reminds people of other events with a similar causal structure or theme, they may be led to abstract out a theme that they think explains a number of events in their lives.

Accounting as Part of a General Model of Cognitive Processes

The knowledge structure approach suggests that processes of attribution, account formation, and explanation can be integrated under a more general framework that describes how people gain an understanding of events they experience in their relationships. This may be an understanding of an isolated partner behavior ("Why did he ignore my attempts to cuddle?"), or it may be a complex and detailed accounting for the failure of an important intimate relationship ("Why did my marriage end?"). Although these explanation situations differ in important ways, we argue that they are linked by the same cognitive processes.

Further, Wilensky (1983), working from a knowledge structure approach, has argued that the understanding of social behavior is intimately involved with the planning and coordination of social interaction (see also Read & Miller, 1989). This involvement occurs in two ways. First, social understanding is central to the coordination of social interaction, because understanding our interaction partner's goals and plans is vital to figuring out our own goals and plans. Second, social understanding involves many of the same processes involved in the planning and coordination of social interaction. According to Wilensky, both understanding and planning require a detailed knowledge of human goals and plans, as well as knowledge of how to put these components together. After all, recognizing someone's plans requires that we put the sequence of behaviors into a coherent plan. Wilensky has provided a detailed account of how understanding and planning can be integrated in a common system.

Thus, the knowledge structure approach is broader in scope than current models and can handle a range of problems and issues (Galambos, Abelson, & Black, 1986; Read, 1987). As such, this model provides a coherent framework for integrating existing work and can serve as a guide for continuing research in this area.

Role of Concrete Social Knowledge in Accounts

As we have argued throughout this paper, people's accounts for relationship events should be strongly dependent on their social knowledge and beliefs. As a result, individuals with different knowledge and beliefs should often explain the same events differently. Although a number of theorists have suggested that individual cognitive models may play an important role in differentiating the attributional patterns of satisfied and dissatisfied couples (e.g., Baucom, Epstein, Sayers, & Sher, 1989; Bradbury & Fincham, 1989; Fincham, 1985a), this topic has received almost no empirical attention. (See Bradbury & Fincham, 1988; Fincham & Bradbury, 1987 for exceptions.) One reason may be the difficulty of making a principled choice among the vast array of individual social knowledge. A first step in making such a choice is to identify theoretical frameworks that specify important aspects of individual models that should be predictive of attribution patterns in relationships. Ideally, these frameworks would also offer a broader model of relationship functioning, of which attribution and social perception is a part.

One such framework that we are currently exploring (Collins, 1990) is provided by recent applications of attachment theory (Bowlby, 1973, 1980, 1982) to adult relationships (Collins & Read, 1990; Feeney & Noller, 1990; Hazan & Shaver, 1987; Levy & Davis, 1988; Shaver, Hazan, & Bradshaw, 1988). A central theme throughout this work is that different adult attachment styles are associated with differences in mental models of self and others. In the following section we describe how one of us (Collins, 1990) is using attachment theory in the study of accounts for relationship problems.

ATTACHMENT STYLES AND MENTAL MODELS

Attachment theory is concerned with the nature and quality of early parent-child relationships and their importance for social functioning throughout the lifespan. According to Bowlby (1980), the attachment system in infants is a goal-corrected behavioral system that has a "set goal" of maintaining "felt security" (Bischof, 1975; Bretherton, 1985; Sroufe & Waters, 1977) and functions to promote the child's security and survival by encouraging proximity to a caretaker.

Bowlby argued that the quality of the attachment relationship is largely determined by the caregiver's emotional availability and responsiveness to the child's needs and that this relationship has a profound impact on the child's developing personality and view of the social world. Through continued interaction with the caretaker, the child develops internal "working models," which contain beliefs and expectations about whether the caretaker is someone who is caring and responsive and whether the self is worthy of care and attention. Ainsworth, Blehar, Waters, & Wall (1978) have identified three different patterns or "styles" of attachment in childhood: secure, anxious/avoidant, and anxious/ambivalent. These attachment styles, and their associated working models, are assumed to have a pervasive influence on perception and behavior in relationships across the lifespan (Bowlby, 1980).

Consistent with these ideas, a growing body of research indicates that the three styles of attachment found in children can also be found in adult close relationships (Collins & Read, 1990; Feeney & Noller, 1990; Hazan & Shaver, 1987; Simpson, 1990). These studies suggest that a person with a *secure* attachment style is comfortable with closeness, able to depend on others, and is not worried about being abandoned or unloved. In contrast, a person with an *avoidant* attachment style is uncomfortable with closeness, feels others are not available when needed, and is not worried about being abandoned or unloved. Finally, an *anxious* attachment style characterizes someone who is comfortable with closeness, somewhat unsure about the availability of others, and very worried about being abandoned or unloved. Thus, underlying the attachment styles are beliefs and expectations that are fundamental to feelings of security in adulthood and central to the maintenance and quality of relationships. Clearly, these beliefs and expectations should have important implications for relationship perceptions and experiences.

Collins and Read (1990) have provided further evidence about the beliefs and models of individuals with different attachment styles. For example, people with a secure attachment style had more positive views of themselves, including a higher sense of self-worth and social self-confidence, and greater sensitivity to and awareness of others. They also had more positive beliefs about others, viewing people as trustworthy, dependable, altruistic, willing to stand up for their beliefs, and able to control the outcomes in their lives. In contrast, people with an anxious attachment style had a more negative view of themselves, including lower self-worth and self-assertiveness. They also had much more negative beliefs about the social world, viewing others as less altruistic, as complex and difficult to understand, and unable to control the outcomes in their lives.

These findings (and related work by Hazan & Shaver, 1987; Feeney & Noller, 1990) provide evidence that attachment styles represent fundamental differences in beliefs about oneself and about others. And we would expect these differences to have important implications for attributions in relationships. Let us examine how these models may influence the explanations of secure people as compared to anxious people.

For secure people, relationship events will be understood and interpreted through largely positive models of self and others. As a result, positive partner behaviors will be easily assimilated and should be explained in ways that confirm positive expectations. Negative events, however, may be discounted or else understood through other knowledge structures that are less relevant to attachment concerns. As a result, secure people should be less likely to interpret negative events as having implications for broader issues of relationship security. In contrast, anxious people will rely on unfavorable models of self and others to help construct explanations for relationship events. As a result, negative partner behaviors will be easily assimilated into existing models and should be explained in ways that confirm negative expectations. Positive partner behaviors may be discounted or else assimilated by attributing them to a partner's underlying negative motives. In addition, because anxious people are chronically worried about being unloved, their partner's behavior may be continually monitored for signs that indicate lack of caring and responsiveness. This "hypothesis testing" (Holmes & Boon, 1990) strategy suggests that attachment-relevant models will be easily activated and, as a result, even minor relationship events may be interpreted as having negative implications for broader issues of relationship security.

Collins (1990) has recently investigated whether subjects' attachment styles are, in fact, related to the nature of their explanations for potentially negative relationship events. Participants who had filled out a measure of adult attachment styles were asked to imagine that they were currently involved in a dating relationship. They were then presented with several potentially negative behaviors and asked to imagine that their boyfriend or girlfriend behaved that way toward them. Among the behaviors included were that your partner: didn't respond when you tried to cuddle, left you standing alone at a party, didn't comfort you when you were feeling down, and wanted to spend the evening by himself or herself. These behaviors were chosen because they were predicted to invoke attachment-related concerns. For each behavior, subjects wrote an explanation for why they thought their partner would behave that way. These explanations were then content coded by independent judges on a variety of dimensions that were both theoretically derived from attachment theory and empirically derived from the work by Collins and Read (1990) on the mental models of individuals with different attachment styles. One dimension had to do with ways in which the explanation reflected subjects' model of self. Included were ratings of the extent to which the explanation reflected a high or low opinion of one's self-worth and ratings of the extent to which the explanation reflected self-reliance. A second set of dimensions had to do with perceptions of love and security in the relationship. A third set involved perceptions of partner warmth and closeness. A fourth set measured whether the explanation reflected perceptions of the partner as responsive to the subject and dependable. A final item rated the extent to which the explanation reflected subjects' trust in the partner.

As predicted, subjects' attachment styles consistently predicted the presence of these themes in their explanations. The explanations of secure subjects, compared to those of avoidant subjects, reflected stronger perceptions of love and security in the relationship, greater partner warmth and closeness, and stronger perceptions of the partner as responsive to the subject and dependable. On the other hand, the explanations of anxious subjects exhibited lower self-worth and self-reliance, less love and security in their relationship, less partner warmth and closeness, less trust in their partner, and lower beliefs that their partner was responsive and dependable. Additional evidence that anxious subjects tended to interpret the behaviors negatively and secure subjects positively was provided by subjects' ratings of their emotional response to these partner behaviors. Anxious subjects were significantly more likely than secure subjects to indicate that they would feel anxiety and distress.

Interestingly, given the current model's emphasis on goals and motives in explanations, attachment styles were also related to the perceived intentionality of the partner's behavior. As another part of the study, subjects were asked to rate their explanations for the extent to which their partner's behavior was intended to have an impact on them (the subject), was voluntary, and was intended to be negative. Secure subjects, compared to avoidant subjects, were less likely to see these potentially negative behaviors as intended to impact them, as voluntary, and as intended to be negative. This study illustrates one way in which a knowledge structure theory can serve as a useful framework for guiding research on attributions in close relationships. Moreover, it highlights the value of examining concrete explanations by showing how they can be used to detect patterns that would otherwise be difficult or impossible to uncover (Collins, 1990).

Interaction Between Social Knowledge and Situational Factors in Constructing Accounts

In addition to emphasizing the role of social knowledge, this model also stresses the importance of considering jointly both the social knowledge that the person brings into the situation and the information available in the environment. This may be especially relevant to research exploring the role of attributions in relationship functioning. Much of the work in this area has found that distressed and non-distressed couples do show different patterns of attributions. And it is often assumed that the distressed couples are providing attributions that are biased and dysfunctional. However, because it is difficult to determine the validity of an attribution, it is unclear whether distressed partners offer dysfunctional attributions or whether their partners really do have negative motives, and so on (Baucom et al., 1989). Although enduring models and expectations will affect and sometimes bias the interpretation of current relationship events, we must also acknowledge that these models will be based in part on actual experiences. And, as our model suggests, both sources of information will be necessary for people to construct coherent explanations for relationship events.

Thus, both existing knowledge and environmental information will be relevant and must be considered if we are to understand the role of attributions in relationship functioning. This person × environment approach is one that a number of relationship theorists have urged us to consider (Baucom et al., 1989; Fincham, 1985a).

Concrete Explanations Versus Abstract Dimensions

Another implication of our model is the need for a strong emphasis on studying concrete explanations rather than the abstract dimensions so favored by attribution researchers. By focusing on the structure and content of the explanations that people offer, we should develop a more accurate model of how people actually construct accounts and of what those accounts look like. The research we discussed earlier on attachment styles and explanations provides an example of how one can use a particular theoretical approach to the study of relationships to explore the role of specific concrete themes in people's explanations.

To investigate people's naturally offered attributions and the knowledge used to construct them, we must gather open-ended explanations rather than have people respond to a fixed set of questions, which is the method most often used in this area. Even when open-ended attributions have been collected, they have simply been coded in terms of abstract dimensions such as internality, stability, globality, and intentionality. As such, the richness and complexity that is present in the content is simply lost (Baucom et al., 1989), and information that may be central to how one should deal with a situation may be totally missed. For example, consider the following two accounts for why your wife came home from work late:

My wife is late because she is having an affair with her secretary.
My wife is late because she is working hard to get ahead in the company.

Both of these accounts are internal, stable, intentional, and controllable. Yet they have different implications for how one should try to deal with the behavior, and they have very different implications for the health of one's marriage.

In fact, researchers in this area are finding that traditional causal dimensions, such as internal-external, are frequently not very useful for differentiating distressed and nondistressed couples (see Bradbury & Fincham, 1990, for a review). However, responsibility attributions (Fincham, 1985b) and attributions about a partner's motives and intentions are often better predictors of relationship functioning—perhaps because they tap into one partner's understanding of the other's goals. Thus, understanding the intentions and goals of the partner become important.

Of course we do not suggest that abstract dimensions are never useful, but that it is time for us to go beyond them. Too much valuable information is lost when we reduce explanations to a limited set of abstract dimensions.

Intervention

This model also has important implications for the form intervention should take. It is not sufficient to suggest that people simply make more benign attributions. Instead, we need to consider the knowledge that maintains these attributions. Such intervention is likely to be complex, including such things as replacing existing structures with alternatives and making unconscious/automatic processing more conscious. We do not have the training to make detailed recommendations on interventions, but it is important to note that a number of clinicians have suggested the limitations of current work for designing interventions. Perhaps the current model, or one like it, may provide greater insights into how people construct accounts and thus provide a more useful basis for intervention.

Conclusion

Work on the role of accounts and attributions in close relationships has taught us a great deal about the kinds of accounts people give in relationships and about the role of these accounts in relationship functioning. However, we know very little about how people construct these accounts. This is particularly true for the story-like, extended accounts that people typically give for important relationship events or when they are trying to provide a coherent account of the history of a relationship. Yet if we truly want to understand accounts in close relationships, we need a much deeper understanding of how people make sense of events in their relationships. We hope that the present model advances our comprehension of the processes underlying the richness of everyday accounts for events in our closest relationships.

References

Abelson, R.P., & Lalljee, M. (1988). Knowledge structures and causal explanation. In D. Hilton (Ed.), *Contemporary science and natural explanation: Commonsense conceptions of causality* (pp. 175–203). London: Harvester Press.

Ainwsworth, M.D., Blehar, M.C., Waters, E., & Wall, S. (1978). *Patterns of attachment: A psychological study of the strange situation.* Hillsdale, NJ: Erlbaum.

Allport, G.W. (1937). *Personality: A psychological interpretation.* New York: Henry Holt.

Alston, W.P. (1970). Toward a logical geography of personality: Traits and deeper lying personality characteristics. In H.D. Krefer & M.K. Munitz (Eds.), *Mind, science, and history* (pp. 59–92). Albany, NY: SUNY Press.

Alston, W.P. (1975). Traits, consistency and conceptual alternatives for personality theory. *Journal for the Theory of Social Behaviour, 5*, 17–48.

Anderson, J.R. (1983). *The architecture of cognition.* Cambridge, MA: Harvard University Press.

Antaki, C. (1987). Performed and unperformable: a guide to accounts of relationships. In R. Burnett, P. McGhee, & D. Clarke (Eds.), *Accounting for relationships: Explanation, representation, and knowledge.* London: Methuen.

Argyle, M., Furnham, A., & Graham, J.A. (1981). *Social situations.* Cambridge: Cambridge University Press.

Bargh, J.A., & Pratto, F. (1986). Individual construct accessibility and perceptual selection. *Journal of Experimental Social Psychology, 22*, 293–311.

Barker, R.G. (Ed.). (1963). *The stream of behavior.* New York: Appleton-Century-Crofts.

Barker, R.G. & Wright, H. (1955). *Midwest and its children.* Evanston, IL: Row Peterson.

Baucom, D.H., Epstein, N., Sayers,S., & Sher, T.G. (1989). The role of cognition in marital relationships: Definitional, methodological, and conceptual issues. *Journal of Consulting and Clinical Psychology, 57*, 31–38.

Bischof, N. (1975). A systems approach toward the functional connections of attachment and fear. *Child Development, 46*, 801–817.

Bowlby, J. (1973). *Attachment and loss: Vol. 2. Separation, anxiety, and anger.* New York: Basic Books.

Bowlby, J. (1980). *Attachment and loss: Vol. 3. Loss.* New York: Basic Books.

Bowlby, J. (1982). *Attachment and loss: Vol. 1. Attachment.* New York: Basic Books. (Original work published in 1969)

Bradbury, T.M., & Fincham, F.D. (1988). Individual difference variables in close relationships: A contextual model of marriage as an integrative framework. *Journal of Personality and Social Psychology, 54*, 713–721.

Bradbury, T.M., & Fincham, F.D. (1989). Behavior and satisfaction in marriage: Prospective mediating processes. *Review of Personality and Social Psychology, 10*, 119–143.

Bradbury, T.M., & Fincham, F.D. (1990). Attributions in marriage: Review and critique. *Psychological Bulletin, 107*, 3–33.

Bretherton, I. (1985). Attachment theory: Retrospect and prospect. *Monographs of the Society for Research in Child Development, 50*, 3–35.

Canary, D.J., Cunningham, E.M., & Cody, M.J. (1988). Goal types, gender, and locus of control in managing interpersonal conflict. *Communication Research, 15*, 426–446.

Carbonell, J.G. (1979). *Subjective understanding: Computer models of belief systems* (Computer Science Tech. Rep. No. 150). New Haven, CT: Yale University.

Cattell, R.B. (1965). *The scientific analysis of personality.* Chicago, IL: Aldine Publishing.

Cody, M.J., Canary, D.J., & Smith, S.W. (in press). Compliance-gaining goals: An inductive analysis of actors' goal types, strategies, and successes. In J. Daly & J. Wiemann (Eds.), *Communicating strategically*, Hillsdale, N.J.: Erlbaum.

Collins, N.L. (1990). *Adult attachment styles and explanations for relationship events: A knowledge structure approach to explanation in close relationships.* Unpublished doctoral dissertation, University of Southern California.

Collins, N.L., & Read, S.J. (1990). Adult attachment, working models, and relationship quality in dating couples. *Journal of Personality and Social Psychology, 58*, 644–663.

Feeney, J.A., & Noller, P. (1990). Attachment styles as a predictor of adult romantic relationships. *Journal of Personality and Social Psychology, 58*, 281–291.

Fincham, F.D. (1985a). Attributions in close relationships. In J.H. Harvey & G. Weary (Eds.), *Attribution: Basic issues and applications* (pp. 203–234). New York: Academic Press.

Fincham, F.D. (1985b). Attribution process in distressed and nondistressed couples: 2. Responsibility for marital problems. *Journal of Abnormal Psychology, 94*, 183–190.

Fincham, F.D., & Bradbury, T.N. (1987). The impact of attributions in marriage: A longitudinal analysis. *Journal of Personality and Social Psychology, 53*, 510–517.

Fletcher, C.R., & Bloom, C.P. (1988). Causal reasoning in the comprehension of simple narrative texts. *Journal of Memory and Language, 27*, 235–244.

Fletcher, G.J.O. (1983a). Sex differences in causal attributions for marital separation. *New Zealand Journal of Psychology, 2*, 82–89.

Fletcher, G.J.O. (1983b). The analysis of verbal explanations for marital separation: Implications for attribution theory. *Journal of Applied Social Psychology, 13*, 245–258.

Fletcher, G.J.O., Fincham, F.D., Cramer, L., & Heron, N. (1987). The role of attributions in the development of dating relationships. *Journal of Personality and Social Psychology, 53*, 481–489.

Ford, D.H. (1987). *Humans as self-constructing living systems: A developmental perspective on behavior and personality*. Hillsdale, NJ: Erlbaum.

Forgas, J. (1979). *Social episodes: The study of interaction routines*. London: Academic Press.

Galambos, J.A. (1986). Knowledge structures for common activities. In J.A. Galambos, R.P. Abelson, & J.B. Black (Eds.), *Knowledge structures* (pp. 21–47). Hillsdale, NJ: Erlbaum.

Galambos, J.A., Abelson, R.P., & Black, J.B. (Eds.). (1986). *Knowledge Structures*. Hillsdale, NJ: Erlbaum.

Gick, M.L., & Holyoak, K.J. (1983). Schema induction and analogical transfer. *Cognitive Psychology, 15*, 1–38.

Harvey, J.H., Agostonelli, G., & Weber, A.L. (1989). Account making and the formation of expectations about close relationships. *Review of Personality and Social Psychology, 10*, 39–62.

Hazan, C., & Shaver, P. (1987). Romantic love conceptualized as an attachment process. *Journal of Personality and Social Psychology, 52*, 511–524.

Heider, F. (1958). *The psychology of interpersonal relations*. New York: Wiley.

Higgins, E.T., & King, G. (1981). Accessibility of social constructs: Information-processing consequences of individual and contextual variability. In N. Cantor & J.F. Kihlstrom (Eds.), *Personality, cognition, and social interaction* (pp. 69–121). Hillsdale, NJ: Erlbaum.

Holland, J.H., Holyoak, K.J., Nisbett, R.E., & Thagard, P.R. (1986). *Induction: Processes of inference, learning, and discovery*. Cambridge, MA: MIT Press.

Holmes, J.G., & Boon, S.D. (1990). Developments in the field of close relationships: Creating foundations for intervention strategies. *Personality and Social Psychology Bulletin, 16*, 23–41.

Holyoak, K.J. (1985). The pragmatics of analogical transfer. In G.H. Bower (Ed.), *The psychology of learning and motivation* (Vol. 19, pp. 59–87). New York: Academic Press.

John, O.P. (1986). How shall a trait be called: A feature analysis of altruism. In A. Angleitner, A. Furnham, & G. Van Heck (Eds.), *Personality psychology in Europe: Current trends and controversies* (pp. 117–140). Berwyn: Swets North America, Inc.

Jones, E.E., & Davis, K.E. (1965). From acts to dispositions: The attribution process in person perception. In L. Berkowitz (Ed.), *Advances in experimental social psychology* (Vol. 2, pp. 219–267). New York, Academic Press.

Kelley, H.H. (1973). The processes of causal attribution. *American Psychologist, 28*, 103–128.

Kintsch, W. (1988). The role of knowledge in discourse comprehension: A construction-integration model. *Psychological Review, 95*, 163–182.

Lalljee, M., & Abelson, R.P. (1983) The organization of explanations. In M. Hewstone (Ed.), *Attribution theory: Social and functional extensions* (pp. 65–80). Oxford: Blackwell.

Leddo, J., & Abelson, R.P. (1986). The nature of explanations. In J.A. Galambos, R.P. Abelson, & Black, J.B. (Eds.), *Knowledge structures* (pp. 103–122). Hillsdale, NJ: Erlbaum.

Levy, M.B., & Davis, K.B. (1988). Lovestyles and attachment styles compared: Their relations to each other and to various relationship characteristics. *Journal of Social and Personal Relationships, 5*, 439–471.

Mandler, J.M. (1978). A code in the node: The use of a story schema in retrieval. *Discourse Processes, 1*, 14–35.

Mandler, J.M., & Johnson, N.S. (1977). Remembrance of things parsed: Story structure and recall. *Cognitive Psychology, 9*, 111–151.

Markus, H., & Smith, J. (1981). The influence of self-schemata on the perception of others. In N. Cantor & J.F. Kihlstrom (Eds.), *Personality, cognition, and social interaction* (pp. 233–262). Hillsdale, NJ: Erlbaum.

Miller, G.A., Galanter, E., & Pribram, K. (1960). *Plans and the structure of behavior*. New York: Holt, Rinehart, & Winston.

Miller, L.C., & Hoffman, V. (1990). *Sexual scripts*. Unpublished data, Department of Communication Arts and Sciences, University of Southern California, Los Angeles, CA.

Miller, L.C., & Read, S.J. (1987). Why am I telling you this? Self-disclosure in a goal-based model of personality. In V.J. Derlega & J. Berg (Eds.), *Self-disclosure: Theory, research and therapy* (pp. 35–58). New York: Plenum.

Miller, L.C., & Read, S.J. (in press). On the coherence of mental models of persons and relationships: A knowledge structure approach. In F. Fincham & G.J.O. Fletcher (Eds.), *Cognition in close relationships*. Hillsdale, NJ: Erlbaum.

Mischel, W. (1973). Toward a cognitive social learning reconceptualization of personality. *Psychological Review, 80*, 252–283.

Pervin, L.A. (1983). The stasis and flow of behavior: Toward a theory of goals. In M.M. Page (Ed.), *Nebraska Symposium on Motivation, 1982* (pp. 1–53). Lincoln, NE: University of Nebraska Press.

Read, S.J. (1987). Constructing causal scenarios: A knowledge structure approach to causal reasoning. *Journal of Personality and Social Psychology, 52*, 288–302.

Read, S.J., & Cesa, I.L. (1991). This reminds me of the time when . . .: Reminding in explanation. *Journal of Experimental Social Psychology, 27*, 1–25.

Read, S.J., Jones, D.K., & Miller, L.C. (1990). Traits as goal-based categories: The importance of goals in the coherence of dispositional categories. *Journal of Personality and Social Psychology, 58*, 1048–1061.

Read, S.J., & Marcus-Newhall, A.R. (1990). *Explanatory coherence in the evaluation of social explanations*. Unpublished manuscript, University of Southern California, Los Angeles, CA.

Read, S.J., & Miller, L.C. (1989) Inter-personalism: Toward a goal-based theory of persons in relationships. In L. Pervin (Ed.), *Goal concepts in personality and social psychology* (pp. 413–472). Hillsdale, NJ: Erlbaum.

Rule, B.G., Bisanz, G.L., & Kohn, M. (1985). Anatomy of a persuasion schema: Targets, goals, and strategies. *Journal of Personality and Social Psychology, 48*, 1127–1140.

Rumelhart, D.E. (1977). Understanding and summarizing brief stories.In D. LaBerge & J. Samuels (Eds.), *Basic processes in reading and comprehension* (pp. 265–303). Hillsdale, NJ: Erlbaum.

Rumelhart, D.E., McClelland, J.L., & the PDP research group. (1986). *Parallel distributed processing. Explorations in the microstructure of cognition. Vol. 1: Foundations*. Cambridge, MA: MIT Press.

Schank, R.C. (1986). *Explanation patterns: Understanding mechanically and creatively*. Hillsdale, NJ: Erlbaum.

Schank, R.C., & Abelson, R.P. (1977). *Scripts, plans, goals and understanding*. Hillsdale, NJ: Erlbaum.

Shaver, P.R., Hazan, C., & Bradshaw, D. (1988). Love as attachment: The integration of three behavioral systems. In R. Sternberg & M. Barnes (Eds.), *The psychology of love* (pp. 68–99). New Haven, CT: Yale University Press.

Simpson, J.A. (1990). Influence of attachment styles on romantic relationships. *Journal of Personality and Social Psychology, 59*, 971–980.

Sroufe, L.A., & Waters, E. (1977). Attachment as an organizational construct. *Child Development, 48*, 1184–1199.

Stein, N.L., & Glenn, C.G. (1979). An analysis of story comprehension in elementary school children. In R.O. Freedle (Ed.), *New directions in discourse processing* (Vol. 2, pp. 83–107). Norwood, NJ: Ablex.

Thagard, P. (1989). Explanatory Coherence. *Behavioral and Brain Sciences, 12*, 435–467.

Wilensky, R. (1983). *Planning and understanding: A computational approach to human reasoning*. Read, MA: Addison-Wesley.

8
Communication Problems in Committed Relationships: An Attributional Analysis

Anita L. Vangelisti

Whenever we got to talking, we always—well, not really always, but often enough that we couldn't miss it—we would very quickly get to the point where there was nothing to talk about any more. We just sat and looked at each other. . . . (Cuber & Harroff, 1965, pp. 122–123).

A cursory review of popular literature on romantic relationships and marriage reveals the term *communication* as a pivotal concept. Popular authors with backgrounds in psychology, sociology, and counseling applaud communication skills as the answer to most, if not all, relational problems. Although theoretical commentaries (e.g., Parks, 1982) and empirical work (Katriel & Philipsen, 1981) have cautioned that these unqualified prescriptions are based on cultural values rather than objective reality, the underlying theme—that communicative behavior is associated with relational satisfaction—seems to have a great deal of validity. James and Wilson (1986) note that "implicit in much of the literature is the central importance of effective communication between partners" (p. 57). Fitzpatrick (1983) similarly states that "interaction is . . . a major predictor of marital success or failure" (p. 49). Longitudinal data collected by Huston (unpublished manuscript) demonstrates that of several indices of satisfaction, communication is the best predictor of overall relational happiness.

Despite such evidence, a number of cognitive researchers and therapists (e.g., Beck, 1988; Epstein & Eidelson, 1981) would argue that many times it is not the communication behavior per se that causes relational difficulties. Rather, it is the way partners think about, represent, and cognitively process behavior that creates dissatisfaction in their relationships. For instance, a single communication behavior (e.g., expressing negative emotions) may be interpreted in several different ways (e.g., "She is doing this . . . because she is a negative person/because she had a bad day/because she trusts me with her feelings/because we have a intimate relationship/because she's trying to get me to do something for her.") In short, a number of different attributions may be assigned to a single communication behavior, and those attributions determine, to a large degree, individuals' satisfaction with their relationships. The study reported in this chapter was conducted to explore the links among perceived communication problems, attributions for those problems, and relational satisfaction.

One place where attributions may play a central role is in the processing people do of the problems they experience in their relationships. Although studies have been conducted on perceived marital problems (e.g., James & Wilson, 1986; Kelley, 1979), those studies tend to take a general rather than a specific approach to communication behavior. Certainly, some broad-based examinations of relational dynamics catalog potentially problematic behaviors couples engage in during relationship dissolution (Baxter, 1984; Cody, 1982; Duck, 1982; Knapp, 1984; Lee, 1984; Vaughn, 1986) and therapeutic treatment (Hickman & Baldwin, 1971; Pierce, 1973; Rappaport, 1976). Knapp (1984) notes, for example, that one of the first signs of relationship dissolution occurs when partners discuss at length "how different" they are from one another. Although communication behaviors such as this one may be seen as problematic because they facilitate the dissolution process, they may be perceived quite differently when performed in another relational context. In addition, there may be a number of communication behaviors deemed problematic by relational partners that are not included in stage-models of relational dissolution or in therapeutic intervention techniques. Few romantic couples would likely make the claim that they have "problem-free" communication, and yet not all of these couples are on their way to relational demise.

If couples' communication problems cannot be defined in terms of their direct association with relational dissolution, what are the qualities that distinguish perceived communication problems from other communication behaviors? At least two of the following three criteria must be fulfilled for a behavior to be deemed problematic: (a) The behavior must be negatively valenced by one or both partners, and (b) it must occur with some degree of frequency, or (c) if it does not occur with some degree of frequency it must be salient enough for one or both partners to remember it and identify it as a continuing source of displeasure or difficulty. When identifying communication problems, then, knowledge concerning the valence of the behavior (negative) and the frequency (or salience) with which the behavior is performed both come into play.

Given the purported centrality of communication to relational satisfaction and the notion that one source of relational dissatisfaction may involve partners' perceptions of their communication problems, the following research question was posited:

RQ1: What are the communication problems that committed, romantic partners commonly perceive in their relationships?

Initially, one would assume that perceived communication problems would be inversely associated with relational satisfaction. However, this may not be the case. In fact, most people can probably identify problematic communication behaviors that occur within the context of very satisfying relationships. These behaviors may be characterized as problems that a couple is "working on together," or they may simply be irrelevant to the couple's overall relational satisfaction. Although a number of studies have demonstrated strong associations between global assess ments of communication quality and relational satisfaction or adjustment, the specific behaviors perceived by relational partners that contribute to their satisfaction have not been examined. A number of works (e.g., Fitzpatrick, 1983; Gottman, 1979; Noller, 1985) have described differences in the ways that satisfied/dissatisfied (or adjusted/maladjusted) couples communicate. But these studies tend to focus on observers' perceptions of communication patterns and characteristics. Whether or not communication problems perceived by relational partners are actually associated with satisfaction is another issue. Given this, a second research question was posited:

RQ2: Is there an association between partners' reports of their communication problems and their relational satisfaction?

Another, perhaps less obvious, issue involves partners' attributions concerning why they have communication problems. When a communication problem arises, people try to make sense of it. This sensemaking process occurs, in part, because something has gone amiss—an expectation about what should happen in the relationship has been violated. Research on attribution has repeatedly demonstrated that one time when people are likely to formulate conscious explanations about events is when their expectations are violated. Moreover, to the extent that problems are particularly salient, couples may develop "stories," "sacred myths" (Katriel & Philipsen, 1981), or accounts (e.g., Harvey, Agostinelli, & Weber, 1989) as ways to explain and remember them. It follows, then, that when people perceive salient communication problems in their relationships, they will more than likely formulate some type of causal explanation for them.

A common criticism of research examining "lay persons'" explanations for social phenomena is that those explanations are distorted by any number of perceptual biases (Nisbett & Ross, 1980). Indeed, the catalog of studies demonstrating that such biases exist is extensive (e.g., Harvey, Harris, & Barnes, 1975; Jones & Nisbett, 1971; Snyder & Swann, 1976; Storms, 1973; Taylor & Fiske, 1975). The fact that people's perceptions and causal explanations are biased, however, negates neither their importance nor their potential effect on intimate relationships. Cuber and Harroff (1965) perhaps put it most clearly when they note that such efforts at self-examination and interpretation may be fraught with inaccuracies and self-deception, but they are still important since they constitute reality for these people *and are the bases for present and future courses of action.* [italics added] (p. 77)

Because individuals' attributions concerning their communication problems in part govern the way they view the behaviors associated with those problems, such attributions play a prominent role in affecting both present and future interactions. Further, if communication is an important component of relational satisfaction, the way committed partners perceive communication problems in their relationships should significantly influence their relational outcomes. With this in mind, a third research question was generated:

RQ3: What types of attributions do partners make for their perceived communication problems?

Finally, the consistent associations found between attribution patterns and relational satisfaction (e.g., Fincham, 1985a, 1985b; Fincham & Bradbury, 1987a; Fincham & Bradbury, 1988) suggest that there may also be an association between the way partners explain their communication problems and how satisfied they are with their relationships. Variables such as causal source, stability, and globality or uniqueness may affect both the way behavior is interpreted and the subsequent responses that will be made to it. This may explain why, in many cases, the same communicative behavior is considered problematic by one partner or couple and is seen as a sign of affection by another (Duck, 1981). Given the purported centrality of attributional processes to relational functioning, an additional research question was put forth:

RQ4: Is there an association between the pattern of partners' attributions for their communication problems and their relational satisfaction?

Method

Subjects

Forty-six committed, romantic couples participated in this study. To be eligible for participation, couples had to be married or cohabiting, engaged to be married, or must have been "serious" (discussing marriage and/or engagement) for at least 2 years. Those who did participate had known their partners for an average of 5.87 years (sd = 5.87) and reported that they were committed to their partners for an average of 4.66 years (sd = 4.57). Eighteen (39.13%) of the couples were married, 3 (6.52%) were cohabiting but neither married nor engaged, 9 (19.57%) were engaged to be married, and 16 (34.78%) were seriously dating.

Forty-three (93.48%) of the couples were heterosexual, and 3 (6.52%) were homosexual. As a whole, the couples spent an average of 24.80 days ($sd = 8.09$) each month together and an average of 22.12 nights ($sd = 9.72$) together.

Participants were solicited using Granovetter's (1976) "network" sampling technique. This technique, adopted by a number of relational researchers (e.g., Dindia & Baxter, 1987), involves obtaining subject participation through subjects' acquaintance with an initial pool of participants. In this case, graduate students enrolled in communication, journalism, and advertising programs were asked to recruit committed couples who would be interested in participating. The couples who participated were then also asked if they knew of others who might be willing to serve as subjects. Respondents either received extra credit in a university class or $10 for their participation.

Procedure

One-on-one interviews were conducted individually with each partner. With the permission of the participants, each interview was audiotaped for later analysis. Following an introduction to the study, participants were asked to think over the past 3 or 4 months and to identify any communication behaviors that they (and/or their partners) engaged in that they would like to change. A window of 3 to 4 months was selected both to aid in respondents' memory and to encourage a focus on daily behavior rather than on behavior associated with a particular relational trauma or turning point. For each behavior described, participants were asked to provide an explanation for why they (and/or their partners) performed the behavior and why it was less than desirable for their relationship. They were also asked to assess how frequently each behavior occurred (average number of times per month), how negative or undesirable they found the behavior (on a 10-point scale), and how global or unique they felt the behavior was (whether it was enacted only in the context of their relationship or whether it was enacted in most relationships). Finally, to close the interview on a positive note, individual partners were asked to identify and discuss communication behaviors that they (and/or their partner) engaged in that helped to keep the relationship close or intimate.

While one person was being interviewed, the other completed a packet of questionnaires eliciting two types of information: (a) demographic information (age, sex, number of months/years acquainted with partner, number of days and nights they spent with their partner each month, and number of months/years "seriously" involved with the partner) and (b) level of relational satisfaction. Due to recent discussions (e.g., Fincham & Bradbury, 1987b; Huston, McHale, & Crouter, 1986) of the potential fallibility of some satisfaction measures, Huston's (Huston, McHale,

& Crouter, 1986) Marriage Opinion Questionnaire (*alpha* = .90) was selected as a measure relational satisfaction. Although other scales (e.g., Spanier, 1976) may be more commonly used in communication studies, the Huston scale is based on evaluations of general affective states and therefore avoids artificially high correlations with interpersonal behaviors (Fincham & Bradbury, 1987b). Spanier's (1976) Dyadic Adjustment Scale was also administered to confirm previously found correlations (Huston, in progress) between the Marriage Opinion Questionnaire and other measures of satisfaction. In this case, the correlation between the two measures was .77 ($p < .01$).

Results

Characteristics of Communication Problems

Prior to analyzing the data, the interview notes were read carefully. Whenever the notes were unclear or incomplete, audiotaped versions of the interviews were used to clarify and/or complete the data. After this, the notes were reread and an initial typology of problematic communication behaviors was developed. Finally, behaviors within each of the categories were refined to eliminate redundancy, and the data were coded. Ninety-one percent of the behaviors listed were codable into the typology. Table 8.1 contains descriptions and examples of the behaviors within each category.

A second coder categorized approximately one third (34.8%) of the couples' interview data to check the reliability of the coding (Guetzkow's $p = .89$) (Guetzkow, 1950). Because each partner could list more than one communication problem, raw frequency scores were adjusted to account for the total number of behaviors listed. Throughout the investigation, when such adjustments were made, arcsine transformations were computed for the resulting proportional values.

Three groups of analyses were conducted to address the first and second research questions. First, frequency counts of each communication problem were conducted. Second, potential differences in communication problems due to marital status, gender, and relational satisfaction were assessed. Third, and finally, four variables designed to measure partners' perceptions of responsibility for their communication problems were computed, and potential associations with relational satisfaction were tested.

TYPES OF COMMUNICATION PROBLEMS

A frequency count revealed that, by far, the most commonly noted communication problem was "withholds expression of negative feelings." This behavior was noted more than three times more frequently than the

TABLE 8.1. Examples of behaviors cited by couples.

Description	Example[a]
Expressive problems	
Withholds expression of negative feelings	"When she's upset, she has problems expressing herself . . . she clams up . . ."
Generally withholds expression of feelings	"He doesn't talk enough about what he's thinking or feeling . . ."
Needs to be more clear about wants and needs	"If she wants attention, just come out and say it instead of hem-hawing around . . ."
Assumes feelings, thoughts, plans and forgets to ask	"We assume that we are thinking the same thing . . ."
Does not express enough affection	"I wish he would express his feelings about our relationship more . . . I think I show more affection . . ."
Says things without thinking that hurt the other	"Sometimes I blurt something out that will hurt him . . ."
Acts silly/teases me at inappropriate times	"He jokingly calls me names . . . Sometimes it hurts my feelings."
Should be more spontaneous/romantic	"He doesn't have an ounce of romance in his body . . ."
Needs to elaborate more when speaking	"Sometimes I'm short, abrupt . . . I'll give a short answer to something that might be more complex"
Has nervous habits/quirks that bother the other when he/she communicates	"She likes to communicate a lot with her hands . . . it can make her look childish and immature . . ."
We need more time together to communicate	"I'd like more time to talk . . . she's tired when she gets home from work . . ."
Responsive problems	
Does not comply with my requests	"He doesn't listen when I ask him to do something . . . he blows it off . . ."
Does not take the other's perspective when listening	"Sometimes he's close-minded . . . he won't listen to what I have to say . . ."
Does not accept the other's opinions/feelings	"She should be more accepting of my dreams . . . she is quick to say that they won't work."

TABLE 8.1. Continued

Description	Example[a]
Does not act sensitive/responsive to the other	"I probably need to listen a little more . . . sometimes I zone out . . . I don't hear her . . ."
Conflictive problems	
Disagrees with me too often	"He argues too much . . ."
Becomes upset/disturbed about inconsequential matters	"I go off the handle too quickly when things don't go my way."
Takes out frustrations on me	"When we spend too much time together, we start to take out our frustrations on each other . . ."
Blames the other for negative occurrences	"Whenever we have a problem, he makes it seem like it's my fault"
Raises his/her voice	"I yell a lot . . . I would like to yell less when I'm angry . . ."
Leaves or withdraws during conflict	"I tend to withdraw when we argue . . . I should be more involved . . ."
Is not logical/rational during conflict	"I'd like her to deal with conflict on a more mature basis . . . she lets her emotions get in the way of solving the problem."
Needs to be less logical/rational during conflict	"I learned to fight in a way that's formal . . . I turn away from the emotion and get rational . . ."

[a] Examples were taken from interviews with committed couples. In some cases words or phrases have been changed to protect the anonymity of the couples.

next most commonly listed behavior. "Does not take my perspective when listening," "generally withholds expression of feelings," and "we need more time together to communicate" were the next most frequently noted problems. Those problems that were noted least included "does not listen/comply to requests," "does not accept my opinions/feelings," and "does not express enough affection." Table 8.2 contains the relevant information.

GROUP DIFFERENCES IN COMMUNICATION PROBLEMS

Several follow-up analyses were conducted to further examine the nature of these frequency counts. First, a series of t tests for proportions were done to determine whether individual behaviors distinguished among

TABLE 8.2. Frequencies of couples' reported Behaviors.

Communication Problem	Overall (N = 92)	Gender: Males (N = 43)	Gender: Females (N = 43)	Satisfaction: High (N = 31)	Satisfaction: Low (N = 22)
Expressive problems	.62	.58	.65	.46	.69
Withholds expression of negative feelings	.32	.35	.27	.22	.46
Generally withholds expression of feelings	.08	.04	.13	.02	.10
Needs to be more clear about wants and needs	.03	.04	.03	.02	.02
Assumes feelings, thoughts, plans and forgets to ask	.06	.04	.08	.06	.02
Does not express enough affection	.00	.00	.01	.00	.00
Says things without thinking that hurt me	.02	.01	.03	.02	.02
Acts silly/teases me at inappropriate times	.01	.01	.01	.01	.03
Should be more spontaneous/romantic	.01	.00	.01	.00	.02
Needs to elaborate more when speaking	.01	.02	.00	.00	.00
Has nervous habits/quirks that bother me when he/she communicates	.01	.01	.01	.00	.00
We need more time together to communicate	.07	.07	.07	.11	.02
Responsive problems	.11	.10	.13	.16	.09
Does not comply with my requests	.00	.00	.01	.00	.00
Does not take my perspective when listening	.09	.07	.09	.11	.07
Does not accept my opinions/feelings	.00	.01	.00	.00	.02
Does not act sensitive/ responsive to me	.02	.02	.03	.05	.00
Conflictive problems	.26	.31	.22	.25	.13
Disagrees with me too frequently	.02	.03	.02	.03	.01
Becomes upset/disturbed about inconsequential matters	.04	.06	.03	.08	.04
Takes frustrations out on me	.01	.01	.00	.00	.00
Blames me for negative occurrences	.02	.02	.01	.02	.00
Raises his/her voice	.03	.04	.03	.07	.00
Leaves or withdraws during conflict	.01	.01	.02	.01	.02
Is not logical/rational during conflict	.03	.02	.03	.04	.04
Needs to be less logical/ rational during conflict	.01	.01	.01	.00	.02
Uncodable	.09	.11	.07		

Frequencies are proportions.

groups. Of particular concern was whether individuals who were seriously dating reported different types of behaviors than those who were married, cohabiting, or engaged. Were these people's perceptions of their communication problems different from those who had made more public declarations of commitment? Should they be treated as a separate sample? *T* tests for differences among the individual behaviors reported indicated that they should not. Reports of the individual behaviors did not significantly differentiate those who were seriously dating from others in terms of frequency.

Similar analyses were conducted to explore potential differences involving gender. The sample was divided according to gender and a series of *t* tests for proportions were conducted.[1] As can be seen in Table 8.2, results did not reveal any significant gender differences in the reports of problematic behaviors.

Finally, potential differences due to relational satisfaction were tested. Individuals who scored one half of a standard deviation above and below the mean on the relational satisfaction measure were selected for the analyses. Proportions for each behavior category were calculated (see Table 8.2), and a series of *t* tests was conducted. Results did not reveal any significant differences for the individual behaviors between high and low satisfied respondents.

PERCEIVED RESPONSIBILITY FOR COMMUNICATION PROBLEMS

Although these tests provide some initial information concerning couples' communication problems, they are limited in two very obvious ways. First, they do not indicate which partner was perceived to be responsible for the problem. Second, the small percentage of individuals reporting some problem categories may mask group differences. To address these issues, a second set of analyses was conducted. The number of problematic behaviors identified were computed in terms of four different variables: (a) the *total* number of behaviors cited, (b) the number of behaviors attributed to the *self*, (c) the number of behaviors attributed to the *other*, and (d) the number of behaviors attributed to *both* partners. These divisions were made with the expectation that the number of problematic behaviors partners reported that they themselves engaged in would be less strongly associated with satisfaction than the number of problematic behaviors they assigned to their partners (Fincham & Bradbury, 1987a).

---

[1] Because part of the purpose of this set of analyses was to explore potential differences between males' and females' perceived roles in close relationships, the homosexual couples were not included in these analyses. Generally, however, comparisons between the data collected for the homosexual couples and the data collected for three randomly selected heterosexual couples did not reveal any significant differences.

TABLE 8.3. Correlations between quantitative behavior measures and relational variables.

	Total	Self	Other	Both
Satisfaction	−.01	.16	−.26**	.11
	(82)	(82)	(82)	(82)
Years known	−.21*	−.12	−.14	−.04
	(90)	(90)	(90)	(90)
Years committed	−.23*	−.10	−.20*	−.03
	(90)	(90)	(90)	(90)

*p < .05; **p < .01.
Sample sizes in parentheses.

Although when examined individually, problematic behaviors did not, for the most part, vary according to which partner was held responsible for the behavior,[2] Pearson correlations using the four summed variables did reveal a significant negative association between the number of behaviors attributed to the *other* and relational satisfaction ($r(82) = -.26$; $p < .01$). The number of behaviors attributed to the self, to both partners, and the total number of behaviors were not significantly associated with individuals' satisfaction with their relationship. Table 8.3 contains the relevant information.

Parenthetically, the total number of problematic communication behaviors was negatively related to the number of years partners reported knowing the other ($r(90) = -.21$; $p < .02$) and to the number of years they were committed to the other ($r(90) = -.23$; $p < .02$). Although these results suggest that those with longer relationships feel they have fewer communication problems, a competing explanation is possible. It may be that relational satisfaction mediates the association between relationship length and the number of communication problems cited. To test this notion, partial correlations were computed, controlling for individuals' satisfaction with their relationship. When satisfaction was partialled out, both correlations decreased (years known: $r(75) = -.16$; $p < .09$; years committed: $r(75) = -.17$; $p < .08$). It appears from these findings that satisfaction plays some part in both associations.

Attributions for Communication Problems

Partners' explanations for their communication problems were analyzed along a number of different dimensions. The first three, commonly used in studies of attribution and personal relationships (e.g., Fincham,

[2]The only problematic behavior that significantly differed between the three groups was "we need more time together to communicate." As would be expected, the responsibility for this problem was attributed to both partners more frequently than it was attributed either to the self or the other partner.

1985a, 1985b; Fincham, Beach, & Baucom, 1987), were the *source* of the problem, its *stability*, and its *globality* or uniqueness compared to other problems. Given that communication problems, by definition, involve behaviors that are negatively valenced and that occur with some degree of frequency (or salience), two additional variables were assessed. These included partners' perceptions of how *negative* the problem was and how *frequently* it occurred. Reliability estimates conducted for each category ranged from .87 to .92 (Guetzkow, 1950). In addition, because explanations were solicited for each communication problem, all frequency counts were adjusted for the number of explanations cited.

SOURCE

Partner's responses concerning the perceived source of each communication problem they noted were coded into one of four categories: internal, external, interpersonal, and relational. Traditionally, attribution studies have utilized an internal-external dichotomy to describe causal sources (Baucom, Epstein, Sayers, & Sher, 1989). However, since Orvis, Kelley, and Butler's (1976) initial discussion of attribution and communication in relationships, scholars have begun to regard attributions as potentially more interactive in nature. Newman (1981), for instance, has argued that interpersonal attributions—those involving one partner's perceptions of the other—provide information relevant to interaction that the traditional internal-external dichotomy does not. Fincham (1985b) extends this argument by distinguishing causal statements that focus on the relationship from those that emphasize interpersonal perceptions. Because the current study is an investigation of romantic partners' perceptions of their *interactions* with one another, the coding scheme was expanded from the traditional internal-external dichotomy to include interpersonal and relational attributions.

Results revealed that, as a whole, partners tended to attribute communication problems most commonly to internal causes (44%). Attributions to external (29%) and to interpersonal (25%) causes were, however, also relatively frequent. Causes focusing on the relationship (3%) were cited least (see Table 8.4).

Analyses were also conducted to test for any differences due to individuals' gender and their relational satisfaction. A series of t tests for proportions failed to reveal any significant differences due to gender. However, similar tests examining the causes in terms of individuals' satisfaction did generate significant results. As would be expected from past studies (e.g., Fincham, 1985a), partners reporting high levels of satisfaction tended to cite external causes more frequently and internal causes (marginally) less frequently than those reporting low levels of satisfaction (see Table 8.4). Pearson correlations also revealed a marginally significant, negative association between partners' satisfaction

TABLE 8.4. Frequencies of attributions for communication problems.

Attribution	Overall (N = 92)	Gender: Male (N = 41)	Gender: Female (N = 39)	Satisfaction: High (N = 28)	Satisfaction: Low (N = 22)
Internal	.44	.39	.56	.38	.55*
External	.29	.25	.24	.37	.14**
Interpersonal	.25	.33	.18	.26	.25
Relational	.03	.03	.02	.00	.06

Frequencies are proportions.
* $p < .06$, ** $p < .05$.

and the internality of their attributions ($r(78) = -.18$; $p < .06$) and significant, positive relationship to the externality of their attributions ($r(78) = .23$; $p < .02$). No significant differences were found between the groups' tendencies to report interpersonal or relational causes.

STABILITY

Explanations provided for each communication problem were also coded as to whether they were stable or unstable. Adjusted frequency counts indicated that the overall sample tended to report stable causes. Stable causes were cited 73% of the time, whereas unstable causes were reported for only 27% of the behaviors. No significant differences in causal stability were found due to gender or relational satisfaction.

GLOBALITY

Respondents assessed the globality or uniqueness of each communication problem using one of three ratings. They reported whether the behavior was performed (a) uniquely in the context of their relationship, (b) only in some relationships, or (c) across all relationships.

As can be seen in Table 8.5, a frequency count of each of the three uniqueness categories revealed that for the overall sample, the majority of the problematic behaviors were seen as relatively global. Over 63% of the time, partners noted that the individual performing the behavior in question did so across all of his or her relationships. Behaviors were described as occurring only in the context of the couples' relationship approximately 20% of the time and in some other relationships in about 17% of the cases.

A series of t tests for proportions revealed that individuals reporting high levels of relational satisfaction were more likely to see problematic behaviors as occurring in the context of some of the performer's other relationships than were individuals with low levels of satisfaction (see Table 8.5). Although a number of explanations for this difference are possible, a cursory review of the interview notes suggested that the majority of the other relationships within which the problematic be-

TABLE 8.5. Frequencies of uniqueness ratings of communication problems.

		Gender		Satisfaction	
Uniqueness	Overall (*N* = 92)	Male (*N* = 40)	Female (*N* = 37)	High (*N* = 28)	Low (*N* = 19)
Unique to this relationship	.20	.26	.16	.14	.16
Occurs in some relationships	.17	.19	.14	.26	.04*
General to all relationships	.63	.53	.70	.60	.77

Frequencies are proportions.
* $p < .05$.

haviors were reported tended to be close or intimate relationships. Rather than implying that these relationships were relatively random as far as level of acquaintanceship, partners made comments such as "Well, she does it around her close friends" and "He only does it with his mother. . . . "

To test whether or not this was actually the case, those individuals who said that they (or their partners) performed the problematic behaviors in some other relationships were separated into two groups. One group consisted of individuals who either reported that the nature of the relationship was irrelevant or who failed to specify the nature of the relationship. The second was composed of people who noted that the other relationships were relatively close or intimate—specifically involving friends or family members. When this was done, more than 66% of the other relationships fell into the second category. Much of the time, when partners said that the problematic behaviors were performed in the context of some other relationships, those relationships were intimate ones. These findings may suggest that partners' ability to define problematic behaviors as intimate, despite their undesirability, is related to their relational satisfaction.

NEGATIVITY

The perceived negativity of each problematic behavior was rated by partners on a scale ranging from (1) not at all negative to (10) extremely negative. Analyses conducted to test for differences between individuals' average negativity rating and their gender and relational satisfaction failed to reveal any significant differences, as did Pearson correlations between negativity ratings and relational satisfaction.

FREQUENCY

Finally, partners were asked to estimate how often each communication problem they identified occurred. Their responses fell into one of six categories: (a) more than once a week, (b) once a week, (c) once every 2 weeks, (d) once a month, (e) once every 2 months, and (f) less than once every 2 months. With the exception of two of the six categories, the frequency values reported did not vary greatly from category to category. Respondents reported problems to occur more than once a week approximately 16% of the time, once a week about 21% of the time, every 2 weeks approximately 19% of the time, and every 2 months approximately 16% of the time. Problematic behaviors were noted as occurring once a month and less than once every 2 months 1% and 4% of the time, respectively—supporting the supposition that communication problems are perceived to occur with relative frequency.

To test whether or not partners' average frequency ratings across behaviors varied in terms of their relational satisfaction, Pearson correlations were conducted using the entire sample. The association between frequency and satisfaction was marginally significant ($r(82) = -.17; p < .06$).

Discussion

One of the central goals of this study was to specify the behaviors that commonly comprise "problematic" communication from the perspective of partners involved in committed relationships. Although an initial typology of problematic communication behaviors was developed, analyses revealed that, at least for the sample interviewed for this study, the type of problematic behaviors that partners noted as occurring in their relationships did not significantly differentiate between "happy" and "unhappy" couples. Negativity ratings assigned to each behavior also failed to strongly distinguish between those who were highly satisfied and those who were not. Rather, the things that distinguished satisfied from relatively dissatisfied individuals were the following: causal attributions for the behaviors, whether the behavior was seen as unique to the couple's relationship, who was described as performing the problematic behavior, and how frequently the behavior occurred.

The distinction between factors that did and did not differentiate between satisfied and dissatisfied couples can, perhaps, best be described in terms of concrete versus abstract conceptualizations of communication problems. The type of communication problem that occurs and how negative that problem is, are comparatively concrete variables. Describing them requires relatively modest cognitive processing: identification of a problem and evaluation of how negative or undesirable it is. On the other hand, assigning causal attributions to the problem, assessing its frequency, and deciding whether the problem occurs across all relationships, some relationships, or only a single relationship require higher level processing. Fincham (1985b), for example, notes that assigning causal attributions "involves monitoring and coordinating information derived from behavior chains of both partners, as well as cognizance of potential causes which lie outside the immediate interaction sequence" (p. 221). Witteman (1988) similarly discusses both problem frequency and problem uniqueness as involving cognitive processes that require cross-situational (and, in this case, cross-relational) comparisons.

The findings of this study suggest that for many couples, partners' conceptualizations of the concrete aspects of their behavior may not differentiate between individuals who are satisfied and dissatisfied with their relationships. Rather, couples' more abstract conceptualizations of those concrete behaviors—in terms of causal attributions and comparisons to other situations and relationships—are the distinguishing factors.

One finding in this study might seem to be an exception to this claim. The total number of problematic behaviors that individuals said their partners performed was negatively correlated with relational satisfaction. On one hand, it could be argued that the number of behaviors performed by "the other" is a relatively concrete variable and that reporting such a variable requires only the identification of a problematic behavior. Although in some cases this may be true, a number of researchers (e.g., Doherty, 1981; Fincham & Bradbury, 1987a) have argued that the assignment of responsibility for a particular behavior is a relatively complex cognitive process. Deciding which partner in a relationship performed a problematic communication behavior requires that the respondent first identify a reoccurring problematic interaction and then decide which partner is responsible for the problem that occurs during such interactions. Subsequent reports of "who done it" are the results of such a decision. Fincham and Bradbury (1987a) carry this argument further by noting that attributions of responsibility are even more complex than attributions of cause:

> Briefly stated, judgments of causation involve establishing what produced an event or outcome and thus involve analysis of past events. Responsibility, in contrast, typically concerns accountability for the outcome once a cause is established. (p. 1107)

It is reasonable to posit, then, that although determining who performed a problematic behavior may seem to be a relatively concrete variable, it actually involves comparatively complex cognitive processes. The notion that the conceptualization of abstract, rather than concrete, aspects of communication problems differentiates between committed couples who are highly satisfied and those who are much less satisfied therefore still holds.

Wilensky (1983) has posited several principles that affect the interpretation of social interaction. One of these, the principle of concretion, posits that people will use concrete knowledge (when it is available) to form inferences. Abstract knowledge is used in the absence of concrete information. Smith and Miller (1983) have further found that people make affective judgments (whether or not they will like a person) more quickly than they make inferences concerning causality (whether a causal source is internal or external). Zajonc (1980) has also argued that people process affective information with relative ease in comparison to cognitive information.

The results of this study, however, suggest that partners' affective judgments concerning their relationship (i.e., their satisfaction) are associated with relatively abstract knowledge. At first glance, these results seem to contradict the previous findings that affective judgments are comparatively simple cognitive tasks. In the current study, affective judgments are associated with more complex cognitive tasks—those involving causal inferences and abstract knowledge. More careful consideration of the relevant variables, however, reveals a fairly clear explanation for this seeming contradiction. The affective judgments made in Smith and Miller's study involved hypothetical assessments of interpersonal liking. Similarly, respondents' initial preferences were examined in Zajonc's study. In contrast to both of these, the current study involved participants' affective judgments of their own, long-term, committed romantic relationship—a very different cognitive task from those examined in the other two studies.

Becoming dissatisfied with one's own long-term, romantic relationship is neither simple nor easy. At the very least, it involves dissonance concerning the validity and accuracy of previous judgments made about the partner ("If the person is so undesirable, why did I become involved in the first place?"). The results of this study suggest two possible models illustrating how individuals become dissatisfied with their relationships. The first model is represented by a two-step process. Given the complexity of this task, it is possible that partners first look to complex or abstract knowledge and then use that knowledge to make global assessments of their relationship. The more complex inferences required in making causal attributions, for example, would be directly linked to relational satisfaction. The second model involves one additional step. It is possible that partners first use concrete information (e.g., type and negativity of communication problems) to assess pleasure/displeasure in specific situations. Then, only after their displeasure reaches a certain threshold, they begin to make more global judgments about their relationship. Finally, they turn to abstract information to support those judgments (and to affect their subsequent assessments of concrete behaviors). Whereas previous theory (e.g., social learning theory) tends to support the latter model, both models have yet to be fully tested and are therefore still subject to scrutiny.[3]

---

[3] Such models may not apply to all problematic behaviors. For example, the concrete aspects of behaviors that are extremely negative (e.g., verbal and physical violence) would, in many cases, prompt enough distress and dissatisfaction for one or both individuals to terminate the relationship. On the other hand, many psychologists argue that people often maintain extremely negative and even harmful relationships because of their abstract conceptualizations of the behaviors that occur within those relationships.

It is important to specify at this point that these findings refer to partners' *conceptualizations* of concrete behavior as opposed to their actual behavior. Numerous studies (e.g., Fitzpatrick, 1983; Gottman, 1979; Sillars, Pike, Jones, & Redmon, 1983) have reported cases in which partners' actual communication behavior differentiates between high and low satisfied individuals. The current study cannot, and does not, make any suggestions concerning the actual communication behavior of relational partners. Instead, the focus is on how the partners themselves perceive and describe their behavior.

A number of methodological limitations further qualify the claims made in this study. First, and perhaps most obvious, couples who were highly distressed and/or were not committed to their relationship were not included in the sample. If one assumes a linear relationship between relational satisfaction and couples' conceptualizations of their communication problems, a study including highly distressed couples would simply strengthen results found in the current study. Other investigations conducted on attribution in distressed and nondistressed couples (e.g., Fincham, 1985a) support the notion that, at least in the case of causal attributions, this would be the case. However, if relational satisfaction has a nonlinear association with partners' conceptualizations of their communication problems, the findings may differ.

Second, and relatedly, because the participants in this study were committed to their relationships, it is possible that their reports of problematic communication were positively biased. Highly committed partners may actually view the communication problems that occur in their relationships differently from partners who are less than committed. Given one of the goals of this study—to identify the behaviors that commonly comprise problematic communication *from the perspective of partners involved in committed relationships*—such a bias would not be problematic. In fact, the findings of the present study suggest that highly satisfied couples (compared to less satisfied couples) do have a sort of positive bias with regard to their attributions concerning the abstract aspects of their communication problems. It would not be surprising (or inconsistent with current results) if committed couples were found to demonstrate similar "biases."

A third limitation of the current study involves the method used to collect data. Because partners were required to cite communication problems in a free-response format, it is not surprising that the problems they cited were seen as relatively frequent (in occurrence) and negative by the entire sample.[4] If partners were required to make comparisons

---

[4] Over 43% of the behaviors cited were reported to occur at least once a week and an additional 22% were noted to occur every other week. With regard to the negativity of problematic behaviors, over 63% were given a rating of "6" or more out of "10."

among a number of previously generated behaviors, it is possible that the variability of frequency and negativity ratings would increase.

It is interesting to note, however, that this methodological "limitation" supports the central claim of this study. Changing the means of data collection from free-response interviews to comparisons of previously generated behaviors would involve a change in the sort of cognitive processing in which the participants engaged. In the case of free-response interviews, participants are simply identifying communication behaviors that they see as problematic; in the case of rating a list of previously generated behaviors, respondents would be required to make comparisons that they might not otherwise make. Any distinctions found using the latter methodology would, therefore, likely involve higher level cognitive processes, such as those involved in making causal attributions and assessing the uniqueness of behaviors. Because the findings of this study suggest that such processes are the ones that distinguish between high and low satisfied individuals, the results would support rather than contradict those found in the current study.

References

Baucom, D.H., Epstein, N., Sayers, S., & Sher, T.G. (1989). The role of cognition in marital relationships: Definitional, methodological, and conceptual issues. *Journal of Consulting and Clinical Psychology, 57*, 31–38.

Baxter, L.A. (1984). Trajectories of relationship disengagement. *Journal of Social and Personal Relationships, 1*, 29–48.

Beck, A.T. (1988). *Love is never enough: How couples can overcome misunderstandings, resolve conflicts, and solve relationship problems through cognitive therapy*. New York: Harper & Row.

Cody, M.J. (1982). A typology of disengagement strategies and an examination of the role of intimacy, reactions to inequity and relational problems play in strategy selection. *Communication Monographs, 49*, 148–170.

Cuber, J., & Harroff, P. (1965). *The significant Americans*. New York: Van Rees.

Dindia, K., & Baxter, L.A. (1987). Strategies for maintaining and repairing marital relationships. *Journal of Social and Personal Relationships, 4*, 143–158.

Doherty, W.J. (1981). Cognitive processes in intimate conflict: 1. Extending attribution theory. *American Journal of Family Therapy, 9*, 3–13.

Duck, S.W. (1981). Toward a research map for the study of relationship breakdown. In S.W. Duck & R. Gilmour (Eds.), *Personal relationships 3: Personal relationships in disorder* (pp. 1–29). London: Academic Press.

Duck, S.W. (1982). A topography of relationship disengagement and dissolution. In S.W. Duck (Ed.), *Personal Relationships 4: Dissolving personal relationships* (pp. 1–30). New York: Academic Press.

Epstein, N., & Eidelson, R.J. (1981). Unrealistic beliefs of clinical couples: Their relationship to expectations, goals and satisfaction. *The American Journal of Family Therapy, 9*, 13–22.

Fincham, F.D. (1985a). Attribution processes in distressed and nondistressed couples: 2. Responsibility for marital problems. *Journal of Abnormal Psychology, 94*, 183–190.

Fincham, F.D. (1985b). Attributions in close relationships. In J. Harvey & G. Weary (Eds.), *Attribution: Basic issues and applications* (pp. 203–234). New York: Academic Press.

Fincham, F.D., Beach, S.R., Baucom, D.H. (1987). Attribution processes in distressed and nondistressed couples: 4. Self-partner attribution differences. *Journal of Personality and Social Psychology, 52*, 739–748.

Fincham, F.D., & Bradbury, T.N. (1987a). Cognitive processes and conflict in close relationships: An attribution-efficacy model. *Journal of Personality and Social Psychology, 53*, 1106–1118.

Fincham, F.D., & Bradbury, T.N. (1987b). The assessment of marital quality: A reevaluation. *Journal of Marriage and the Family, 49*, 797–809.

Fincham, F.D., & Bradbury, T.N. (1988). The impact of attributions in marriage: Empirical and conceptual foundations. *British Journal of Clinical Psychology, 27*, 77–90.

Fitzpatrick, M.A. (1983). Predicting couples' communication from couples' self-reports. In R.N. Bostrom (Ed.), *Communication Yearbook 7* (pp. 49–82). Beverly Hills, CA: Sage.

Gottman, J.M. (1979). *Marital interaction: Experimental investigations*. New York: Academic Press.

Granovetter, M. (1976). Network sampling: Some first steps. *American Journal of Sociology, 81*, 1287–1303.

Guetzkow, H. (1950). Unitizing and categorizing problems in coding qualitative data. *Journal of Clinical Psychology, 6*, 47–58.

Harvey, J.H., Agostinelli, G., & Weber, A.L. (1989). Account-making and the formation of expectations about close relationships. *Review of Personality and Social Psychology, 10*, 39–62.

Harvey, J.H., Harris, B., & Barnes, R.D. (1975). Actor-observer differences in the perceptions of responsibility and freedom. *Journal of Personality and Social Psychology, 32*, 22–28.

Hickman, M.E., & Baldwin, B.A. (1971). Use of programmed instruction to improve communication in marriage. *Family Coordinator, 20*, 121–135.

Huston, T.L., Huston, T.L. (in progress). *When the honeymoon's over: Strain and adaptation in marriage* (Unpublished manuscript).

Huston, T.L., McHale, S.M., & Crouter, A.C. (1986). When the honeymoon's over: Changes in the marriage relationship over the first year. In R. Gilmour & S.W. Duck (Eds.), *The emerging field of personal relationships* (pp. 109–132). Hillsdale, NJ: Erlbaum.

James, S.L., & Wilson, K. (1986). *Couples, conflict, and change: Social work with marital relationships*. New York: Tavistock.

Jones, E.E., & Nisbett, R.E. (1971). *The actor and the observer: Divergent perceptions of the causes of behavior*. Morristown, NJ: General Learning.

Katriel, T., & Philipsen, G. (1981). "What we need is communication": Communication as a cultural category in some American speech. *Communication Monographs, 48*, 301–317.

Kelley, H.H. (1979). *Personal relationships: Their structures and processes*. New York: Wiley & Sons.

Knapp, M.L. (1984). *Interpersonal communication and human relationships*. Boston: Allyn and Bacon.

Lee, L. (1984). Sequences in separation: A framework for investigating endings of the personal (romantic) relationship. *Journal of Personal and Social Relationships, 1*, 49–74.

Newman, H. (1981). Communication within ongoing intimate relationship: An attributional perspective. *Personality and Social Psychology Bulletin, 7*, 59–70.

Nisbett, R., & Ross, L. (1980). *Human inference: Strategies and shortcomings of social judgment*. Engelwood Cliffs, NJ: Prentice-Hall.

Noller, P. (1985). Negative communications in marriage. *Journal of Social and Personal Relationships, 2*, 289–301.

Orvis, B.R., Kelley, H.H., & Butler, D. (1976). Attributional conflict in young couples. In J.H. Harvey, W. Ickes, & R. Kidd (Eds.), *New directions in attribution research* (Vol. 1, pp. 353–386). Hillsdale, NJ: Erlbaum.

Parks, M.R. (1982). Ideology in interpersonal communication: Off the couch and into the world. In M. Burgoon (Ed.), *Communication yearbook 5* (pp. 79–107). New Brunswick, NJ: Transaction Books.

Pierce, R.M. (1973). Training in interpersonal communication skills with the partners of deteriorated marriages. *Family Coordinator, 22*, 223–227.

Rappaport, A.F. (1976). Conjugal relationship enhancement program. In D.H.L. Olson (Ed.), *Treating relationships* (pp. 41–66). Lake Mills, IA: Graphic Press.

Sillars, A.L., Pike, G.R., Jones, T.S., & Redmon, K. (1983). Communication and conflict in marriage. In R.N. Bostrom (Ed.), *Communication yearbook 7* (pp. 414–429). Beverly Hills, CA: Sage.

Smith, E.R., & Miller, F.D. (1983). Mediation among attributional inferences and comprehension processes: Initial findings and a general method. *Journal of Personality and Social Psychology, 44*, 492–505.

Snyder, M., & Swann, W.B. (1976). When actions reflect attitudes: The politics of impression management. *Journal of Personality and Social Psychology, 34*, 1034–1042.

Spanier, G. (1976). Measuring dyadic adjustment: New scales for measuring the quality of marriage and similar dyads. *Journal of Marriage and the Family, 38*, 15–27.

Storms, M.D. (1973). Videotape and the attribution process: Reversing actors' and observers' points of view. *Journal of Personality and Social Psychology, 27*, 165–175.

Taylor, S.E., & Fiske, S.T. (1975). Point of View and perceptions of causality. *Journal of Personality and Social Psychology, 32*, 439–445.

Vaughn, D. (1986). *Uncoupling: How relationships come apart*. New York: Random House.

Wilensky, R. (1983). *Planning and understanding: A computational approach to human reasoning*. Reading, MA: Addison- Wesley.

Witteman, H.R. (1988). Interpersonal problem solving: Problem conceptualization and communication use. *Communication Monographs, 55*, 336–359.

Zajonc, R.B. (1980). Feeling and thinking: Preferences need no inferences. *American Psychologist, 35*, 151–175.

9 Attributions and Maritally Violent Men: The Role of Cognitions in Marital Violence

AMY HOLTZWORTH-MUNROE

Despite increasing attention from researchers and clinicians, marital violence remains a poorly understood phenomenon. Although a variety of theoretical models have been proposed, only recently have researchers begun to study the potential role of cognitive processes in marital violence. Specifically, there has been a recent interest in examining the attributions, or accounts, offered by violent couples (see Holtzworth-Munroe, 1988a, for a review; see chapter by Andrews, current volume).

As outlined by Holtzworth-Munroe (1988a), one can examine several different categories of attributions in this research area; for example, one can study attributions offered by the offender or those offered by the victim (e.g., Andrews, Chap. 10, this volume). The present chapter will examine attributions offered by violent husbands. First, the research literature that examines how men explain their own violence will be reviewed. Second, studies that examine the attributions offered by violent husbands for more global relationship events (e.g., marital problems) and for negative wife behaviors will be reviewed. By examining the attributions offered by violent husbands for each of these levels of events, we hope to gain some insight into the correlates, and possible etiology, of marital violence.

Husbands' Attributions for Their Violence

Researchers have recently begun to address the question of how violent husbands explain and rationalize their violence. Retrospective explanations for violence are viewed as important because they may help us to understand the ways in which violent men "neutralize self-punishment for reprehensible behavior" (Dutton, 1986, p. 382, discussing Bandura's model). Thus, "the purpose of accounts is persuasive, not merely descriptive. By bridging action and expectation, they function to neutralize potentially deviant behavior. Within this frame of reference, the importance of accounts is assessed by their social function, not by their validity"

(Bograd, 1988, p. 62). To date, only a few studies have directly examined the attributions offered by violent men for their violent behavior.

In an early study, Shields and Hanneke (1983) interviewed 69 men who had been violent toward a female partner. The majority of these men were identified through social service agencies and self-help groups. They were asked why they had been violent, and their answers were coded into one of two general categories measuring the locus of causality: internal (e.g., actor's state or characteristics or attitudes) versus external (e.g., circumstances, other people) attributions. Using this coding system, it was discovered that the men tended to offer external attributions for their violence. In fact, the most frequently given explanation was that the wife was responsible for the man's violence; 42% of the men offered this attribution.

In a similar study, Bograd (1988) interviewed 15 violent men, recruited from domestic violence programs. She asked the men to describe the first, the most recent, and the worst episodes of violence in their marriages; this resulted in a total of 40 accounts of violence. Coding the data, she found that the men tended to attribute causality for their violence to the victim; 58% of the men said that they were violent because their wife had failed to fulfill the obligations of a good wife, and 28% said that they were violent because their wife had been physically or verbally aggressive. In addition, men tended to blame external stressors (35%) and transient states (e.g., 40% attributed causality to alcohol or drugs, and 33% attributed causality to transient psychological states such as internal pressure); percentages add to greater than 100% because subjects could list more than one cause. When explicitly asked about their intent, one third of the men said that they had not had a goal when engaging in the violent behavior. However, the majority of the men who admitted having a goal stated that they had used violence to achieve a positive objective (e.g., to stop the fight or aid communication). When asked whether or not the violence was justified, 80% of the men felt that it was; the major justifications given were that the wife had failed to meet the husband's expectations or had been aggressive or that the husband had no other way to handle the conflict.

In a more comprehensive study, Dutton (1986) interviewed 75 men who had been violent toward their wives and were seeking treatment for domestic violence; 25 of the men were self-referred and 50 were court-referred to therapy. Dutton interviewed the men and categorized subject responses using several coding systems. First, Dutton coded the locus of causality (i.e., who or what caused the violence); differences were found between the self-referred and the court-referred men. Among self-referred men, 52% attributed causality to themselves, 32% attributed their violence to the situation, and only 16% attributed their violence to their partner. In contrast, only 16% of the court-referred men attributed their violence to themselves, whereas 44% attributed their violence to the situation, and 42% attributed it to the victim. Thus, self-referred men were more likely to attribute causality to themselves, whereas court-referred men were more likely to blame the victim.

Next, Dutton coded whether men offered excuses (i.e., denying personal responsibility) or justifications (i.e., accepting personal responsibility but attempting to justify the act) for their violence. Justifications were offered more frequently than excuses; 79% of court-referred and 92% of self-referred men offered justifications. Finally, by comparing the men's reports of their violence to reports offered by the men's wives and other sources (e.g., probation officers), Dutton classified the amount of minimization each man used when describing his violence. Minimization could occur in three ways: minimizing the number of violent incidents, the severity of those incidents, or the consequences of those incidents. Using this coding system, men were classified as high (i.e., minimized all three factors), moderate (minimized one or two of the three factors), or non- (did not minimize on any factor) minimizers. Self-referred men were more likely than court-referred men to be categorized as high minimizers. In addition, men who attributed the cause of their violence to their wife were the most likely to fall into the high-minimizer category.

Examining the data across his coding systems, Dutton outlined three basic strategies used by violent men to neutralize self-punishment for their violence. One group of violent men tended to view the wife as the cause of the violence and engaged in high levels of minimization regarding their actions. Another group attributed causality to themselves but engaged in high levels of minimization. The third group attributed their violence to the situation and engaged in moderate levels of minimization. Unexpectedly, a fourth group, consisting of 17% of the subjects, emerged; this group attributed causality to themselves and did not engage in any minimization. Dutton suggests that, given cultural norms, the men in this group may view their violence as acceptable and thus do not excuse or minimize it.

Finally, Holtzworth-Munroe (Holtzworth-Munroe, Jacobson, Fehrenbach, & Fruzetti, 1990) examined the attributions offered by 24 maritally violent men seeking therapy. In the other studies reviewed here, researchers had coded subjects' attributions; however, in Holtzworth-Munroe et al. (1990), the subjects rated their own attributions along a series of attributional dimensions. Also in this study, subjects offered attributions for specific violent behaviors (e.g., "I slapped my wife") rather than for more global violent incidents. In addition to offering attributions for their violent behaviors, subjects offered attributions for nonviolent/negative relationship behaviors (e.g., "I ignored my wife when she asked for my attention"). Thus, attributions for self-initiated violent behaviors were compared to attributions for self-initiated nonviolent, negative behaviors. The data demonstrated that—relative to their attributions for nonviolent, negative behaviors—the men viewed their own violence as less stable and as more attributable to their transient state at the time of the action (i.e., less attributable to their personality traits). In addition, trends in the data indicated that, relative to their attributions of their nonviolent behavior, men were more likely to attribute their violence to their wives and to view the violence as having less global causes.

Summary: Results from these four studies are very consistent, demonstrating that violent men do not attribute the cause of their violence to themselves. Instead, they excuse their violence by attributing it to external factors, including their wife or external stressors, or to transient states within themselves, such as having been drunk or angry. In addition, even when violent men attribute violence to themselves, they use other methods, such as justifications and minimization, to explain their behavior.

This self-justifying attributional pattern may reflect informational and attentional processing biases, because actors do not observe themselves acting but rather focus their attention on the situation and the other people involved (Jones & Nisbett, 1971). Or these attributions may represent self-serving motivational biases, either a conscious desire to present oneself positively or an unconscious motivation to justify one's behavior.

Whatever the cause of such attributions may be, it is likely that this pattern of attributions would allow a violent man to continue his violence. By denying responsibility for his actions, or by justifying his violence as necessary, a violent husband does not have to change his behavior. By believing that he will not be violent again (e.g., by attributing his actions to temporary factors), the violent husband does not acknowledge that his violence is an ongoing problem that requires help. This attributional pattern matches clinical descriptions of violent men, which portray violent husbands as reluctant to seek therapy and resistant to therapeutic interventions. These data suggest that clinicians will need to challenge violent men's explanations of their violence in order to help men recognize their need for help.

The results reviewed also suggest the importance of examining sampling issues in future studies. Dutton (1986) found differences in the attributions offered by self-referred and court-referred violent men; this group difference has important implications for clinicians who work with both groups of men. In addition, the attributions offered by violent men in the community, who are not seeking therapy and have not been arrested, should be examined; their attributions may differ from those offered by either court-referred or self-referred men. Finally, Dutton found a subgroup of violent men who did not seem to use the "standard" methods for neutralizing their violence (i.e., they did not excuse or minimize their violence); these men should receive further empirical attention.

Husbands' Attributions for Relationship Events and Negative Wife Behavior

The studies just reviewed examined husbands' after-the-fact explanations for their violence. However, another approach to the study of attributions in marital violence has recently been taken: Researchers have begun to examine the attributions offered by violent husbands for nonviolent relationship events. The potential fruitfulness of such work is suggested by two related research literatures.

First, work examining the role of attributional processes in marital distress may be relevant, given the overlap of marital violence and marital distress (e.g., Rosenbaum & O'Leary, 1981). Distressed and non-distressed couples have been found to offer different types of attributions for their partners' behavior, in a manner that may maintain, or even cause, their respective marital satisfaction levels. Relative to happily married spouses, distressed spouses are more likely to attribute negative partner behavior to the partner and to view the partner's behavior as having stable and global causes; they are also more likely to view such behavior as having been done with negative intent and selfish motivation and as being blameworthy (see Bradbury & Fincham, 1990, for a review of this work).

In another research area, Dodge and his colleagues have examined the role of attributional processes in childhood aggression (e.g., Dodge, 1991; Dodge & Coie, 1987). Relative to nonaggressive boys, aggressive boys are more likely to attribute hostile intent to a peer in an ambiguous situation (e.g., a peer destroys a child's puzzle, but it is not clear whether the peer did so purposefully or accidentally). This "hostile attributional bias" may be related to the use of aggression, as the child "retaliates" against a supposedly hostile peer.

These data, in the areas of marital distress and childhood aggression, suggest the potential usefulness of examining the attributions offered by violent husbands for nonviolent relationship events. One would predict that maritally violent men would interpret negative wife behaviors as having been done with hostile intent. Such attributions might increase the probability that a husband would act violently, because violence would seem justified as a retaliation against the wife's hostile actions. To date, only three studies have examined the attributions of violent husbands for negative, nonviolent relationship events.

Murphy, Vivian, O'Leary, & Fincham (1989) asked couples seeking marital therapy to rate the cause of their marital conflict along several causal and responsibility attributional dimensions; couples ranged from those with no history of violence to those experiencing severe violence. Correlations between husbands' attributions and their level of marital satisfaction were significant. However, correlations between husbands' attributions for marital conflict and the presence, or extent, of husbands' violence were nonsignificant.

Holtzworth-Munroe (Holtzworth-Munroe et al., 1990) examined husbands' attributions for negative wife behavior. In the study introduced above, Holtzworth-Munroe et al. recruited 24 maritally violent men seeking therapy and two control groups: 16 nonviolent, maritally distressed men seeking marital therapy and 14 nonviolent, nondistressed men. Each subject was presented with nonviolent, negative wife behaviors (e.g., "My wife did not pay attention to me when I was trying to discuss something important") that he had indicated were occurring in his marriage. The subject then rated whether or not his wife acted with negative intent when engaging in each of these behaviors. Relative to men in the nonviolent control groups, violent husbands were significantly more likely to attribute negative intent to their wives' negative behavior. This group difference in attributional content remained significant even when group differences in marital distress level (i.e., the violent men were significantly more distressed than men in the distressed/nonviolent group) were statistically controlled. Interestingly, the two groups of nonviolent men (i.e., distressed and nondistressed) did not differ significantly from one another in their attributions of wives' negative intent.

Thus, these two studies generated different findings in regard to the attributions offered by maritally violent men for nonviolent relationship events. The Holtzworth-Munroe et al. (1990) study suggests that violent men are particularly likely to attribute negative intent to their wives' negative behavior. In contrast, the Murphy et al. (1989) study did not identify attributions for marital conflict that were unique to violent men.

In interpreting these studies, several methodolotical issues must be considered. Perhaps differences in the type of events used to elicit attributions led to the differing results across the studies, because attributions unique to violent men were demonstrated when examining husbands' attributions for wives' behavior (Holtzworth-Munroe et al., 1990) but not when examining husbands' attributions for marital conflict in general (Murphy et al., 1989). In addition, the data from one previous study (Dutton & Browning, 1988) suggest that *certain types of wife behaviors* may be particularly problematic for violent men. Dutton and Browning (1988) asked violent and nonviolent men to view videotapes of couples having a disagreement; subjects rated their anger and were asked what they would do in the situations. Relative to control groups, violent men reported more anger and offered more negative behavioral intentions (e.g., more aggression and less constructive reasoning). However, this group difference was strongest for the videotape depicting the wife's "abandonment" (i.e., the wife wanted to spend more time with her friends and join a women's group); group differences were not as strong for the tapes presenting other types of negative wife behavior, including "engulfment" (i.e., the wife wanted the man to spend more time talking to her and to share his feelings more) and arguments about neutral topics (i.e., where to go for vacation). Thus, it is possible that certain types of wives' behaviors are particularly problematic for violent men; it would be predicted that such situations would elicit attributions that would differentiate violent and nonviolent men.

A final methodological issue to be considered is the attributional questionnaires used in studies of marital violence. Murphy et al. (1989) used global, composite measures of causal and responsibility attributions, and did not find an attributional pattern unique to violent men; in contrast, Holtzworth-Munroe et al. (1990) measured the specific dimension of negative intent and did find an attributional pattern unique to violent men. In addition, both of these researchers "borrowed" measures that were originally designed to study the role of attributions in marital distress; thus, neither group designed measures to capture attributions unique to violent husbands.

We attempted to deal with some of these issues in a recently completed study; the goal of the study was to differentiate the attributions offered by violent husbands from those offered by nonviolent husbands (Holtzworth-Munroe & Hutchinson, 1990). We chose to measure husbands' attributions for specific, negative wife behaviors rather than for marital conflict in general. In addition, given that certain types of wife behavior may be particularly problematic for violent men, we attempted to design such situations as stimulus events for soliciting attributions. Using a method originally developed by Goldfried & D'Zurilla (1969) and later used by McFall (e.g., Freedman, Rosenthal, Donahoe, Schlundt, & McFall, 1978), we designed a series of hypothetical vignettes depicting negative wife behaviors that we believed would be particularly problematic for violent men (e.g., jealousy, wife's "abandonment"). For example, one situation is the following: "You are at a social gathering and you notice that for the past half-hour your wife has been talking and laughing with the same attractive man. He seems to be flirting with her."

We also considered the issue of attributional measures. As with the previous studies, we included a questionnaire "borrowed" from the marital distress literature (Bradbury & Fincham, 1989); as with the Murphy et al. (1989) study, this questionnaire measured the global concept of responsibility attributions (i.e., negative intent, selfish motivation, and blameworthiness of the wife's behavior). However, we also chose to focus on the measurement of negative intent and developed a new measure, which we believed included negative intentions that would be particularly important to maritally violent men. For example, we had subjects consider the possibility that "my wife was trying to put me down"; we assumed that this might be a particularly relevant attribution for violent men, because they are described in the clinical literature as being very sensitive to threats to their competency. On our new measure, subjects rated the extent to which they agreed/disagreed that their wife was acting with specific negative intentions: She was . . . trying to make me angry, trying to hurt my feelings, trying to put me down, trying to get something for herself, and trying to pick a fight.

We recruited 22 maritally violent men who were arrested for domestic violence; this group was also maritally distressed. Through newspaper advertisements, we also recruited two nonviolent control groups, including 17 maritally distressed men and 17 nondistressed men. The violent/distressed and nonviolent/distressed groups did not differ in level of marital distress.

After each hypothetical situation was presented to a subject, his attributions for the wife's behavior in the situation were assessed. First, he completed the attributional measure of responsibility attributions "borrowed" from the marital distress literature; a subject's ratings on these scales were averaged to form a composite score measuring responsibility attributions. Next, the subject completed our new attributional measure of specific negative wife intentions; a subject's ratings on these items were averaged to form a composite score of the wife's negative intentions.

Across situations and groups, we first compared subjects' ratings on the composite measure of responsibility attributions. Using this measure, the violent and nondistressed/nonviolent groups differed significantly from one another; however, the mean of the distressed/nonviolent group fell in-between the two extreme groups and did not differ significantly from either.

In contrast, examining subjects' ratings on our new attributional measure, the violent group differed significantly from both of the control groups, being more likely to attribute the wife's actions to negative intentions; the distressed and nondistressed control groups did not differ significantly from one another. In addition, we examined subjects' score on our new attributional measure for each of the situations. There were five situations on which the violent men's attributions differed significantly from those offered by both the distressed/nonviolent and the nondistressed/nonviolent groups, whereas the two control groups did not differ significantly from each other. In other words, these situations seem to elicit attributions unique to violent men. Two of these situations involve jealousy themes: (1) A man calls for the subject's wife and says that he is her friend but won't leave his name. (2) The subject's wife is talking and laughing with an attractive man at a party, and the man seems to be flirting with her. Two of the situations involve the wife's rejection of the subject: (1) The subject wants sex and his wife is not interested. (2) The subject buys a shirt and is unsure whether he made the right choice; however, he can't return the shirt. When he asks his wife for her opinion, she begins to giggle, tells him that it looks funny, and suggests that he return it to the store. The final situation involves potential public embarrassment: The subject has made special plans with friends, for a special event. However, his wife wants him to cancel these plans. The fact that these situations were uniquely problematic for violent men is consistent with Dutton and Browning's (1988) finding that violent husbands were particularly angered by situations portraying the wife's possible "abandonment" of the husband; the jealousy and rejection situations in our study can easily be viewed as representing possible "abandonment" by the wife.

Summary: Data from the three studies examining husbands' attributions for relationship events and negative wife behavior suggest that attributions unique to maritally violent men can be identified. However, several issues must be addressed by researchers in order to do so. First, it is clear that the stimulus events used to elicit attributions deserve more attention from researchers. Although attributions unique to violent men have been identified in the two studies examining men's attributions for negative wife behavior (Holtzworth-Munroe et al., 1990; Holtzworth-Munroe & Hutchinson, 1990), the same group differences were not found when examining men's attributions for marital conflict in general (Murphy et al., 1989). In addition, our new data (Holtzworth-Munroe & Hutchinson, 1990) suggest that some situations (e.g., jealousy, rejection, and public embarrassment) are uniquely problematic for violent men and are particularly likely to elicit attributions unique to violent men.

Second, it appears that attributional measures deserve more attention from researchers. Studies examining responsibility attributions, using measures "borrowed" from the marital distress literature (Holtzworth-Munroe & Hutchinson, 1990; Murphy et al., 1989), did not identify attributional patterns unique to violent men. However, when negative intent is measured (Holtzworth-Munroe et al., 1990; Holtzworth-Munroe & Hutchinson, 1990), such attributions were identified. Thus, future researchers should carefully consider the types of attributions that might be unique to violent men.

Clinical Implications of Husbands' Attributions for Wife Behavior

Discovering attributional patterns unique to marital violence has important clinical implications. Armed with knowledge regarding the types of situations that are problematic for violent men and the types of attributions violent men are likely to make in these situations, therapists could identify a client's dysfunctional attributions and help the client to consider alternative interpretations of his wife's behavior. For example, consider David, a man who was referred to therapy after being arrested for assaulting his wife, Susan. David and his wife had been having financial problems. Both worked at a local factory; however, recently David had been laid off. They had discussed how to handle the bills that were piling up, but had not agreed what to do. One day, David walked into the house and heard Susan on the phone with a creditor. She was telling the creditor that David had been laid off (i.e., a case of public embarrassment). David, in a rage, grabbed the phone from her hand and slammed it down. He pushed Susan and she fell against a table, breaking her arm. When asked about this incident in therapy, David stated that he had been furious because his wife was "trying to put me down; she wanted to humiliate me by telling that guy on the phone what a loser I was, that I can't even hold down a job." The therapist worked with David to help him consider alternative explanations, including the possibility that Susan had been explaining David's job situation not to humiliate him, but merely to get the creditor to give them some extra time to pay their bills. Obviously, in such cases, it is important that therapists consider a client's attributions.

Summary

Although marital violence remains a poorly understood phenomenon, recent research examining the attributions offered by violent husbands has increased our knowledge in this area. First, data have consistently demonstrated that violent husbands excuse and justify their violence. Such explanations serve to neutralize self-punishment and thus may help to maintain the violence, because a man making such attributions is unlikely to seek help for himself. Second, researchers are beginning to identify a pattern of attributions, offered for negative wife behaviors in problematic marital situations, that are unique to violent men. These data may help us to better understand why a man chooses to use violence in a particular situation.

However, much work remains to be done, and future researchers should proceed carefully. Research that simply applies measures and ideas from other clinical areas (e.g., marital distress) to the problem of marital violence may not be productive, because such efforts often fail to consider what is unique about the role of attributions in marital violence. Instead, it is likely that future work will be most fruitful if it is based on theoretical development.

References

Bograd, M. (1988). How battered women and abusive men account for domestic violence: Excuses, justifications, or explanations? In G.T. Hotaling, D. Finkelhor, J.T. Kirkpatrick, & M.A. Straus (Eds.), *Coping with Family*

Violence: Research and Policy Perspectives (pp. 60–70). Newbury Park, CA: Sage.

Bradbury, T., & Fincham, F. (1989, November). An instrument for assessing attributions in marriage: Rationale and initial validation. Paper presented at the annual convention of the Association for the Advancement of Behavior Therapy, Washington, D.C.

Bradbury, T., & Fincham, F. (1990). Attributions in marriage: Review and critique. *Psychological Bulletin, 107*, 3–33.

Dodge, K.A. (1991). The structure and function of reactive and proactive aggression. In D.J. Pepler & K.H. Rubin (Eds.), *The development and treatment of childhood aggression*. Hillsdale, NJ: Erlbaum (pp. 201–218).

Dodge, K.A., & Coie, J.D. (1987). Social-information processing factors in reactive and proactive agression in children's peer groups. *Journal of Personality and Social Psychology, 6*, 1146–1158.

Dutton, D.G. (1986). Wife assaulter's explanations for assault: The neutralization of self-punishment. *Canadian Journal of Behavioral Science, 18*, 381–390.

Dutton, D.G., & Browning, J.J. (1988). Concern for power, fear of intimacy, and aversive stimuli for wife assault. In Hotaling, G., Finkelhor, D., Kirkpatrick, J.T., & Straus, M.A. (Eds.), *Family abuse and its consequences: New directions in research* (pp. 163–175). Newbury Park, CA: Sage.

Freedman, B.J., Rosenthal, L., Donahoe, C.P., Schlundt, D.G., & McFall, R.M. (1978). A social-behavioral analysis of skill deficits in delinquent and nondelinquent adolescent boys. *Journal of Consulting and Clinical Psychology, 46*, 1148–1462.

Goldfried, M.R., & D'Zurilla, T.J. (1969). A behavioral-analytic model of assessing competence. In C.D. Spielberger (Ed.), *Current topics in clinical and community psychology* (Vol. I, pp. 151–194). New York: Academic Press.

Holtzworth-Munroe, A. (1988a). Causal attributions in marital violence: Theoretical and methodological issues. *Clinical Psychology Review*, 8, 331–344.

Holtzworth-Munroe, A. (1988b). *Causal attributions offered by violent and nonviolent couples for relationship events*. Paper presented at the meeting of the Association for the Advancement of Behavior Therapy, New York.

Holtzworth-Munroe, A., & Hutchinson, G. (1990). Attributions offered by violent and nonviolent husbands for negative wife behavior in problematic marital situations. Manuscript in preparation.

Holtzworth-Munroe, A., Jacobson, N.S., Fehrenbach, P.A., & Fruzetti, A. (1990). *Causal attributions offered by violent married couples for relationship behaviors*. Manuscript submitted for publication.

Jones, E.E., & Nisbett, R.E. (1971). *The actor and the observer: Divergent perceptions of causes on behavior*. Morristown, NJ: General Learning Press.

Murphy, C.M., Vivian, D., O'Leary, K.D., & Fincham, F. (1989, November). *Cognitive factors in marital violence*. Paper presented at the meeting of the Association for the Advancement of Behavior Therapy, Washington, D.C.

Rosenbaum, A., & O'Leary, K.D. (1981). Marital violence: Characteristics of abusive couples. *Journal of Consulting and Clinical Psychology, 49*, 63–71.

Shields, N.M., & Hanneke, C.R. (1983). Attribution processes in violent relationships: Perceptions of violent husbands and their wives. *Journal of Applied Social Psychology, 13*, 515–527.

10
Attribution Processes in Victims of Marital Violence: Who Do Women Blame and Why?

BERNICE ANDREWS

There is a growing body of literature concerning the attributions of those involved in interpersonal conflict and marital distress (e.g., Fincham & Bradbury, 1988; Holtzworth-Munroe & Jacobson, 1985; Orvis, Kelley, & Butler, 1976; Sillars, 1981). The focus in this literature has often been on an actor's perceptions of his or her partner, and the studies reveal that those involved in such conflict are likely to attribute blame to the stable characteristics of their partners or adversaries. Furthermore, distressed married couples have been distinguished from the nondistressed by their propensity to make such attributions (Fincham, Beach, & Baucom, 1987). Most of these studies treat actor and partner as equals in their relationship struggles, so that neither is perceived as being a victim of the other. Research has concentrated on the consequences of attributions for subsequent marital satisfaction, and there has therefore been no apparent need to consider in any depth the origins of attributions and whether they are in fact justified.

In contrast to this work are studies of the attributions of those involved in marital violence and nonmarital rape. The focus here is usually on the aggrieved recipient of the abuse, and it is assumed that the balance of power is uneven in any struggle the subject has experienced. Indeed, in the case of rape there is often no prior relationship between the victim and perpetrator, so attributions have not been formulated by researchers in terms of the role of a "partner". In the case of marital violence the partner does figure, but because the emphasis has been on the cognitive-affective state of the victim and not on the marital relationship per se, attention has more often been focused on self-blame and its potentially deleterious effects. Interest in the phenomenon of self-blame in the context of victimization has increased alongside growing attention to its relation to depression and self-esteem (Abramson, Seligman, & Teasdale, 1978; Brewin, 1986; Ickes & Layden, 1978; Janoff-Bulman, 1979). Recent studies of the effects of marital violence on the victims have shown such violence to be associated with a high incidence of depression and other related disorders (Andrews & Brown, 1988a; Gelles & Harrop, 1989;

Hilberman, 1980; Walker, 1983). It has therefore been of considerable interest to know how far such women blame themselves for the violence and, if they do, why they do so and what aspects of themselves they single out for blame.

So, paradoxically, blaming the partner has been interpreted as maladaptive for wives in studies concerning attributions for negative spouse behaviors (e.g., Fincham et al., 1987), whereas self-blame has been viewed as a problem for victims of violence (Janoff-Bulman, 1979; Peterson & Seligman, 1983). In this chapter, this paradox will be examined in the context of victims' attributions of blame for past and present marital violence, a highly aversive and at times life-threatening situation for which spouses appear to be the most salient cause and self-blame might be unexpected. Attention is paid both to the origins and consequences of such attributions.

Although marital distress has been related to partner blame and self-blame has been found to be a common response among victims of nonmarital rape (Burgess & Holmstrom, 1974; Janoff-Bulman, 1979; Medea & Thompson, 1974), the small body of research conducted on the attribution processes of women involved in marital violence has produced conflicting results. Whereas some studies have found a tendency to self-blame (Hilberman, 1980; Walker, 1979), others have not (Frieze, 1979; Shields & Hanneke, 1983). A possible resolution is suggested by the finding that there is a tendency to self-blame with regard to the first violent episode but not in general (Frieze, 1979). This suggests that the high rate of self-blame found in the rape victim studies may be due to the fact that nonmarital rape usually happens only once. Marital violence tends to involve repeated incidents, and this may lead to shifts in blame over time. Furthermore, a recent extensive review indicates that existing studies of marital violence do not distinguish attributions made by women in current violent relationships from those made by women whose violent relationships have been in the past (Holtzworth-Munroe, 1988). Here again, blame may shift toward the violent spouse after the woman has left him, thus reflecting disaffection with the relationship (Fincham et al., 1987). The literature on attributional processes has for the most part described the attributions people make in somewhat static terms. The possibility that attributions for the same event (in this instance violence by the husband) change over time, as social or marital circumstances change, has so far not been examined.

If women do blame themselves for marital violence, the question arises as to the form this is likely to take. In a study exploring self-blame in rape victims, it was shown that on the whole the women involved did not see themselves as personally deserving or provoking the rape. Rather, they blamed the attack on some modifiable aspect of their behavior. For example, they judged that they could have been more careful or not have been out so late at night (Janoff-Bulman, 1979). In contrast, it has been suggested that those who are repeatedly assaulted or mistreated may be more likely to blame their character; they may feel that there must be something wrong with them if such an event happens more than once (Silver & Wortman, 1980). However, it may also be argued that such a consistent experience at the hands of the same individual may just as easily lead to the belief that there is something wrong with the perpetrator of the abuse.

What might lead one woman involved in a violent marital relationship to blame herself and another to blame her assailant? An extensive review of research into the antecedents of attributions has defined three main areas of investigation: individual beliefs, motivations, and situational information (Kelley & Michela, 1980). One of the most important situational cues when violence is experienced might be its severity (see Holtzworth-Munroe, 1988), and the making of stable attributions concerning the partner demonstrated in studies of marital distress may in part be reflecting the serious nature of the negative behaviors focused upon. But in situations like marital violence, social influences may play a particularly important role in the formation of attributions, not least because of the reported tendency of perpetrators and observers to blame the victim (Davis & Jones, 1960; Glass, 1964; Lerner & Miller, 1978). It has been suggested that in such situations, self-blame may be reinforced by the reactions of others (Silver & Wortman, 1980). A consistent finding in the literature on family abuse is that it seems to occur in the context of psychological exploitation, where abusers use their power to manipulate victims' perceptions of reality (Finkelhor, 1983). Abused wives may be persuaded by their husbands that they are incompetent, hysterical, and frigid (Walker, 1979). But although victims' perceptions of who is to blame may be influenced by the perpetrators of their victimization, it is possible that positive support from an existing social network may also play a potentially important role by disconfirming such accusations.

Social influences on current attributions may also extend further back in time. Abused children are often told by their parents that they are bad and unlovable (Herbruck, 1979), and of some relevance here is a recent study that has shown an association between the experience of inadequate parenting in childhood and subsequent low self-esteem in adulthood (Andrews & Brown, 1988b). Following from this, it is possible that those who have been abused or maltreated in childhood will be more likely than others to respond to later abuse by blaming their character. In the context of attribution theory, it would be predicted that consistent abuse across different situations and at the hands of different individuals would be likely to result in dispositional self-blame (Kelley, 1967). Evidence of greater dispositional self-blame for hypothetical bad events in people who have been sexually victimized in childhood has recently been reported by Gold (1986).

I turn now from the possible influences on victims' attributions of blame for marital violence to consideration of their potential consequences. It has already been mentioned that wives' stable attributions involving the partner are likely to be related to marital dissatisfaction, and it is therefore possible that these same attributions might also influence their strategies for dealing with the situation. For example, help-seeking has been shown to be a common response to marital violence, although there is some question as to how effective it may be (Borkowski, Murch, & Walker 1983; Frieze, 1979; Stark, Flitcraft, & Frazier, 1979). Help and advice may be sought from members of one's social network or, alternatively, from health professionals, lawyers, and the police. A person's willingness to seek help may depend, however, on her beliefs about the cause of the problem, those causes being seen as more stable presumably being more in need of outside intervention if change is to be effected. In addition, blaming the partner's character may facilitate approaches to other people, whereas blaming oneself may inhibit such approaches. However, there is evidence to suggest that women who blame themselves for marital violence are somewhat more likely than others to seek help from therapists (Frieze, 1979).

The attributions that women give for marital violence may not only influence help-seeking strategies but may also affect the women's mental state. Marital violence has been associated with a greater risk of concurrent depression, and rates of depression for women no longer in violent relationships are as high or higher than those of women still in such relationships (Andrews & Brown, 1988a; Walker, 1983). A possible explanation for this persistence of episodes of depression after the point of separation from a violent partner, and one that is consistent with learned helplessness theory (Abramson et al., 1978; Alloy, Abramson, Metalsky, & Hartlage 1988), is that such persistence is associated with the making of internal stable attributions for negative outcomes, or what has been referred to as characterological self-blame (Janoff-Bulman, 1979). It has in fact been specifically proposed that victims of crime who make such attributions will react with greater deficits to emotional well-being (Peterson & Seligman, 1983). The effects of having once made an attribution of characterological self-blame could endure for some time and may even persist or recur despite what appears to be a significant change in circumstances.

To summarize, the major focus of this chapter is on the attributions of blame women make while they are in violent marriages. In particular, the study to be described considered whether situational and social factors—such as current marital situation (i.e., whether still in or out of the abusive relationship), childhood experiences, and social network response—influence different types of attributions and, in turn, whether certain attributions are related to help-seeking and depression. Some of these data are presented in more detail elsewhere (Andrews & Brewin, 1990).

Background to the Study

The material to be reported is drawn from a subsample of women who took part in a longitudinal community study of women in Islington, an inner-city area of London, England. The study was designed to investigate the onset and course of depressive disorder over a period of 3 years. The main enquiry required a group of women who were at high risk of developing clinical depression, and the study therefore concentrated on working-class women with at least one child at home. Screening questionnaires were sent out to women between 18 and 50 years old, registered with seven doctors' offices. The screening procedure resulted in 438 suitable women being identified, but 7% refused to participate. The original sample of 407 women included 25% who were single mothers. (For futher details of selection see Brown, Andrews, Harris, Adler, & Bridge, 1986). We saw the women at three points in time of approximately 1 year apart. A total of 286 women participated in all three waves of the study and did not differ from the original sample in terms of marital status and incidence of depression. Marital violence was not specifically considered at the inception of the larger investigation. However, spontaneous comments concerning such violence were common responses to more general questions about the quality of past and current marital relationships in the first stages of the study. At the third and final stage, it was therefore decided that it warranted more detailed investigation, and all of the women were asked: "Are you now or have you ever been in a relationship where your partner has been physically violent toward you?" Any woman who answered yes, or hinted at such a situation, was asked a further series of questions about her experiences. Seventy-two of the women reported that they had experienced marital violence, and in 92% of the cases this was classified as severe according to Straus's criteria (Straus, Gelles, & Steinmetz, 1980). The remaining 6 women were reluctant to reveal the full extent of the violence, but all reported that it was a regular feature of the relationship and not a onetime occurrence. Two of these 6 women refused to be questioned further, and the present report is based on data from the 70 women who agreed to answer further questions. Of these women, 27 had been in a violent relationship in the 3-year study period. The remaining 43 had had a violent relationship that had ended before the beginning of the study period and were no longer living with a partner who had been violent. At the point of interview, 19 were currently in a violent relationship.

Measurement

The approach to measurement in our research is investigator-based. Tape recorded, semistructured interviews allow women to talk freely, and measures are in the form of numerical ratings by the investigator, based on the woman's verbal descriptions in response to questioning. Information is transcribed, and interviewers made ratings after the interview on the basis of a number of predetermined indicators and with reference to a series of examples. Some ratings used in the present study were dichotomous and aimed to establish the presence or absence of key variables such as clinical depression, which was measured using a well-established standardized interview, the Present State Examination (Wing, Cooper, & Sartorius, 1974). Most of the remaining ratings were based on nominal scales and, where they were not, equal intervals between the points could not be assumed. We therefore selected nonparametric techniques as the most appropriate form of statistical analysis.

The measures used in this study, described in detail elsewhere (Andrews & Brewin, 1990), include measures of repeated physical and sexual abuse in childhood and measures relating to the circumstances surrounding the marital violence—such as the severity of the violence, confiding and support received from social networks, and help-seeking from more formal contacts, such as health professionals and legal agencies. However, because the focus of this chapter is on the attributions that the women in our study made for violence, a more detailed description is given of the way these attributions were collected and categorized.

Our investigation was concerned with attributions of *blame* and not those of *causality*; all of the women were asked, "How far do/did you feel personally responsible or in any way to blame for the violence?" and "How far do/did you blame your husband for what happened?" A further series of probes was used where necessary to ascertain the degree of self- or partner blame. In addition, those whose violent relationships had been in the past were asked, "Are your feelings about who was to blame any different now from what they were at the time?" and their responses rated in terms of both past and current attributions. Responses were rated on a 3-point scale, ranging from predominantly blamed self to predominantly blamed partner, the midpoint being equal blame.

Judgments were also made about whether attributions were predominantly characterological or not. In the case of attributions of self-blame, a distinction was made between whether the attribution was predominantly characterological or predominantly behavioral (Janoff-Bulman, 1979). Examples of characterological self-blame were where women blamed themselves for being incompetent, unattractive, or provocative by nature. Examples of behavioral self-blame were where a woman blamed herself because she answered back or nagged. In attributions implicating the partner, he was always blamed for the way he had behaved (i.e., for using violence). A distinction was therefore made between blame predominantly implicating his character and blame predominantly implicating his response to specific situations. Examples of characterological partner blame were where the violence was seen as a consequence of his being alcoholic, psychopathic, or schizophrenic. Examples of blaming partner's responses to specific situations were where the violence was seen as a consequence of his response to outside stress, such as work pressure or response to the women's pregnancy. The four women who attributed blame equally to self and spouse were included in the category of partner's situational response. In all four instances the partner was blamed for the way he responded to the woman's behavior (for which she blamed herself as well).

In order to control for the possibility of bias, all of the transcribed attributions were removed from the context of the rest of the interview and rated by a second independent judge, who was unaware of any information about the subject, including her abuse status. Overall, agreement between the two raters for the self/partner dimension and the behavioral/situational versus characterological distinction was high. Weighted kappa was 0.95 and 0.80 respectively. Disagreements between raters were resolved by discussion.

Changes in Self-Blame

The first consideration was whether blame for violence changes with marital circumstances. Table 10.1 shows the distribution of self- and partner blame according to different marital circumstances.

Among those no longer in a violent relationship at interview, the current rate of self-blame was lower than that reported for the past (i.e., that felt while in the relationship, Table 10.1, col. 1 and 2). But whereas 61% (11/18) of those who had originally blamed themselves, blamed their partners after they were out of the relationship, only 1 of the 33 women who had originally seen her partner to blame while in the relationship currently blamed herself. The significance of this change was investigated using McNemar's test ($\chi^2 = 7.69$, $p < .01$).

The results therefore indicate that women show a greater tendency to self-blame while still involved with an abusive partner, but after the relationship is over there is greater tendency to blame ex-partners. This finding is given further support by evidence that past reports of self-blame while in a violent relationship did not differ from the reports of women currently in such a relationship (Table 10.1, col. 1 and 3; $\chi^2 = 1.08$, $1df$, n.s.). In contrast, women no longer in a violent relationship reported significantly less current self-blame than those still in such a relationship (Table 10.1, col. 2 and 3; $\chi^2 = 11.39$, $1df$, $p < .001$). We were unfortunately not able to question the same women both before and after they left violent relationships and therefore have to rely on their own convictions that their attributions had indeed changed. The women in the study, however, showed little difficulty in answering questions about blame and gave every indication of having considered the issues at length. This extended to their ability to report past as well as current attributions

TABLE 10.1. Women's attributions of blame for marital violence while still in violent relationship and when out of relationship.

Type of blame	Still in relationship				Out of relationship	
	n	% past blame	*n*	% current blame	*n*	% current blame
Self-blame	18	35	7	14	10	53
Partner blame	33	65	44	86	9	47

From Andrews & Brewin, 1990. Used by permission.

with ease. Women reported that their understanding of who was to blame had changed since the relationship had ended. In a typical response, one woman reported:

When I was married I used to think I must be encouraging him because I wouldn't shut my mouth. I've got it all worked out now, it wasn't me that was aggravating him, it was him that was aggravating him and he had to have an excuse for being the way he was. I believe that I really do. I think he would have been the way he was anyway because he was that way before I met him, he liked his drink.

This example of attributional change illustrates the process and lends insight into what might be underlying it. The verbatim reports of many of the women indicate that they systematically thought through the issue of blame in a way similar to that suggested by Kelley's covariation model (Kelley, 1967). Consensus, consistency, and distinctiveness information all appeared to have been considered in the formation of attributions. Some women reported how they seriously questioned what they had done to deserve the abuse before coming to the conclusion that it could not be their fault, because they had tried their best but were still getting hit. This realization led a number of them to blame their husbands for the violence, although others still blamed themselves and went on trying harder. Blaming the spouse often involved consideration of his violent or otherwise aberrant behavior in other situations. Often, however, this process did not take place until after the relationship had ended, because it was only then that more information became available. For example, some women reported that their ex-spouses had started cohabiting again and had been violent in these subsequent relationships. One stopped blaming herself when her former partner was arrested and sent to prison for a violent offense. She said, "I though that's it, if you can do that to your kids, why should I worry about you." Women also changed their attribution in the context of subsequent relationships with nonviolent men where they could conclude that they were not to blame for the original violence, because their current partner did not react toward them in the same way.

Types of Blame While in the Violent Relationship

Some understanding has been gained about the switch from self- to partner blame demonstrated among women no longer living with violent men. We go on now to consider in greater detail the different types of attribution for blame contained within these two broad categories. In order to do this, attributions made by women currently in violent relationships and reports of past attributions made by those no longer in such relationships were combined to ascertain the types of attribution women make when living in violent relationships. Overall, 40% (28/70) of women reported self-blame. However, more blamed their behavior (68%—19/28) than their character (32%—9/28). Of those who blamed their partner, more implicated his character (67%—28/42) than his situational response (33%—14/42). Overall, the least common attribution for marital violence while involved in the relationship was own character (13%), followed by partner's situational response (20%) and own behavior (27%). As would be predicted by the marital distress and interpersonal conflict studies cited above, most of the women blamed their partners' character (40%). The most common aspects of spouse's character singled out for blame involved his general inadequacy, mental instability (including being alcoholic), and his jealous and possessive temperament.

Social and Situational Influences on Attributions

But what led women to make these different types of attributions? Did other experiences of abuse that happened much earlier in life influence the formation of these later attributions for abuse in adulthood? Following Kelley's (1967) theory, it was hypothesized that where there was self-blame, those with a history of repeated abuse in childhood would be likely to blame their characters, whereas those without such a history would be likely to blame their behavior. The women had been questioned in detail about their experiences throughout childhood (before the age of 17), and specific questions were asked about the occurrence of repeated incidences of physical violence or sexual abuse at the hands of a family member or other adult. These two types of early adverse experience were included in an index of early repeated abuse. Around one fourth (18/70) of these women with experiences of marital violence had also experienced early repeated abuse. Overall, there was no difference in the rates of self-blame between women with early abuse and those without—50% (9/18), compared to 37% (19/52). However, when self-blame was reported, those with early abuse tended to blame their character, and women without abuse tended to blame their behavior. Thirty-three percent (6/18) of those with abuse blamed their character, compared to only 6% (3/52) of the rest of the women ($\chi^2 = 6.77$, 1*df*, $p < .01$). There was no difference between those with early abuse and those without in rates of blaming partner's character and partner's situational response.

Consideration is now given to whether there are other proximal influences on the formation of attributions. Turning first to social influences, the response of others in the woman's social network at the time when marital violence was being experienced is shown in Table 10.2. Emotional and practical support was rated on a 7-point scale ranging from marked support to reaction positively destructive, and the rating was determined by the predominant response. Women rated on the top 3 points were defined as having received a negative response. Confiding was rated on a 4-point scale ranging from marked, moderate, and some to little or none, and those rated on the first 3 points were defined as having confided. Those with characterological self-blame at that time reported that they received much less social support. Only one of the nine women involved received any support at all, compared to 65% (35/54) of the rest of the women ($\chi^2 = 7.0$, 1*df*, $p < .01$). However, they were just as likely to have confided in their social network as those without characterological self-blame—56% (5/9) did so, compared to 67% (36/54) ($\chi^2 = 0.07$, 1*df*, n.s.). But although there was no difference in rate of confiding, Table 10.2, column 3 also shows that those women with characterological self-blame who did confide received different responses from their social networks. They were significantly more likely than the other women to have received a negative response from those they confided in about the violence. It could be argued that those who reported such responses may have had some negative bias in their reporting style, so that it was the perception rather than the reality of the response that was the crucial factor. However, the style of measurement was investigator-based, and the interviewer required the respondent to provide actual examples of

TABLE 10.2. Confiding in and response from social network by type of attribution while in relationship.

	% support		% confiding		% negative response to confiding		
Attribution	11	(1/9)	56	(5/9)	80	(4/5)	
Own character	56	(9/16)	56	(9/16)	11	(1/9)	
Partner's character	75	(18/24)	75	(18/24)	6	(1/18)	6
Partner's situational response	57	(8/14)	64	(9/14)	0	(0/9)	(2/36)
	$\chi^2 = 10.91^*$		$\chi^2 = 1.95$		1-v-2,3 & 4 $\chi^2 = 13.97^{**}$		

From Andrews & Brewin, 1990. Used by permission.
* $p < .05$, 3*df*; ** $p < .001$, 1*df*.

behavior in order to make ratings on what we see as objective scales such as social support. A typical response from a woman rated as having received a negative response illustrates this point:

Only once I told his mum and dad because he stopped me feeding the baby—he used to lock me up and that. They said it was his business what he did, he could do what he liked. The next day his sister said I shouldn't have told them because they were so upset, it made them ill.

Another proximal factor that was considered with regard to its potential influence on attribution was the severity of the marital violence. Ratings were made on a 3-point scale ranging from very severe to severe to less severe. Women had been asked about the degree and frequency of violence they had experienced (particularly whether they had been injured in any way), the extent of their injuries, and how often they had been injured. Around one third of the women had experienced very severe abuse, involving prolonged beatings that led to broken bones and other serious consequences, such as miscarried pregnancies and stillbirths. Nearly 80% (19/24) of these women attributed blame to their own or their partner's characters, compared to 39% (18/46) of those who experienced severe or less severe violence ($\chi^2 = 8.60$, 1*df*, $p < .01$). Very severe violence was experienced by 67% (6/9) of those who blamed their own character and 46% (13/28) of those who blamed their partner's characters; only 16% (3/19) of those who blamed their behavior and 14% (2/14) who blamed their partner's situational response experienced such extreme violence—$\chi^2 = 11.39$, 3*df*, $p < .01$.

What Are the Consequences of Attributions?

In the last stage of the analysis, two possible consequences of the women's attributions are considered: help-seeking from formal contacts and depression. With regard to help-seeking, three-fourths (21/28) of those who sought help from the caring professions went to their own doctor, three of the remaining seven women consulted a social worker, and four saw a therapist. Table 10.3 shows that women with characterological self-blame appeared to be less likely than the others to seek help from health professionals, although this difference failed to reach significance. This was in contrast to those with behavioral self-blame who seemed particularly likely to seek such help.

With regard to help-seeking from police or lawyers, two thirds (18/27) of the women who sought such help went to the police and the remaining one third consulted a lawyer only. Table 10.3 shows that those who blamed their partners' characters were the most likely to have had recourse to the law. It is also of interest to note that whereas those with

TABLE 10.3. Help-Seeking from formal contacts by type of attribution while in relationship.

Attribution	Health professionals (% help-seeking)	Police or lawyer (% help-seeking)
Own character	11 (1/9)	*22* (2/9)
Own behavior	58 (11/19)	*16* (3/19)
Partner's character	46 (13/28)	*64* (18/28)
Partner's situational response	21 (3/14)	*29* (4/14)
	$\chi^2 = 8.15^*$	$\chi^2 = 13.58^{**}$

*p < .05, 3*df*; **p < .01, 3*df*.

behavioral self-blame were particularly likely to have consulted a member of the caring professions, they were most unlikely to have gone to the police or a lawyer. One third (3/9) of those with characterological self-blame sought help from any formal contact, compared with two thirds of the rest (40/61), but this difference was not significant.

I turn now to the relationship between attributions and depression among women who had experienced marital violence in the 3-year study period and among those who had left such a relationship at least 1 year before the 3-year period. There was no association between attributions and depression among those who had experienced marital violence in the 3-year study period. However, there was an association among those who had experienced marital violence outside of the study period. Women who said that in the past they had blamed their own character had a higher rate of depression in the study period than the rest of the women. Six of the seven had been depressed at some time in the 3-year study period, compared to 33% (12/36) of the other women ($\chi^2 = 4.62$, 1*df*, $p < .05$). The strength of this association was unexpected because five of the seven women reported that they no longer blamed themselves after the relationship had ended. It could be argued that retrospective and current reports of attributions were distorted by women's mood at the interview. In fact, only 8 women were depressed at the interview, and they did not favor any one particular type of attribution. There is also the possibility that retrospective reports were describing attributions made by women who were depressed at the time of the violent relationship, so that it is prior depression that accounts for the relationship between attributions and subsequent depression. However, there was no association between depression and any type of attribution in women who were in violent relationships in the study period. Taken together, these findings suggest that attributions are not primarily related to current depression and that the results are not likely to have been influenced by current or past mood. (Further details regarding these results on attributions and depression can be found in Andrews & Brewin, 1990).

Discussion and Conclusions

The view that emerges from this investigation of victims of marital violence is of attribution as a very social process, one that depends crucially on interactions with other people. The finding that women do retrospectively report a change in attributions after they leave violent relationships has gone some way toward resolving the conflicting evidence in existing studies about the preponderance of self-blame and partner blame. It would appear that differences in results may be due to a failure to distinguish women no longer in violent relationships from those who remain. Overall, the results show a substantial proportion made an attribution of self-blame. But, whereas over one half of the women currently living with violent spouses blamed themselves for the violence inflicted upon them, only a small proportion of those no longer in such a situation blamed themselves for the past violence. Furthermore, having taken social and situational factors into account, many of the latter women reported that their understanding of who was to blame had changed. With one exception, the direction of the change since ending the relationship was from self-blame to blame of the ex-spouse.

Consistent with studies of marital distress, the most common type of attribution for violence made by the women while still in the relationship was blaming partner's character. Such blame was related to the severity of the violence, and it is therefore possible that the propensity to blame partner's character, found among women in distressed marriages, may be a reflection of the serious nature of the partner's actual negative behavior. Women who blamed their own characters (the least common attribution) were similar to those who blamed their partner's characters in the degree of violence they sustained. Both sets of women were more likely than the others to have experienced very severe violence. It may be that when violence is extreme, own behavior or other situational factors are seen as insufficient causes, compared with either own or partner's character. Which form of characterological blame is chosen may be a result of earlier experiences, current social network response, or even the partner's influence.

As already mentioned, husbands may convince wives that they deserve the violence (Walker, 1983). It is therefore possible that while in the relationship, the spouse's influence may be strong enough to prevent any serious questioning of his behavior. Unfortunately, women were not questioned systematically about their husband's attributions for violence. Nevertheless, four of the nine women with characterological self-blame mentioned spontaneously that their husbands had told them they had deserved the violence because of the sort of person they were, compared with only 7% (4/61) of the other women. Of those who blamed their characters, one was told by her spouse that she was inadequate and not a proper human being, another that she was not fit to be a mother, a third that she was a whore, and the last that she was "off the air" and mentally inadequate.

However, more systematic evidence has been presented in regard to the importance of other social influences on the development of attributions. Childhood experiences of repeated physical and sexual abuse were shown to be related to characterological self-blame when in the violent relationship. The responses of others at that time were also related to such self-blame. The women involved received significantly less support from their social network and experienced more negative reactions in response to the abuse they sustained at the hands of their spouses. This finding is consistent with a recent study of sexual assault victims where it was shown that nonempathic confidant reactions to the assault were associated with less successful coping (Harvey, Orbuch, Chwalisz, & Garwood, 1990).

Confiding in others but receiving no positive support in return characterizes the syndrome of nonoptimal confiding that has already been described in a larger study of personality characteristics and social support (Andrews & Brown, 1988b). Women with adverse childhood experiences were more likely than others to turn to unsuitable or inappropriate people for support. In the present study, those who blamed their own character may, therefore, have met with negative reactions and lack of support because of the kind of people they turned to. Unfortunately, the data were not sufficiently detailed for a judgment to be made of whether the people they approached were more unsuitable than those approached by other women. However, only one of the nine approached anyone she could describe as a close friend or confidant compared to more than one half (23/54) of the other women for whom we collected the relevant information.

Turning now to possible consequences of attribution, women with characterological self-blame were as likely as the other women to confide in a social network member but somewhat less likely than the others to seek help from a health professional or from any other formal source. It may have been that a low self-image led such women to believe they were not deserving of professional help. In contrast, well over one half the women with behavioral self-blame consulted a health professional. Because of the unstable nature of their attributions, it may have been than such women held out some hope that professionals could offer advice that would help them change their own behavior, or at least alleviate the effects of the violence. However, women with behavioral self-blame were among the least likely to have recourse to the law. As expected, it was those who blamed their partners's character who were the most likely to seek such help. This would be a logical course of action given they they did not expect their partners to change. It is of interest that such attributions may be functional for women in the context of marital violence in so much as they relate to strategies of self-protection.

In contrast, research into the attributions of distressed couples indicates that these types of attributions are dysfunctional in terms of marital satisfaction and also affective impact (Fincham, Beach, & Nelson, 1987; Fincham & Bradbury, 1988).

With regard to the affective impact of attribution in the present study, it was expected that characterological self-blame would be associated with depression both during and after the termination of a violent relationship. However, depression was not associated with characterological self-blame for violence for the women who were in violent relationships in the study period. Neither was it associated with blaming partner's character, a finding that is at variance with that of Fincham and his colleagues. However, the measurement of clinical depression used in this study involved the use of a standardized clinical interview and stringent criteria for "case" depression. Other types of self-blame not directly measured in this study may also be associated with depression among women currently involved with violent partners. For example, self-blame for not being able modify the continuation of the abuse or self-blame for tolerating the violence (see Miller & Porter, 1983). Alternatively, the severity of their objective situation may in itself have been a sufficient cause of depression quite independently of their causal beliefs (cf. Holtzworth-Munroe, 1988).

Characterological self-blame was only related to depression among women who were no longer in violent relationships in the study period. All but one of the seven women involved had been depressed at some time in the study period. Most of these women no longer believed they were to blame for this violence, and it is possible that a propensity to blame one's own character may be part of a long-term latent pattern of negative thinking that is only primed by certain situations (Alloy et al., 1988; Brewin, 1989; Riskind & Rholes, 1984). The results presented indicate that in such situations, characterological self-blame may further be reinforced by lack of support and negative reactions by others.

It remains to consider whether the paradox noted at the beginning of this chapter has been resolved or elucidated by the results presented here. What has been made clear is that whether attributions are judged as dysfunctional or not may depend more on the context in which marital distress is experienced than has been generally acknowledged. Where marital distress is associated with marital violence, the very attributions that may be maladaptive for the future of the marriage, blaming partner's character, may in fact be functional for the safety of the women involved because they lead to seeking help from law enforcement agencies. Moreover, blaming one's own character for the violence may lead to lasting deficits long after the marriage is over. Marital violence has been shown to be a common occurrence in representative community samples (e.g., Straus et al., 1980; Andrews & Brown, 1988a), affecting more than one in four married people in their lifetime, and presumably such violence is even more common in distressed marriages. But research involving attributions of distressed couples has yet to take into account the possibility of violence. Many studies involve couples who are self-selected and some who have come forward for marital therapy. It is possible that the occurrence of violence in these samples is low given that some are seeking help and others presumably have nothing to hide. This would, however, restrict the generalizability and implications of their findings for marital distress in the general population.

The results presented here go some way toward explaining women's different responses to victimization and elucidating the consequences of such responses. Keeping in mind the need for replication, the research has important implications for those involved in counseling both single victims of marital violence and distressed couples, and it points to a need for further research into the attributions of the perpetrators of abuse.

Acknowledgments. The research in Islington was supported by the Medical Research Council. I am grateful to the women who took part and to the general practitioners in the area who collaborated with us. I am indebted to Zsuzsanna Adler, Antonia Bifulco, Julia Brannan, Linda Bridge, Jessica Mayer, and Eileen Neilson, who participated in the interviewing, and to Chris Brewin for helpful comments on an earlier version of this chapter.

References

Abramson, L.Y., Seligman, M.E.P., & Teasdale, J. (1978). Learned helplessness in humans: Critique and reformulation. *Journal of Abnormal Psychology, 87*, 49–74.

Alloy, L.B., Abramson, L.Y. Metalsky, G.I., & Hartlage, S. (1988). The hopelessness theory of depression: Attributional aspects. *British Journal of Clinical Psychology, 27*, 5–21.

Andrews, B., & Brewin, C.R. (1990). Attributions for marital violence: A study of antecedents and consequences. *Journal of Marriage and the Family, 52*, 757–767

Andrews, B., & Brown, G.W. (1988a). Marital violence in the community: A biographical approach. *British Journal of Psychiatry, 153*, 305–312.

Andrews, B., & Brown G.W. (1988b). Social support, onset of depression and personality: An exploratory analysis. *Social Psychiatry and Psychiatric Epidemiology, 23*, 99–108.

Borkowski, M., Murch, M., & Walker, V. (1983). *Marital Violence: The community response*. London: Tavistock.

Brewin, C.R. (1986). Internal attribution and self-esteem in depression: A theoretical note. *Cognitive Therapy and Research, 10*, 469–475.

Brewin, C.R. (1989). Cognitive change processes in psychotherapy. *Psychological Review, 96*, 379–394.

Brown, G.W., Andrews, B., Harris, T., Adler Z., & Bridge, L. (1986). Social support, self-esteem and depression. *Psychological Medicine, 16*, 813–831.

Burgess, A.W., & Holmstrom, L.L. (1974). Rape trauma syndrome. *American Journal of Psychiatry, 131*, 981–985.

Davis, K.E., & Jones, E.E. (1960). Changes in interpersonal perception as a means of reducing cognitive dissonance. *Journal of Abnormal and Social Psychology, 61*, 402–410.

Fincham, F.D., Beach, S., & Baucom, D. (1987). Attribution processes in distressed and nondistressed couples: 4. Self-partner attribution differences. *Journal of Personality and Social Psychology, 52*, 739–748.

Fincham, F.D., Beach, S., & Nelson, G. (1987). Attribution processes in distressed and nondistressed couples: 3. Causal and responsibility attributions for spouse behavior. *Cognitive Therapy and Research, 11*, 71–86.

Fincham, F.D., & Bradbury, T.N. (1988). The impact of attributions in marriage: Empirical and conceptual foundations. *British Journal of Clinical Psychology, 27*, 77–90.

Finkelhor, D. (1983). Common features of family abuse. In D. Finkelhor, R. Gelles, G. Hotaling, & M. Straus (Eds.), *The dark side of families: Current family violence research*. 17–28 London: Sage.

Frieze, I. (1979). Perceptions of battered wives. In I. Frieze, D. Bar-Tal, & J.S. Carroll (Eds.), 79–108 *New approaches to social problems*. San Francisco: Jossye-Bass.

Gelles, R.J., & Harrop, J.W. (1989). Violence, battering and psychological distress among women. *Journal of Interpersonal Violence, 4*, 400–419.

Glass, D.C. (1964). Changes in liking as a means of reducing cognitive discrepancies between self-esteem and aggression. *Journal of Personality, 32*, 531–549.

Gold, E.R. (1986). Long-term effects of sexual victimization in childhood: An attributional approach. *Journal of Consulting and Clinical Psychology, 54*, 4, 471–475.

Harvey, J.H., Orbuch, T.L., Chwalisz, K.D., & Garwood, G. (1990) Coping with sexual assault: The roles of account making and confiding. Unpublished manuscript, University of lowa.

Herbruck, C. (1979). *Breaking the cycle of child abuse*. Minneapolis, MN: Winston Press.

Hilberman, E. (1980). The "wife-beater's wife" reconsidered. *American Journal of Psychiatry, 137*, 1336–1347.

Holtzworth-Munroe, A. (1988). Causal attributions in marital violence: Theoretical and methodological issues. *Clinical Psychology Review. 8*, 331–344.

Holtzworth-Munroe, A., & Jacobson, N.S. (1985). Causal attributions of married couples: When do they search for causes? What do they conclude when they do? *Journal of Personality and Social Psychology, 48*, 1398–1412.

Ickes, W.J., & Layden, M.A. (1978). Attributional styles. In J.H. Harvey, W.J. Ickes, & R.F. Kidd (Eds.), *New directions in attribution research (Vol. 2)*. Hillsdale, NJ: Erlbaum.

Janoff-Bulman, R. (1979). Characterological versus behavioral self-blame: inquiries into depression and rape. *Journal of Personality and Social Psychology, 37*, 1798–1809.

Kelley, H.H. (1967). Attribution theory in social psychology. In D. Levine (Ed.), *Nebraska symposium on motivation, Vol. 15*. Lincoln, NE: University of Nebraska Press.

Kelley, H.H., & Michela, J.L. (1980). Attribution theory and research. *Annual Review of Psychology, 31*, 457–501.

Lerner, M.J., & Miller, D.T. (1978). Just world research and the attribution process: Looking back and ahead. *Psychological Bulletin, 85*, 1030–1051.

Medea, A. & Thompson, K. (1974). *Against rape*. New York: Farrar, Strauss & Giroux.

Miller, D.T., & Porter, C.A. (1983). Self-blame in victims of violence. *Journal of Social Issues, 39*, 139–152.

Orvis, B.R., Kelley, H.H., & Butler, D. (1976). Attributional conflict in young couples. In J.H. Harvey, W.J. Ickes, & R.F. Kidd (Eds.), *New directions in attribution research (Vol. 1)*. Hillsdale, NJ: Erlbarum.

Peterson, C., & Seligman, M.E.P. (1983). Learned helplessness and victimization. *Journal of Social Issues, 39*, 105–118.

Riskind, J.H., & Rholes, W.S. (1984). Cognitive accessibility and the capacity of cognitions to predict future depression: A theoretical note. *Cognitive Therapy and Research, 8*, 1–12.

Shields, N.M., & Hanneke, C.R. (1983). Attribution processes in violent relationships: Perceptions of violent husbands and their wives. *Journal of Applied Social Psychology, 13*, 515–527.

Sillars, A.L. (1981). Attributions and Interpersonal Conflict Resolution In J.H. Harvey, W. Ickes, & R.F. Kidd (Eds.), *New Directions in Attribution Research (Vol. 3)*. Hillsdale, NJ: Erlbaum.

Silver, R.L., & Wortman, C.B. (1980). Coping with undesirable life events. In J. Garber & M.E.P. Seligman (Eds.), *Human helplessness: Theory and applications*. 279–340 New York: Academic Press.

Stark, E., Flitcraft, A., & Frazier W. (1979). Medicine and patriarchal violence: The social construction of a "private event." *International Journal of Health Services, 9*, 461–493.

Straus, M., Gelles, R., & Steinmetz, S. (1980). *Behind closed doors: Violence in the American family*. New York: Anchor.

Walker, L.E. (1983). The battered woman syndrome. In D. Finkelhor, R. Gelles, G. Hotaling, & M. Straus (Eds.), *The dark side of families: Current family violence research*. 31–48 London: Sage.

Walker, L.E. (1979). *The Battered Woman*. New York: Harper & Row.

Wing, J.K., Cooper, J.E., & Sartorius, N. (1974). *The Measurement and classification of psychiatric symptoms*. Cambridge: Cambridge University Press.

11
Attribution and Emotion in Patients' Families

CHRIS R. BREWIN

The importance of the family environment to patients suffering from medical and psychiatric disorders can scarcely be overestimated. To take three examples, depression, agoraphobia, and alcoholism have been shown to be closely tied to the quality of the marital relationship, an observation that has led to a number of successful attempts to treat these disorders with marital therapy or spouse involvement (Gotlib, 1990; O'Leary & Beach, 1990; N.S. Jacobson, Holtzworth-Munroe, & Schmaling, 1989). The course of a number of disorders—such as depression, schizophrenia, bipolar affective disorder, and obesity in women—has also been shown to be sensitive to the presence of expressed emotion (specifically, critical comments, hostility, and emotional over-involvement) in other members of the family (Vaughn, 1989). These findings have also led to family interventions that have been successful in changing the family's emotional climate and bringing about improvement in patients' relapse rates (e.g., Leff, Kuipers, Berkowitz, Eberlein-Vries, & Sturgeon, 1982; Leff et al., 1989).

The emotional responses of family members may also have less direct effects on patients, for example in mediating their willingness to be involved in the treatment of the patient. Parents of enuretic children are more likely to withdraw their child prematurely if they report feeling less tolerant of the bedwetting (Butler, Brewin, & Forsythe, 1986). This is likely to be a significant factor affecting treatment outcome, because the management of many conditions, from substance abuse to agoraphobia, is often enhanced by the effort and involvement of relatives. Finally, it should be noted that relationship conflict and breakdown carry with them an enhanced probability of marital violence and consequent depression in the victim (Andrews & Brown, 1988), and of the abuse or neglect of children. This abuse and neglect, and the presence of parental discord, are in turn associated with a greater risk of later psychopathology (Bryer, Nelson, Miller, & Krol, 1987; Harris, Brown, & Bifulco, 1986; A. Jacobson & Richardson, 1987). Understanding the causes of dysfunctional emotions in families would therefore appear to be of immense clinical significance.

Perhaps the emotions most commonly encountered in the literature on families and disorder are anger, criticism, and hostility. In a recent statement of the relation between attribution and emotion, Weiner (1986) proposed that anger toward another is experienced when a negative outcome is attributed to a cause controllable by that person. This suggestion has received support from studies of various clinical and nonclinical groups. There is now extensive evidence that marital dissatisfaction and distress are associated with locating the cause of negative outcomes in the intentional, controllable, or blameworthy actions of the partner (Bradbury & Fincham, 1990). Butler et al. (1986) investigated the emotional reactions of mothers of children with nocturnal enuresis. Mothers' attributions concerning the degree of control by the child were associated with the mothers' tolerance for the disorder, greater control being linked to less tolerance. Less tolerance was in turn highly associated with greater feelings of anger. Applying these ideas to research on expressed emotion (EE) in families, Brewin (1988) suggested that patients' symptoms and negative behaviors would elicit hostility and criticism in relatives to the extent that they perceived the patient as being able to control those symptoms or behaviors.

In some ways, however, the context of caring for an ill person may be unlike those in which attributional analyses of the emotions were developed. There is some recent evidence that in professional caregivers anger is not associated with perceived controllability on the part of the patient (Sharrock, Day, Qazi, & Brewin, 1990). Unlike a student who has received a request to lend his class notes (a situation typically used in basic research on attribution, emotion, and helping behavior), professional caregivers and relatives may perceive that they have a long-term duty of care to the sick person, who may be occupying a "sick role," in which personal responsibility is diminished. An alternative hypothesis suggested by Leff & Vaughn (1985) is that the emotional reactions of criticism and hostility may be linked to the belief that negative behaviors reflect the patient's enduring personal characteristics and idiosyncrasies, rather than indicating the presence of a legitimate illness.

Turning to explanations for emotional overinvolvement by relatives, a separate component of expressed emotion, it has been suggested that among the underlying emotions are relatives' feelings of protectiveness and guilt concerning the patient's condition (Leff & Vaughn, 1985). Weiner's (1986) analysis proposes that guilt is experienced when a negative outcome is attributed to a cause internal to and controllable by oneself. Protectiveness, on the other hand, may be related to experiencing pity. According to Weiner, pity arises from seeing another person as experiencing negative outcomes caused by external and uncontrollable factors. In the research reported below, we test the hypothesis that greater overinvolvement is associated with the opposite pattern of causal beliefs to criticism and hostility, that is, perceiving less controllability on the part of the patient and more controllability on the part of the relative.

Studies with the Relatives of Patients with Schizophrenia

In this chapter I shall focus mainly on current research we are conducting concerning the relation between attributions and expressed emotion in the families of patients with schizophrenia (a more detailed account of some of the material can also be found in Brewin, MacCarthy, Duda, & Vaughn, in press). Relatively little research on the origin and correlates of these emotional characteristics has been conducted, and we wished to investigate whether relatives' emotions would be related to their beliefs about the causes of the patients' illness, behavior, and symptoms. Because the symptoms of schizophrenia are unfamiliar and extremely diverse, and because little education is typically given to the relatives of diagnosed schizophrenic patients, we anticipated that many relatives would experience considerable attributional uncertainty.

Do Relatives Make Attributions?

Our starting point was to ask whether family members spontaneously made attributions about their ill relatives. Causal beliefs are prominent and easily elicited from patients themselves (e.g., Brewin & Antaki, 1987), from people in close relationships (e.g., Harvey, 1987), and, more generally, from anyone faced with an unexpected or unwelcome event (Weiner, 1985). But as far as we were aware, nobody had investigated attributional processes in the relatives of diagnosed psychiatric patients. We were fortunate to have available in the MRC Social and Community Psychiatry Unit audiotapes from a number of earlier studies of expressed emotion (Vaughn & Leff, 1976a; Vaughn, Snyder, Freeman, Jones, & Falloon 1984; Leff, Berkowitz et al., 1989; Leff, Kuipers, et al., 1982). Expressed emotion is rated from a semistructured interview, the Camberwell Family Interview, which is carried out individually with each relative, lasts for about an hour, and inquires about the onset of the illness, current symptoms and behavior, and impact on the relationship between patient and relative.

From this interview, raters count the number of critical comments and positive remarks, and make global judgments about the degree of hostility, emotional overinvolvement, and warmth shown by the relative. (See Vaughn & Leff, 1976b, for the specific criteria employed.) These judgments, which can be based on tone of voice as well as the content of what is said, are quite reliable when made by appropriately trained raters.

It has been shown that it is primarily the presence of critical comments, hostility, and emotional overinvolvement that predicts subsequent relapse by the schizophrenic patient (Vaughn, 1989). At the time the Camberwell Family Interview was designed and the data for these earlier studies collected, no thought had been given to the possible role of attribution theory, and respondents were not explicitly asked for their causal beliefs. All of the causal material was therefore in the form of spontaneous statements by relatives.

To define and rate causal statements, we relied primarily on the Leeds Attributional Coding System (LACS: Stratton et al., 1986). After discussions with Peter Stratton and Christine Barrowclough, a more detailed set of guidelines was drawn up to assist in the identification of causal attributions. For the purposes of this particular study, attributions were defined as statements that identified a factor or factors that produced or contributed to a specific negative outcome. The outcome could be a symptom, the onset of illness, a negative life event or any behavior or characteristic, such as social withdrawal or swearing, judged by the relative to be undesirable. The outcome could not, however, be hypothetical and had to be locatable in time and space. There also had to be a stated or implied causal relation between some factor and the outcome.

To be rated, attributions also had to be the relative's own (not, e.g., statements attributed to the doctor), and they had to be currently held (attributions held in the past were excluded). We included all statements regardless of the degree of doubt the relative expressed about the causal relationship, which could vary between a confident assertion of cause and effect and a tentative suggestion about a contributory causal factor. In another departure from the LACS, which recommends rating each individual cause-effect pair regardless of how many causes are offered for the same event, we chose to rate passages of text that contained relatives' complete explanations of a given outcome.

We initially extracted causal statements directly from the audiotapes of interviews with 25 relatives, 24 of whom had previously been rated as high on one or more of the three crucial indices of expressed emotion (criticism, hostility, and emotional overinvolvement). These relatives made a total of 175 attributions (mean 7, range 1–21). A second sample of 33 relatives was added, some high and some low in expressed emotion, but in this instance attributions were extracted from typed transcripts of the audiotaped interviews. This procedure yielded a further 858 attributions (mean 26, range 1–59). Unfortunately, it is not possible to say why there was the discrepancy in the numbers of attributions extracted. The data from the two samples differed not only in the use of audiotapes versus transcripts but also in the distribution of expressed emotion, in the interviewers used, and to some degree in the nationality of the respondents (but, as we show later, the pattern of attributions was identical in both samples).

What can be concluded is that relatives do make spontaneous causal statements about negative outcomes associated with the ill member of the family. However, in both samples there was considerable individual variation in the number of attributions, and this appeared to reflect two different styles of responding to the semistructured interview format. One, which we may call the *narrative* style, depended on a detailed historical reconstruction of significant episodes ("I said this, then he said that. The next thing that happened was that his father . . ."). Little attempt was typically made to extract key elements for the interviewer, and this style was associated with relatively few causal statements. The alternative *analytic* style involved a much less detailed narrative, with more highlighting of specific events and interpretation of their significance in terms of the respondent's theories. This style was usually associated with a high frequency of causal statements, often of a complex kind.

What Were the Most Common Attributions?

The range of individual causal factors mentioned by relatives was extremely wide (see Brewin et al., in press, for examples), and not readily classifiable by content. Attributions were frequently complex and multifaceted. Thus, one father initially stated, "He drove us mad with the way he'd crawl up and down the stairs, limping, accentuating his weakness . . . deliberately. And yet at hospital he's been walking quite normally." A little later in the interview he elaborated, "When he was a bit low he was walking deliberately a lot slower then . . . he took his time getting up and down the stairs . . . a sympathetic reflex action, he wanted sympathy and love." It is striking how the second attribution introduces a number of relatively uncontrollable causal or temporal elements ("feeling low," "reflex action") into the explanation of what appeared initially to be fully controllable actions. Other relatives clearly possessed interactional models and pointed to the conjunction of various causal factors: "I think she's too placid, she doesn't speak up enough for herself. She's the type that can be pushed around for the sake of peace, but then people can go too far and that's when she'll really let go."

These extracts were then rated using a slightly modified version of the LACS system. The LACS provides for binary ratings of each attribution to be made on five dimensions: stable-unstable, global-specific, internal-external, personal-universal, and controllable-uncontrollable. The LACS has two features that distinguish it from other methods for rating spontaneous data such as the Content Analysis of Verbatim Explanations (Peterson, Schulman, Castellon, & Seligman, in press). First, it has a second "internality" dimension, labeled personal-universal. This captures judgments based on consensus information and differentiates (personal) causes seen as unique to the actor from (universal) causes common to many others in the actor's situation. Ratings on the internal-external dimension, by contrast, are concerned with whether the cause is located within the actor or outside the actor. Second, the LACS provides for separate ratings to be made of whether causes are internal, personal, and controllable to the speaker (the relative in our study) and to the target (the patient).

In all cases we rated the speaker's knowledge, beliefs, and assumptions, not those of the rater or of a notional "man in the street." In addition to the binary coding of each dimension, a third code was available for use whenever the information was in any way ambiguous or insufficient, or when the extracts mentioned causal factors at opposite ends of the same dimension (e.g., they identified a combination of internal and external causes). The reliability of the 3-point ratings in this sample was good, the only exception being the global-specific dimension (see Brewin et al., in press, for details). Because of its poor reliability this dimension is omitted from further analyses.

The overall frequency of different types of attribution was as follows (numbers do not sum to the same totals because on each dimension a different percentage of attributions could not be rated): Attributions were predominantly unstable rather than stable (518 vs. 186). As far as the patient was concerned, they were largely internal rather than external (464 vs. 209), universal rather than personal (503 vs. 333), and uncontrollable rather than controllable (600 vs. 237). As far as the relative was concerned, they were overwhelmingly external rather than internal (904 vs. 39), uncontrollable rather than controllable (961 vs. 50), and universal rather than personal (980 vs. 11). In view of this great imbalance in attributions concerning the relative, further analysis was conducted only on the four attributional dimensions that concerned the patient.

Possible Methodological Artifacts

Mean causal attribution scores were calculated by dividing relatives' total score on a particular dimension by the number of ratable attributions contributing to that total. Only ratings that fell at one or the other end of the dimension were included, and all scores fell in the range 1–2. We then conducted a number of checks to see whether the method of extracting spontaneous causal statements from interview material was subject to any obvious biases. One possible problem was the fact that interview length varied considerably, longer interviews naturally being associated with greater numbers of attributions ($r = .71$, $p < .001$). There was no evidence, however, that the total number of attributions a relative made was systematically related to the direction of their causal beliefs (largest $r = .24$, $p > .05$).

In order to examine whether there were systematic differences in the attributional data obtained from the transcripts and the audiotapes, we

TABLE 11.1. Mean causal attribution scores by type of problem.

	Illness	Negative symptoms	Antisocial behavior	Interpersonal problems	*F* (*df*)
Stable (1)-unstable (2)	1.80	1.67	1.86	1.38	9.82*** (3,75)
Internal (1)-external (2)	1.40	1.23	1.33	1.29	1.08 (3,57)
Personal (1)-universal (2)	1.68	1.65	1.48	1.50	3.07* (3,75)
Controllable (1)-uncontrollable (2)	1.87	1.72	1.51	1.77	5.40** (3,72)

From Brewin et al. in press. Used by permission.
* $p < .05$; ** $p < .01$; *** $p < .001$.

compared a subsample of 15 of each. The two subsamples consisted of relatives matched exactly for being high or low on criticism, hostility, and emotional overinvolvement. A series of *t* tests indicated that there were no significant differences among the subsamples on any of the attributional dimensions (largest $t = 1.53$, $p > .10$).

Another important point about the assessment of attribution-emotion processes in naturalistic settings is that the settings may differ objectively (e.g., Bradbury & Fincham, 1988). Different patterns of attribution may reflect different situational factors as well as differences in relatives' perceptions, and we therefore attempted to classify the events for which relatives made attributions. Although there were insufficient numbers of explanations for positive symptoms such as delusions and hallucinations for these to be included as a separate category, content analysis indicated that 83.3% of the events could be classified as either (a) onset or exacerbation of the illness, or specific symptoms (this category is subsequently referred to as *illness*); (b) the *negative symptoms* of schizophrenia, such as slowness, apathy, self-neglect, and social withdrawal; (c) *antisocial behavior*; (d) *interpersonal problems*. Two independent raters assigning a sample of 163 events to these four categories achieved 87% agreement.

Table 11.1 shows the mean causal attribution score on each dimension for these four different classes of event. The analysis is restricted to those relatives who provided attributions in all four categories. Repeated measures analyses of variance on these data indicated that the different categories of event did not differ on the internality dimension. However, negative interpersonal behaviors were seen as much more stable than illness or antisocial behaviors, with negative symptoms falling in between. Interpersonal and antisocial behaviors were perceived as having more personal causes than were illness and negative symptoms. Finally, antisocial behaviors were perceived as having more controllable causes than the other categories of event.

Attribution and Expressed Emotion

Our eventual sample of 58 relatives consisted of 26 mothers, 11 fathers, 7 husbands, 4 wives, 2 sisters, 3 stepfathers, 1 male guardian, 1 foster mother, 1 foster father, 1 boyfriend, and 1 female cohabitee. Relatives were initially classified as being high or low on the individual expressed emotion (EE) variables. Critical relatives were likely to be more hostile ($r = .58, p < .001$), but emotional overinvolvement (EOI) was unrelated to either criticism or hostility (largest $r = .05, p > .10$). They were then divided into four groups. The *low EE* group ($N = 15$) were low on all expressed emotion indices. The *critical* group ($N = 21$) were high either on criticism (six or more critical comments), on hostility (score of at least 1 on a global rating of hostility), or on both, but were low on emotional overinvolvement. The *high EOI* group ($N = 9$) were high on emotional overinvolvement (score of at least 3 on a global rating of overinvolvement) but low on criticism and hostility. The *mixed high EE* group ($N = 13$) were high on emotional overinvolvement and high either on criticism, hostility, or both.

Table 11.2 gives the mean attribution scores in the four groups of relatives: the low EE, critical, high EOI, and mixed high EE.

A series of one-way ANOVA's were conducted on these data with the EE group as the grouping variable. There were no significant effects of group on the stability or internality scores, but the groups differed markedly on the personal/universal and controllable dimensions. Post hoc comparisons indicated that critical relatives made the most personal attributions, followed by those with mixed high EE. Low EE and high EOI relatives made the most universal attributions and did not differ significantly from each other. The critical relatives also made the most controllable attributions, and the low EE and high EOI relatives the least controllable attributions. Once again, the mixed high EE group fell in between these two extremes.

A series of analyses of covariance were then conducted to rule out the possibility that these results could be explained by the influence of third

TABLE 11.2. Mean attribution scores by expressed emotion group.

	Low EE	Critical	High EOI	Mixed High EE	F (3,54)
Stable(1)-unstable(2)	1.76	1.64	1.84	1.73	1.56
Internal(1)-external(2)	1.26	1.25	1.45	1.34	1.60
Personal(1)-universal(2)	1.74c	1.34a	1.79c	1.53b	11.69*
Controllable(1)-uncontrollable(2)	1.84b	1.50a	1.81b	1.64ab	6.18*

From Brewin et al., in press. Used by permission.
*p < .001.
Means with different subscripts are significantly different ($p < .05$).

variables. Covariates entered at this stage included the length of the interview, but this did not alter the basic ANOVA results reported above. The fact that attributions had been shown to vary both with the relative's emotional characteristics, but also with the type of event explained (see Table 11.1), led us then to consider the possibility that the different groups of relatives were offering attributions for different types of event. We therefore entered the proportion of each individual's attributions that concerned illness, negative symptoms, antisocial behavior, and interpersonal difficulties into the analysis as additional covariates, but the basic ANOVA results were once again unaffected.

Change in Attributions and Emotions

Part of our interview data came from studies attempting to reduce expressed emotion in high EE families with the use of relatives' groups and family therapy sessions (Leff, Berkowitz, et al., 1989; Leff, Kuipers, et al., 1982). In addition to the initial pretreatment interviews included above, we also had available repeat Camberwell Family Interviews carried out 9 months later in these samples. We were therefore able to test whether changes in criticism and hostility are accompanied by corresponding attributional change. To date, we have analyzed before-and-after data on 18 relatives. On levels of criticism, following the intervention, 12 changed from high to low, 3 remained high, and 3 remained low. On hostility, 6 changed from high to low, 3 remained high, and 9 remained low.

In the group as a whole, the only significant change was on the personal-universal dimension. At initial assessment this subsample of high EE relatives differed from the total sample in making predominantly personal attributions, but at follow-up they had changed to making predominantly universal attributions ($\bar{X} = 1.39$ versus $\bar{X} = 1.61$, $t(17) = 2.28$, $p < .05$). The main hypotheses, however, concerned the relation of change in criticism and hostility to change in attributions, and we calculated partial correlations between attribution scores and EE measures at Time 2, controlling for the corresponding attribution and EE scores at Time 1. Reductions in criticism were associated with shifts toward more universal ($r = -.52$, $p < .05$) and more uncontrollable attributions ($r = -.47$, $p < .05$). Reductions in hostility were similarly associated with a shift toward more universal attributions ($r = -.55$, $p < .05$), although the association between changes in hostility and controllability just falls short of significance ($r = -.41$, $p < .10$). As expected from the lack of any association at Time 1, changes in emotional overinvolvement were unrelated to attributional change.

If we consider just the six individuals whose hostility was eliminated following the intervention, their mean attributions changed from being predominantly personal at Time 1 ($\bar{X} = 1.21$) to predominantly universal

($\bar{X}$ = 1.83) at Time 2. Five out of the six changed in this direction (data were missing for the remaining one). Their attributions also changed from being predominantly controllable at Time 1 ($\bar{X}$ = 1.39) to predominantly uncontrollable ($\bar{X}$ = 1.71) at Time 2, once again five out of six showing this pattern. To further illustrate this change I have selected a mother who went from being high on criticism and hostility before the intervention to low on both indices. Before the intervention she made this attribution for her son's behavior: "He leaves the TV on all night, he leaves the lights on all night, he leaves hot taps running and he goes off. . . . That's normal Gary anyway, and that's what I said to Dr. P, 'If you want him to be normal, you won't ever, because he's eccentric'." Her attribution for disturbed behavior after the intervention showed that she was much more aware of her son's mental state and how it might affect him: "Then he started throwing all that furniture about. I mean why didn't he tell them he was frightened of the patients and that's why he was aiming cushions at them?"

Discussion and Conclusions

The overwhelming impression left by our investigations was of the sheer complexity and variety of the attributions made, even by the same individual—and this, we believe, attests to the difficulty relatives frequently experienced in understanding the patient's behavior. Often they appeared to be testing out plausible hypotheses concerning the patient's problems: "I did lose a daughter just over a year ago . . . that may have pulled him down, you know. He was very close to Barbara." Or again: "He's had a pretty rough life in the past, along with his mother being mentally ill. . . . I think she's been ill for years, even before she had the children. . . . It wouldn't be hereditary, would it?" To some degree this reflected the fact that not all relatives knew that a diagnosis of schizophrenia had been made, although all were aware that the patient had received hospital treatment. The effect of the intervention program in generally promoting attributions to more universal causes was probably due to the educational component in which relatives were taught about schizophrenia and its effects. But even when the diagnosis is known, the symptoms are so varied that it may be difficult to decide what is a symptom and what is not. There appears to be almost no aspect of a patient's life and behavior that cannot be touched in some way by the illness.

Also striking was the complexity and sophistication of the beliefs mentioned. We have already noted an example of how causal factors were thought to interact. Causal chains, as described by Kelley (1983), were also common: "He was particularly sensitive about the way he looked, about the fact he was missing out on quite a lot, depressed, because he hadn't any friends. . . . I moved quite a lot after the time when he was born and we never seemed to get settled and build up many friendships with people who had children around Melvyn's age." The existence of such chains raises important questions about the relative role played by distal and proximal causes. For example, is the link between anger and a proximal controllable cause attenuated by an uncontrollable distal cause? It is plausible that the affect aroused by intentional actions with negative consequences could be at least partially diffused if the relative were aware of contributory background causes such as a harsh, unloving parent. Needless to say, these subtleties cannot be captured by questionnaire methods.

In accord with the literature on the situational determinants of attributions, relatives' causal beliefs varied considerably according to whether the outcome was the illness itself or specific manifestations such as negative symptoms or antisocial behavior. These differences reflected variation in such factors as the severity and the temporal and cross-situational stability of behaviors. What was clear was that we were not measuring some kind of general attributional style that was evident in all of the causal judgments made by a relative. Nevertheless, despite the variability introduced by these situational determinants, and despite other attempts to rule out objective differences between the patients involved (see Brewin et al., in press, for details), the type of attribution made was still a powerful predictor of criticism and hostility. Although these data are only correlational, they are consistent with the hypothesis that some emotional attitudes arise at least in part from specific types of causal belief. However, contrary to our prediction that emotionally overinvolved relatives should blame themselves more and blame the patient less, their attributions were not found to differ from those of low EE relatives. Some possible reasons for this are discussed by Brewin et al. (in press).

Further support for the attribution-emotion link came from the data on change during the course of a structured intervention. Although these were preliminary findings on only 18 subjects, the marked correspondence between emotional and attributional change was consistent with the view that criticism and hostility are at least in part mediated by relatives' causal beliefs. Since these data were collected, another study has been published that suggests that by attending meetings of a national self-help organization relatives of patients with schizophrenia can be induced to reattribute the patient's problems more to organic causes and less to an adverse family environment (Medvene & Krauss, 1989). Taken together, the implication is that the mechanism behind existing intervention packages for high EE relatives (e.g., Leff, Berkowitz, et al., 1989; Leff, Kuipers, et al., 1982) is some kind of attribution retraining that brings about change in their previous causal analysis. Obtaining this reattribution will not necessarily be a simple matter, however. There is evidence that merely educating relatives about schizophrenia is insufficient to bring about significant change either in their expressed emotion or in the patient's outcome status (Tarrier et al., 1988), and brief attributional interventions aimed at the families of delinquent adolescents have similarly proven ineffective (Alexander, Waldron, Barton, & Mas, 1989).

The analysis of spontaneous explanations is a relatively new technique that has already generated a variety of interesting findings (Peterson, 1991). It allows the investigator to capture the often-noted richness and complexity of causal beliefs (e.g., Harvey, 1987), rather than restricting them to predetermined causal categories or dimensions. In the present investigation we were able to demonstrate that the attribution-emotion links survived the effects of independent situational influences on attributions. We also found that emotions were asociated with the new personal/universal dimension identified by Stratton et al. (1986), a dimension that largely reflects consensus beliefs among family members about the frequency of the behavior in question. The fact that comparable differences were not obtained on the internal/external dimension reinforces the view that they are conceptually separate dimensions and makes a persuasive argument for using the Leeds Attributional Coding Scheme in future studies.

A number of limitations of the method must also be noted. Perhaps chief amongst these is the fact that, because subjects do not all generate similar quantities or types of data, there is no way of knowing whether their spontaneous attributions always reflect equally well the structure of their causal beliefs. A related concern is whether mean scores based on a small number of spontaneous attributions are as useful an estimate of causal beliefs as mean scores based on many attributions. Data we present elsewhere (Brewin et al., in press) indicate that means based on small numbers of attributions do introduce noise and should be treated with caution. Yet another issue is whether attributions for certain key events, which may have individual predictive power, are swamped by aggregating data without regard to the events being explained. At present there is no evidence pertinent to this concern. Thus, although the sampling of spontaneous attributions appears to be a promising method, and one that can yield rich and interesting data, it should be complemented by standardized techniques of eliciting attributions.

Our data further support the hypothesis that at least some negative family emotions, such as criticism and hostility, are intimately linked with attributional processes (although other emotions, such as overinvolvement, may not be attributionally mediated). Like the findings of Butler et al. (1986), these data were obtained under conditions of considerable attributional uncertainty in relatives, which may have accounted for the ability of the structured intervention to bring about an alteration in causal beliefs. In terms of a recent theory of cognitive change processes (Brewin, 1989), the intervention may be presumed to have acted by correcting misconceptions in verbally accessible knowledge about schizophrenia in general and about the behavior of the ill patient in particular.

It remains to be seen whether in cases of marital distress, where there is generally no ill relative and hence less uncertainty, commensurate attributional change is brought about through therapy. It is, however, noteworthy that attributional theories of the emotions were supported in a context where relatives had a duty of care to a patient who in almost all cases they knew to have received hospital treatment. It appears that in this situation relatives do not behave like Sharrock et al.'s (1990) professional caregivers but are influenced emotionally by their causal beliefs. Given the importance to health of family processes, it seems likely that family reattribution training may in the future come to be seen as an important adjunct to the treatment of a large number of physical and psychiatric conditions.

References

Alexander, J.F., Waldron, H.B., Barton, C., & Mas, C.H. (1989). The minimizing of blaming attributions and behaviors in delinquent families. *Journal of Consulting and Clinical Psychology, 57*, 19–24.

Andrews, B., & Brown, G.W. (1988). Marital violence in the community: A biographical approach. *British Journal of Psychiatry, 153*, 305–312.

Bradbury, T.N., & Fincham, F.D. (1988). Assessing spontaneous attributions in marital interaction: Methodological and conceptual considerations. *Journal of Social and Clinical Psychology, 7*, 122–130.

Bradbury, T.N., & Fincham, F.D. (1990). Attributions in marriage: Review and critique. *Psychological Bulletin, 107*, 3–33.

Brewin, C.R. (1988). *Cognitive foundations of clinical psychology*. London: Erlbaum.

Brewin, C.R. (1989). Cognitive change processes in psychotherapy. *Psychological Review, 96*, 379–394.

Brewin, C.R., & Antaki, C. (1987). An analysis of ordinary explanations in clinical attribution research. *Journal of Social and Clinical Psychology, 5*, 79–98.

Brewin, C.R., MacCarthy, B., Duda, K., & Vaughn, C.E. (in press). Attribution and expressed emotion in the relatives of patients with schizophrenia. *Journal of Abnormal Psychology*.

Bryer, J.B., Nelson, B.A., Miller, J.B., & Krol, P.A. (1987). Childhood sexual and physical abuse as factors in adult psychiatric illness. *American Journal of Psychiatry, 144*, 1426–1430.

Butler, R.J., Brewin, C.R., & Forsythe, W.I. (1986). Maternal attributions and tolerance for nocturnal enuresis. *Behaviour Research and Therapy, 24*, 307–312.

Gotlib, I.H. (1990). An interpersonal systems approach to the conceptualisation and treatment of depression. In R.E. Ingram (Ed.), *Contemporary psychological approaches to depression*. New York: Plenum.

Harris, T.O., Brown, G.W., & Bifulco, A. (1986). Loss of parent in childhood and adult psychiatric disorder: The role of lack of adequate parental care. *Psychological Medicine, 16*, 641–659.

Harvey, J.H. (1987). Attributions in close relationships: Research and theoretical developments. *Journal of Social and Clinical Psychology, 5*, 420–434.

Jacobson, A., & Richardson, B. (1987). Assault experiences of 100 psychiatric inpatients: Evidence of the need for routine enquiry. *American Journal of Psychiatry, 144*, 908–913.

Jacobson, N.S., Holtzworth-Munroe, A., & Schmaling, K.B. (1989). Marital therapy and spouse involvement in the treatment of depression, agoraphobia, and alcoholism. *Journal of Consulting and Clinical Psychology, 57*, 5–10.

Kelley, H.H. (1983). Perceived causal structures. In J. Jaspars, F.D. Fincham & M. Hewstone (Eds.), *Attribution theory and research: Conceptual, developmental, and social dimensions* (pp. 343–369). London: Academic Press.

Leff, J., Berkowitz, R., Shavit, N., Strachan, A., Glass I., & Vaughn, C.E. (1989). A trial of family therapy versus a relatives group for schizophrenia. *British Journal of Psychiatry, 154*, 58–66.

Leff, J., Kuipers, L., Berkowitz, R., Eberlein-Vries, R., & Sturgeon, D. (1982). A controlled trial of social intervention in the families of schizophrenic patients. *British Journal of Psychiatry, 141*, 121–134.

Leff, J., & Vaughn, C.E. (1985). *Expressed emotion in familes*. London: Guilford Press.

Medvene, L.J., & Krauss, D.H. (1989). Causal attributions and parent-child relationships in a self-help group for families of the mentally ill. *Journal of Applied Social Psychology, 19*, 1413–1430.

O'Leary, K.D. & Beach, S.R.H. (1990). Marital therapy: A viable treatment for depression and marital discord. *American Journal of Psychiatry, 147*, 183–186.

Peterson, C. (1991). The meaning and measurement of explanatory style. *Psychological Inquiry*, *2*, 1–10.

Peterson, C., Schulman, P., Castellon, C., & Seligman, M.E.P. (in press). The explanatory style scoring manual. In C.P.Smith (Ed.), *Thematic content analysis for motivation and personality research*. New York: Cambridge University Press.

Sharrock, R., Day, A., Qazi, F., & Brewin, C.R. (1990). Explanations by professional care staff, optimism, and helping behaviour: An application of attribution theory. *Psychological Medicine, 20*, 849–855.

Stratton, P., Heard, D., Hanks, H.G.I., Munton, A.G., Brewin, C.R., & Davidson, C. (1986). Coding causal beliefs in natural discourse. *British Journal of Social Psychology, 25*, 299–313.

Tarrier, N., Barrowclough, C., Vaughn, C., Bamrah, J.S., Porceddu, K., Watts, S., & Freeman, H. (1988). The community management of schizophrenia: A controlled trial of a behavioural intervention with families to reduce relapse. *British Journal of Psychiatry, 153*, 532–542.

Vaughn, C.E. (1989). Expressed emotion in family relationships. *Journal of Child Psychology and Psychiatry, 30*, 13–22.

Vaughn, C.E., & Leff, J. (1976a). The influence of family and social factors in the course of psychiatric illness. *British Journal of Psychiatry, 129*, 125–137.

Vaughn, C.E., & Leff, J. (1976b). The measurement of expressed emotion in the families of psychiatric patients. *British Journal of Social and Clinical Psychology, 15*, 423–429.

Vaughn, C.E., Snyder, K.S., Freeman, W., Jones, S., & Falloon, I.R.H. (1984). Family factors in schizophrenic relapse. *Archives of General Psychiatry, 41*, 1169–1177.

Weiner, B. (1985). "Spontaneous" causal thinking. *Psychological Bulletin, 97*, 74–84.

Weiner, B. (1986). *An attributional theory of motivation and emotion*. New York: Springer-Verlag.

12
Attributions and Apologies in Letters of Complaint to Hospitals and Letters of Response

SALLY LLOYD-BOSTOCK

Formal complaints against hospitals (in common with formal complaints in most areas) are typically made in letters, and the response to the complainant is typically a letter back. A complaint file, therefore, does not merely contain a record of the complaint: it contains the complaint itself. From the complainant's perspective, the files contain the essence of the story. The process of complaining, from the complainant's perspective, consists in that exchange of letters. The complainant's letter *is* his or her complaint. The letter back to the complainant is, very often, all the complainant gets.

Access to hospital complaint files therefore offers the opportunity to study the dynamics of complaining—the act of complaining and the act of responding to a complaint. Taken together, the interchanges between complainant and respondent might be described in Schönbach's terminology as an account epoisode (Schönbach, Chap. 3, this volume). In the letter of complaint, the hospital is held responsible for the violation of a normative expectation held by the complainant (Phase 1—the *failure event*); and the complainant frequently reproaches the hospital or responds in some other way as indicated in Schönbach's Phase 2—the *reproach phase*. The reply to the complainant constitutes Phase 3—the *account phase*. However, Schönbach's Phase 4—the *evaluation phase*—is usually absent from the files. In the majority of cases, the complainant does not communicate again with the hospital. If he or she comes to an evaluation of the account and/or the hospital in the light of the account, that evaluation is not usually communicated to the hospital. From the point of view of the hospital staff concerned, the complaint has gone away following the reply to the complainant, and the file is regarded as closed. Interestingly, the absence of any further communication from the complainant struck us, as researchers, as leaving the episode incomplete. We are conducting interviews with complainants that will fill the gap in the story by asking how they felt about the replies they received.

Complaining to hospitals can be viewed as a social act that takes place within the relationship between the complainant and the hospital staff concerned. Relationships between complainants and hospital staff take rather varied forms. They can be long-term or short-term, close or remote, and continuing or noncontinuing. The circumstances that bring people into contact with hospitals are sometimes such that their relationships are emotionally charged and prone to become distressed. There is often a background of stress, anxiety, or grief in the complainant's life arising from whatever led to the episode of hospital contact; and the complainant may be experiencing feelings of powerlessness, anger, or confusion. Even if the circumstances are a happy event, such as giving birth to a healthy child, few people enjoy being in the hospital.

The pursuit of complaints and negligence claims indicates a relationship that is perceived as unbalanced. In equity theory terms, one party (the complainant) views the other (the hospital, or member of the hospital staff) as a harmdoer, or wrongdoer, and takes a particular kind of social action toward remedy. It is a relationship into which the law is likely to intervene. First, the process of handling complaints against a public body such as the National Health Service is governed by law; second, where a negligence claim is involved, the law of torts becomes relevant. Previous research on complaining in a wide range of contexts has shown the relative weakness of the complainant's position (e.g., Nader, 1980). Although the law in both the above areas seems at first glance to provide protection and remedy for the complainant or victim, it is questionable whether these are its effects in practice.

The method of analysis capitalizes on the fact that the process of complaining, investigating complaints, and responding to complaints typically takes place totally in writing. It consists in categorizing phrases or passages from letters of complaint, and their replies. The acts of complaining and responding can be broken down into component acts that are being carried out or attempted in the letters. Accounts offered by each side can be analyzed as packages of attrtibutions about the correct state of affairs. For example, letters may describe events, argue that they are complaintworthy, offer justifications, portray the complainant as incompetent; apologize, and so on. The framework of analysis draws on concepts from attribution theory, the social psychology of explanation and accounting, and from Goffman's work on apologies (e.g., Kelley, 1967; Goffman, 1971; Antaki, 1988).

The chapter is based on in-depth analysis of approximately 30 hospital complaint files, together with the reading of a larger number, conducted as the first phase of continuing research on complaints against National Health hospitals in Great Britain. A multidisciplinary research group at the Centre for Socio-legal Studies in Oxford is studying complaints against hospitals from the perspectives of psychology, economics, and law. Psychological questions include the following: What motivates individuals to complain? What factors affect the satisfaction of complainants? How does the process of complaining affect the crystallization of a complaint?

Complaints against British hospitals are something rather different from complaints against hospitals in the United States, not least because of the existence of the National Health Service (NHS) in Great Britain. Patients in the NHS are not consumers to be wooed and kept satisfied. It is very noticeable that hospitals in the United States are much more concerned that their patients should feel they would use the hospital again or recommend it to their friends. In Great Britain, complaining against a hospital is more like making a complaint against the police than making a normal consumer complaint. Moreover, because patients have not usually paid anything at all for treatment they receive, they are not prompted to complain by being sent a bill—a frequent stimulus to complaint in the United States.

I first fill in briefly some background on hospital complaints procedures in Great Britain, the nature of the complaints that are made under those procedures, and the relationship between complaints and negligence claims. I then describe the research in more detail.

Hospital Complaints Procedures

Procedures for handling complaints against National Health hospitals in Great Britain are governed by Department of Health circulars. Circulars issued under the 1985 Hospital Complaints Act have statutary backing, which means that Health Authorities have been obliged to establish a complaints procedure along the lines dictated by the Department of Health.

The complaints procedure currently in operation is largely governed by HC(88)37. According to this, each unit (usually consisting of one hospital) must have a "designated officer" who is in charge of handling complaints. The designated officer is required to coordinate responses to a particular complaint, asking for information from the staff involved in the treatment and on that basis composing a reply to the complainant.

If the complainant is still dissatisfied, the designated officer may prepare another reply, or arrange a meeting between the hospital staff, clinicians, and the complainant. If still dissatisfied, the complainant can do one of two things. If the complaint relates to clinical aspects of care, then the complainant can refer it to the Regional Medical Officer. If it concerns administrative matters (i.e., nonclinical), he or she can refer it to the Health Service Commissioner, or Ombudsman. The Regional Medical Officer has the discretion, after meeting with the complainant, to refer the matter to an Independent Professional Review Panel made up of two peers of the consultant involved. The panel reports to the Regional Health Authority on its findings.

The first stage in the process is a *formal* complaint from a complainant—that is, a complaint made in writing or (much less often) orally to the designated complaints officer. There is no filter at this stage as to the substance of complaints, which means that complaints going through the complaints machinery may concern anything from those that on most criteria would be regarded as somewhat trivial to the extremely serious. Probably the most trivial complaint we have so far encountered was a complaint from a National Health patient that his boiled egg was smaller than the boiled egg served to a private patient.

People complain about a tremendous range of things. Around one half of all hospital complaints are nonclinical. Some of the most common are complaints about waiting times and about rudeness of staff. For example, a list of complaints about one hospital over a 3-month period included the following:

Waiting time at out-patients
Missing flowers
Unavailability of funding for a specialist operation for a deaf child
Closing of a ward
Rudeness of staff
Failure to provide treatment because of breakdown of machinery
Inadequacy of aftercare arrangements made by the hospital
Laziness of portering staff
Failure of an ambulance to turn up
Hospital waiting lists
Reduction of services because of cuts
Charges for contact lens solution
Unavailability of pioneering operations on the NHS
Blindness caused by alleged medical negligence of junior medical staff

It is interesting to note that most formal complaints are made, not by a patient, but on behalf of a patient by someone else. That person is most often a woman, usually the patient's mother, wife, or daughter.

Legal Advice, Complaints, and Negligence Claims

The complainant may sometimes obtain the help of an agent such as a member of parliament, or the local Community Health Council; but it is rare for the complainant to use a lawyer. (Community Health Councils are part of the NHS. Among other things, their staff members are available to provide assistance and advice to patients with complaints.) If a complainant does use a lawyer, the complaint is likely to be channeled into the Health Authority's system for processing negligence claims and to be responded to as a claim or potential claim, bringing in the Health Authority's own lawyer and doctors' defense societies.

It is tempting to think of complaints against hospitals as mini-negligence claims or as potential negligence claims—part of the rest of an iceberg of dissatisfaction and potential litigation, whose tip is those claims that patients actually bring. It is true that some negligence claims originate as complaints and that some complaints could become quite major negligence claims but never do so. But where complaints against British National Health hospitals are concerned, this is a very partial picture of what passes through hospital complaint procedures. Of 113 claims made in one district, only 17 started out as complaints. The most usual route was straight in as a claim.

Although claims and complaints, in Great Britain at least, are two different things, the existence of the tort system for medical negligence cases does appear to affect the processing of complaints. Public law in relation to hospital complaints operates in the shadow of private law: fear of claims evidently influences the processing of complaints, to the detriment of both complainant satisfaction and quality of services. The defensive way in which complaints are responded to by the hospitals suggests that hospital administrators do tend to think of complaints as some kind of mini-claim, and this casts a shadow over their relationship with the complainant. Most complaints are handled by attempts to dismiss the complaint by denying, excusing, or justifying the events complained of. A complaint is regarded as successfully handled if the complainant goes away. Only rarely are complaints regarded as providing useful feedback from patients.

Research Questions

As mentioned above, my interest within the project is the complainant's perspective. There are three broad research questions here: First, who complains and why? This question is set against the fact that the vast majority of potential grievances are never acted on. Why do certain people complain? The question is of some importance if complaints are to be used in any way as an information resource for quality management purposes. Complaints are clearly a biased source of information, but, more precisely, in what ways is the information biased?

Second, how do complaints crystallize? The hypothesis here is that grievances do not come into being fully formed when the event in question occurs. They crystallize over time—in the sense of becoming clearer, harder, and more fixed—as a result of such things as social contacts, the procedures that exist for handling complaints, and the experience of using those procedures. Complaint procedures and responses to complainants may themselves actively contribute to the crystallization of a complaint, for example, by structuring the perceptions of potential complainants and giving momentum to their complaints. In some cases the complainant may be propelled toward bringing a negligence claim.

Third, what features of procedures and outcomes affect the satisfaction of complainants? Do complainants get what they want?

Important data on these questions will come from interviews with complainants and a matched group of noncomplainants, which are being planned as the next stage of research. But the fact that so much takes place in writing raises the possibility of analyzing letters to explore questions about the dynamics of complaining itself.

This possibility casts a fascinating slant on the questions raised above. To understand why people complain and what affects their satisfaction, it is clearly important to understand what they are doing when they complain. Are they trying to get something specific done in response? Do they want something, or is the complaint an end in itself? Through study of the letters themselves, we can ask; What is the complainant actually doing when he or she complains? What is the respondent doing when he or she replies to the complaint?

One would obviously expect the satisfaction of complainants to be affected by whether or not they get what they want in response to their complaint. But do they say what they want? Do they *know* what they want? Or is it like what most people say about art: "I don't know anything about art but I know what I like." It may be that complainants do not always know what they want but know when they (don't) get it. Perhaps we need to take the question back a step. Rather than asking whether complainants get what they want, perhaps we should ask: Do they actually want anything? How crystallized are complaints at the stage a letter of complaint is written? Are complainants clear about what happened, their view of it, and what they think should be done now? Techniques of handling consumer complaints recognize that very often the complaint is a "blasting off" with no further specific goal. The most important part of satisfying the complainant is to agree that something worthy of complaint has occurred and to indicate that the matter is taken seriously (Finkelman & Goland, 1990).

Conversely, in looking at letters of reply, one can ask what the hospital administrator (or other respondent) is doing in the reply. Is he or she trying to mollify the complainant, to offer help or redress, or to undermine and dismiss the complaint? Is the administrator interested in correcting the situation? Or in making the complaint go away? Again, because the letter of reply is usually all the complainant gets, analysis of what social acts the respondent is performing in the reply should help explain the complainant's satisfaction or dissatisfaction with the complaints procedure and its outcome.

The Framework of Analysis

The analysis of letters initially aimed to document the range of different things that complainants and responders to complaints do in their letters. Subsequently, we hope to to extract an extensive data set from a sample of approximately 200 complaint files, which can be related to interview data on such variables as the satisfaction or otherwise of the complainant.

In essence, the analysis consists of categorizing phrases or passages from letters. Taken together, each exchange of letters between complainant and respondent constitutes an account episode (Schönbach, Chap. 3, this volume). As mentioned above, the framework that has been developed draws on concepts from attribution theory, the social psychology of explanation and accounting, and from Goffman's work on apologies. Thus, much of what complainants are doing in their letters of complaint is arguing for the complaintworthiness of an event and justifying the fact that they are complaining. Attribution theory provides a framework for analyzing ways in which the causes of behavior, events, or circumstances are located in people or in sources external to people, for example, by pointing to ways in which the behavior or event is distinctive, stable, and controllable. Replies frequently contain some form of apology. Goffman's analysis of the components of a true apology provides a framework for analyzing apologies into full apologies, and incomplete, or pseudoapologies (Goffman, 1971).

The actual categories used in the analysis were derived from many hours spent reading complaints files in five hospitals. This stage of the work was carried out with the assistance of a second researcher, Linda Mulcahy. Because the procedure was necessarily somewhat subjective, a third researcher, Ann Bullen, provided a check. She was given 20 letters of complaint and their replies. Using cards, she was asked to split the content into different things that it seemed to her the complainant or respondent was doing, continuing until she had categorized everything in the letters. She independently arrived at a very similar set of categories.

Letters of Complaint

Complaints, as we have seen, vary considerably. Not only the substance of the complaint varies, but also the way it is expressed, the reasons the complainant gives for complaining, the extent to which the complainant pursues it, and many other aspects.

Eight major categories of statement emerged from the study of letters of complaint: statements setting out the substance of the complaint, statements about why what occurred was worthy of complaint, statements of action taken by the complainant to correct the situation, consensus/distinctiveness information locating the cause of the complaint in the event, statements explaining or justifying the act of complaining, statements about the complainant's status, anticipated excuses or justifications that might be offered, and statements of what the complainant wants.

Every letter, by definition, contains a statement of what is complained of, which may be anything from a short sentence to a lengthy account running to several pages and documenting events with times and dates. This is commonly followed by supplementary evidence of the event's seriousness. Complainants may give reasons why what occurred was important to them or why a seemingly trivial event is not in fact so. Thus, the offhand manner of a member of staff is significant "because my mother is 80 years old, frail and suffering from angina and osteoporosis. . . . I wonder what effect such a man has on people visiting patients about whom they are desperately worried. . . ." Or (concerning some lost flowers); "It may seem a small thing to you, but it was very important to me." Complainants often remark that dignity, politeness, and comfort are important to patients. For example,

> I had to use the toilet in the same room. Again, another person . . . came in and out of the room part of the time and though I felt almost too ill to care I found it very humiliating. . . . I realise that to the hospital staff this is a familiar routine but to the patient it is not. . . . I left the hospital feeling angry at being degraded. I only pray that I'll never be asked to go through this experience again because it would take very much persuasion.

Reference may be made to worse outcomes that could have occurred, though nothing happened this time, and to expected professional standards—doctors should know what they are doing; nurses should have a more caring attitude. For example:

> As you should know, any personal matter should be considered confidential and I would expect you and your staff to realise that a matter that is connected with anything as private as pregnancy must be treated as a highly confidential mattter.

The complainant's or patient's feelings are commonly mentioned—I was disgusted, embarrassed, broken-hearted, and so on.

Consensus and distinctiveness information is particularly commonly offered. Letters of complaint frequently include statements that seem designed to preempt the recipient of the complaint from explaining the complaint as somehow a product, not of objective, complaintworthy circumstances, but of the complainant's complaining nature. Statements may be made that the complainant is not someone who usually complains or that other people also found the event or circumstances complaintworthy, thus showing that the complaint is not simply a product of the complainant as a person but of the external circumstances. Complainants may praise other aspects of their hospital experience, thus providing distinctiveness information. They may the refer to the fact that they are complaining as something they feel compelled to do, or they may give altruistic reasons for complaining—"I wouldn't want anybody else to have to go through what I have been through over the past few days. . . ."

Anticipation of excuses from the Health Authority may again be designed to preempt or lessen their effectiveness, by signaling in advance that the complainant is aware of the possible explanation, but still wishes to complain. Writing "I know emergencies must take precedence, but surely a six hour wait is unacceptable" makes it less possible for the hospital simply to reply that emergencies must take precedence.

Although letters of complaint often contain relatively large amounts of material arguing for the complaintworthiness of the event complained of, complainants are much less often specific about what they want from the complaint. Often, nothing is said at all, or there may be a general statement that "something should be done," or "you should know. . . ." It may be that in some cases the complaint is an exercise in itself, as is recognized in the consumer world. Some complainants do specifically state that they want an apology, an explanation, compensation, or their appointment sorted out. Others may wish primarily for their complaint to be acknowledged and taken seriously. The interview phase of the research will provide an opportunity to pursue some of these questions further.

In addition to analyzing particular phrases, the analysis aims to characterize complaints more broadly. Certain clusters of complaints emerge from the data. For example, one cluster is complaints following a death. Consistent with other findings in the United States on negligence claims, it seems that sometimes complaining may be a reaction to the death. It may be that certain kinds of illness or treatment similarly tend to give rise to complaints. Such complaints may not necessarily concern treatment; a daughter very distressed at her mother's illness may complain about the attitude of the staff or even parking difficulties.

Some complaints are a more general statement of problems and difficulties with life, containing a catalog of woes, perhaps with a general plea for help. For example, a long letter from a woman about her husband's poor recovery after an operation included this passage:

> Here I am with my pension cut nearly in half with the same bills to pay as well as having to keep buying more and more clothes for my husband. His clothes keep having to be in the wash as well as getting torn trying to get them on him . . . [and so on for two handwritten sheets].

Or again,

> It has made me a widow and I am broken hearted and this treatment that he had in the last weeks of his life does not make me feel any better . . . the dirty dinner dishes well into the afternoon . . . I was very tired when I got home, after all I am 67 and did the journey too. . . .

Complaints also vary in specificity. Some are quite global—"the dreadful time I had on Ward X"; others are very specific—"the missed fracture on the x-ray."

Replies to Letters of Complaint

The converse of the analytical framework developed for complainants' letters is often appropriate. The complainant is putting the case that something was complaintworthy; the response corrects the facts stated by the complainant or in other ways undermines the complaintworthiness of the event. This is sometimes done by undermining the competence of the complainant, implying that he or she should have complained earlier or that he or she doesn't understand medical matters. It is common for details of the complainant's account to be corrected, even if the facts corrected are not relevant to the substance of the complaint, for example, names of medical conditions, dates, or details of treatment. Doubt may be cast on whether the event occurred at all, and statements made to the effect that if the event did occur, it was not complaintworthy.
For example:

> I don't think the bath would actually have been uncleaned for the whole week [the patient] was in hospital—but it is certainly possible that the bath wasn't clean whenever she went.

Or again:

> I know no-one likes having a barium enema done, but we do try to be as nice as we can.... One has to expect a little bit of non-privacy in an x-ray department.... As for the room opening from the room where you were examined, this is the main dark room and film sorting area and we cannot expect people there to be entirely quiet.

In the same way as complainants attempt to preempt the implication that they are complaining people, respondents may comment that no one else has complained. Explanations (or excuses) for events often place the matter out of the hospital's hands—for example, the hospital is aware of the problems, but is underfunded.

While the majority of replies to complainants are defensive, not all are so. Some replies to complainants thank them for the useful feedback, agree that the event complained of occurred and was unacceptable, apologize *that it happened*, and set out the steps that are being taken to prevent a recurrence. These replies shine out from the rest; interviews will reveal whether complainants who receive them are more satisfied.

In analyzing responses, particular attention is being paid to apologies. Goffman (1971) suggests that apologies have several elements, including that the person making the apology must acknowledge that something blameworthy occurred and must sympathize with the censure of others. Many of the apologies offered in letters to complainants might be called pseudoapologies. They contain such words as "apology," "apologise" or "sorry", but they do not acknowledge that anything complaintworthy happened and indeed often manage to imply that it is a little strange of the complainant to complain, or shows his or her ignorance. The phrasing of the apology itself is important. If an apology states, "I apologise *if you felt that*, the doctor was rude," it does not actually concede that the doctor was rude. Also important is whether or not the rest of the letter acknowledges that something complaintworthy happened.

Here is an actual example of a real apology rather than a pseudo apology (at the end of a letter acknowledging that the complainant is quite right):

> Can I also offer to you and your sister my apologies and assurances that we will do everything we can to avoid inflicting such discomfort on our patients in the future

Another, concerning a rude remark by a nurse:

> We have identified the person concerned. . . .
> May I once again offer you my apologies on behalf of the hospital and nursing staff and thank you for drawing the problem to my attention, as without important feedback we may never have known.

Contrast these with some pseudoapologies, which do not acknowledge that anything worthy of complaint has actually occurred, let alone give any indication of intention to correct the situation:

> The nurse in question was very sorry *if you found* her manner to be one of indifference as this was certainly not her intention.

> I am sorry *that you felt as* you did, but we try to be as kind as we can and I think that our staff go out of their way to do this

> I apologise for *any misunderstanding that may have arisen* over the reason for her visit.

What at first glance appears to be an apology may not in fact be one at all, but rather an expression of regret over something noncomplaintworthy—often that a patient has not recovered well or, indeed, that the complainant has complained:

> I was sorry to receive your letter and learn of your husband's continued illhealth.

> I am sorry that you felt you had to complain.

> I am sorry that you don't like the new chairs.

The predominantly defensive and unrepentant response of hospitals to complainants may, as already suggested, owe something to the fear of negligence claims. The reaction of the hospital is to admit nothing. On the analysis offered here, the attitude is probably counterproductive. When complainants do state what they want, it is very rarely compensation—it is an explanation, an investigation, someone disciplined, an assurance that the event will not recur, an individual punished, a (genuine) apology. It is probable that some complainants go on to litigate because they cannot achieve these things through the complaints machinery. The law in this context would appear to be worsening interpersonal relationships through its efforts to repair them.

References

Antaki, C. (Ed.). (1988). *Analysing Everyday Explanation: A Casebook of Methods*. London: Sage.

Finkelman, D. & Goland, T. (1990). The Case of the Complaining Customer. *Harvard Business Review, 90*(3), 9–25.

Goffman, E. (1971). *Relations in Public*. Harmondsworth, England: Penguin.

Kelley, H.H. (1967). Attribution theory in social psychology. In D. Levine (Ed.), *Nebraska Symposium on Motivation*, Vol. 15. Lincolin, NE: University of Nebraska Press.

Nader, L. (Ed.). (1980). *No Access to Law*. New York: Academic Press.

13
Accounts of Intimate Support Relationships in the Early Months of Mothering

ROSALEEN CROGHAN and DOROTHY MIELL

If mothering is difficult, the fault lies not in individual failings, but in the social structure in which mothering occurs. (Wearing 1984)

Introduction

The months following the birth of the first child represent an acute transitional period in which mothers are called upon to reassess existing accounts of their personal relationships and to revise their views of parenting (Cowan, Cowan, Coie, & Coie 1978; La Rossa & La Rossa, 1981). A number of factors will have an effect on mothers' ability to successfully navigate this transition, among them the stress that mothers experience at this time and their access to and use of support. Parents under social and psychological stress are more likely, at the worst, to become physically abusive and, at the best, to have impaired relationships with their children (Gelles, 1979). Beyond such relational factors, however, are other structural factors, such as poverty, poor housing, unemployment, and isolation, which have been repeatedly associated with depression and with impairment of the mother-child relationship (Graham, 1984).

In this chapter research is reported that examines mothers' accounts of how such relational and structural factors affect their experience in the early months of mothering. In particular, we will be concentrating on the intimate relationships that might be expected to provide mothers with the most support. The close support relationships that surround mothers in the early months play an important part in shaping the quality of the mothers' experience. These relationships will be influenced by ideological expectations that define both the amount of stress that a mother may be assumed to experience and the acceptable limits of support. While offering a measure of practical help and support, intimate relationships can also bring stress because they impose their own expectations on the mothers' role. Relationships with the sexual partner in particular can bring conflict because they are based on a sex role ideology that characterizes motherhood as intrinsically rewarding and fathers' contributions as an optional extra, given as a gift not as a right (La Rossa & La Rossa, 1981). Thus, a relationship previously seen as equitable may, after the birth, be characterized by a shift back to traditional gender roles and conflict over the imbalance in parental workload (Bloode & Wolfe, 1960).

The way in which mothers define their role and the limits they place upon their responsibilities will profoundly affect their expectations of support and their view of themselves as parents. The accounts mothers give of their experiences following the first birth, and in particular of their relationship with their sexual partner, are indicative of their struggle to come to terms with the unequal allocation of power and status within the context of a close and notionally reciprocal relationship (Pleck, 1979, 1982).

The Study

The accounts discussed in this chapter are taken from interviews with 25 first-time mothers recruited in an English university city in the year following the birth of their first child. Because it was hypothesized that early experience would influence later patterns of support, the mothers were drawn from two distinct groups. Ten came from disrupted family backgrounds (defined as a period of 12 months or more in residential care before the age of 16) and 15 were from more stable backgrounds with no such early history. Mothers from both disrupted and stable backgrounds were included in order to contrast the support networks of each and to examine the way in which the greater fragmentation in the "ex-care" mothers' networks, together with their lower social and economic status, affected their parenting experience.

The "stable" group was contacted through postnatal clinics, and the ex-care mothers through statutory and voluntary agencies dealing with disadvantaged parents. The mothers ranged in age from 17 to 33. The stable mothers were between 19 and 33 years old with a mean age of 26.33, whereas the ex-care mothers were considerably younger, aged between 17 and 25 with a mean age of 19.5. The mothers fell into three broad categories according to their sexual relationships. They were either married (12 of stable group and 3 of ex-care group) or in stable cohabitations (defined as a cohabitation of more than 6 months' uninterrupted duration; 2 stable, 1 ex-care), or single parents (1 stable, 6 ex-care). Among the married group, 10 stable and 3 ex-care mothers had been married less than 2 years.

Data were collected by means of a combination of in-depth interviews and a 24-hour time use diary, which recorded both mother's activities and the allocation of responsibility for the child in the sample period. The approach adopted here has been essentially to view mothers' accounts as valid within their own terms, rather than assessing their accuracy as representations of internal dispositions. In this we follow Wilkinson's (1981) suggestion that, "If we are attempting to study a person who actively interprets reality in her own terms, then her account of those terms is the only acceptable primary source of data". As a result of taking this approach, interviews were designed to allow mothers to express and examine any inherent contradictions within their accounts. Such contradictions were seen as a reflection of the complex interaction between social and ideological influences on what are usually conceived of as private intimate relationships.

In the accounts they offer of their parenting experience, mothers are engaged in making sense of and reconstructing their experience in the context of their personal relationships. It is therefore necessary to understand the function of accounts and their relationship to the social and emotional context in which they occur (Gergen & Gergen, 1987). This dictates a focus that moves away from a search for the "real self" and an assessment of the accuracy of accounts, toward the way in which discourse is used to *construct* and *mediate* meaning (Potter & Wetherall, 1987). Because there is no assumption here that the self exists as a unified, relatively discoverable entity, there can be no question of assessing the accuracy of accounts of the representation of that self. Instead, the variability in accuracy is seen as evidence of the range of strategies that mothers employ in the construction and interpretation of events.

Acknowledging this "indexicality of discourse" leads us to focus upon the way in which the information available to individuals and its salience for them will vary in different social situations. As Jones & Nisbett (1971) have shown, the different perspectives of actors and observers in interactional situations will lead them to emphasize different features in the social context. Researchers, in the role of observer, have tended to focus on internal and dispositional attributions at the expense of environmental attributions, whereas the actor, with greater access to knowledge of her particular situation, is instead inclined to emphasize the immediate situational context. Psychology has traditionally been concerned with revealing the internal dispositions of actors and has underestimated the bias inherent in the perspective of the observer. In order to take account of both relationships and structure, accounts need to be placed in their social and situational context, viewing them as both internally *and* externally derived (Nisbett & Wilson, 1977).

Motherhood as Work: Evidence from the Time-Use Diary

Women are habitually cast in the role of caregiver, whether of young children or of the sick and elderly. They are expected to perform these tasks out of love and are not assumed to need rewards in the form of either status or remuneration (Graham, 1983). Motherhood as work is characterized by long hours of often monotonous and unremitting labor that is disproportionately allocated to women (Oakley, 1976). In addition to the maternal role, women are laden with various role prescriptions that place conflicting demands on their time and energy as they are expected to fulfill the function of emotional caretaker for the family (Graham, 1984). Pleck (1979) observes this to be the case whatever the woman's paid work commitments are outside the home.

The diary data was analyzed with reference to both the extent of mothers' workload and to the relative allocation of tasks within the household. By examining the allocation of work and leisure over a 24-hour period it was possible to make a more accurate comparison of the maternal and paternal contribution and to avoid the pitfalls of other studies that have looked at the allocation of tasks rather than at the distribution of work and leisure. A more accurate appraisal of the relative commitment of each partner was obtained by weighting time periods within the 24 hours according to the level of responsibility each partner carried. Particular attention was paid to times when couples were together and to the way responsibility was allocated at these times. Thus, an hour in which partners shared the care of the child equally added .5 to both the maternal and the paternal workload, whereas an hour when the mother was merely accompanied by her partner (i.e., when he did not share the baby's care) added a full hour to the maternal day.

Using this method of assessment revealed that the mothers in the present study worked on average 13.36 hours per day and that the practical support offered by the partner was surprisingly limited, despite their designation as the main source of support. Men had sole care of the child for between 0 and 2 hours on the diary day, a mean contribution of around 20 minutes. Even when the times in which couples shared the care of the child are taken into account, the average male contribution was just 1 hour 20 minutes over the 24-hour period.

Although the mothers interviewed differed widely in their early history and in the current parenting context, they shared a common experience of the work of mothering. As the following extracts show, the diary data revealed not only the extent of mothers' workload but the way in which it was organized and the personal pressure this induced:

Paula: 5:10 a.m.—Seamus woke me up crying. He was wet and so was the sheet underneath him. Changed him and the cot sheet. Fed him—mistake—he threw up violently. Gave him his dummy and put him back in his cot—wide awake.

Kim: Kier awake at 12:30, gave him bottle. Went back to sleep until 3.00. Gave him another bottle. He cried for a while. Picked him up and put him in bed with me. Fell asleep eventually until 4:30.

Judi: 10 a.m.–11 a.m. Getting annoyed with Tom cause he's getting under my feet while I'm trying to Hoover up. Sorting out the clothes that need ironing and what don't. Tom has just hit his head and is screaming like mad. I have to keep stopping him going into the back room which is causing hassle.

In the follow-up interview mothers talked at length about the stress that the sheer volume of work induced and the frustration of undertaking a task that has no set limits:

Anne: Until he was ten or eleven months I was up five or six times at night. I used to be up every night with him. I used to get very tired with me working nights.

Paula: It's continuous, you are required to work hard and it might be completely the wrong time.

Sharon: I found it really difficult not being able to find the time to have a bath and wash my hair. I got this feeling I must have a bath.

The relationships within the first year of motherhood cannot be divorced from the central reality of the *work* of motherhood and the stress it entails. Not only are relationships affected by the stress brought about by an increase in mothers' workload, but the relationships themselves place further stress on the mother, creating demands on her time and emotional energy. As Brannen & Wilson (1983) have shown, it is the work of parenting that often forces mothers to reappraise their gender beliefs and to call into question the very nature of their relationship with their sexual partner. The extent to which mothers are able to meet the demands placed upon them will depend on their ability to negotiate for and to annex resources as their own. "The extent to which a mother can afford to meet her child's demands, how much food and attention she can give and when, how much crying she can permit or tolerate, must be strongly influenced by her position in the system of production and consumption" (Ingleby, 1974, p. 298).

Motherhood as Ideology

It is the ideology of motherhood that legitimizes the subordinate, economically dependent and relatively powerless position of women in contemporary society. The mother's role is perpetuated and women's adherence to current ideals of motherhood is assured by the system that allocates to her primary child care responsibility (Wearing, 1984). The sole responsibility for parenting that devolves upon mothers actively constructs and informs their experience, and in the first year of the first child's life mothers need to come to terms with the lack of fit between ideology and experience. The existing positive definitions of intimate relationships, particularly the relationship with the sexual partner, are severly strained by mothers' experience of stress in parenting.

Motherhood has identifiable attributes, foremost among which is the designation of the mother as primary parent and the primacy of the child's needs over those of the mother (Rappoport & Rappoport, 1977). Much research, for example, Gavron (1966) and Rainwater (1959), has highlighted the close identification of women with the maternal role and their need to identify themselves as good mothers. The ideology of the "good" mother is a vivid reality in these accounts:

Mary: I felt I was a good mother, what I was doing was . . . I was good enough.

Di: If Des was here now he'd tell you. I'm a good mother, it just took me time to adapt.

Mothers seek to both delimit the attributes of the good mother and to define themselves within those limits by appraising the mothering skills of others:

Di: I mean she could make a good mother—it's just that she doesn't want to spend time with her baby. I speak to her and I try to give her advice, because I am like the mother hen round here. I've looked after my Step Mum's kids and I know what responsibility is. I can cope.

Sharon: I'm not putting her down or anything but she leaves him with anyone, the kids from the estate. All day they take him out in that pram. I just don't know how she does it, because I just couldn't do it. She leaves him with anyone.

Good mothering implies a denial of self in favor of the needs of the child:

Diana: Now I've had him he comes first. He is my own family. He is something that no-one else can take away from me.

In their accounts of childbirth, it is the child's well-being and not the mothers' distress that is stressed. Fathers are actively protected from the more negative aspects of childbirth:

Tess: He thought it was painful but I didn't think about it. Looking back it wasn't actually the contractions that were painful. It was the birth, just his head coming out. Andy said, "I can't cope any more. I can't stand seeing Tess in this much pain." I tried to explain to him what I was feeling and that it wasn't as painful as it looks that you groan—and you're crawling around the floor on all fours. I tried to explain, it wasn't as bad as what I was making it out to be.

Paula: I was quite prepared for him to pop out and have a few fags, you know poor bloke having to go through his wife's labour.

In recounting their day-to-day experience, fatigue, like pain, is minimized:

Anne [who has paid night employment]: I stay up through the day and I go to bed when my husband gets home. I don't think it's fair on him not to. I still keep going, and as I say it keeps me stimulated as well. It's not as bad as it sounds actually. Most people who don't work nights think, "God, No." But it really isn't that bad.

All the mothers interviewed saw themselves as the main parent, whatever their marital or ideological status.

Denise: I do most of the planning as far as she is concerned, like it's me who decides when she gets fed and all those sorts of things. Unless it's obvious that her nappy needs changing, I'll say he wouldn't necessarily do it. I sort of do, I make the rules.

Jane: I knew he was helping but it felt like it was ultimately my responsibility to look after her.

Mary: Certainly I seem to take the main responsibility for her, even if we are together. He will help out and get her a drink or change her: a generous gift to me. Or if I am going out I will take her with me, like now he'll just take her off to the other room. And I forget perhaps these things, because I feel the total responsibility.

Because of this acceptance of primary responsibility, all other roles were secondary to the maternal role. Work, even for those with established careers, was subordinate to this and might be seen simply as a preparation for the "real task" of child care.

Eve: Yes, I think the fact that I've done nursing has helped because it is a very kind of time-consuming, emotionally-draining job. So I kind of went when Sam came along, "Oh, here we go again!" Um . . . It was quite, you know, in some ways it was quite good preparation, you know . . . just that constant demand and stress.

Many mothers found it impossible to reconcile their responsibility for their child with the need to find adequate substitute care. An underlying theme was that all substitute care was by definition second best.

Jane: I think I would have gone back for the extra money so that we wouldn't have to worry—but I couldn't and when it comes down to who you leave it with—who I'd leave Charlotte with.

Anne: I don't think I could have left Simon. I know some people go back to work really early. I did try to leave him with the childminder, but it was only one afternoon a week, and I really felt guilty about that, but I felt as if I wanted to do something for myself on one afternoon a week.

References to paid employment were hedged about with an elaborate framework of justification, central to which were accounts that emphasized the benefits to others rather than to the self. The most commonly used justification was that of economic necessity.

Marian: And I think you're made to feel guilty as well, "Who's got her, who's looking after her?" or "I don't agree with these mum's who've gone back to work." But some poor women have no choice. I mean, really, we haven't got a choice, I mean we scrape by for a few months, but. . . .

Fiona: Yes. We've got a mortgage to pay, so that's the bottom line. And in someways it made it easier, because there wasn't a choice there.

Part-time work was favored because it was clearly subordinate to the maternal commitment.

Anne: I think it's good to keep your hand in, because when I've finished the family, I'll want to go back full time, to fit in with sort of school and things.

Marian: I definitely will have more children, but I won't start getting further in my career till they have grown up a bit.

Those who opted to work full-time in the early years experienced a marked degree of conflict as they tried to reconcile the demands of both roles.

Fiona: I went back full time, and I was very miserable doing full time. So I've now just started a job share for one year, and then after that I'll see if I want to carry on doing a job share.

The maternal role is clearly given primacy in these accounts. In order to adequately fulfill the role of the good mother, women must subordinate their needs and ambitions to those of those of their family, absorbing the stress of parenting and protecting them from its outcome.

Coping with Motherhood

The primary identification of mothers with the maternal role means that they feel obliged to meet the requirements of that role, whatever the personal cost. Mothers frequently refer to their ability "to cope." The concept of coping implies that mothers' capacities must expand to meet the needs of the situation (Graham, 1982).

Denise: I coped with the getting up for the feeds a lot better than I thought I would. I mean I've always been somebody who needs eight hours or they are in a rotten mood. But I coped with it quite well. And I did just sleep when she slept if I was tired in the day.

Coping is seen as a female attribute. When the domestic burden increases, it is women who are expected to cope. Men's capacities are finite and are bounded by their primary identification with work outside the home.

Fiona: He's the one who tends to go down instead of me, I cope, I don't always feel happy but I cope, whereas he is somebody who far more gets the glooms.

Coping also functions as a way of relocating responsibility, away from others and back onto the self.

R: You said the first three months were quite bad?

Jane: That was my feeling of not being able to cope. It wasn't how anybody else made me feel.

The attempt to cope meant that mothers were pushed to the limit, and sometimes beyond the limit, of their resources.

Judi: He's kept out sometimes till half ten at night, which doesn't help me because I don't get a break. When you look at it like that it sounds really bad. . . . How do I cope? Oh dear. I don't know how I cope myself. I think I'll go loopy some of the time.

In the face of extreme stress, the designation of mothers as the primary caretaker is severely stretched. Women feel themselves to be culpable if they cannot cope, however difficult the task (Graham, 1982). Guilt is a necessary corollary of an acceptance of ultimate responsibility; it is experienced when mothers feel they have transgressed ideological constraints—for example, where they feel they may be putting their own interests above those of their child:

Anne: I wasn't happy about leaving him there, maybe, that is why he didn't settle but I felt very guilty, even if it had have worked, I don't think I could have done it for that long. Because I just felt so guilty. I felt guilty that perhaps I shouldn't be doing something that I wanted to.

Or if they have asked for support when they should have been able to cope:

Anne: There would always be some problem that Sean [husband] couldn't have coped with. I'd come back and he'd say, "He was crying all the time you were away." It used to make me feel so guilty, that I thought, "I won't go this week," and I think that's why I gave it up.

They were able to reconcile this conflict only if they could feel satisfied that there was a correspondence between their own and their child's interests:

Di: I didn't feel guilty, because I just felt that what was good for me was good for her. That was my theory and it seemed to work. I followed it through I didn't feel guilty.

Dally (1982) has argued that these expectations of motherhood place an intolerable burden of responsibility upon women from which there can be no effective relief, since the primacy of the mother-child bond is regarded as sacrosanct. Women who have been thus socialized have defined themselves as centrally and ultimately responsible. Such an ideology places severe limitations on the extent and nature of acceptable support and defines involvement by others in childcare as tangential. The mothers in the current study struggle to come to terms with their experience within the terms of this limited definition of support. Married and cohabiting mothers carry with them a commitment to a relationship that is defined as naturally supportive and mutually rewarding, and they have to come to terms with the lack of fit between their expectations of support and their partner's limited contribution.

Defining the Limits of Support

Paternal Support

There is some evidence that attachment relationships, because of their steady accessibility, may be of primary importance for adequate social functioning and that all other relationships are organized around these central emotional ties (McFarlane, Norman, Streiner, & Roy, 1983). Gottlieb (1978) analyzes support by function, reasoning that only a rich and varied network will meet all an individual's support needs. However, for first-time mothers the access to such a network is very limited. The first birth brings about a retrenchment in social ties for women, who are cut off from previous social contacts (particularly if they were previously in full-time employment) and who are prevented by the long hours and sleepless nights of early mothering from reforming social bonds (Veroff & Feld, 1970). Graham & Mckee (1983) found that this sense of isolation was at its most acute in the first 6 months, when mothers have to come to terms with the isolation and loss of status that mothering brings with it. The relative poverty of the environment of the new mother means that she is thrown back on her intimate relationships, particularly on her relationship with the partner who is most often the main confidante following the transition to parenthood (Moss, Bolland, Foxman, & Owen, 1985).

The primary support relationship is the one most often associated with adequate mental health (Miles, 1988). All of the mothers, both married and unmarried, who were in stable cohabitations identified the partner as both the main and preferred source of support. The sexual relationship was for many mothers the focus of both their social and emotional lives and the one around which all others were organized; however, the practical support that could be derived from this relationship was severely proscribed by mothers' assumption of primary child care responsibility.

A comparison of partners' work commitments shows that at no time does the father's contribution equal that of his partner. In addition, men were highly selective in their domestic and child care contribution, favoring play activities over routine child care.

Tess: He won't change a dirty nappy, that's one thing he won't do. He says he can't stomach it just yet. [baby 4 months old]

Gwen: We worked it out and then Karl decided to give him a bath, and that was because of realising that on the one hand it's a chore, but it's also very enjoyable.

For mothers who accept that the responsibility for parenthood lies with them, to blame the father for not contributing equally would necessitate a major ideological shift. For this reason, they cast around for other explanations that do not call the relationship into question. So embedded are mothers in their emotional context that they are inclined to see external rather than internal factors as salient (Nisbett & Wison, 1977) and to choose accounts that distance stress and conflict from their intimate relationships. Their accounts emphasize the equivalence of sexual roles in which each partner fulfills gender-role expectations, making an equivalent though not an equal contribution to the relationship. The issue therefore becomes, not the inequality in the division of labor, but the ability of each partner to fufill his or her assigned role. It therefore becomes illegitimate to ask the male to increase his participation in child care, because to do this would be to expect him to exceed male gender norms.

Paula: I know you say this is work, but this is my work completely, isn't it? So I should be able to do it.

Judi: He takes work when he's there. I mean he's been very busy lately. He's also starting up his own business, him and a friend, so if people phone up he's got to fit them in at night time or whatever. So I can't really expect him to come home and start doing housework.

Anne: He's busy at work. Being an architect they have sort of dead lines for things and they can't refuse business at the moment while he's building it up. . . .

The function of these accounts appears to be to locate the responsibility for change with some external agency and not within the power structure of the marriage or sexual relationship. The division of labor is seen as a constant, fixed by an external order, and dictated by economic necessity.

Judi: If Eamonn cut down on his hours we wouldn't have the money to go out anywhere, so I don't resent it.

One strategy for dealing with inequalities in the division of labor is to undervalue the maternal contribution, either by emphasizing the importance of paid work or by denigrating child care and treating it as nonwork.

Paula: He's been at work all day. So for him to come home, I know his job is really difficult, and then to come home to me, and he's still got more work on top of that, you know. . . .

Claire: He used to walk up and down with her in the back yard. . . . Especially after he'd done a days work; it was really good of him. He was doing this research, that was his sort of commitment.

Even when experiencing acute stress, mothers resisted locating the responsibility in their marital partner, opting for explanations that stressed social-structural factors such as bad housing or low-income factors, or naturally arising personality differences, rather than active choice and responsibility.

Eve: It's not that he's not willing to, I think he's just, he's one of these distractable people, he's always kind of off somewhere else. Uh, not that he's neglectful, but I think, like Leo's nappy needs changing now, and I'll go and do that whereas he'll just kind of not realise till the last minute. That makes him sound awful, but he's not.

Denise: I'm just more of an organiser than he is anyway. He's quite happy to do things. He'll feed her and change her and he bathes her and he'll put her to bed and all the rest of it, so I mean he will do everything but I have to tell him to do it.

If the man's contribution is optional, and his "help" with child care and domestic work is evidence of his goodness, then the mother's anger becomes illegitimate. In the following account Kathy allocates responsibility to and then withdraws it from her spouse.

Kathy: I resented having to go back to work and I blamed Stuart. It wasn't Stuart's fault but I blamed him. When I had to go back to work the problem was really the tiredness.

Attempting to make sense of the problem of equity within the relationship brought about a sense of confusion because mothers were unable to find an objective yardstick against which to measure the paternal contribution.

Jane: I used to try to work out in my head what was fair and not reach any conclusions. I still do that a bit now.

Gwen: I don't know if he does his share; it's very difficult to be objective about it.

Because the father's role only carries with it partial responsibility, the onus is upon the mother to request assistance. Work done by the father thus has the status of a gift to the mother:

Jane: If I ask he will do it, and if I really can't do anything then I will ask. Like if I've been ill then he's very good.

Tess: I have to ask; he won't do it off his own bat which is a shame because sometimes I get a bit irritable.

Mothers need to establish special circumstances in order to enlist paternal support.

Mary: I say I'm pregnant and I feel sick, can you do her nappy? I think I play on it a bit too much really.

Tess: If he sees that I'm tired or if I've already told him earlier on in the evening that I've got a headache, then he will say, "Would you like me to feed him and you can go to bed if you have got a headache?"

Because of their uncertainty, mothers often felt guilty about raising questions of work sharing and were easily defeated if their partners were unwilling to cooperate.

Deidre: Ken always maintains that I have to ask him, that he doesn't know automatically, and then he sort of accuses me of martyring, of deliberately not asking.

The confusion about the distribution of power and resources is reflected in women's ambivalence towards the male contribution. Men are either seen as incapable (Judi: "I'd have frying pans up to the ceiling if

I let him do it.") or are assumed to be suffering from role overload because the conventions of support have been violated:

Jane: We are very lucky. Chloe is really very good, but I think because he sees his friends and they are all off to play rugby or whatever and he still has to battle with Chloe he feels a bit hard done by.

Over one half of the women in the sample reported that their partner had difficulties in coming to terms with fatherhood. Mothers recounted dealing with both their own and their partner's adjustment to parenthood. This was presented in terms of their partner's personal difficulties in coming to terms with an essentially alien task.

Tess: At first he was very . . . he didn't want hardly anything to do with him, I think he thought that he was too small.

The task of helping men to adjust placed an additional burden upon mothers' already overstretched resources, as they struggled to place this response within the ideology of a companionate relationship. Mothers attempt to account for this in terms of personality traits.

Kathy: There was a lot of stress, because I had problems with Stuart well towards the end—he threw a wobbly about becoming a Dad. . . . He suddenly decided he didn't want to—I think what did it was—he's always been a worrier and I'm not I never have been and whereas I was syaing, "It'll all work out"—as the mortgage interest rate went up he got more and more worried and then I think it was all a bit too much for him.

Deidre: He got quite screwed up about it. I think he was worried about the financial responsibility.

Because of their responsibility to maintain and service men, the central supportive relationship can create rather than diminish work. In these accounts mothers struggle to come to terms with an experience of stress and work that is incompatible with the designation of the sexual relationship as primarily supportive. Whereas the married and cohabiting mothers cling to their definition of this relationship as supportive, almost all of the single mothers interviewed were aware that men could be a source of stress, and in their accounts they treated male company as a stressful luxury rather than as a means of support.

Sharon: I've never lived with a bloke, but I think that I cope much better on my own than I would with a bloke around.

Kim: It's so many questions and answers, "where have you been? who have you seen? don't do this with him," that I like it, I like being here. You get no hassle from anyone.

These mothers relied primarily on family and friends for support, and often perceived sexual relationships as too costly because they represented a drain on their already overstretched resources.

Marie: If you've got a baby and he wakes you up at night then you are always worrying in case it wakes him up. Um and you've got to spend as much time with them, because you've got to start cooking their dinner, and you've got times more washing. It's not worth it. . . . My Mum always helped me if I needed anything. You just have to go up there. We just help each other.

Extended Family Support

For the married and cohabiting mothers, support relationships were derived from and organized around the central male-female relationship. The expectation that male support would be the norm placed limits on the availability of other sources of support (Mcintyre, 1976). Married and cohabiting mothers had a strong commitment to the nuclear family, and alternative sources of support were perceived as most helpful when they respected the boundaries of the nuclear family.

Jaquie: I didn't want anybody there; I wanted it to be just us three when I came out of hospital.

Marian: She [mother] doesn't interfere with what I am doing; she won't say, "Don't do it like that."

The extended family was a significant source of support for less than one half of the mothers interviewed. Both married and cohabiting mothers used their own mothers for practical assistance and guidance when they lived nearby, and this relationship acted as a buffer against any stress in the sexual partnership. However, less than one fourth of the mothers had intimate maternal relationships, and there were limitations placed on the extent and intimacy of maternal support. For those who had been in residential care, many of whom were single parents, family ties were, at best, conflicted and full of remembered bitterness and, at worst, a source of continuing stress. For almost all of the respondents, the nuclear family and not the extended family was the main focus of meaning and support. While offering support, the extended family often placed additional burdens on mothers by defending existing gender-role prescriptions and underlining the attributes of good motherhood.

Deidre: Thinking of my extended family, they would just reinforce the man. All they would say would be to the woman, "Pull yourself together." They'd come and take over because I was lacking. My mother thinks its absolutely wonderful that Ken does the cooking. I have to keep quiet about how much he actually does.

The husband's family in particular were perceived as reinforcing the traditional female role.

Fiona: His mother sees me as responsible. Or when they realise that he's done it, or he has cooked dinner, the praise he gets is just extraordinary.

Gwen: His Mum was very undermining when she visited. It's like she's the better mother and all that sort of thing. "You go out, we'll look after him."

Fathers and fathers-in-law reinforced gender stereotypes by confining themselves to traditional male tasks:

Marian: He keeps out of the other things, but he likes to sort of play with him. He's really good with him, he's sort of doting on him.

This equivocal support, in which help was offered within prescribed limits, underlined the mother's primary responsibility and increased her sense of isolation, creating a pressure to succeed as a mother whatever the personal cost.

Friends

Friends could provide an alternative to this social pressure by reaffirming the mother as a person in her own right. However, the isolation of new parenting limited mothers' abilities to form and maintain friendship ties.

Anne: I mean Sean still goes out for a drink in the evening with his friends. I don't do anything that I used to do. I used to play squash and do aerobics and all sorts but I don't do anything any more.

Few mothers had intimate friendships that could offer the kind of support that might have acted as a buffer to the primary relationship, and many felt obliged to present themselves in terms of the ideal even to close friends.

Deidre: I think the conspiracy of silence is almost worse than the work or the exhaustion.

They were reluctant to share the negative aspects of parenting, although when they did so, the relief could be enormous.

Kathy: I was in the middle of telling her, and I had one of me crying fits, I told her and she told Sue and the next thing I knew they were both saying, "We've been feeling awful." They hadn't told each other either and then the three of us felt better because we thought we're not alone, and they said, "Next time you're up at two in the morning give me a ring."

Power and Conflict

In the mothers' accounts, men were accorded disproportionate power over economic resources, which they could both dispense and withhold, deciding when and how they should be used. Mothers treated these inequalities as externally imposed. They became so integrated into the structure of the relationship that they became invisible. Economic support was seen as a personality attribute, evidence of goodwill rather than a feature of differential economic power.

Tess: He's very good. If I ask for something and he's got enough then he will buy it. He's very money conscious when it comes to spending out on things that are silly.

The voluntary nature of this contribution is underlined by according to the man the right to question the way money is spent.

Tess: Sometimes he gets very uptight when I ask him for a bit of money or if I go out and spend a bit more than I should have done or if I've bought things we didn't need. Um he still considers his wages as his own, and he gets very uptight if he hasn't got any money in his pocket.

Women betray a consciousness of men's potential power in describing their partners as good not only in terms of what they do but also of what they might do if they chose.

Deniece: Alex expects the least. I mean some husbands like their shirts ironed and all the rest of it.

Paula: He's not one of these people saying my dinner should be on the table.

The traditional view of gender relations rests on an assumption of a mutuality of interests between partners and a denial of the differential possession of power within the relationship. Each performs his or her assigned role and makes not an equal but an equivalent contribution (Parsons & Bales, 1955). Mothers who have previously defined their sexual relationship as mutually beneficial are faced with the task of accounting for the inequality within their relationship in terms that will not disturb this interpretation. They typically employ strategies that involve a reappraisal of child care in terms other than the simple division of labor, either by emphasizing the equivalence of maternal and paternal roles or by treating child care as nonwork that could not be equated with the male paid work commitment.

The powerful ideological apparatus surrounding motherhood mystifies the experience and makes it difficult for women to identify structural inequality and to negotiate for improved access to resources. Inequality is not always perceived as such, hedged in as it is by an ideology of mutual fulfillment within personal sexual relationships (Bernard, 1975). As Lukes (1974) argues, the exercise of power enables a dominant group or individual to define the world of a subordinate group, who are then prevented from having grievances and shaping their perceptions in such a way that they accept their role because they can see or imagine no alternative. Where ideology conflicts with reality, mothers experience great difficulty in reappraising the social construction of their experience. They can only express their acute shock and accept suffering as a part of "normal" motherhood:

Di: He was a total disappointment. I thought it's a wonderful thing and its going to be good you know. And I found out it's not so good.

Kathy: I didn't realise just how exhausting it would be. Even at the time I couldn't understand why I was so tired.

Deidre: I felt as if I was in a glass jar or something. I couldn't feel anything properly. It's peculiar. I think it was just the shock of becoming a parent and having to spend 24 hours a day looking after a child.

The unremitting nature of the task and the lack of support available to mothers make stress an inevitable part of new parenting. This ideological overload is commonly experienced by mothers as acute stress, which damages the relationship between mother and child.

Judi: Sometimes I could throw him out the window. I'd never hurt him for nobody. If anyone touched him I'd kill 'em, when he's on a bad day teething or something.

Kathy: One or two times when you are holding them and they are crying its so tempting to just squeeze that bit too hard. And to think that pillow's just handy, and you have to put him down and walk away, and that frightened me.

These accounts are embedded in inherent structural imbalances in gender roles, which bring about an unequal distribution of power and resources (Leonard-Barker & Allen, 1976). The central sexual relationship is one that is heavily scripted and influenced by ideological and social structures. As Pahl (1980) observes, custom accords certain privileges to the male breadwinner, among them a right to make decisions about what is fair and equitable in the distribution of resources. With the birth of the first child, resources of time and energy become scarce and the negotiation for these becomes central to the currency of the relationship, a social and emotional rate of exchange. Bloode and Wolfe (1960) describe how at this time the balance of power shifts, consolidating the basis of male power by confirming the woman's dependent status as she loses the independence that had accrued to her through paid employment. The birth of the first child typically brings about a loss in financial status and a reappraisal of priorities, and women must negotiate from a newly allocated position of weakness at a time when their social and economic autonomy is depleted.

Anne: I don't complain because if I complain he'll think, "She doesn't appreciate it, so I won't do it."

Gwen: When Karl does things for him, I'll tend to say, "Thanks for doing that." And I do feel if I say, "Thank you," maybe he'll do it more often. Praise him. It's kind of subtle . . . managing men.

Those mothers who had a dual commitment to motherhood and to paid work were more aware of the imbalance in gender roles. They were able to see that their roles were clearly equivalent and thus took active steps to increase their partner's contribution.

Gwen: I've taken time off work to look after him so I'll do that, and I'll do all the things that go with it, and then I'll only do my half of the rest, and Karl can do his half. Yes, you see, I can rationalise it to myself, because Karl is a social worker and he's only just qualified, and he's earning less than I was, I'm still paying my half of the mortgage, so he's not keeping me, he's not keeping us. So I don't feel Oh yeah, I've been having a nice time all day I should do more of the housework, I feel o.k.

In contrast to the more traditional mothers, these mothers acknowledged that there might be a conflict of interests between partners who were both competing for the same scarce resources. However, their negotiations for a more equitable distribution of labor failed to produce an improvement in their conditions. Participation in paid work did *not* reduce mothers' domestic work contribution. Instead, their overall workload was *increased*. The two mothers in full-time work both worked in excess of 16 hours per day. If anything, there was an inverse relationship between the father's contribution and the mother's paid work. Whereas the mean paternal contribution was 1 hour, 35 minutes for mothers not in paid employment it was 1 hour, 15 minutes for those who worked between 10 and 30 hours per week, and it averaged only 30 minutes for mothers in full-time work. Women took up paid work without relinquishing any of the responsibilities of the maternal role, and any increase in their paid work commitment could be expected to increase their overall levels of work and stress.

It is clear from this that consciousness of inequality and a degree of economic autonomy are in themselves insufficient to secure an equitable division of labor. The payoff from the sexual relationship comes from emotional rather than practical support, and mothers will go to great lengths to preserve their vision of the companionate marriage striving to maintain harmony and to avoid overt conflict.

Paula: I don't ever have a go at him about it though, because if you started using the baby against each other it would be hell. "Who cares enough for this baby?" It would just be awful. I know he loves him, we were just tired and fed up really.

Women put a high premium on affection and communication in their sexual relationships, and as long as these are present, they are willing to accept a marked degree of inequality (Brannen & Collard 1982).

Cherie: I wouldn't have been able to survive. Not if there had been no-body there. You can't relate to a baby, you can't sit there and tell a baby. A baby can't give you a hug and make you feel better. If I didn't have Martin I think I would have killed myself. I really do.

It is only when there is overt conflict that women's perceptions are likely to shift and self-interest is placed above the preservation of the relationship. Mothers in violent or unstable relationships were jolted out of their belief in a mutuality of interest between partners and began to take steps to preserve their financial and emotional independence.

Martina: He used to get the money and just spend it on drink. So now I claim in my name.

Although more traditional mothers emphasized the equivalence of gender role and the value of mutual support, experience had taught them to expect minimal levels of support. They accepted the total responsibility for child care, seeing men as having little or no role in their child's upbringing. Without the expectation of mutual support, they had no common ground on which to negotiate or to effect change.

Martina: I'm still wary but what can you do? Steve he's really bad when he's drunk, but he's alright when he's sober. He goes out and gets drunk and he hits me and I'm really frightened then, but its not all the time. Its about once a month or every few weeks.

For these mothers an awareness of conflict was combined with a knowledge that confrontation was likely to bring about a violent response.

Belinda: He was alright, but no matter how big or small the argument he would always turn nasty.

Martina: He drunk all the time, and he got violent as well, really violent towards me. I was scared of him.

Belinda: I tried one night to go and take him with me. And he came home and I got caught red-handed. He dragged me in and he beat me up as well when I got back in.

Because of the nature of their relationships, these women were forced to rely on practical rather than emotional strategies in order to effect change.

Martina: Now I kick him out the moment he starts hitting me. He stays away then for about a week. I'm not having it.

Belinda: I got the injunction out when he started making phone calls—because he knows my number, and he started making threatening phone calls.

The balance of power in the sexual relationships of all the mothers interviewed was weighted in favor of the male and conferred on the male the right to give or to withhold support. In a few relationships this power was reinforced by violence or the threat of violence, and in many it was underlined by the mother's economic dependence. However, for most mothers the parameters of support were set by their unwillingness to put pressure on the relationship, which was the primary focus of their emotional support, at a time when they felt most vulnerable.

Conclusion

In this chapter ideology is used as a linking concept between the traditional psychological focus upon personal relationships and the sociological concern with context. The function of accounts cannot be divorced from the social situation in which they occur, nor is it possible to treat accounts of relationships as purely personal discourse because to do so is to ignore the parameters of power and control in which they are embedded, which will shape the way in which relationships are construed (Gergen & Gergen, 1987).

The stress that mothers experience is directly related to the ideological structure in which mothering occurs, and the accounts that mothers employ are grounded in a realistic appraisal of the benefits that accrue from and the costs of disrupting the dominant construction of gender relations. In their accounts, mothers are actively engaged in coming to terms with the lack of fit between experience and ideology, while at the same time protecting their view of their intimate relationships as beneficial and supportive. The conception of marriage and sexual relationships as mutually supportive and that of child care as effortless and fulfilling both obscure and invalidate mothers' sense of grievance and preempt any attempt to establish alternative sources of support. They are inhibited from a public declaration of their experience of motherhood both by their own assimilation of gender norms and by the power of the dominant reality to punish and to categorize as abnormal any deviance from the ideal (Spender, 1980). As Shender (1981) observes, power is tolerable only when a good deal of its workings are concealed. At the heart of these accounts lies a conflict that cannot be resolved without taking apart the very meaning that motherhood has been ascribed and reappraising intimate relationships in terms of conflict rather than support. In their attempts to deconstruct and revalue their experience, mothers are brought up against the structural basis of men's power, which places limits on both their ability to understand and to change their experience.

Diedre: The problem is, in this society authority rests with the male point of view and there is no-body who can stand up and say, "You men are wrong" except women, who are discounted anyway.

References

Bernard, J. (1972). *The future of marriage*. Chicago: Aldine.

Bernard, J. (1975). *Women wives and mothers, values and options* Chicago: Aldine.

Bloode, R.O. & Wolfe, D. (1960). *Husbands and wives: The dynamics of married living*. New York: Free Press.

Brannen, J. & Collard, J. (1982). *Marriages in trouble: The process of seeking help*. London: Tavistock.

Brannen, J. & Wilson, T. (1987). *Give and take in families*. London: Allen and Unwin.

Cowan C.P. Cowan, R.A., Coie L., & Coie, J. (1978). Becoming a family: The impact of the first child on the couple's relationship. In B. Miles & I.F. Newman (Eds.), *The first child and family formation* (pp. 296–234). Chapel Hill, NC: University of North Carolina, Carolina Population Centre.

Dally, A. (1982). *Inventing motherhood*. London: Burnett Books.

Gavron, H. (1966). *The captive wife*. Harmondsworth: Penguin.

Gelles, R.J. (1979). Family violence. Beverly Hills, CA: Sage.

Gergen, M.M., & Gergen, K.J. (1987). Narratives of relationships. In R. Burnett, P. McGhee, & D. Clarke (Eds.), *Accounting for relationships*. London: Methuen.

Gottlieb, H. (1978). The development and application of a clasification scheme of informal helping behaviour. *Canadian Journal of Behavioural Science, 70*, 110–115.

Graham, H. (1982). Coping, or how mothers are seen and not heard. In S. Friedman & S. Elizabeth (Eds.), *On the problem of men*. London: Women's Press.

Graham, H. (1983). A labour of love. In J. Finch & C. Groves (Eds.), *A labour of love* (pp. 12–30). London: Routledge & Kegan Paul.

Graham, H. (1984). *Women, health and the family*. London: Wheatsheaf Books.

Graham, H. & Mckee, L. (1980). *The first months of motherhood* Research Monograph No.3, London Health Education Council.

Ingleby, I. (1974). The psychology of child psychology. In M. Richards & P. Light (Eds.), *The integration of the child into the social world*. Cambridge: Cambridge University Press.

Jones, E.E., & Nisbett R. (1971). *The actor and the observer*: Divergent perceptions of the causes of behavior. Morristown, NJ: General Learning Press.

La Rossa, R., & La Rossa, M.M. (1981). *The transition to parenthood*. Beverly Hills, CA: Sage Publications.

Leonard-Barker, D. & Allen, S. (Eds.). (1976). *Dependence and exploitation in work and marriage*. London: Longman.

Lukes, J. (1974). *Power: A radical view*. London: Macmillan.

McFarlane, A.N., Norman, G.R.D., Streiner, L. & Roy, R.G. (1983). The process of social stress in stable, reciprocal and mediating relationships *Journal of Health and Social Behavior, 24,* 122–31.

Mcintyre, S. (1976). The social construction of instincts. In D. Leonard & S. Allen (Eds.), *Sexual divisions in society* (pp. 150–173). London: Tavistock.

Miles, A. (1988). *Women and mental illness*. London: Wheatsheaf Books.

Moss P., Bolland, G., Foxman, R., & Owen, C. (1985). *Marital relations during the transition to parenthood*. London: Thomas Coram Research Unit Paper.

Nisbett, R.E. & Wilson T.D. (1977). Telling more than we can know: Verbal reports on mental processes. *Pschological Review, 84*, 231–259.

Oakley, A. (1976). *The sociology of housework*. Oxford: Martin Robertson. Pahl, J. (1980). Patterns of money management within marriage *Journal of Social Policy 9(3)*, 313–335.

Parsons, T., & Bales, R.C. (Eds.). (1955). *Family socialisation and integration*. Chicago: Free Press.

Pleck, J. (1979) Men's family work: Three perspectives and some new data. *Family Co-ordination, 28*, 481–488.

Potter, J., & Wetherall, M. (1987). *Discourse and social psychology*. London: Sage.

Rainwater, L. (1959). *Working man's wife: Her personality, world and lifestyle*. New York: Oceana.

Rappoport, R., & Rappoport, R. (1977). *Fathers, mothers and others* London: Routledge & Kegan Paul.

Shender, A. (1981). *Michel Foucault: The will to truth*. London: Tavistock.

Spender D. (1980). *Man made language*. London: Routledge & Kegan Paul.

Veroff, J. & Feld, S. (1970). Marriage and work in america. New York: Van Nostrand.

Wearing, B. (1984). *The ideology of motherhood*. Sydney, Australia: J. Allen & Unwin.

Wilkinson, S. (Ed.). (1981). The psychology of ordinary explanations of social behaviour. In Antaki, C. (Ed.), *Personal constructs and private explanations* (pp. 203–219). London: Academic Press.

Commentaries

14
Richness and Rigor: Advancing the Study of Attributions and Accounts in Close Relationships

FRANK D. FINCHAM

Mundus vult decipi: the world wants to be deceived.
The truth is too complex and frightening. (Walter Kaufman, *I and You*)

As practitioners we know that when a client presents for psychotherapy it is important to find out why he or she is presenting *this* symptom(s) at *this* time. Donning our caps as scientists, however, we sometimes forget that the same question should be asked about scholarly endeavors. If the intellectual reasons for addressing this question are not compelling, it must nonetheless be confronted at the pragmatic level in deciding what should occupy the space on our bookshelves. This commentary therefore addresses the question: "Why this book at this particular time?" The response to this question is organized into three sections. First, the book is placed in an historical perspective. Second, its contribution to future research is examined by considering several desiderata for work on accounts in close relationships. The final section attempts to integrate earlier observations by discussing a theme implicit in earlier sections of the commentary.

Looking Back: A Historical Perspective

In 1978, Huston and Levinger noted that most psychological research on relationships involved people who were "personally irrelevant" to each other. Since then, this circumstance has changed dramatically, and psychologists have made substantial contributions to our understanding of close relationships. In clinical psychology a large body of literature now documents the behaviors shown in marital interactions, and more recent work has turned to examine the covert (e.g., thoughts and feelings) factors that migh influence such behavior. The present volume is germane to this new genre of research and therefore particularly timely. Research on close relationships has also mushroomed in social psychology. Although interest in how intimates explain and account for relationship events has been evident since the inception of this work, it has not gained attention commensurate with its potential to advance our understanding of close relationships. This book is again timely in that it is likely to stimulate such attention.

Despite the evident progress, psychological research on close relationships has been hindered by disciplinary myopia; psychologists tend to overlook the fact that family sociologists began systematic studies of the family shortly after the turn of the century, long before the study of close relationships gained acceptance in psychology. As a consequence, psychological writings informed by scholarship in other disciplines are relatively rare (cf. Duck, 1983), and the failure of psychologists to benefit from the experience of other social sciences remains an enigma.*

This volume is a welcome exception to such disciplinary myopia: The attempt to represent perspectives from various disciplines and to facilitate interdisciplinary communication is exemplary (see Harvey, Orbuch & Weber, Chap. 1, this volume). Given that most of the contributors are psychologists, the diversity of perspective is especially encouraging. This feature of the book is also noteworthy because it points psychologists toward well-established literatures in related disciplines and has the potential to remedy the ahistorical nature of most psychological writings on close relationships.

The integration of work informed by attribution theory (a child of psychology) and by writings on accounts (with its roots primarily in sociology) is indeed timely. For different reasons, each domain is in danger of stagnation, and the infusion of ideas from one to the other is likely to foster interesting advances in each. Specifically, work on accounts has been dominated by the derivation of account topologies and, more recently, by qualitative analyses that use examples of actual accounts to demonstrate their importance in relationships. With notable exceptions (e.g., Harvey and colleagues, McLaughlin and colleagues, Schönbach), theoretically driven empirical studies have been rare. Thus, the promise shown by earlier conceptual analyses of accounts in sociology has never been realized in the eyes of more empirically oriented scholars (cf. Hewstone, 1989).

On the other hand, applied studies on attribution have been plentiful in the last decade, yet this domain also faces a serious challenge. Many

---

* The earliest systematic studies on close relationships in psychology involved a rejection of earlier sociological research, particulary its reliance on self-report. Although understandable at the time, psychologists do not appear to have since incorporated the insights of sociologists in their work. For example, family sociologists address a variety of topics that have not gained the attention of psychologists and even in areas of overlapping interest each discipline has the potential to enrich the other. (For a more complete historical account, see Fincham & Bradbury, 1990.)

areas of applied attribution studies represent first-generation research in which the importance of attributions for the field in question is established, usually by documenting an association between attributions and the phenomenon of interest and then ruling out third variable explanations for the association. Although typically informed by some of the assumptions found in the early attribution literature (the writings of Heider, Kelley, Jones, and Weiner), sophisticated theoretical statements that address specifically the applied issues at hand, and that might advance attribution research in the area, are rare. This circumstance is particularly relevant to attributional research on close relationships. In addition, there is some sentiment that attribution research on close relationships fails to capture the richness of explanations that are offered in such relationships, a circumstance that does not characterize research on accounts. The continued vitality of attribution research on close relationships is likely to rest on the infusion of new ideas from the accounts literature and on careful conceptual analyses of attributional phenomena in close relationships.

In sum, several considerations make this book timely. Those already mentioned speak to the identification of an important topic that needs to be addressed and point to a new domain of integrative research. Although useful, the contribution of the book would be strengthened further were it to advance our understanding of the topic identified. This issue is therefore addressed in the next section, where some desiderata are offered for research on accounts. In doing so, an attempt is made to highlight the further contributions of the book as well as some of its limitations.

Looking Forward: Some Desiderata for Future Research

The chapters in this book speak to at least five desirable features of research on accounts that are discussed in this section, namely, clarity of constructs, formulation of testable theory, identification of replicable phenomena, methodological sophistication, and an appreciation of the role of context.

An Account Is Not an Account Is Not an Account

The term *account* has a variety of referents, and in this respect it is very similar to the term *attribution*. (For further discussion see Antaki; 1987, Fincham, in press.) By integrating work that falls under both of these labels, the present book is innovative and challenges us to specify the relation between the discrete, causal/responsibility attributions offered for events in close relationships and the more extensive tales/accounts that intimates weave about those same events. The success with which we meet this challenge will depend, in part, on the care we take to specify precisely the constructs under inquiry, the manner in which they are operationalized, *and* the context in which they are studied (see later section, "Accounts in Context"). Stated in more general terms, increasing the scope of inquiry that falls under the rubric of research on accounts increases the obligation of each writer to be precise about the object of his or her study. The belief that "account" has the same referent across authors or that it has a single, accepted referent when it does not is likely to promote confusion inimical to scientific progress.

The chapters in this book are testimony to the variety of constructs incorporated under the umbrella of accounts research in close relationships and, without exception, the object of their inquiry is clear. However, a fundamental conceptual distinction emerges from the attempt to integrate the chapters that is not always recognized within each chapter. The distinction is between accounts as private events involving purely intrapersonal processes and as public events or social acts that necessarily entail overt behavior. Accounts are, by definition, public events in some seminal writings (e.g., Scott & Lyman, 1968). Indeed, to account or explain is a three-place predicate (someone accounts/explains for something to someone) and therefore implies social action. However, like attribution, which originally refered to external acts such as assigning, giving or paying, account can also be used to refer private, intrapersonal events. These two classes of events most likely influence each other, but it is a mistake to assume that they are equivalent; despite possible overlap, each is likely to have different correlates, to be influenced by different factors, to serve different functions, and so on (cf. Bradbury & Fincham, 1988). In fact, Baumeister and Stillwell (Chap. 4, this volume) present evidence to show that public and private accounts for success do indeed differ. By housing work pertaining to private and public accounts, this book invites us to address the important question of how they are related, and the answer that emerges may well vary depending on our conception of the account construct.

Testable Theory

A second conceptual issue that deserves attention is the formulation of testable theory. Many of the earlier theoretical statements that stimulated interest in accounts have not yet led to systematic bodies of programmatic research. This is reminiscent of the hiatus that followed Heider's seminal writings on attribution—it was the translation of Heider's insights into testable theories (evidenced in the work of Kelley, Jones, & Davies, Weiner, and others) that lead to the explosion of basic attribution research in the late 1960s and in the 1970s.

It is clear that the generation of testable theory relating to accounts is underway (e.g., Harvey et al. Chap. 1, this volume; Schönbach, Chap 3, this volume). The work in this book leads to two further observations about theory generation. First, the material incorporated into theoretical statements is impressive in scope, and the promise of rich, broadly inclusive theoretical statements is great (e.g., Read & Collins, Chap. 7, this volume). Second, the willingness to question traditional assumptions about the task of understanding close relationships, the nature of relevant theory, what constitutes acceptable data, and so on is exciting (see Shotter, Chap. 2, this volume). Like many of the newer, radical perspectives in social psychology (emanating largely from Europe), it has the potential to revolutionize the discipline when translated into testable theory that will allow its importance to be demonstrated empirically.

Finally, a note of caution is appropriate. Just as we need to be clear about our constructs, it is equally important to be precise about the subject of our theories. Do the theories pertain to behavior in close relationships, or are they really theories about lay conceptions of accounts and related behavior? It is not always appreciated that some research on accounts (especially when it involves vignettes about hypothetical others) may tell us more about respondents' knowledge of the culture and its behavioral norms than about their behavior in close relationships. Presumably, such cultural knowledge informs individual behavior in relationships, but whether it does so inexorably is very much open to question. Recognition of this possibility is a prerequisite to research that allows us to evaluate the breadth of a theory's applicability.

Replicable Phenomena

Integral to the generation of testable theory is the identification of replicable phenomena that the theory explains. Although important in establishing the need to study accounts and in providing a rich source of hypotheses, the qualitative analyses of accounts found in the close relationships literature do not appear as yet to have spawned a cumulative body of empirical research that investigates replicable phenomena (a possible exception is research on relationship dissolution). The empirical rigor found in the attribution literature, together with ideas and methods found in basic research on accounts (see Cody, Kersten, Braaten & Dickson, Chap. 6, this volume; Schönbach, Chap. 7 this volume), has the potential to provide the conditions that will accelerate the identification of new accounts phenomena.

The present book shows that identification of such new phenomena is also underway. Several chapters offer insights that point to empirical research programs in close relationships (e.g., Baumeister & Stillwell, Chap. 4; Croghan & Miell, Chap. 13; Lloyd-Bostock, Chap. 12; Read & Collins, Chap. 7), whereas others present studies that are likely to represent the beginnings of a new genre of accounts research (e.g., Andrews, Chap. 10; Brewin, Chap. 11; Holtzworth-Munroe, Chap. 9;

Vangelisti, Chap. 8). It is especially noteworthy that the studies are informed by related research findings (e.g., attributions in marriage) but does not assume that the findings can be generalized to the domain investigated (e.g., attributions pertaining to marital violence).

Equally noteworthy, however, is the paucity of attention given to accounts as dynamic, rather than static, phenomena. It is conceivable that the most important feature of accounts is not their stability but their variability. Indeed, whether accounts are marked by stability versus variability might vary as a function of the stage of the relationship, with variability dominating the beginning and end phases of the relationship. The need for longitudinal studies of accounts is critical.

Methodological Advances

The marriage of research on accounts and on attributions in close relationships is timely for yet another reason: Work on accounts lacks the methodological rigor found in attribution research, whereas, as noted, work on attribution lacks the richness of material found in the accounts literature. Close relationships are complex, and if we are to gain a more complete understanding of them, we need to combine the best of these two research traditions.

The most immediate gains are likely to emerge from the derivation of reliable and valid methods to study the kind of material reported in the accounts literature. Several chapters show that the methodological chasm separating research on accounts and attributions is narrowing. From the perspective of attribution research, the studies on open-ended attribution responses (e.g., Andrews, Chap. 10; Vangelisti, Chap. 8) and on spontaneous attributions (e.g., Brewin, Chap. 11; Holtzworth-Munroe, Chap. 9) focus attention on methodologies that have been underutilized in the attribution literature and that hold considerable promise for infusing this literature with the richness and complexity found in the explanations offered by intimates. In a similar vein, the studies presented within the framework of accounts show the kind of methodological rigor that is likely to advance this domain of inquiry (e.g., Schönbach, Chap. 3; Cody et al., Chap. 6). The chapters that integrate the two research traditions and that suggest promising methodologies toward this end (e.g., Baumeister & Stillwell, Chap. 4; Harvey et al., Chap. 1 Read & Collins, Chap. 7) also bode well for future research.

Accounts in Context

Consistent with earlier observations, there is also a need for greater precision in specifying the context in which accounts are obtained. Brewin (Chap. 11, this volume) offers the insightful observation that we need to develop standardized techniques for obtaining data because the manner in which attributions/accounts are elicited is likely to influence what is obtained. This is not simply an issue of methodology; the context in which accounts are studied is likely to have profound implications for what is learned about them. Surprisingly little attention has been devoted to this topic, and the remainder of this section therefore attempts to illustrate its importance.

At the most pragmatic level, inattention to context is likely to result in seemingly contradictory findings. For example, far fewer spontaneous attributions have been identified in the conversations of married partners (Holtzworth-Munroe & Jacobson, 1988) than in family therapy sessions (Stratton et al., 1986). Although this discrepancy could be due to several factors, we need only consider one in the present context. Unlike marital conversations, family therapy sessions involve the presence of at least one stranger (the therapist) who does not have the same shared knowledge about the family as family members. Unless the therapist is totally ignored, more attributions are likely to be offered by family members simply to make family events intelligible to the therapist, attributions that might otherwise be redundant if articulated because they represent knowledge shared by family members (cf. Bradbury & Fincham, 1988).

Context is also likely to be important for understanding accounts at a conceptual level. For example, what constitutes an appropriate account is likely to vary as a function of cultural or subcultural context. Thus, it may be impossible to study accounts without studying the cultural context (and its rules about relationship behavior) in which they are embedded (see Croghan & Miell, Chap, 13, this volume). As a second example, consider accounts that occur in formal contexts, such as complaint letters to hospitals, and in informal contexts, such as close relationships. As Lloyd-Bostock (Chap. 12, this volume) notes, the very structure of the health system is likely to influence the occurrence and nature of letters of complaint. Consequently, the findings obtained in such contexts may reveal a different picture than that obtained from research on accounts in close relationships. A lesson from the attribution literature is instructive. Although research on responsibility attribution has been advanced by legal writings, it is now equally apparent that some of the distinctions investigated are not relevant for understanding psychological functioning and reflect only institutionalized, legal processes.

Context is particularly salient for understanding accounts in close relationships because "the reality of the world is sustained through conversation with significant others" (Berger & Kellner, 1970) and because "in close relationships we often explain our own actions to our partner; we also often tell our partner why she or he acted in some particular way" (Kelley, 1977, p. 87). To understand accounts we therefore need to view them as part of the fabric of everyday conversation (cf. Shotter, Chap. 2, this volume).

The study of accounts in the conversations of intimates is not easy because a couple's shared history allows each partner to draw on a vast repertoire of implicit, common assumptions and meanings in their conversation. Moreover, access to this repertoire is often hindered by the use of telegraphic utterances that may not even cue the outsider to the elaborate story conveyed by them. Finally, adherence to conversational maxims, such as informativeness (Grice, 1975), may further restrict the occurrence of easily recognized accounts and attributions; they may occur only at the time of novel expectancy violations that are truly surprising to the partner (accounts for other forms of expectancy violation may comprise part of shared knowledge and would not therefore be informative) and may not occur explicitly in subsequent conversations (they would comprise part of existing knowledge and their use may therefore violate the maxim of informativeness).

Viewing accounts in their conversational context draws attention to the fact that dialogue (whether written or verbal) between social scientist and informant is only one (quite unusual) type of conversation. How do conversational maxims such as informativeness, manner, relevance, and truthfulness influence the accounts obtained from respondents? Can accounts offered to different audiences be analyzed similarly? Are conversational maxims followed fully in close relationships, and, if not, how does deviation from them differ across different types of relationships (e.g., happy versus distressed)? In short, viewing accounts as talk harnesses useful perspectives (e.g., the theory of speech acts) and tools (e.g., conversational analysis) that are likely to advance our understanding of this topic (cf. Fincham, in press). At the same time, it multiplies the challenge of our task by illuminating further the complexity of our subject matter.

Conclusion

Like the present book, this commentary traverses a great deal of territory. Addressing the question "Why this book at this particular time?", several observations were offered to show that from an historical perspective the book is timely in identifying the need to integrate attribution and accounts literatures. It went on to illustrate the book's substantive contribution by considering several desiderata for future research and noting the extent and manner in which the chapters address each of them.

A theme throughout the commentary is that accounts in close relationships provide researchers with rich, complex material. Faced with the challenge of understanding such material, social scientists have sometimes appeared to shrink from the challenge, especially in the eyes of the impatient and the layperson. What emerges in the research literature appears to be a barely recognizable derivative of the naturally observed phenomenon that stimulated research interest. It is important to recognize that simplifying and dissecting phenomena in research is important in advancing knowledge. It is equally important, though less often acknowledged, that studying the phenomenon as a whole, in all its complexity, is critical to a complete understanding. But confronting complex phenomena directly is fraught with danger: It can cause us to question cherished epistemological assumptions (e.g., about what constitutes adequate data) and can easily lead us down a cul-de-sac.

It is comforting to believe that the truth is simple and will yield itself to the familiar, traditional methods of our chosen discipline. To think otherwise, to allow for complexity, requires courage. In transcending familiar boundaries and attempting to understand accounts in all their complexity, this is above all a volume that reflects considerable courage—it will not allow us to deceive ourselves.

Acknowledgments. The author thanks Susan Kemp-Fincham and John Grych for their comments on an earlier version of this chapter. Preparation of this chapter was supported by Grant MH44078-01 from the National Institute of Mental Health and by a Faculty Scholar Award from the W.T. Grant Foundation.

References

Antaki, C. (1987). Performed and unperformable: A guide to accounts of relationships. In R. Burnett, P. McGhee, & D. Clark (Eds.), *Accounting for relationships*. New York: Methuen.

Berger, P., & Kellner, H. (1970). Marriage and the construction of reality. In H.P. Dreitzel (Ed.), *Recent sociology: Patterns of communicative behavior*. New York: Macmillan.

Bradbury, T.N., & Fincham, F.D. (1988). Assessing spontaneous attributions in marital interaction: Methodological and conceptual considerations. *Journal of Social and Clinical Psychology, 7*, 122–130.

Duck, S. (1983). Review of *Close relationships. Journal of Social and Personal Relationships, 1*, 132–133.

Fincham, F.D. (in press). The account episode in close relationships. In M.L. McLaughlin, M. Cody, & S.J. Read (Eds.), *Explaining one's self to others: Reason-giving in a social context*. Hillsdale, NJ: Erlbaum.

Fincham, F.D., & Bradbury, T.N. (1990). Psychology and the study of marriage. In F.D. Fincham & T.N. Bradbury (Eds.), *The psychology of marriage: Basic issues and applications* (pp. 1–12). New York: Guilford.

Grice, H.P. (1975). Logic and conversation. In P. Cole & J.L. Morgan (Eds.), *Syntax and semantics 3: Speech acts* (pp. 41–58). New York: Academic.

Hewstone, M.R. (1989). *Causal attribution: From cognitive processes to collective beliefs*. Oxford: Basil Blackwell.

Holtzworth-Munroe, A., & Jacobson, N.S. (1988). Toward a methodology for coding spontaneous causal attributions: Preliminary results with married couples. *Journal of Social and Clinical Psychology, 7*, 101–112.

Huston, T.L., & Levinger, G. (1978). Interpersonal attraction and relationships. *Annual Review of Psychology, 29*, 115–156.

Kelley, H.H. (1977). An application of attribution theory to research methodology for close relationships. In G. Levinger & H. Raush (Eds.), *Close relationships: Perspectives on the meaning of intimacy*. Amherst, MA: University of Massachusetts Press.

Scott, M.B., & Lyman, S. (1968). Accounts. *American Sociological Review, 33*, 46–62.

Stratton, P., Heard, D., Hanks, H.G.I., Munton, A.G., Brewin, C.R., & Davidson, C. (1986). Coding causal beliefs in natural discourse. *British Journal of Social Psychology, 25*, 299–313.

15
Toward a Deeper Understanding of Close Relationships

MILES HEWSTONE

Ten commandments for marriage, etc.: You ought not to say "you ought." You ought not to blame o. You ought not to infringe on o's territory. Always the egocentric evaluation: each thinks other infringes, violates commandments—he does not. (F. Heider, 1988, p. 162)

Introduction

Social psychology has, somewhat belatedly, come to recognize the importance of close, long-term relationships between individuals (e.g., Argyle & Henderson, 1985; Brehm, 1985; Clark & Reis, 1988; Duck, 1984; Kelley et al., 1983; Levinger, 1980). Although, with hindsight, causal and other forms of commonsense attributions would seem to be an important component of such relationships, just as the epigram from Heider's *Notebooks* shows, research on this topic tended to lag behind work on information-processing aspects of attribution (see Hewstone, 1989). This book provides the latest piece of evidence that attribution theory, in part via its link with the closely related field of interpersonal accounts, is now taking close relationships very seriously indeed.

Before the publication of this book, social psychologists had already contributed a great deal, theoretically and methodologically, to the study of relationships. Attribution researchers had also proposed that attribution processes were integrally related to the core stages of relationships: formation, maintenance and dissolution. Thus Fincham (1985) suggested that during the formation phase, attributions would help to reduce ambiguity and to ease the processing of information about behavior in the relationship. During the maintenance phase, attributional activity should decrease; the existence of stable conceptions (dispositional attributions) will increase predictability and reduce the need to make causal attributions. In the dissolution phase, attributions are again likely to be functional in helping partners to understand what is happening in the relationship.

What, then, do the chapters in this book contribute to this flourishing area? In the small space available, I will limit myself to a few comments under three broad headings: conceptual issues, methodological issues, and insights into close relationships.

Conceptual Issues

Attributions and Accounts

As Harvey, Orbuch, and Weber (Chap. 1) correctly convey, the fields of attribution theory and accounts have emerged, not only in different disciplines, but "along parallel but seldom intersecting avenues of logic" (p. 1). Yet because of their obvious conceptual overlap, there is a need to integrate the findings of both fields, as Harvey et al. attempt to do.

Attribution theory is concerned with commonsense explanations and perceptions of the causes of behavior; it has also merged into attributions of responsibility and blame, judgments that have more moral connotations. It has the advantages and disadvantages of being tied to a relatively small number of core theoretical statements (Heider, 1958; Jones & Davis, 1965; Kelley, 1967), and it has proved eminently translatable into empirical, primarily experimental, work. Attribution theory's bequest is evident through many chapters in the present volume: Jones and Nisbett's (1972) actor-observer hypothesis is extended to offender-victim and mothering relationships (see Holtzworth-Munroe, Chap. 9, this volume; Croghan & Miell, Chap. 13, this volume); Weiner's (1986) work on the fundamental dimensions underlying causal attributions is picked up in many chapters, to which I return below; and even Kelley's (1967) three core informational dimensions (consensus, consistency, and distinctiveness) are identified in the verbatim reports of female victims of marital violence (see Andrews, Chap. 10, this volume). This last finding is of some interest, given studies that indicate the low propensity of experimental subjects to seek out these kinds of information (e.g., Garland, Hardy, & Stephenson, 1975; Major, 1980).

Accounts are more difficult to define. Their study was initiated by Scott and Lyman (1968), who defined them as "statements made to explain untoward behavior and bridge the gap between actions and expectations" (p. 46). In contrast to attribution theory's concern with the informational antecedents and rules of causal inference, the focus of accounts was on linguistic forms. Harvey et al. in their introductory chapter, take a commendably broader approach, which deliberately emphasizes the form of accounts as "story-like constructions that contain a plot, or story line, characters, a time sequence, attributions, and other forms of expression such as affect" (p. 3). Over time, certainly, there has been a broadening of work on accounts, justifying Harvey et al.'s definition. This is most evident in Cody, Kersten, Braaten and Dickson's chapter (Chap. 6, this volume), which charts the move away from what they refer to as "accounts as remedial work" (p. 98), to include forms such as "concession," "apologies," and "denials," serving functions such as intimidation, ingratiation, and supplication (see also Schönbach, Chap. 3, this volume).

Harvey et al.'s interpretation of accounts as stories aims to accommodate a richer variety of psychological processes, inform about emotion and affect-laden memory, forge a link with the literatures on narrative and story telling, and emphasize both the private and public nature of account-making. These are all criteria in terms of which these chapters can be evaluated and in terms of which the volume can be judged, broadly, successful. But questions remain about exactly how attributions and accounts differ and what is to gained by their integration in the field of relationships. Harvey et al. acknowledge the theoretical limitations of the work on accounts, but they fail to give a precise answer as to how the two approaches trade off against each other. One of the shortcomings of the volume, and this is as much a reflection on the two fields as on the editors or contributors, is that it brings together one set of chapters "mainly on attributions" (Read & Collins, Chap. 7, this volume; Vangelisti, Chap. 8, this volume; Holtzworth-Munroe, Chap. 9, this volume; Andrews, Chap. 10, this volume; and Brewin, Chap. 11, this volume) and another set of chapters "mainly on accounts" (Shotter, Chap. 2, this volume; Baumeister & Stillwell, Chap. 4, this volume; Croghan & Miell, Chap. 13, this volume; Schönbach, Chap. 3, this volume; and Planalp & Surra, Chap. 5, this volume). Only the chapters by Cody et al. (Chap. 6, this volume) and by Lloyd-Bostock (Chap. 12, this volume) connect the two approaches.

Knowledge Structures

The most ambitious theoretical advance offered in this book is the knowledge structure approach put forward by Read and Collins (Chap. 7, this volume). The starting point for this relatively new approach is that people's explanations of human behavior depend on detailed social and physical knowledge, a topic not addressed in the classic theories of attribution. Read and Collins propose a general model of understanding that centers on goal-based and causal links among the elements of an account.

I was particularly struck by the way these authors linked work on stories with accounts and narratives via their insight that stories and behavioral episodes have the same general form. Read and Collins argue that people are not imposing a story form on events but rather that this form is "actually the basic form of human behavioral episodes" (p. 118). This parallel leads to a more specific view of what people must do to construct accounts than any other model of which I know. According to Read and Collins, people must discern the goals of the actors, the factors that instigate those goals, and what happened to those goals; they must then work out how the actors' behaviors fit into the plans and strategies that were followed in pursuit of the goals.

This model is fleshed out with a daunting armamentarium of elements of social knowledge, including scripts, plans, goals, themes, explanatory patterns, and so on. Any of these knowledge structures can be the source of an expectancy that is violated, leading to the search for an account, and one begins to wonder about the viability of such a complex model. Its cognitive sophistication is not in question, but this very refinement seems a long way from the type of naturally offered explanations that Read and Collins wish to investigate. In sum, I admire this chapter's breadth, but I worry that the knowledge structure approach has yet to provide empirical research that has kept up with its conceptual developments.

Causal Dimensions

The one point on which I disagree with Read and Collins (Chap. 7, this volume) concerns the utility of traditional causal dimensions such as internal-external, stable-unstable, controllable-uncontrollable, and global-specific. According to Read and Collins, these dimensions "are not very useful for differentiating distressed and nondistressed couples" (p. 138). My reading of the relevant literature suggests, on the contrary, that these dimensions have been tremendously useful in this, as in other, respects. Happily married (or nondistressed) spouses tend to give their partners credit for positive behaviors by citing internal, stable, controllable, and global factors to explain them. Negative behaviors, on the other hand, are explained away by ascribing them to causes viewed as external, unstable, uncontrollable, and specific. As Holtzworth-Munroe and Jacobson (1985) have noted, these attributions maximize the impact of positive behavior and minimize the impact of negative behavior; they can therefore be viewed as "relationship enhancing." Distressed couples, in contrast, tend to give exactly the opposite pattern of attributions, which can be thought of as "distress maintaining" (see Hewstone, 1989, Chap. 5).

These dimensions are, moreover, central to Weiner's (1986) work on the affective consequences of causal attributions. Weiner has specified the roles of each of the three main underlying dimensions for his general theory of motivation and emotion (e.g., that locus is related to self-esteem, stability to hopelessness, and controllability to anger and pity).

Several chapters in this book also rely heavily on the causal dimensions. For example, Vangelisti (Chap. 8, this volume) analyzes partners' explanations for their communication problems in terms of locus, stability, and globality dimensions. Cody et al. (Chap. 6, this volume) investigate the relationship between controllability of a relational problem and the decision to withdraw from a relationship. Brewin (Chap. 11, this volume) analyzes spontaneous attributions using the Leeds Attributional Coding

System (LACS; Stratton et al., 1986), which uses five underlying dimensions. There are certainly still many unanswered questions about how causal dimensions relate to affective and other consequences of causal attributions, but I suggest that future work on close relationships will continue to rely heavily on fundamental attributional dimensions.

Communication

Notwithstanding my positive assessment of causal dimensions, attention to them should not rule out research on concrete, ordinary-language explanations. The links among attributions, accounts, and communication have been emphasized at least since Orvis, Kelley, and Butler's (1976) influential chapter on attributional conflict in young couples, and Sillars's (1981) chapter on attributions and interpersonal conflict resolution. Attribution, like communication, is typically a circular process, yet disciplinary borders between social psychology and communication have yet to be effectively breached.

Vangelisti (Chap. 8, this volume) has tried effectively to link communication and attribution by developing a typology of "problematic communication behaviors" and finding that causal attributions for the behaviors differentiate between satisfied and less satisfied couples. She also makes the point that a number of different attributions may be assigned to a single communicative behavior and that these attributions determine, to a large extent, how satisfied individuals are with their relationships.

Cody et al. (Chap. 6, this volume) also focus on strategic communication in relationship dissolution, and their definition of accounts is operationalized for communication research, "messages used to cope with social predicaments of failure events" (p. 94). They provide an interesting summary of work mapping "tactical preferences" (e.g., "positive tone," "deescalation," and "justification") onto three general types of relationship problems ("faults," "failure to compromise," and "constrained").

This kind of work has led to a better understanding of the *process* of relationship disengagement than has been obtained by a purely attributional approach. It is, however, probably no accident that these two chapters focusing on communication are the work of scholars based in departments of communication. Social psychologists wishing to work in this area should be equally ready to step across the disciplinary boundaries.

Methodological Issues

Open-Ended versus Closed-Ended Measures

As I wrote above, it is not alwasys clear from this book where and how attribution-based research differs from accounts-based research on relationships. Methodologically, attribution research tends to make more use of questionnaires with closed-ended questions, whereas accounts research tries to do justice to the richness of the spoken or written word by analyzing open-ended responses. One reason for this distinction is that attribution researchers have a much stronger theoretical basis on which to select specific questions. But this distinction is only a trend, not an absolute contrast, and it raises a number of issues.

Read and Collins (Chap. 7, this volume), for example, make a strong plea for open-ended rather than closed-ended questions: "To understand explanations we need to focus on their structure and content. Therefore we must investigate people's naturally offered attributions and the knowledge used to construct them. . . To do so requires that we gather open-ended explanations rather than have people respond to a fixed set of questions" (p. 137–138). Attribution research has certainly relied heavily on the use of rating scales, and open-ended measures can be very useful in exploring the vocabulary of commonsense explanations, especially at the pilot stage of research. It should be acknowledged, however, that open-ended questions are not unproblematic; they are time-consuming for respondents and researchers alike, and they have been found to have poorer intertest validity and reliability than structured response measures (Elig & Frieze, 1979).

Vangelisti (Chap. 8, this volume) has noted some of the limitations of the free-response format. Frequency ratings of self-generated communication problems seem to have been subject to an availability bias (Tversky & Kahneman, 1973), and Vangelisti notes the possible advantages of comparing open-ended and structured responses in terms of the sort of cognitive processing in which respondents have to engage. Unfortunately, sophisticated statistical comparisons of open-and closed-ended measures are few in number and should remain on the agenda of future research (see Elig & Frieze, 1979; Howard, 1987; Miller, Smith, & Uleman, 1981).

Coding Schemes

Within the category of open-ended attributions and accounts, the range of methodological possibilities is wide. Baumeister and Stillwell (Chap. 4, this volume) refer to a continuum from "micronarratives" to "broadly focused life stories," and their chapter will be useful to anyone first contemplating what type of data to collect and analyze. Their use of the autobiographical method is an interesting one that might usefully be integrated with recent work on autobiographical memory (e.g., Neisser, 1988; Neisser & Winograd, 1988). The relevance of the work on memory for the study of close relationships is evident from Neisser's view that the main function of autobiographical memory is not the accuracy of one's past, but the creation and maintenance of relationships with family and others.

Wherever on Baumeister and Stillwell's continuum the collected open-ended responses are located, the researcher must choose how to *analyze*. The only exception is the chapter by Croghan and Miell (Chap. 13, this volume), which, in my view, weakens a potentially interesting study of the mothering relationship by its failure to undertake any empirical analysis of accounts. Many social psychologists will welcome the attention paid to discourse by "discourse analysis," but they will lament the failure to undertake any real analysis.

At this stage in the development of the field of close relationships, we also need analyses comparing different coding schemes based on attributions and accounts (see Dutton, 1986; Henderson & Hewstone, 1984), and respondent-rated versus researcher-coded attributions (an issue raised by Holtzworth-Munroe, Chap. 9, this volume). As Brewin (Chap. 11, this volume) agrues, we need to use different types of analysis to complement each other.

Where most of these chapters tend to disappoint is in what they actually do with open-ended data. They neither develop new, general typologies of accounts, nor do they provide sophisticated linguistic analyses of content, form or structure. Schönbach (Chap. 3, this volume) is the major exception to this criticism, with his analysis of account episodes carried out in exquisite detail. Only this kind of approach can reveal that the variety of accounts masks a common underlying pattern. Baumeister and Stillwell (Chap. 4, this volume) also report interesting findings linking self-esteem to the tense used in accounts of past failures: People with high self-esteem linked their past failures up to the present more than did people with low self-esteem.

A new approach to such data that holds great promise is Semin and Fielder's (1988) Linguistic Category Model. This model distinguishes four linguistic categories that may be used in describing other people—the same behavioral episode may be encoded at four different levels of abstraction, ranging from the most concrete level ("descriptive action verbs") through gradually more abstract verbs ("interpretive action verbs" and "state verbs"), to the highest level of abstraction ("adjectives"). An interesting consequence of how something is encoded is that more abstract encoding implies greater stability over time and generality across settings and interaction partners. Abstract statements are perceived as less verifiable, imply greater temporal stability, and are perceived as revealing more about the person and less about the situation than are concrete statements. This sort of approach could easily be applied to many of the types of data reported in this volume to provide a reliable and sophisticated analysis of open-ended responses.

Longitudinal Research

Without wishing to minimize the difficulties of conducting longitudinal research, these chapters provide numerous illustrations of why we need it. Consider Baumeister and Stillwell's (Chap. 4, this volume) conclusion that autobiographical accounts enable respondents to "include, delete, or distort material as they see fit" (p. 68). It would be fascinating to study exactly what, and when, people delete from and distort their accounts over time.

Longitudinal research would also speak to the potential bias associated with retrospective methodology, as widely used in research on accounts. Holtzworth-Munroe (Chap. 9, this volume), for example, raises the question of whether after-the-fact attributions for marital conflict are as "important" as on-line attributions during marital interaction. Andrews (Chap. 10, this volume) reports interesting retrospective data on self blame during and after violent relationships, findings that one would like to see verified in a longitudinal design. There exist only a few studies of how attributions change over time (see Miller & Porter, 1980; Moore, Sherrod, Liu, & Underwood, 1979; Peterson, 1980), and this issue ought to be revived in the content of close relationships.

By raising these methodological issues, I am not trying to be hypercritical. Many of the accounts cited in this volume are genuinely moving, and this renders it all the more imporant to analyze them soundly. As Harvey et al. (Chap. 1, this volume) point out, attributions in close relationships do not come as "easily condensed or summarized structures of thought or feeling" (p. 9), but it should surely be a goal of the scientific study of relationships to provide that systematization and structure. I think this is a goal that many, but not all, the contributors would endorse.

Insights into Close Relationships

Traditionally, the study of close relationships has been the study of dating or married heterosexual couples. The sheer variety of topics studied in this volume attests to a broadened approach. The kinds of relationships and relationship issues studied include: dating couples (Read & Collins, Chap. 7, this volume; Cody et al., Chap. 6, this volume), committed relationships (Vangelisti, Chap. 8, this volume; Planalp & Surra, Chap. 5, this volume); masochistic relationships, unrequited love (Baumeister & Stillwell, Chap 4); marital violence (Holtzworth-Munroe, Chap. 9, this volume; Andrews, Chap. 10, this volume); families of schizophrenics (Brewin, Chap. 11, this volume); complainant-hospital staff relationships (Lloyd-Bostock, Chap. 12, this volume); and mothering (Croghan & Miell, Chap. 13, this volume). The insights into close relationships are evident and sometimes profound.

A strong claim made for the accounts or narrative approach is that some phenomena can only be studied by this method of research (Baumeister & Stillwell, Chap. 4, this volume). This certainly seems to be true of topics such as masochistic relationships and unrequited love; as these authors rather laconically state "laboratory experiments probably cannot simulate unrequited love effectively" (p. 65). One may have to rely on samples of convenience and problematic data bases (e.g., the letters pages of S&M magazines), but these authors report counterintuitive findings and provide interesting interpretations for them. For example, they claim that the appeal of masochism can be better understood in terms of fantastic escapes from the mundane than motivations of guilt, self-dislike, or sexual inadequacy and that the objects of unrequited love ultimately experience more negative affect than do the rejected suitors. A strength of Baumeister and Stillwell's approach is that several themes reappear across a variety of phenomena, suggesting that concepts such as time, self-esteem, egocentrism, and guilt are central parts of the conceptual vocabulary of relationships.

I am especially impressed by the insights gained from three of these chapters. The first two complement each other, with Holtzworth-Munroe (Chap. 9, this volume) examining violent husbands' perceptions and Andrews (Chap. 10, this volume) investigating women's self-blame in violent relationships. Holtzworth-Munroe's chapter starts from the troubling finding of previous research, that men tend to explain away, excuse, or justify their violence. Her careful analysis, however, which controls for group differences in marital distress, found no difference between violent/distressed and nonviolent/distressed husbands' attributions for negative but nonviolent partner behaviors. Thus, attributional data do not yet help us to differentiate among those men who choose to use, or not use, violence.

Andrews's chapter (Chap. 10, this volume) begins with the fundamental inequality of partners in violent marital relationships, as contrasted with the neutral roles of actor and observer (Jones & Nisbett, 1972). She reports the interesting finding that women's retrospective reports of self-blame, for the time when they were still involved with an abusive partner, are higher than when the relationship has been terminated. She also distinguishes between characterological and behavioral self-blame, reporting that when self-blame was reported by women, those who had suffered early abuse tended to blame their character, whereas those without abuse tended to blame their behavior. The analysis is pushed as far as the behavioral consequences and functions of these attributions, but Andrews' interpretation is commendably cautious. The tendency for women with characterological self-blame to be less likely to seek help from health professionals was not significant, but those who blamed their partner's character were the most likely to seek legal help. Thus in both these chapters we see the role of attributions carefully investigated, but not oversold.

Brewin's contribution (Chap. 11, this volume) shows just what can be gained from detailed, quantitative analysis of spontaneous causal attributions, coded from videotapes and written materials. His collection, analysis, and reporting of data are exemplary, while providing an honest assessment of the strengths and weaknesses of different methods. I am filled with admiration at the time demands and complexity of coding required by the LACS method, about which we ought to be reading more in the future. Brewin's unique data on relatives' attributions of diagnosed psychiatric patients reveal wide individual variation in the number and type of responses. Attributions were found to predict both criticism and hostility, but Brewin acknowledges implicitly that future work must tackle the difficult question of how to analyze chains of distal and proximal causes. This question continues to be practically ignored by researchers (for exceptions see Brickman, Ryan, & Wortman, 1975; Fincham & Schultz, 1981; Kelley, 1983; Vinokur & Ajzen, 1982), but the story-like definition of accounts espoused by this volume's editors cries out for such an analysis in the context of long-term relationships.

Conclusions

At the end of this book, it is only reasonable to pose to the editors their own question: In their synthesis of attributions and accounts for close relationships, are they "trying to assimilate too much diversity"? (Harvey et al., Chap. 1, this volume, p. 14). Quite the contrary. I admire the breadth of approach, the variety of relationships studied, and questions asked as well as answered. We appear nowhere near a point of closure in this fascinating field, and I have tried to raise some of the questions that I hope will occupy future researchers. If the conceptual and methodological issues are faced, not avoided, then future insights will accrue at an even faster rate, and this volume will have been an important landmark on the road toward a deeper understanding of close relationships.

References

Argyle, M., & Henderson, M. (1985). *The anatomy of relationships*. London: Penguin.

Brehm, S.S. (1985). *Intimate relationships*. New York: Random House.

Brickman, P., Ryan, K., & Wortman, C.B. (1975). Causal chains: Attribution of responsibility as a function of immediate and prior causes. *Journal of Personality and Social Psychology*, *32*, 1060–1067.

Clark, M.S., & Reis, H.T. (1988). Interpersonal processes in close relationships. *Annual Review of Psychology*, *39*, 609–672.

Duck, S.W. (Ed.). (1984). *Personal relationships* (Vol. 5). London: Academic Press.

Dutton, D.G. (1986). Wife assaulter's explanations for assault: The neutralization of self-punishment. *Canadian Journal of Behavioral Science*, *18*, 381–390.

Elig, T.W., & Frieze, I.H. (1979). Measuring causal attributions for success and failure. *Journal of Personality and Social Psychology*, 37, 621–634.

Fincham, F.D. (1985). Attributions in close relationships. In J.H. Harvey & G. Weary (Eds.), *Attribution: Basic issues and applications*. Orlando, FL: Academic Press.

Fincham, F.D., & Shultz, T.R. (1981). Intervening causation and the mitigation of responsibility for harm. *British Journal of Social Psychology, 20*, 113–120.

Garland, H., Hardy, A., & Stephenson, L. (1975). Information search as affected by attribution type and response category. *Personality and Social Psychology Bulletin, 4*, 612–615.

Heider, F. (1958). *The psychology of interpersonal relations*. New York: Wiley.

Heider, F. (1988). *The notebooks* (Vol. 5) (M. Benesh-Weiner; ed.) München-Weinheim: Psychologie Verlags Union.

Henderson, M., & Hewstone, M. (1984). Prison inmates' explanations for interpersonal violence: Accounts and attributions. *Journal of Consulting and Clinical Psychology, 52*, 789–794.

Hewstone, M. (1989). *Causal attribution: From cognitive processes to collective beliefs*. Oxford: Basil Blackwell.

Holtzworth-Munroe, A., & Jacobson, N.S. (1985). Causal attributions of married couples: When do they search for causes? What do they conclude when they do? *Journal of Personality and Social Psychology, 48*, 1398–1412.

Howard, J.A. (1987). The conceptualization and measurement of attributions. *Journal of Experimental Social Psychology, 23*, 32–58.

Jones, E.E., & Davis, K.E. (1965). From acts to dispositions: The attribution process in person perception. In L. Berkowitz (Ed.), *Advances in experimental social psychology* (Vol. 2). New York: Academic Press.

Jones, E.E., & Nisbett, R.E. (1972). The actor and the observer: Divergent perceptions of the causes of behaviour. In E.E. Jones, D.E. Kanouse, H.H. Kelley, R.E. Nisbett, S. Valins, & B. Weiner (Eds.), *Attribution: Perceiving the causes of behaviour*. Morristown, NJ: General Learning Press.

Kelley, H.H. (1967). Attribution theory in social psychology. In D. Levine (Ed.), *Nebraska symposium on motivation* (Vol. 15). Lincoln, NE: University of Nebraska Press.

Kelley, H.H. (1983). Perceived causal structures. In J.M.F. Jaspars, F.D. Fincham, & M. Hewstone (Eds.), *Attribution theory and research: Conceptual, developmental and social dimensions*. London: Academic Press.

Kelley, H.H., Berscheid, E., Christensen, A., Harvey, J.H., Huston, T.L., Levinger, G., McClintock, E., Peplau, L.A., & Peterson, D.R. (1983). *Close relationships*. New York: Freeman.

Levinger, G. (1980). Toward the analysis of close relationships. *Journal of Experimental Social Psychology, 16*, 510–544.

Major, B. (1980). Information acquisition and attribution processes. *Journal of Personality and Social Psychology, 39*, 1010–1023.

Miller, D.T., & Porter, C.A. (1980). Effects of temporal perspective on the attribution process. *Journal of Personality and Social Psychology, 39*, 532–541.

Miller, F.D., Smith, E.R., & Uleman, J. (1981). Measurement and interpretation of situational and dispositional attributions. *Journal of Experimental Social Psychology, 17*, 80–95.

Moore, B.S., Sherrod, D.R., Liu, T.J., & Underwood, B. (1979). The dispositional shift in attribution over time. *Journal of Experimental Social Psychology, 15*, 553–569.

Neisser, U. (1988). Time present and time past. In M.M. Gruneberg, P.E. Morris & R.N. Sykes (Eds.), *Practical aspects of memory: Vol. 2. Current research and issues*. Chichester: J. Wiley.

Neisser, U., & Winograd, E. (Eds.). (1988). *Remembering reconsidered: Ecological and traditional approaches to the study of memory*. New York: Cambridge University Press.

Orvis, B.R., Kelley, H.H., & Butler, D. (1976). Attributional conflicts in young couples. In J.H. Harvey, W.J. Ickes, & R.F. Kidd (Eds.), *New directions in attribution research* (Vol. 1). Hillsdale, NJ: Erlbaum.

Peterson, C. (1980). Memory and the "dispositional shift." *Social Psychology Quarterly, 43*, 372–380.

Scott, M.B., & Lyman, S. (1968). Accounts. *American Sociological Review, 33*, 46–62.

Semin, G.R., & Fiedler, K. (1988). The cognitive functions of linguistic categories in describing persons: Social cognition and language. *Journal of Personality and Social Psychology, 54*, 558–568.

Sillars, A.L. (1981). Attributions and interpersonal conflict resolution. In J.H. Harvey, W.J. Ickes, & R.F. Kidd (Eds.), *New directions in attribution research* (Vol. 3). Hillsdale, NJ: Erlbaum.

Stratton, P., Heard, D., Hanks, H.G.I., Munton, A.G., Brewin, C.R. & Davidson, C. (1986). Coding causal beliefs in natural discourse. *British Journal of Social Psychology, 25*, 299–313.

Tversky, A., & Kahneman, D. (1973). Availability: A heuristic for judging frequency and probability. *Cognitive Psychology, 5*, 207–232.

Vinokur, A., & Ajzen, I. (1982). Relative importance of prior and immediate events: A causal primacy effect. *Journal of Personality and Social Psychology, 42*, 820–829.

Weiner, B. (1986). *An attributional theory of motivation and emotion*. New York: Springer-Verlag.

16
Attributions, Accounts, and Close Relationships: Close Calls and Relational Resolutions

MARY M. GERGEN and KENNETH J. GERGEN

As Adele sat in the fading light, I was again struck by how elegant she appeared in her long brocade caftan. Few women of any age, much less 93, could claim such social presence as she. As she patiently ended her answer to my previous question, I glanced at my questionnaire, gritted my teeth and plunged ahead with the interview schedule. "Have you ever thought of marrying again?" She laughed, her light, tinkling, Tiffany laugh, and then paused thoughtfully for a moment before responding. "No, Mary, I really haven't. There hasn't been a man since Maurice died that I would want to marry." I scribbled a few notes on the interview sheet, and quickly checked the voluntary-internal (VI) column in the attribution list. The interview continued.

Adele died almost 2 years ago, at 101, without remarrying or losing a whit of her charm and grace. More than 10 years have passed since this interview and the reduction of this richly variegated life to a few simple categories. During this time, alternative research procedures and new perspectives on the nature of social understanding have emerged within psychology, procedures and perspectives that might have been more sensitive to this life in motion. We would like to summarize how we see the changes that have taken place in the research on attributions and accounts in the study of close relationships, and how the chapters of this book contribute to this shift. Further, we shall attempt to scan the trajectory of these pursuits, and to explore possibilities that seem most fruitful for the future.

As more fully described in the introductory chapter of this book by Harvey, Orbuch, and Weber, the study of close relationships has been primarily divided into two communities of researchers, each working in parallel rather than in intersecting fashion. Often the boundary line has been geographic, with American social psychologists frequently working separately from their European colleagues. The conference on which this book is based provided a significant interchange between these groups, and the results may be seen as a collection of outreachings and consolidatings among the two strands of endeavor. Our previous work on narratives (cf. Gergen & Gergen, 1986, 1988) has become a part of these various approaches, and we have been invited to comment on these papers primarily in view of this overlapping interest. As our comments will make clear, it is our hope that the future will enable "American" and "European" lines of endeavor (and others as well) to coalesce within a new form of what may be termed "relational" inquiry.

Rather than viewing the distinction in orientation as geographic in character, let us consider certain differences in grounding assumptions. On the one hand we find what may be viewed as a *natural science* or empiricist orientation to close relations. In this case investigators generally assume that there are fundamental—that is, transhistorical or universal—laws of human nature and that it is the task of the investigator to observe, record, and report their functioning. Currently, within this approach, cognitive processes are typically emphasized as the major determinants of human behavior. In order to isolate the relevant processes, experimental work is required in which the psychologist must place strong constraints over the research procedure—manipulating and controlling variables and observing the outcomes.

Within the study of close relationships, this orientation is primarily represented by psychologists indebted to the long and venerable line of attribution investigation. For example, using the classic covariation model of Kelley (1967), Andrews's (Chap. 10, this volume) contribution to the present book explores the attributions of women who have been victims of marital violence. In particular, she focuses on the types of blame that these women assigned in making sense of the violence—self-blame or partner blame. In addition, she relates these attributions to other variables, such as mental health indicators and responses to violence. In a similar vein, the studies of attributions of violent men, as reported in Holtzworth-Munroe's chapter (Chap. 9, this volume), exemplifies this research style. The justificatory accounts of abusive husbands are coded into internal Versus external categories; wife-blame is often given as a cause of the violence. It is assumed within this research strategy that a husband's attributional processes are independent of interactions with his wife and others, and that they are causally related to his violence.

One feature of the traditional attributional paradigm has been to look at the person making attributions as a rational problem solver. Either the choice of attribution makes sense of another's behavior, or it is a way of handling a problem of logical inference or self-presentation. In the chapter by Cody, Kersten, Braaten, and Dickson (Chap. 6, this volume), for example, the authors describe their interest in "strategic communication" between the two partners in a relational dissolution.

> We view the individual communicator as a problem solver who utilizes perceptions of causality and beliefs about everyday problems as a road map for knowing how to navigate around inexcusable relational problems, implement plans concerning how "solvable" problems can be remedied, and withdraw from relationships that are too costly. (p. 94)

In their work the focus is on the individual actor; the type of interchange preferred is dependent on an internal calculus of success. The chapter by Read and Collins (Chap. 7, this volume) takes a similar stance, emphasizing the cognitive aspects of the individual account-producer. Although the authors use the language of accounts, which we shall discuss below, the formation of the research is dependent on a general model of understanding derived from Schank and Abelson's (1977) knowledge structure approach and theories of text comprehension and cognitive science. As it is presumed, people use the same cognitive processes to "read" external social events as they do in reading a written text. Isolated individuals glean knowledge from their social networks, and their accounts furnish public representations of these inner processes.

Work on communication problems in committed relationships by Vangelisti (Chap. 8, this volume) also shares many similarities with the attribution orientation. A cognitive model is basic to her theorizing. People assess and give more or less accurate accounts of their internal processes. These can be correlated with measures of relational satisfaction. Her central finding, that dissatisfied partners gave more abstract answers to the communication problems between romantic partners than satisfied ones, is explained via various competing hypothetical cognitive models (i.e., Model 1: complex inferences associated directly with satisfaction assessments vs. Model 2: assessing concrete information in specific situations and making global judgments after a certain threshold has been reached).

The natural science orientation, as realized most clearly by attribution research in the present context, does have certain assets. On the most general level, the research undertaking is full of optimism for improving close relationships, promising as it does that there are identifiable foundations to personal relations and that each research finding places one more piece in the universal puzzle. Thus, one might anticipate that as we know increasingly more about the basic forms of attribution, their antecedents, and their effects on relationships, we would finally possess the kind of knowledge from which widespread benefit might be derived. The focus on cognition further suggests that the parameters to the puzzle are delimited and that their study is generally looked upon favorably within the scientific community. Further, attribution assumptions themselves yield an array of interesting questions about close relationships. They suggest that beneath the observable interchanges in which people are engaged, there lie a range of secret dispositions. As these dispositions are brought to light, we elucidate the grounds on which relationships are made solid or shaky. The above research achieves just these effects and leads in every case to conclusions that are interesting and far-reaching.

At the same time, many investigators find the natural science orientation deeply problematic—and most specifically so when applied to relationships of intimacy. For one, the natural science orientation is relatively insensitive to the cultural and historical context in which close relationships occur. Indeed, as many argue, the very conception of intimacy presumed by contemporary research is a notion vulnerable to many historical exigencies, and perhaps specific to Western culture in a particular period of its history. In the same way, it is argued, the natural science orientation tends to overlook the ever-shifting context and complexities of ongoing relationships. It tends to see the individual as possessing relatively fixed and stable dispositions and as relatively insensitive to patterns of change—both within relationships and within the immediate social context. Also, the natural science orientation tends toward an almost exclusive emphasis on the internal processes of the single individual. That which is *social* about relationships is thus secondary and derivative of the properties of single individuals. Finally, the natural science orientation favors deductive research endeavors in which the investigator searches for data relevant to a specific set of theoretical assumptions. This means that research is relatively insulated from the perspectives of the participants themselves, their own understandings of what is taking place, and the complex nuances of various forms of relationship. As in the case of Adele, the research tends to reduce the richness of ongoing interchange to a set of preselected categories.

It is in this context that many researchers in close relationships have adopted what may be termed a *social science* orientation to investigation. In this case there is a broad recognition of the cultural and historical contingency of the subject matter and a more general appreciation of the shifting character of ongoing relationships and their social milieu. The emphasis shifts from the internal, cognitive processes of the individual to the social context, action patterns, and consequences of action. And because in a world of complex and ever-shifting pattern one can never be too sensitive, there is a tendency to avoid deductive research procedures and to remain relatively open to the perspectives of the research participants themselves.

Within the present book this orientation is most fully realized in the various investigations of social accounting, or the means by which people describe, explain, or otherwise lend meaning to actions. Here it is generally assumed that people can and do explain their behaviors, internal states, feelings, thought processes, and so on, and have a "right" to be right about themselves. The individual actor thus becomes the author of his or her own meanings, and the psychologist generally works interpretively from this body of material. The researcher attempts to avoid altering, reforming, denying, or discouraging the sense of meaning produced within these accounts but rather attempts to amplify the intelligibilities around which interaction takes place.

In the present book, the various chapters on accounts move significantly in the social science direction. The chapter by Croghan and Miell (Chap. 13, this volume) on the accounts of women concerning their first year of mothering is one of the most direct expressions of the social science orientation. Through in-depth interviews and 24-hour time use diaries, mothers recorded their daily lives. "The approach . . . has been essentially to view mothers' account as valid within their own terms, rather than assessing their accuracy as representations of some supposed internal dispositions. . . . [The mother's] account . . . is the only acceptable primary source of data." (p. 222–223). These authors do not try to smooth out the accounts so as to create clear, univocal data, but allow the contradictions within the accounts to stand. Accepting these conflicting messages means, to them, that social and ideological forces of various powers influence in complex ways the mothers' interpretations of reality. Mothers are seen as constantly making and remaking sense of their lives in a continuous process of relating. For these researchers, social environmental influences are crucial. Because the mothers are viewed as structuring their own realities, the chapter is heavy with verbatim quotations, provided in part so as to allow the reader a sense of independent access to the field of inquiry.

Ironically, the conclusions drawn by the authors do differ from the realities of the mothers. Drawing from a critical perspective they detect in the mothers' accounts a form of false consciousness derived from living in a world under an ideology of male power. The mystification of experience that results "makes it difficult for women to identify structural inequality and to negotiate for improved access to resources. Inequality is not always perceived as such, hedged in as it is by an ideology of mutual fulfillment within personal sexual relationships" (p. 241–242).

Lloyd-Bostock's (Chap. 12, this volume) work, analyzing patient complaints to the National Health Service hospitals in Great Britain, is also clearly formed along the social science lines. Her method involved categorizing passages from letters of complaint, as well as responses, in order to better understand the relationship of writer to hospital authorities, and particularly the perspective of the complainant. Interestingly, she sees the complaint process, that is the process of social accounting, as a reality-construing means. Until the social process of complaining is completed, writers do not fully apprehend the nature of their complaints. While vested in a social accounting method (cf. Antaki, 1988), and informed by Goffman's (1971) writings on spology, Lloyd-Bostock also utilizes Kelley's (1967) covariation model to analyze her data. While basically following an accounts orientation, her conclusions attempt to synthesize a broad range of perspectives.

The chapter by Baumeister and Stillwell (Chap. 4, this volume) on autobiographical accounts also has a strong affinity with the social science domain. Within their research, accounts provide means for studying intimate relationships, for example, differences among couples in how they construct social realities. In order to illustrate the perspectival nature of accounts, they frequently ask subjects to write two autobiographical accounts, one from each of two, often oppositional, perspectives. In studies on unrequited love, for example, subjects wrote both as a rejected lover and as the object of the unreturned love (Baumeister & Wotman, 1990). The findings indicated that stories written from the perspective of the "heartbreaker" usually included references to their feelings of emotional distress at being loved by someone they do not love in return. When the same subjects wrote stories of being rejected, they never indicated that the heartbreaker was suffering from receiving unwanted affection. It seemed as if the knowledge of what went into the story was limited by the perspective from which it was told. The suffering of the heartbreaker is not a part of the rejected lover's story. The import of this finding is that the power of the cultural form of the narrative is more potent than the ability of the single teller to overcome the boundary between one teller's story and another's—even if the teller is the same person.

Although Baumeister and Stillwell's chapter nicely illustrates the importance of autobiographical accounts in the lives of individuals, they are, at last, reluctant to abandon the natural science orientation. In order to explain the forms of account, they discuss the "naturalized processes" of motivation, emotion, and personality. There is further a perfunctory apology for using naturalistic methods of research. While they indicate that their autobiographical method is valuable, it also "must be considered inferior to laboratory methods for isolating variables and testing hypotheses about causal processes." (p. 55). For the fully committed social scientist/analyst, such an apology would be unnecessary; indeed, it would be the laboratory technician who should apologize for the artificial, narrowly focused, and context-stripping character of laboratory methods.

Let us shift consideration to the third orientation to relationship research, an alternative to both the natural science and the social science views. By way of doing so, however, let us consider differing definitions of accounts located within the chapters of this book. Specifically, within these contributions, four meanings of accounts can be located: (a) explanations or stories that help one understand or describe a particular situation; (b) justifications for actions that have been raised as problematic by others; (c) excuses, that is, ways of admitting wrongful or unseemly behavior while not accepting responsibility for it; and (d) denials of wrongful behavior. It is important to distinguish among these definitions because there are important implications for both the way in which research is viewed, as well as future theories of close relationships. Specifically, whereas the first definition is ontologically neutral, the latter three presume the possibility of accurate as opposed to inaccurate portrayals of action. That is, to view accounts as means of helping people to make sense of their world makes no commitment concerning the relationship between the sense making and the world itself. Or, to put it another way, one can imagine a multiplicity of possible descriptions and explanations, with no means of determining which is the superior (except by falling back on yet another description). In contrast, by viewing accounts as justifications, excuses, and denials, it is presumed that individuals can and often do report incorrectly on their worlds.

The implications of these differing orientations are important. First, consider the methodological level. To take the former position is to give the research participant a full right to his or her interpretations of the world. This is not to say that the accounts furnished within the research setting will necessarily be identical to those given elsewhere or that couples may not favor certain accounts within a relationship over others. However, it is not to presume that the research relationship is shot through with dissimulation and defensiveness and that it is the researcher's task to move past the surface to detect the underlying truth. In effect, the first of these definitions lends itself to a trusting or "appreciative" (Srivastva & Cooperrider, 1990) mode of inquiry.

On the theoretical level, the first of these definitions of accounts also promotes theories of close relationships that place a stronger emphasis on the process of relating than on the makeup of the individuals forming the relationship. If accounts are the means by which people justify, excuse, and deny, then theories of close relationships will tend to emphasize the individual dynamics, rational calculus, and strategic planning giving rise to actions within relationships. Given the true nature of affairs, the theorist is prompted to ask, why does the individual engage in giving an account that differs from this state? In contrast, if accounts are the means by which persons make sense of life, they may be viewed as fundamental to the formation and sustenance of relationships themselves. That is, accounts may be the essential means by which persons in a relationship generate a jointly agreeable sense of the real and the good. As it may be argued, without the achievement of these localized realities, relationships could not successfully proceed.

These distinctions are important because they introduce a third mode of inquiry into close relationships: *social constructionist*. From the constructionist perspective, the world does not in itself demand or require any particular form of description. There are an unlimited number of ways of characterizing the same state of affairs, and no single language can justifiably claim transcendence or status as the one true description. For the constructionist, the emphasis on internal or psychological processes is also replaced by a focus on social interdependence. Because conceptions of the individual mind are products of language, and language is inherently a social activity, social processes are considered prior to (or more fundamental than) individual, psychological ones. That is, linguistic constructions cannot be the sole property of individual minds; a private language cannot form the basis for meaningful communication. Meaningful description, then, grows out of relational process. (Or in Vygotsky's sense, all that takes place within the private reaches can be viewed as the social world internalized.) In any case, for inquiry into close relationships, the constructionist emphasis is likely to depend on forms of ongoing interdependence.

There is a strong tendency among constructionists to favor the interpretive techniques of the social scientist over the hypothesis-testing strategies of the empiricist. This is not because interview data are truer to life, but because such techniques generally operate to broaden—as opposed to narrow—the range of possible interpretations. From the constructionist perspective, the participants' accounts are viewed as the outcome of prior and ongoing social practices, influenced by cultural forms that constrain the narrative options available to the actors. Thus, accounts are seen as neither accurate nor inaccurate, but as useful or not, valid or not, according to the communal group where they are offered. Additionally, the relationship of the interviewer and the respondent is seen as creating meaning. No interview, questionnaire, or experimental activity can be seen as providing "pure" information. Rather, the individuals' actions are seen as embedded within ongoing social process. Thus, what any action means is never closed or clear. In the case of the interview with Adele, for example, Adele's responses may be seen, in part, as an outgrowth of the relationship between her and the interviewer, who are historically, culturally, and socially bound together in multiple, often tangled, ways. Ultimately, for the constructionist, research participants might be viewed as colleagues who join the investigator in the search for understandings.

Within the present book there are many moves congenial to a constructionist orientation. As the Chapters move from the natural science to the social science base, they also acquire an increasing number of constructionist attributes. Thus, as we find, assumptions built into much of the accounting literature lends itself to a constructionist orientation. Schönbach's chapter (Chap. 3, this volume) is especially interesting in this regard. Schönbach's work most fully realizes the constructionist emphasis on relational description. As he demonstrates, if failure is attributed to a participant in a close relationship, then reproach is likely to follow, with excuses or justification following reproach and evaluation occurring after justification. In this sense, excuses or justification are built into a particular scenario of relating— or to put it otherwise, they are steps in a relational dance that gain their meaning only by virtue of their place in the dance. Further, Schönbach indicates that "a negotiation of identities" is implied as the participants try to cope with a specific conflict. Yet, even though Schönbach's description is relational, his choice of explanation falls back on natural science assumptions. As he proposes, the individual actors are motivated to maintain or regain a sense of control and self-esteem; in this case interaction is a by-product of individual minds, and interaction is an artificial by-product of individuals.

Also consistent with the constructionist perspective is Vangelisti's (Chap. 8, this volume) finding that dissatisfied couples tend to produce more abstract complaints about communications problems. If these complaints were seen as moves in a relational game in which irreparable damage is being claimed (and not as a report of the actual nature of their problems), it would be possible to interpret their statements as signaling a loss of hope for the relationship's survival. The communication problems are neither one type or another—until negotiated into a reality by the coparticipants. Andrews's (Chap. 10, this volume) finding that, over time, women who left their abusive situation shifted from a self-blame to a partner blame may also be viewed relationally. As the woman becomes involved in new social networks, she constructs a new non-self-blaming social reality. Brewin's chapter (Chap. 11, this volume) on schizophrenic relapse among family members suggests a form of relational theory in method, interpretation and in therapeutic interventions. By using spontaneous causal statements from relatives concerning negative outcomes associated with the acts of afflicted people, the researchers were able to compare various ways of talking about the illness and to attempt some retraining of family caretakers so as to reduce symptoms of the disorder. The description of this work is framed primarily in traditional attributional language, and the use of standard empirical research practices is prevalent. However, the notion that family interactions generate schizophrenic behaviors and that "changing the families' emotional climate" brings about improvements in patients' relapse rates moves toward a rclational approach to close relationships.

Shotter's (Chap. 2, this volume) contribution is the most speculative and forward-looking in terms of this direction in the study of close relationships. Shotter's major hope is that researchers will eschew the natural science goals of creating theory for purposes of predicting and controlling behavior (a traditional attributional theory goal) and accept the consequences of engaging in the study of human behavior as a practical science, one in which circumstances of living from moment to moment influence action and meaning, and in which moral and ideological issues are constant dilemmas for actors and investigators alike. A second contribution to relational theory is Shotter's concept of "joint actions" as a basis for analyzing behavior. Joint actions are those that can be accomplished by no single individual alone but that are, inevitably, social.

The full challenge of a constructionist orientation has scarcely been confronted. However, we see within this book possibilities that are both promising and intriguing. Within the introductory chapter, the editors of this book raise the key question of how the two major approaches to studying close relationships can be merged. They point to the methodological strengths of the attributional, or natural science, approach and claim that given the "wealth of stimulation and evidence" it has amassed "it would be folly to disregard this literature" (p. 15). They also praise the accounts, or social science, position for the focus on contextualized narratives of respondents. They note the problems of integrating experimental methodology and cause-effect relations with naturalistic methods and hermeneutic-interpretive metatheory. Clearly, there is evidence within the book of researchers trying to fuzz the lines between the two approaches. In each case the attempt seems to be to try to get the most from each type of work—methodological rigor from the first and ecological validity from the second. In our view, however, this blurring of distinctions between these competing orientations avoids rather than solves the problem of their differential assumptions. Constructionism, we believe, could furnish a means of viable resolution.

From the natural science position, researchers make a strong case for the importance of attributional processes. Research in this book is fully compelling on this score. However, the importance of attributional dispositions is not at all denigrated by viewing them as forms of social accounting. Further, for the constructionist, all social accounts may be viewed as inherently social—forms of discourse embedded within cultural and historical conditions, and within the network of relationships of which people carry out meaningful lives. By making this final move, neither of these lines of research loses its significance. Rather, the domain of relevant research inquiries expands manifold. The investigator is invited, for example, to extend his or her concerns by exploring the forms of relationship in which attributional and other accounts are sustained, examining their effects on the course of relationships, investigating the broader network of relationships supporting or influenced by various accounting practices, and exploring the historical and cultural circumstances in which accounting processes gain their intelligibility. Further, one finds the investigation of accounts in close relationships informed and enriched by inquiry into rhetorical processes, literary construction, and ideological critique. And perhaps most invitingly, from the constructionist perspective the investigator's role is not limited to description and explanation (forms of scientific accounting), but expands as well into the realm of the imaginary. That is, like the creative artist, the constructionist investigator faces the challenge of envisioning and making intelligible new forms of accounting, alternatives means of relating, to replace those that may currently be problematic. In effect, the investigator takes an active part in the construction of cultural life.

References

Antaki, C. (Ed.). (1988). *Analysing everyday explanations: A casebook of methods*. London: Metheun.

Baumeister, R.F. & Wotman, S.R. (1990). Autobiographical accounts of unrequited love. Manuscript in preparation. Case Western Reserve University, Cleveland, OH.

Gergen, K.J., & Gergen, M.M. (1986). Narrative form and the construction of psychological science. In T.R. Sarbin (Ed.), *Narrative psychology: The storied nature of human conduct* (pp. 22–44). New York: Praeger.

Gergen, K.J., & Gergen, M.M. (1988). Narrative and the self as relationship. In L. Berkowitz (Ed.), *Advances in experimental social psychology. Vol. 21.* (pp. 17–56). San Diego, CA: Academic Press.

Goffman, E. (1971). *Relations in public.* Harmondsworth, England: Penguin.

Kelley, H.H. (1967). Attribution theory in social psychology. In D. Levine (Ed.), *Nebraska Symposium on motivation.* Lincoln, NE: University of Nebraska Press.

Schank, R.C., & Abelson, R.P. (1977). *Scripts, plans, goals and understanding.* Hillsdale, NJ: Erlbaum.

Srivastva, S., Cooperrider, D.L., & Associates. (1990). *Appreciative management and leadership. The power of positive thought and action in organizations* San Francisco: Jossey-Bass.

17
A Meta-Account

ANN L. WEBER

Introduction: The Power of Closure

In the course of chairing two recent symposia on the topic of attributions, accounts, and close relationships, I discovered the importance of constructing the "big pictures," especially for those in the audience who were hopeful about their interest in the subject but unfamiliar with its history and terminology. Three strategies seem important to invite new interest and involvement in this area: explicit definitions; coherent, common models; and gut-level appeal. Throughout this volume, contributors have provided explicit definitions for such terms as account, although no two contributions feel constrained to employ the same definitions. In this brief afterword, then, I offer my own versions of the common models underlying much of the work reviewed here. To that end, I begin this afterword with my own gut-level appeal, a "meta-account," a story about the power of stories.

My account involves no traumatic stressors or relationship failures, but it serves to illustrate most of what I continue to find uniquely appealing about work in attributions and accounts, and what I perceive to be essential common threads. One summer evening when I was 15 years old, I was dropped off too early at a community meeting house in my suburban neighborhood, where I planned to attend an organizational meeting of a new club I was interested in joining. To kill the half hour or so I had to wait, since no one else was around, I explored the meeting hall, which was cluttered with boxes of books and other goods for an upcoming rummage or jumble sale. In one of the boxes I found a book of short stories, thumbing through until I found an interesting beginning: "The man who expected to be shot lay with his eyes open, staring at the upper left-hand corner of his cell." I read on, several paragraphs describing the prisoner and his introspections, and came across a powerful description that has stayed with me ever since. The man's glasses had been broken, and the story's author succeeded in conveying the sense of security and clarity that glasses give to myopic persons like myself. The lines said something about how one puts on one's glasses first thing in the morning, and the out-of-focus world snaps into view, so all is well. I read on a while but was interrupted by other early arrivals to the meeting and had to set the book aside. When the meeting was over, the books had been repacked and I was unable to retrieve the one I had been reading. I remembered the story, however, and intended to try to find it again. I knew the title had something to do with martyrs, and the author's last name was Benét. I vaguely intended to use that information to find the story again.

The years passed. I grew up, went on to college and graduate school, and became a psychology professor far away from my home town. But I never forgot those first few pages of the story, at least in a general sense. In particular I had liked the insightful description of the martyr's near-sightedness and his reliance on his glasses, and the connection between literal vision and one's figurative perception of the world. I told and retold that metaphor about the world itself seeming out of focus until glasses simply put it right again.

About 8 years ago, in the campus library on a psychology-related mission, I stumbled (more or less) across a shelf of books by the American poet and writer, Stephen Vincent Benét. The details of my long-ago short story flashed into my mind, and I compulsively ran through the books until I found a short story whose title clicked: "The Blood of the Martyrs." It began as I remembered, and there was the unforgettable passage about the glasses:

> He could see more clearly with his glasses on, but he only put his glasses on for special occasions now—the first thing in the morning, and when they brought the food in, and for interviews with the General. The lenses of the glasses had been cracked in a beating some months before, and it strained his eyes to wear them too long. Fortunately, in his present life he had very few occasions demanding clear vision. But, nevertheless, the accident to his glasses worried him, as it worries all near-sighted people. You put your glasses on the first thing in the morning and the world leaps into proportion; if it does not do so, something is wrong with the world. (Benét, 1942, pp. 444–445)

It was immensely satisfying to reread and then finish the story I had begun and started to search for so long before. Yet even today I cannot tell you much about the rest of the story. The details I recalled and hung onto for so many years were part of the unfinished business of my first reading of the story. I was the classic victim of the Zeigarnik effect, who, like one of Bluma Zeigarnik's (1938) original subjects, found that I had much better recall for a task I had been prevented from completing.

By the time I reread this story, of course, I knew about the Zeigarnik effect and other Gestalt principles of life experience. My point here is about the power of closure and the relevance of such simple guidelines as obsessive recall in daily life. We are meaning-seeking creatures; we undertake quests; we remember just enough to renew old searches, to open old diaries, investigations, or wounds. Causal attributions for behavior and story-like accounts for such events as failure, trauma, and relationship loss are elaborate forms of the same process as that involved in hanging onto a tiny literary detail and searching through a library for its antecedents. When we add to this concept the greater relevance and human poignance of personal relationships in our lives, it seems hardly surprising at all, almost artlessly obvious, that the quest for meaning and closure in our relationships might become a focused personal endeavor; a driving force; an expressive, emotional performance.

My purpose in telling this particular story has been to emphasize the value of the gut-level appeal of accounts and explanations for behavior and experiences. By the end of this book, the reader must feel invited to conclude that accounts and attributions are common, ubiquitous, available, and even essential to relationship processes. They are also useful, both to the weaver of the attributional account and to the researcher who hopes better to understand the experience of this weaver. For my part, in accounting for accounts—weaving my own meta-account—I hope I have begun with a tale to provoke sympathetic recognition and satisfaction.

A Synthesis of Subplots

My review of the chapters in this book suggests that a levels-of-analysis approach is appropriate for a synthesis of models. In some cases our definitions may differ importantly, but in the main we are examining different levels of the same set of events. With this expectation in mind, among the symposia I chaired and cochaired in the summer of 1990, I found five levels, or perspectives, represented: (a) accounts in the wake of events/attributions, (b) account-making as part of actor's intrapsychic activity, (c) account-making as part of a general response to stress or loss, (d) the roles and manifestations of attributions within accounts, and (e) a synthesis of these views: account-making as intrapsychic and/or interactive activity.

Accounts in the Wake of Events/Attributions

Schönbach's (Chap. 3, this volume) pattern of an account episode depicts an account "phase" as part of an interaction between an actor and an opponent. In this sequence, the actor experiences or commits (a) a failure event, prompting (b) a reproach from an opponent. As a result of both the failure event itself and the immediacy of the reproach, the actor formulates and presents (c) the account, of which the opponent then offers (d) an evaluation. Although the actor's failure experience has prompted or shaped the account, account-making is central to the *interaction* between actor and opponent. Its form is delimited and qualified by the reproachful opponent's expectations.

In a similar formulation, the interaction pattern proposed by Cody, Kersten, Braaten, and Dickson (Chap. 6, this volume) is basically the same as Schönbach's. In Cody et al.'s version of events, (a) a failure event is attributed to the actor (accurately or not) by a partner or other who confronts the actor with (b) a reproach. The actor offers (c) the account, as a response to this reproach, and incorporates thereinto apologies, excuses, justifications and/or denials, as appropriate. The partner/other considers the content of the account, and offers (d) an evaluation, responding to the account and indicating the impressions communicated, intentionally or otherwise, by the actor's account. The emphasis in the work of Cody et al. has thus far been on the justificatory slant of the actor's account, offered as it is in response to a reproach that has resulted from an attribution of a failure of flaw.

Both Schönbach's model and the work of Cody et al. have in common their understanding of the power of attributions in shaping interpersonal relations, particularly in prompting specific interactions. One's expectations and understandings of a partner are vital to self and future; surprises or disappointments must be noted, reproached, explained. At this level of analysis, the social human is always in a state of "account readiness," hopeful that no other will notice a blunder or express a reproach, but ready to respond in the event. To the extent that we commit attributional errors by blaming persons for situational outcomes, we will hear—and probably repeat—our share of apologies, excuses, justifications, or denials.

Account-Making as Actor's Intrapsychic Activity

As Schönbach has hinted above, however, one may not need a reproachful "opponent" or "other" to feel prompted to ponder the whys and wherefores of relationship experiences. Surra and Planalp and their colleagues (Planalp & Surra, Chap. 5, this volume; Huston, Surra, Fitzgerald, & Cate, 1981; Surra, 1985), for example, present a view of account-making as part of an actor's own subjective assessment of a relationship in the wake of (perceived) change. Their version of the account-making sequence represents the following stages: (a) The actor maintains a preliminary subjective assessment of the relationship; (b) something happens or time passes, and the actor reformulates (c) a subjective assessment of the now-changed relationship, considering the new state of affairs and (d) wondering "Why?" In the course of asking and answering this question, the actor himself or herself formulates (e) accounts, which include and foster altered (f) beliefs and (g) understandings regarding the nature of the relationship and its current status. Further, in a feedback loop, any new beliefs (step f) go back to affect the actor's assessment of the relationship and relationships in general (step a), and any new understandings (step g) go back to affect future assessments of relationship change (step c).

Central to this model of account-making is the process of asking the question "Why?" in reference to apparent relationship change. Perceiving change, wondering and investigating why, formulating an explanatory account, and honing new beliefs and understandings are all in the private, subjective domain of the actor's own cognitive-affective activity. Such processing is not necessarily prompted by the queries or accusations of another, nor vocalized or expressed to anyone else. Unlike the interactive pattern assumed by Schönbach and Cody et al., the sequence hypothesized by Surra and Planalp and colleagues is essentially an intrapsychic process, which may or may not be drawn on or drawn into overt dyadic interaction.

Account-Making as Response to Stress or Loss

Harvey, Orbuch, Weber and colleagues (Chap. 1, this volume; 1990; Harvey, Weber, & Orbuch, 1990; Orbuch, 1990) have somewhat simplified the model-comparison business by grafting their own conceptualization of account-making onto an accommodating stress-response sequence developed by Horowitz (1986). As reviewed earlier in this book (Chap. 1) and elsewhere (Harvey, Orbuch, & Weber, 1990; Harvey, Weber, & Orbuch, 1990), the sequences of this stress-response model of account-making proceed as follows: (a) A traumatic event occurs, followed by (b) an outcry. The individual may attempt (c) denial, but will, over time, experience (d) intrusion of the painful memories and emotions. Eventually, during the course of (e) working through adjustments to the stress or loss, one achieves a measure of (f) completion of the process of responding, with a resultant (g) identity change. Central to Harvey et al.'s sequence of account-making is the suggestion that one's account, initially triggered by the traumatic event, is only really formulated as a result of the persistent intrusion of memories and affect, is developed in the course of working through and completion, and is key to the central "story" of one's subsequent new identity.

Attributions Within Accounts

In this book, the different but related works of Andrews (Chap. 10, this volume), Brewin (Chap. 11, this volume), and Holtzworth-Munroe (Chap. 9, this volume) all focus on the roles and manifestations of attributions within the content or context of more complex or protracted accounts of events in close relationships. Different as they are in specific focus and application, still a sequence of events can be discerned among them. This sequence includes a stimulus, usually a behavior (such as marital violence) or behavior pattern (such as family illness); an attribution (by self or other); and a continuing, broadening account, including cognitions, emotions, behavioral intentions, and other consequences. Across this relatively simple stimulus-attribution-account sequence I would now apply the focus of either the actor or the significant other. Thus the actor has his or her version of the stimulus, attribution, and account; and the significant other has his or her versions as well. The actor's attribution might be "my fault" while the significant other's attribution is "her/his/its fault." In the actor's account, the cognitions are likely to be memories; the emotions likely will include guilt, sense of control, and sense of power; and the behavioral intentions focus primarily on identity change as well as some network change. In contrast, in the significant other's account, the cognitions are primarily causal analyses and rationalizations; the emotions may vacillate between acceptance and anger; and the behavioral intentions focus on network change (rather than self-change).

The major difference between this model and those foregoing is that, in this model, less interest or attention is allotted to *why* the attribution—right or wrong—has been made, and more is devoted to the manifestations of attributions in subtler qualities of their enfolding accounts, and the consequences of these accounts in future behavior.

A Synthesis

Can these various viewpoints be reconciled and drawn together? At this point the effort is less a Gestalt "tying up" than a Procrustean "smashing together" of models into the same bed, perhaps an apt relationshiop metaphor. Nonetheless, there are enough commonalities of definition and sequence to justify this synthesis; these works and patterns do not make such strange bedfellows.

My synthesis of the foregoing works encompasses account-making as either an intrapsychic or an interactive process. Intrapsychically, the account-maker, as actor, may interpret, question, formulate an account, and experience the consequences all independently of any interaction with another. Interactively, the account-maker may offer the account to an other in response to the other's reproach, inviting the other's evaluation of the account, and the subsequent consequences of that evaluation. This synthesis is summarized in Figure 17.1.

At any point, of course, the "track" of the account-making may shift from intrapsychic to interactive, or vice versa. For example, the intrapsychic account-maker may offer an account to an audience, whether first reproached or not. After the account is offered to another in any form, it becomes a unit of exchange and interaction. Likewise, an

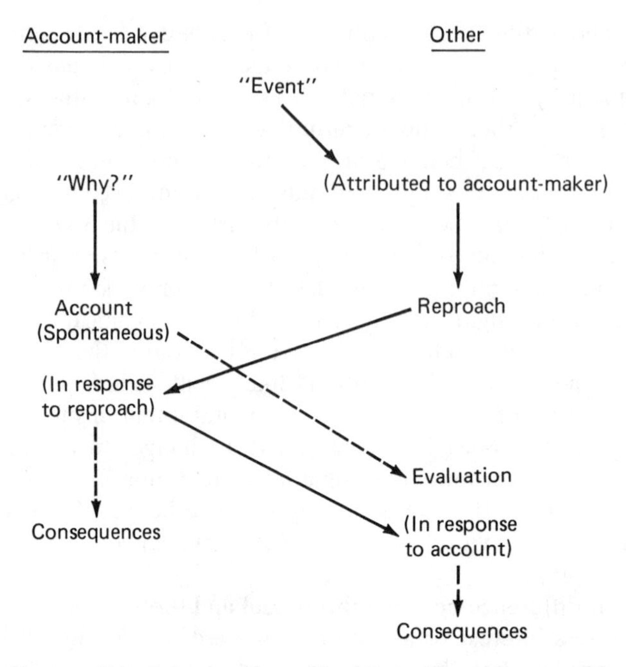

FIGURE 17.1. Intrapsychic and/or interactive account-making.

interactive exchange may provoke an account-maker to become more introspective, less concerned with audience evaluation, and more concerned with self-discovery or identity change.

This synthesis leaves much to be desired, especially because it relegates to "other consequences" the many diverse phenomena of search for control or closure, new memories, perceived likability of the account-maker, audience empathy for the account-maker, and so on. On the other hand, the chief value of this synthesis may lie in its very arrogant simplicity. It encompasses the three basic events in every foregoing sequence: a *question* (usually "Why?") about the attribution of an event, real or imagined; an *account*, whether spontaneous or in response to another's reproach; and the convenient catch-all category of *consequences*, including evaluation by self or others, and internal as well as social adjustments.

The reader will offer reactions and retorts to this model. I hope so, as I hope such reactions generate an exchange of models and countermodels. At this early stage in the development of account theory, it seems appropriate that we engage in more dialogue than dialectic. Whatever our present stage of understanding, account-making is clearly a process of consequence. In this review and synthesis I have sought to suggest a clarity rather than impose a structure. Our understanding of this topic has only begun. It is more likely that the reader of these pages will become a fellow storyteller than a fan. This meta-account, at least, is probably better considered as a welcome, or perhaps a send-off, than as operating instructions. What Coles (1989) termed "the call of stories" is likely to be the thread that links us in our efforts to understand the role of accounts and attributions in close relationships. Whatever our models and definitions, our common interest and experience represent in many ways a familiar call, and a call to action.

References

Benét, S.V. (1942). *Selected works, Volume 2: Prose*. New York: Farrar and Rinehart, Inc.

Coles, R. (1989). *The call of stories*. Boston: Houghton Mifflin.

Harvey, J.H., Orbuch, T.L., & Weber, A.L. (1990). A social psychological model of account-making in response to severe stress. *Journal of Language and Social Psychology, 9*(3), 191–207.

Harvey, J.H., Weber, A.L., & Orbuch, T.L. (1990). *Interpersonal accounts: A social psychological perspective*. Oxford: Basil Blackwell.

Horowitz, M.J. (1986). *Stress response syndromes (2nd ed.)*. Northvale, NJ: Jason Arowson.

Huston, T.L., Surra, C.A., Fitzgerald, N.M., & Cate, R.M. (1981). From courtship to marriage: Mate selection as an interpersonal process. In S. Duck & R. Gilmour (Eds.), *Personal relationships 2: Developing personal relationships* (pp. 53–88). London: Academic Press.

Orbuch, T.L. (1990, July). Person perception through accounts. Paper presented at International Conference on Personal Relationships, Oxford, England.

Surra, C.A. (1985). Courtship types: Variations in independence between partners and social networks. *Journal of Personality and Social Psychology, 49*, 357–375.

Zeigarnik, B. (1938). On finished and unfinished tasks. In W.D. Ellis (Ed.), *A sourcebook of Gestalt psychology*. London: Routledge and Kegan Paul.

Author Index

Subject Index